ASPECTS OF THE THEORY OF TARIFFS

Aspects of the
Theory of Tariffs

by Harry G. Johnson

*Professor of Economics, The London School of Economics
and Political Science and the University of Chicago*

Harvard University Press
Cambridge, Massachusetts
1972

First published in 1971

© George Allen & Unwin Ltd., 1971

SBN 674–04991–8
Library of Congress Catalog Card No. 73-173414

Printed in Great Britain

TO KAREN

Contents

Introduction

This book has its origins in a series of five lectures on the theory of tariffs that I was invited by the late Professor Ely Devons to offer at the London School of Economics and Political Science in January—February 1964. The five lectures dealt respectively with the standard theory of tariffs, the arguments for protection, the cost of protection, the theory of tariff structure, and tariffs and economic development. I had originally intended to reproduce those lectures as originally delivered, in a short monograph under the title of this book. But other activities intervened, and the monograph never materialized. Meanwhile, two of the original lectures have been published elsewhere: one on the standard theory of tariffs,[1] more or less in its original form, and the other on tariffs and economic development,[2] in a substantially revised and extended form. The former struck me on re-consideration for this book as less scientifically valuable than the prior work on which it had been founded; the latter, which contains the introduction to the original lecture series and in one sense is a summary of that series, is reprinted below as Chapter 3 of Part I. Its inclusion at that point is premature and awkward, as it anticipates and builds on some concepts developed fully only in later chapters; but since I have subsequently devoted a great deal more attention to the question of the effects of commercial policies on development,[3] it has seemed to belong near the beginning rather than near the end of my studies of tariff theory.

[1] 'The Standard Theory of Tariffs,' *The Canadian Journal of Economics*, Vol. II, No. 3 (August 1969), pp. 333—52.

[2] 'Tariffs and Economic Development: Some Theoretical Issues,' *The Journal of Development Studies*, Vol. I, No. 1 (October 1964), pp. 3—30, reprinted as Chapter 3 below.

[3] Harry G. Johnson, *Economic Policies Toward Less Developed Countries* (Washington: The Brookings Institution, and London: George Allen & Unwin, 1967), also Chapters 12 and 13 below.

Chapter 3 apart, the first four Parts of the book represent work I have done before and since in the areas of the first four lectures of the LSE series.

Chapters 1 and 2 of Part I present my efforts to construct a truly general, though simplified, model of trade and tariff theory incorporating the distribution of income, and my joint work with Jagdish Bhagwati on the generalization of the theory of tariffs to include alternative assumptions about the nature of government and of economic welfare.

Part II is essentially about the arguments for protection. The long-established optimum tariff theory has become so familiar that the interesting arguments for protection have come to centre on domestic distortions in resource allocation, a category that includes the equally familiar — but still difficult — infant industry argument for protection. Chapter 4 surveys these arguments. Chapter 5, though it has nothing to do with tariff theory as such, takes up an interesting technical puzzle that emerged in the analysis of distortions and tariffs, the effect of factor-market distortions on the shape of the transformation curve; this puzzle has very recently become a subject for exploration by more mathematically-gifted trade theorists than myself.[4] Chapter 6 is concerned with a basic empirical question raised in the lectures, the magnitude of the gains derivable by exploitation of 'optimum tariff' power. The two notes presented in Chapter 7 are concerned with an interesting question raised by the existence of tariffs and domestic distortions, whether economic growth in these circumstances can lead to economic loss for the growing country.

Part III, on the costs of protection, originated in the work of J.H. Young on the Canadian tariff and of W.M. Corden on the Australian tariff. Corden developed the theory of the cost of protection, but stopped short of operational methods of quantification; Young posed the intriguing question of efficiency in the establishment of a tariff structure designed to secure some non-economic objective. Chapter 8 presents my own analysis

---

[4] Rigorous analyses by M.C. Kemp and H. Herberg, J. Bhagwati and T.N. Srinivasan, and R.W. Jones are in process of publication. These consider aspects of the problem going far deeper than my own paper.

of the issues they raised. In essence, it can be described rather satirically as applying two general principles originated at the University of Chicago. The first of these principles is Stigler's Law:[5]

All Demand Curves are Inelastic, and
All Supply Curves are Inelastic Too.

The second, which belongs to the oral rather than the written tradition of Chicago, is the Harberger Principle:

If you multiply enough small fractions together, you can forget about the answer.

Together, these principles imply that the cost of protection, or of any other governmental intervention in free competition, is likely in normal circumstances to be a very small fraction of any interesting aggregate. This implication is confirmed by the quantitative exercise of Chapter 9, which contains appropriate warnings against placing too much emphasis on the result. Chapter 10 develops Young's concept of the scientific tariff, developed in more detail at the end of Chapter 8, into a positive theory of protectionism, tariff bargaining, and the formation of customs unions.

Part IV is concerned with the theory of effective protection, which was novel in 1964 but has been developing very rapidly since. Chapter 11 deals with a special aspect of the subject, the theory of content protection; my attention was drawn to this problem by my fellow-student at the University of Toronto and subsequent colleague for a year at the University of Chicago, J.H. Dales, then editor of *The Canadian Journal of Economics and Political Science*. Chapter 12 reprints my first effort to work out the implications of the theory of effective protection for world trade and development, a 'scarce tract in political economy' if there ever was one. Chapter 13 presents a much later summary of the literature as it then stood, and draws heavily on my Brookings monograph already referred to. Chapter 14 is an attempt, admittedly crude, to meet a problem raised by A.C. Harberger, the reconciliation of the basically

---

[5] George J. Stigler, *The Intellectual and the Market Place*, (New York: The Free Press of Glencoe, 1963), Chapter 7, pp. 45–56.

partial-equilibrium theory of effective protection with the theory of general international equilibrium, including the requirements of international monetary equilibrium. The defects of effective protection theory, as a theory recognizing the general equilibrium problem insofar as it admits the existence of many goods linked in an input-output production system, but avoiding it on the side of the supply of factor services by failing to incorporate the usual assumption of constant-returns to scale production functions, have been exciting the interest of pure trade theorists very recently. Chapter 15, newly written for this book, attempts to state and resolve some of the issues.

Part V admittedly has no direct connection with the rest of the book. It emerges from a quite separate line of my work, concerned with the practical problems of moving towards free trade in the world economy. I have included it because the subject is important, yet not much has been published about it, and the original place of publication of the study is not readily accessible to interested scholars.

I am grateful to the editors of *The Canadian Journal of Economics*, *Econometrica*, *Economica*, *The Economic Journal*, *The Journal of Development Studies*, *The Journal of Political Economy*, *Oxford Economic Papers*, *The Quarterly Journal of Economics*, and *The Review of Economic Studies*, and to the North-Holland Press, the University of Toronto Press, The Graduate Institute of International Studies, Geneva, and the Private Planning Association of Canada for permissions to re-publish material collected in this volume. I am also grateful to Jagdish Bhagwati, Richard Caves, Max Corden, and Harry Eastman, for helpful advice on what should and what should not be included in the book. Finally, I should like to record my gratitude to those who invited me to the London School of Economics in 1964, and entertained me while I was there — Sir Sydney Caine, Mr. M.D. Steuer, and the late Professor Ely Devons — both for their hospitality and for a challenging opportunity which suggested a variety of new problems that have occupied much of my work in the field ever since.

HARRY G. JOHNSON
The London School of Economics and Political Science
October 1970.

PART I:
The Positive Theory of Tariffs

1. International Trade, Income Distribution, The Offer Curve, and the Effects of Tariffs*

Theoretical analysis of two important problems — the effects of protection on real wages, and the effects of free international trade on factor prices — has clarified the relationship between the commodity prices established in international trade equilibrium and the corresponding prices of factors of production, within the framework of the Heckscher-Ohlin model of international trade.[1] Both the central theoretical principle — that an increase in the relative price of a commodity shifts production towards that commodity and so increases the demand for and marginal productivity of the factor in which the good is intensive — and the diagrammatic apparatus for analysing it — the Edgeworthian production-contract box, and the functional relationship between relative commodity prices and relative factor prices — are now well established in the literature of international trade

* Reprinted with abridgments from *The Manchester School of Economic and Social Studies*, Vol. XXVII, No. 3 (September 1959), pp. 241—60 and Vol. XXVIII, No. 3 (September 1960) pp. 215—42.

[1] For the effect of protection on real wages, see W.F. Stolper and P.A. Samuelson, 'Protection and Real Wages,' *Review of Economic Studies*, Vol. IX, No. 1 (November 1941) pp. 62—69, reprinted as Chapter 15 in *Readings in the Theory of International Trade*, ed. by H.S. Ellis and L.A. Metzler (Philadelphia, 1949) pp. 335—57: L.A. Metzler 'Tariffs, the Terms of Trade and the Distribution of National Income', *Journal of Political Economy*, Vol. LVII, No. 1 (February 1949) pp. 1—29; K. Lancaster, 'Protection and Real Wages: A Restatement', *Economic Journal*, Vol. LXVII, No. 266 (June 1957) pp. 199—210; and Jagdish Bhagwati, 'Protection, Real Wages and Real Incomes,' *Economic Journal*, Vol. LXIX, No. 276 (December 1959) pp. 733—48. Some remarks in a preliminary version of this last showed the need for a technique of relating income distribution back to the offer curve and led to the present chapter. For the relation between international trade and factor prices, see the present writer's 'Factor Endowments, International Trade and Factor Prices', *Manchester School*, Vol. XXV, No. 3 (September 1957) pp. 270—83, reprinted as Chapter I in H.G. Johnson, *International Trade and Economic Growth* (London, 1958) pp. 17—30, which contains references to the earlier literature on the subject.

theory. But the parallel interconnection between the distribution of income between factors and the country's demand for imports, which is one determinant of the equilibrium of international trade, has not so far been explored with the same thoroughness. On the contrary, the offer curve is generally derived without reference to the distribution of income, usually from a set of community indifference curves assumed to be invariant. This assumption implies either a social policy governing income distribution or identity of tastes and factor ownership among residents, both of which make the problem of the effect of trade on factor prices uninteresting. Moreover, without an analysis of the connection between distribution and international demand, the general equilibrium model of international trade is logically incomplete — a state of affairs not only aesthetically unsatisfactory but also (as will appear subsequently) capable of permitting erroneous theoretical conclusions to be drawn.

This chapter attempts to fill the gap, by introducing the distribution of income between factors into the derivation of the offer curve itself. Part I states that assumptions of the analysis and develops two alternative methods of representing the distributions of income corresponding to points on the transformation curve between commodities; the technique for doing this was originally developed in connection with the general equilibrium analysis of excise tax incidence.[2] Part II derives the country's free-trade offer curve, analyses the nature of international trade equilibrium with a given foreign offer curve and the effects of shifts in the foreign offer curve, and discusses briefly the effect of trade on welfare. Part III discusses the nature of the displacement of the offer curve resulting from

[2] See Paul Wells, 'A General Equilibrium Analysis of Excise Taxes', *American Economic Review*, Vol. XLV, No. 2 (June 1955) pp. 345–59. Wells gives joint credit for the development of the technique to John Fei. His own exposition of it does not explore the role of income distribution and factor-owners' tastes in the determination of general equilibrium, introducing instead a superfluous apparatus of contract curves; and he errs in treating the division of income as a *pro-rata* allocation of each commodity between factor-owners, who are assumed to trade with each other. See H. G. Johnson, 'General Equilibrium Analysis of Excise Taxes: Comment,' *American Economic Review*, Vol. XLV, No. 1 (March 1956) pp. 151–6, for criticism of Wells' treatment and an early version of the technique developed below.

the imposition of a tariff, and the 'normal' effect of a tariff on international equilibrium, Part IV analyses two well-known 'exceptional' cases; Part V considers in greater detail the effects of the tariff on internal income distribution, and Part VI analyses the conditions on which a tariff may reverse the direction of a country's trade.

PART I. THE DISTRIBUTION OF INCOME

The following analysis assumes, in general conformity with the Heckscher-Ohlin model of international trade, that there are two countries, the home country and the foreign country, producing and trading two commodities, X and Y. For present purposes, the foreign country may be represented simply by its offer curve, expressing the quantities of one good it is prepared to exchange for quantities of the other at the price expressed by the ratio of the two quantities; the foreign offer curve will be assumed to have the normal Marshallian shape. The home country is assumed to have a fixed endowment of two factors, labour and capital, which can be used according to given production functions to produce the two commodities; each production function is assumed subject to constant returns to scale and diminishing marginal rate of substitution between factors, and X is assumed to be more labour-intensive than Y. Perfect competition is assumed, so that factors are paid the values of their marginal products, which are equal in the two industries; and the tastes of the factor owners are assumed to be given, and describable, for each factor separately but not for the two together, by a set of indifference curves of the normal shape, neither good being 'inferior' in the consumption of either factor. It is further assumed that foreign demand is such that X will be the home country's import good, and Y its export good.

The home country's factor endowment and the available technology determine its production possibilities, which can be represented by a transformation curve between the two commodities. For each combination of the commodities on the transformation curve, there is an allocation of labour and capital between the two industries, a corresponding ratio between their marginal productivities common to the two industries, and, since their quantities are fixed, a corresponding distribution

5

of the national product between them. Since there are only two factors, this distribution can be conceived of in terms of the total output, and the income earned by one factor, since the residue is the income of the other. The income earned by a factor, in turn, can be envisaged in two alternative ways: as an amount which the factor itself produces, and as a share of the total which both factors together produce. The former notion leads to the concept of a 'production block' representing the income the factor would produce for itself at different relative commodity prices, the latter to the concept of an 'income-distribution curve' showing the share of total output the factor would receive at different points on the country's transformation curve. Both of course amount to the same thing, but each has its own advantages and disadvantages.

The concept of the income-distribution curve is fairly obvious, as is its chief characteristic: that the share of a factor rises as production shifts along the transformation curve towards the good which uses that factor relatively intensively. The concept of a factor's production block requires more explanation, since factors always produce in co-operation with each other; and it involves introducing the concept of negative production of a commodity. But the central idea is simply an extension of existing analysis, notably the Rybczynski proof [3] that if commodity prices are constant, an increase in the supply of one factor must reduce production of the good which uses that factor relatively less intensively.

The initial problem is to determine, given the amounts of X and Y produced by the economy with both factors together, how much X and how much Y can be said to be produced by one factor — say labour — alone. The answer is derived along the following lines: At the factor prices corresponding to the total quantities of X and Y produced in the economy, there is an optimum capital: labour ratio in each industry, and this ratio is higher in Y than in X by assumption. Now suppose all labour is employed in producing X; to do so efficiently, labour must be assisted by capital in the optimum ratio. Where is this

[3] T.M. Rybczynski, 'Factor Endowment and Relative Commodity Prices', *Economica*, New Series, Vol. XXII, No. 88 (November 1955) pp. 336–41.

capital to come from? Suppose that negative production of Y is possible; this will release capital and labour, which can be put to producing still more X; and since the capital: labour ratio in Y is higher than in X, there will be a net release of capital which can be put to co-operating with the initial stock of labour. Thus labour can be conceived of as contributing to total production a positive quantity of the labour-intensive good (larger than the economy's actual production of it) and a negative quantity of the capital-intensive good, the negative production of the latter providing all the capital and some of the labour required to produce the former. Similarly, capital can be conceived of as producing a positive quantity of the capital-intensive good (larger than the economy's actual output of it) and a negative quantity of the labour-intensive good; and total output of each good can be conceived of as comprising a positive contribution by one factor and a negative contribution by the other. The combination of positive quantities of one good and negative quantities of the other 'produced' by a factor at different points on the economy's transformation curve constitute the 'production block' for the factor; like the transformation curve, and for the same reasons, the production block will be characterized by a diminishing marginal rate of transformation of one good into the other.

The derivation of the income-distribution curve and the factor production blocks just described from the factor endowment and technology of the economy is illustrated in Figure 1, which reproduces the familiar production contract box. $O_x A = O_y B$ represents the economy's labour endowment, $O_x B = O_y A$ its capital endowment; production indifference curves for X originate at O_x, for Y at O_y, their tangency points tracing out the production contract curve $O_x P O_y$. Initially, production is at P, with $O_x P$ of X and $O_y P$ of Y being produced, the price of capital in terms of labour being the slope of the common tangent FF, and the labour: capital ratios in the two industries being the slopes of $O_x P$ and $O_y P$ (with respect to the horizontal).

The shares of the two factors in the national product are determined by drawing $O A'$ parallel to $FF: AA'$ is the value of capital's contribution to production, measured by the quantity of labour it will command, whereas $O_x A$ is the value of labour's

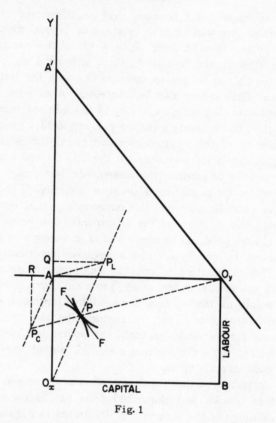

Fig. 1

contribution measured the same way; hence AA'/O_xA' is capital's share, and O_xA/O_xA' is labour's share, in total income. As the production point shifts towards O_y, more X and less Y being produced, the labour:capital ratio in both industries declines, the slope of FF consequently decreases, labour's share rises and capital's share falls; and conversely when the production point shifts towards O_x, more Y and less X being produced.

To derive the points on the factor production blocks corresponding to total production of O_xP of X and O_yP of Y, draw AP_L parallel to O_yP and AP_c parallel to O_xP to the north-east and south-west of A respectively; distances along these lines from A represent negative production of Y and X respectively. The intersection of these lines with O_xP and O_yP produced give the production points for labour and capital respectively; negative production of AP_L of Y releases QP_L of capital and QA of labour, which together with O_xA of labour can produce O_xP_L of X; similarly negative production of AP_C of X releases RP_C of labour and RA of capital which together with O_yA of capital can produce O_yP_C of Y. The points on the factor production blocks corresponding to the other points on the contract curve may be derived in the same fashion.

The relationship between the transformation curve, the income distribution curve, and the factor production block is shown in Figure 2, with labour as the factor whose income or income share is of special interest. In the Figure, TT is the transformation curve for the economy as a whole, WW' the income-distribution curve, and LL the labour production block. WW' is so drawn that it intersects the vector from the origin to any point on the transformation curve in the ratio in which income is divided between labour and capital; for example, if production is at P_1 and the intersection at W_1, labour's share is OW_1/OP_1. The income actually received by labour is obtained by drawing the budget line $M_L N_L$ through W_1 parallel to the tangent to the transformation curve at P_1. Alternatively, labour's budget line $M_L N_L$ is given by the tangent to LL (at L_1) which has the same slope as the tangent to the transformation curve at P_1; and its share can be obtained by finding the intersection of the vector OP_1 with this budget line. Thus the income-distribution curve can be derived directly from the factor production block; the converse derivation, though possible in principle, can be regarded as impossible in geometrical practice. It should be noted that the WW' curve may rise from left to right over part of its range — this is consistent with the requirement that the budget line through each point W_1 must lie outside the budget line through any point on WW' left of W_1; also that, once the country becomes completely specialized, the LL curve becomes irrelevant, and distribution is fixed at the relevant extreme point on the WW' curve.

The factor production block technique has the advantage of relating distribution to production directly and so avoiding possible errors: the income-distribution curve has the advantage of diagrammatic simplicity, and of remaining relevant when the

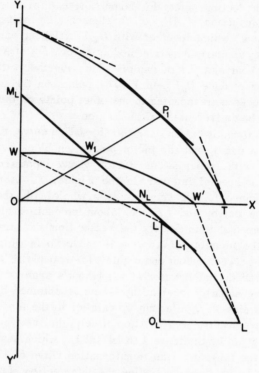

Fig. 2

country is completely specialized. The income-distribution curve will be employed in the remainder of this chapter. Both techniques can readily be extended to the case of distribution between two factor *owners* owning the factors in different ratios. In this case, part of the factor (i.e. factor-owner) production block may intrude into the north-east portion of Figure 2. [4] If factors are owned in the same ratio as the country's overall endowment, the income-distribution curve becomes a contracted form of the transformation curve, distribution is constant, and analysis in terms of the transformation curve and a community indifference curve becomes legitimate.

[4] See H.G. Johnson, 'General Equilibrium Analysis of Excise Taxes: Comment,' *loc. cit.*

PART II. THE OFFER CURVE AND FREE TRADE EQUI-LIBRIUM

The offer curve shows, for each international price ratio between the commodities, the quantity of exports the country would supply and the quantity of imports it would demand in exchange. Under free trade, the internal price ratio is the same as the international (external); and the point on the offer curve corresponding to a particular international price ratio represents the excess of the quantity of one good that the country would produce over what it would consume, and the excess of the quantity of the other it would consume over what it would produce, at that price ratio. Given the price-ratio, which determines the country's production point and the distribution of income between the factors, the consumption of the two goods and therefore the point on the offer curve corresponding to the price ratio is determined by the preference systems of the factors. An increase in the relative price of the imported good has in addition to the usual income and substitution effects, the effect of shifting domestic production towards producing more of that good and less of the export good, and re-distributing income towards the factor used relatively intensively in producing that good, thus altering the weights of the preference systems of the two factors in determining aggregate demand for the goods. While the income,[5] substitution, and production effects of the price increase will tend to reduce the quantity demanded, the re-distribution effect may work in either direction. It will tend to reduce the quantity demanded if each factor prefers the commodity which employs it relatively less intensively, and to increase the quantity demanded if each factor prefers the commodity which employs it relatively more intensively, 'preference' being defined as having a higher marginal propensity to consume the good than does the other factor.[6] In the latter case, the re-distribution effect may outweigh the other effects over a certain range of the offer curve, so that the quantity of imports demanded increases as their relative price rises and decreases

[5] Inferior goods are excluded by assumption.

[6] 'Preference' in this sense may be the consequence of differences in either tastes or level of income.

as their relative price falls, thus producing the equivalent of the 'Giffen case' even though imports are by assumption not an inferior good. It is even possible that, as the price of the imported good falls, the re-distribution effect will convert the country from an importer to an exporter of the good concerned, though again this can only occur over a certain range of the offer curve, as at a sufficiently low price the country must specialize on the other good and rely on imports for its consumption of this one. The re-distribution effect therefore introduces new possibilities of instability and multiple equilibrium not suggested by the standard offer curve analysis.

The derivation of the offer curve is illustrated in Figure 3 which reproduces the transformation and income-distribution curves of Figure 2. The indifference curves for labour are drawn in the usual north-east direction, with the fixed origin O, and the quantities of X and Y demanded by labour are determined by the tangency of an indifference curve with labour's budget line as given by the production point on the transformation curve and the income distribution curve. The indifference curves for capital, on the other hand, are drawn in the south-west direction from the shifting origin of the production point on the transformation curve; and the quantities of X and Y demanded by capital are determined by the tangency of one of these indifference curves with labour's budget line, determined as above and extended as necessary to intersect the axes of capital's indifference map, which represents capital's budget line viewed from the point on the transformation curve as origin. The excess or deficit of the total quantity of a good demanded by both factors together, as compared with the amount of it produced, is the country's import demand or export supply of it, and is measured by the overlap or gap between the two factors' consumption points with respect to the axis for that good.

Thus, in Figure 3, with the price ratio equal to the slope of MN, the production point is P_1, with OB of X and OA of Y being produced, total income is given by the budget line MN, and labour's budget line is $M_L N_L$. Labour's consumption point is C_L, involving a demand for OX_L of X and OY_L of Y; capital's consumption point is C_C, with capital demanding BX_C of X and

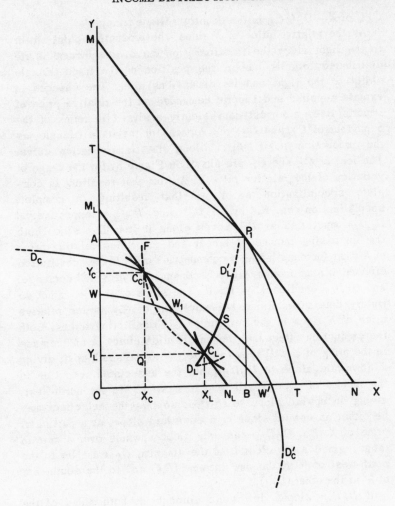

Fig. 3

AY_C of Y. There is therefore an excess of demand for X over domestic production (a demand for imports) of $X_C X_L$, and an excess of production of Y over domestic demand (a supply of exports) of $Y_C Y_L$, at the given price ratio. More simply, at the terms of trade given by the slope of $C_C C_L$, the country will supply exports of $C_C Q$ of Y in exchange for imports of

13

$C_L Q$ of $X - C_C Q C_L$ is the country's 'trade triangle'.

As the relative price of X rises, the production point shifts to the right along the transformation curve, and income is redistributed towards labour, the position of the trade triangle shifts to the right and its dimensions alter. The changes in exports supplied and imports demanded as the relative price of imports rises are most conveniently analysed in terms of the behaviour of C_L and C_C, the vertices of the trade triangle, as the production point shifts along the transformation curve. The loci of C_L and C_C are shown in Figure 3, for the range of variation of the relative price of X from that resulting in complete specialization on Y to that resulting in complete specialization on X, by $D_L D_{L'}$ and $D_C D_{C'}$ respectively.[7] $D_L D_{L'}$ must rise as C_L moves along it from D_L, since both the increasing income of labour and the rising relative price of X must increase labour's consumption of Y; if the substitution effect is strong enough, labour's consumption of X will decrease, and $D_L D_{L'}$ bend back on itself. The slope of $D_C D_{C'}$ is not so rigidly determined since the movement of C_C as the relative price of X rises is the net outcome of conflicting forces. Both the production effect and the substitution effect of an increase in the price of X will tend to move C_C to the south-east, giving a downward slope to $D_C D_{C'}$; but the associated reduction in the income of capital will tend to move C_C to the north-west, giving an upward slope to $D_C D_{C'}$; so that the net effect may be either an upward slope or a downward slope, at a particular price of X. But $D_C D_{C'}$ can only slope upwards over a certain range, since as is clear from the diagram, C_C must lie to the north-west of W at the one extreme (D_C) and to the south-east of W' at the other ($D_{C'}$).

If $D_C D_{C'}$ slopes downwards throughout, both sides of the trade triangle diminish as the price of X increases; and the

[7] Once the country is completely specialized in one industry, the distribution of income between the factors is rigidly fixed by their relative marginal productivities in that industry, and shown by the relevant terminal point of the income-distribution curve. As the price of X varies beyond that at which specialization occurs, the budget line rotates about the terminal point of the WW curve, and both factors gain from the cheapening of the imported good. The continuations of $D_L D_{L'}$ and $D_C D_{C'}$ after specialization occurs are shown in Figure 3 by the dotted lines; the shapes of these curves are determined by the usual income and substitution effects.

country's offer curve has the normal ('elastic demand for imports') shape, less of X being demanded and less of Y supplied as the price of X rises (Y falls). But if $D_C D_{C'}$ slopes upwards in the relevant range, abnormal shapes of the offer curve become possible: (a) the vertical side of the trade triangle may increase as the price of X increases, indicating an increase in the quantity of Y supplied as the price of X rises ('inelastic demand for imports'); (b) both sides of the trade triangle may increase as the price of X increases, indicating an increase in the quantity of X demanded as its price increases ('perverse elasticity of demand for imports'); (c) as the price of X decreases, the trade triangle may shrink to nothing and invert over a certain range before reverting to normal ('perverse reversal of trade direction').[8] This last possibility requires that $D_C D_{C'}$ and $D_L D_{L'}$ intersect three times, which means that there are three possible closed-economy equilibrium points, at successively higher prices of X and larger incomes for labour, of which the middle one is unstable.[9]

The possibility that the quantity of imports of X demanded will increase as the price of X increases, common to cases (b) and (c) above, is illustrated in Figure 4, which is designed to demonstrate, in a general way, the conditions required for that possibility to emerge. With the price of X shown by the slope of $M_L N_L$, the production point is P, labour's budget line $M_L N_L$, and the trade triangle $C_C Q C_L$; when the price of X rises to that shown by the slope of $M_{L'} N_{L'}$, the production point shifts to P', labour's budget line to $M_{L'} N_{L'}$, and the trade triangle is $C_{C'} Q C_{L'}$, such that $Q' C_{L'}$, the new quantity of imports demanded, is greater than $Q C_L$, the quantity formerly demanded.

The shift of labour's consumption point from C_L to $C_{L'}$ can be divided into two parts: $C_L D$, the 'income-re-distribution

---

[8] Since the country must specialize completely on the production of X at a sufficiently high price, importing its requirements of Y, there must be a reversal of trade direction as the price of X rises.

[9] There may be a larger (odd) number of intersections of $D_c D_{c'}$ and $D_L D_{L'}$, and a corresponding number of reversals of trade direction as the price of exports rises.

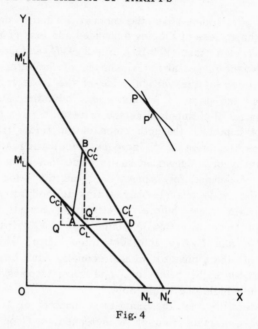

Fig. 4

effect' of the price change, defined as the change in labour's consumption that would have occurred if labour had been moved to its new budget line but prices kept constant by appropriate tax and subsidy arrangements, and $DC_{L'}$, the 'cost-compensated substitution effect' of the price change.[10] Similarly, the shift of

[10] In principle, two income effects of a price change are discernible, one operating by changing the purchasing power of a given income — the income-effect of consumer theory — and the other operating by re-distributing income between the factors. In the present model there seems to be no point in distinguishing them. The effort to do so would in fact create unnecessary complexities, since if the point on the income-distribution curve is taken to define labour's initial income, and the budget line through it rotated to represent the non' re-distributive effects of the price change, the consumption income effect will be positive or negative according as C_L is initially above or below that point on the budget line — that is, if its share is constant labour gains from an increase in the price of X if it consumes a larger proportion of Y as compared with X than the economy produces, and conversely. The same proposition applies to capital, though both factors taken together must lose by an increase in the price of X, since X is imported. Since the consumption income effect of a price change is ambiguous and the total effect is not, the latter is evidently the better to work with.

16

capital's consumption point can be divided into three parts: $C_C A$, corresponding to the shift in the origin of capital's indifference curves from P to P' due to the production effect of the price change; AB, the income-redistribution effect of the price change on capital's consumption, and BC'_C, the cost compensated substitution effect of the price change. It is obvious from the diagram that the necessary condition for the country's demand for imports to increase is that AB should be steeper than $C_L D$; that is, that as income is re-distributed from capital to labour, capital should reduce its consumption of Y more, and of X less, than labour increases its consumption of these goods. In other words, each factor must have a preference for (relatively higher marginal propensity to consume) the commodity which employs it relatively more intensively. The diagram also suggests that the case is more likely, the smaller the substitutability of the goods in consumption, the smaller the production shift, and the larger the re-distribution of income between the factors.

The production shift will be smaller, the smaller are the elasticities of substitution between factors in production.

The equilibrium volume and terms of international trade are determined by the intersection of the home country's offer curve with the foreign offer curve. The determination of international trade equilibrium can be depicted in either of two ways. One is to introduce the foreign offer curve into Figure 3, the technique being to slide the origin of the foreign offer curve along $D_L D_{L'}$ (or $D_C D_{C'}$) until its intersection with $D_C D_{C'}$ (or $D_L D_{L'}$) lies on the labour budget line through its origin; for example if the foreign offer curve were $C_L C_C F$ in Figure 3, $C_L Q C_C$ would represent the equilibrium volume and terms of trade. The other method is to draw the two offer curves on a separate diagram. The first has the advantage of relating trade equilibrium directly to the distribution of income, while the second facilitates the analysis of the nature of equilibrium and the effects of changes in trade conditions on it.

The new possibilities introduced by taking explicit account of the distribution of income in the derivation of the offer curve are the cases (b) and (c) mentioned above. Case (b) introduces the possibility of multiple equilibria, and unstable equilibrium,

17

even when the foreign demand for the country's exports is elastic — on the usual analysis, both demands must be inelastic for multiplicity and instability of equilibrium to be possible. It also allows the possibility that an increase in foreign demand will lead to a reduction in the volume of both goods traded between the two countries. These possibilities are illustrated in Figure 5. where $H'OH$ is the home offer curve, and $F'OF$ is the (elastic) foreign offer curve; T_1, T_2, T_3 are possible trade

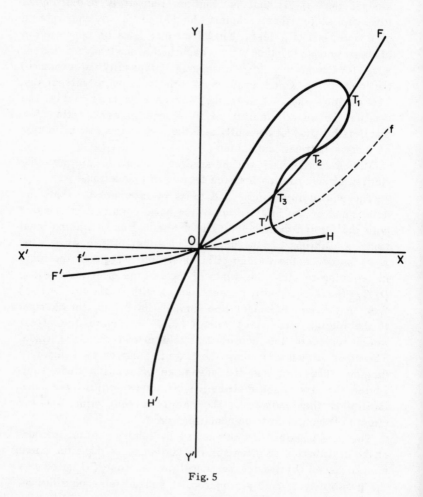

Fig. 5

equilibrium points, T_2 being unstable; and an increase in foreign demand to $f'Of$ would shift the equilibrium to T', at which point smaller quantities of both goods are exchanged, at terms of trade more favourable to the home country.

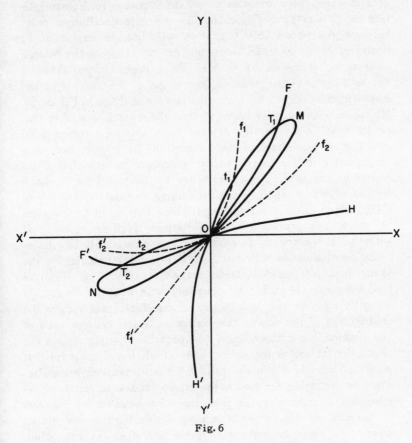

Fig. 6

Case (c) is the more interesting. The offer curve in this case, which is represented in Figure 6 by the curve $H'OMONOH$, makes a closed loop in both the north-east and south-west quadrants of the diagram.[11] This allows not only

[11] A larger number of closed-economy equilibrium points would give rise to an offer curve of an even more intricate floral pattern.

the previous possibility of three equilibria in which the country exchanges Y for X, but also the possibility of two stable equilibria, one at a relatively high price of X in which the country exports Y in exchange for X, and one at a lower price of X in which the country exports X in exchange for Y, exemplified by T_1 and T_2 in Figure 6. The unstable equilibrium point between the two stable equilibria will involve export of Y, export of X, or no trade, according as the slope of the foreign offer curve at the origin is less steep than, steeper than, or (as in Figure 6) the same as the slope of the portion of the domestic offer curve common to the two loops (NOM in Figure 6). Moreover, with an offer curve of this shape, it is possible that an increase in the foreign demand for a country's export good will lead to a reversal of trade direction, the country becoming an ●importer of its former export good and an exporter of its former import good. This possibility is illustrated in Figure 6 by the effect of an increase in foreign demand from $f' O f_1$ to $f_2' O f_2$, which alters the trade equilibrium from t_1, at which point the country is importing X at a relatively high price, to t_2, at which point the country is exporting X at a relatively low price.

In conclusion to this section, a few brief remarks on the gains from international trade are appropriate. The effect of free international trade, as compared with self-sufficiency, is normally to raise the real income of one factor and reduce the real income of the other. The exception is the extreme case of trade which leads the country to specialize completely on the production of one of the goods, *and* establishes a price for that good sufficiently above the price at which complete specialization is profitable for the factor whose income in terms of exportables is reduced to be more than compensated for the loss by the relative cheapening of imports. Excluding the exceptional case, free trade benefits one factor and damages the other. Whether free trade, as compared with self-sufficiency, benefits or harms the nation as a whole is therefore a question whose answer requires a balancing of gains against losses, and can only be decided by reference to the country's social welfare function.[12] In the absence of a social welfare function, the question can only be discussed in terms of potential welfare, that is, of whether it would be possible by transfers between factors (compensations) to make both factors better off (in the limit, no worse off) under free trade than in the absence of trade. This in turn requires a definition of what the change introduced by free trade consists in. If it is taken to consist in the change in the actual collection of goods available for the economy's consumption, it is possible that the collection of goods purchased in the free trade equilibrium could not be re-distributed so as to make both factors as well off as they would be with the self-sufficiency collection.[13] But if, as seems more sensible, it is taken to consist in the opportunity to trade, either at the free-trade price ratio or along the foreign offer curve, it can easily be shown that the country is potentially better off with free trade than under self-sufficiency, since

[12] It is arguable that the social welfare function should be deduced from the revealed preferences of the community, as expressed in governmental decisions, rather than imposed (or denied existence) by the observing economist. Governmental decisions show a preference for trade over no trade, but not for free trade over trade subject to governmental interference.

[13] See Erling Olsen, 'Udenrigshandelens Gevinst,' *Nationalokonomisk Tidskrift*, Årgang 1958, Haefte 1—2, pp. 76—9, which criticizes Samuelson's classic article on 'The Gains from International Trade' (*Canadian Journal of Economics and Political Science*, Vol. V, pp. 195—205, reprinted in *Readings in the Theory of International Trade*) on these grounds. Olsen does not seem to appreciate the distinction drawn here between the opportunity to trade, on which Samuelson bases his argument, and the collection of goods made available by trade, on which his criticism of it is based; for a more elaborate development of the distinction, see R.E. Baldwin, 'The New Welfare Economics and Gains in International Trade,' *Quarterly Journal of Economics*, Vol. LXVI, No. 1 (February 1952) pp. 91—101.

The possibility that the collection of goods obtained in trade cannot be re-distributed to make both factors as well off as before can be illustrated by an elaboration of Figure 3. Through S, the self-sufficiency equilibrium point, passes a price-line to which indifference curves for each factor are tangent. Free trade displaces total production north-west along the transformation curve to the left of P_1, and total consumption south-east of the new production point along a line parallel and equal to $C_C C_L$, thus shifting the no-trade point on capital's indifference system (drawn with reference to the post-trade collection of consumption goods) somewhere to the right of the original price-line through S. If the new location of capital's no-trade consumption point is north-east or south-west of S, capital's original indifference curve may fail to intersect with labour's original indifference curve, in which case capital cannot compensate labour for the effect of trade without being worse off.

on either assumption the effect of free trade is equivalent to an outward movement of the country's transformation curve.[14]

PART III. THE DISPLACEMENT OF THE OFFER CURVE BY A TARIFF[15]

Under conditions of free trade, the internal and world-market commodity price ratios are identical; and the quantities of imports demanded and exports supplied at a particular world-market price ratio are determined by the effects of the identical internal price ratio on the pattern of production, income distribution, and demand for commodities. When a tariff is in force, this is no longer true: the internal and external price ratios differ to an extent determined by the tariff rate, and the quantities of imports demanded and exports supplied at the external price ratio are determined by the effects on the domestic economy of the (different) internal price ratio together with the way in which the recipients of the tariff revenue dispose of it. To put the same point another way, the effect of a tariff is to displace the point on the offer curve corresponding to a particular internal price ratio to a new location such that the external price of imports is lower than the internal by the proportion of the tariff in the domestic price, and that the quantity of imports demanded is greater, and of exports supplied is less, by the amounts demanded by the recipients of the tariff proceeds. The exact nature of the displacement is determined by the rate of the

---

[14] Except at the point on the transformation curve with slope equal to the foreign self-sufficiency price ratio (or, if there is no such point, at one extreme of the transformation curve). For demonstration, see R.E. Baldwin, 'Equilibrium in International Trade: A Diagrammatic Analysis,' *Quarterly Journal of Economics*, Vol. LXII, No. 1 (February 1948) pp. 748–62.

[15] An export duty has exactly the same effects as an import duty at the same rate. See the classic article by Abba P. Lerner, 'The Symmetry Between Import and Export Taxes,' *Economica*, N.S. Vol. III, No. 11 (August 1936) pp. 306–13; the argument of this and the following section is to a large extent a re-working of Lerner's analysis on the assumption that tariff proceeds are distributed to factors instead of being spent by the government. Needless to say, the following argument, like Lerner's, arrives at conclusions about the possible effects of a tariff already familiar in general terms to the classical writers on international trade.

tariff and the way in which expenditure of the tariff proceeds by their recipients is divided between exportables and importables.

Since the way in which the proceeds of the tariff are spent by their recipients helps to determine the resulting displacement of the offer curve, it is necessary to specify these recipients and their behaviour. For some problems in tariff theory, it is most appropriate to consider the government as a separate consumer with its own preferences, receiving the income from the tariff and spending it according to those preferences.[16] For the present analysis, where the emphasis is on the distribution of income between factors, it is more appropriate to assume that the tariff proceeds are redistributed to factor owners according to some principle of distribution which may range from giving all the proceeds to labour to giving them all to capital, and are spent by the recipients in the same way as would be increments of earned income. This permits the displacement of the offer curve by the tariff to be related to the marginal propensities to spend on imports of the tariff recipients.

The displacement of the offer curve by the tariff is illustrated in Figure 7, which reproduces the relevant parts of the central portion of Figure 3 with some additional detail. $C_C Q C_L$ defines a point on the country's offer curve, which in the subsequent argument will be assumed to be the free-trade international equilibrium point. Now suppose that a tariff is imposed at the proportional rate $C_C R / RQ$, so that for the internal price of imports to be equal to the slope of $C_C C_L$ the external price must be equal to the slope of $R C_L$; and that the whole proceeds of the tariff are received by capital. With the same internal price ratio and distribution of earned income, and no share in the tariff proceeds to spend, labour's consumption point must remain at C_L. Thanks to the addition of the tariff receipts to its earned income, however, capital's consumption point will move down its income-consumption line through C_C to C'_C on $C_L R$ produced. C'_C will be capital's equilibrium consumption point, because at this point total consumption of imports $Q' C_L$ from earned incomes plus tariff receipts is just equal to what

---

[16] This is the technique employed by Lerner, *loc. cit.*

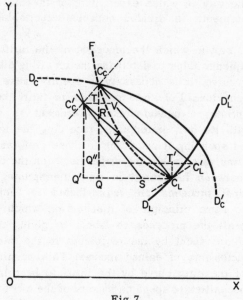

Fig. 7

can be paid for at world market prices by the excess $C'_C Q'$ of the country's production of exportables over the demand for them from earned income plus tariff receipts. The country exports $C'_C Q'$ of Y in return for $Q'C_L$ of X, of which $SC_L = C'_C V$ accrues to capital as tariff receipts; of these receipts, $C'_C T = Q'Q$ is consumed directly by capital, and TV is used to buy $C_C T$ of Y that would otherwise have been exported. Thus the quantity of X demanded by the country is increased by QQ', and the amount of Y supplied reduced by $C_C T$, these quantities being determined by the tariff rate $C_C R/RQ$ and the ratio $C_C T/C'_C T$ in which the capital divides marginal consumption between X and Y. This latter ratio is determined by capital's marginal propensity to spend on imports and exports; since these sum to unity, the ratio can be said to depend on either propensity alone.[17]

When all tariff proceeds go to capital, the point on the new tariff-inclusive offer curve corresponding to the same internal price ratio as the point on the free trade offer curve defined by $C_C Q C_L$ is defined by $C'_C Q' C_L$, where C'_C is determined by

24

the intersection of the tariff-reduced external price ratio line through C_L with capital's income-consumption line through C_C. In the opposite case, when all tariff proceeds go to labour, the point on the tariff-inclusive offer curve corresponding to $C_C Q C_L$ is defined by $C_C Q'' C_L'$, where C_L' is determined by the intersection of labour's income-consumption line through C_L with the line through C_C of slope equal to the tariff-reduced external price-ratio. In this case the quantity of X demanded by the country is increased by $T' C_L'$, and the quantity of Y supplied reduced by $C_L T' = Q Q''$, these quantities being determined by the tariff rate and the ratio $C_L T'/T' C_L'$ in which labour divides marginal expenditure between X and Y, which is determined by labour's marginal propensities to spend on imports and exports. In the general case in which both factors share in the tariff proceeds, the apices of the new triangle corresponding to $C_C Q C_L$ will lie on $C'_C C_L$ and $C_L C_L'$ respectively, and the displacement of the offer curve will be determined by the tariff rate, the income-consumption lines of the two factors, and the principle of distribution of tariff proceeds; the last two of these factors can be combined conceptually in the form of a weighted-average income-consumption line, and represented diagrammatically by a line running south-east through C_C or north-west through C_L, whose slope depends on the weighted-average marginal propensities to spend on imports and exports of the tariff recipients.

[17] The ratio of the increase in the quantity of Y to the increase in the quantity of X consumed as income increases is

$$\frac{dY}{dX} = \frac{\frac{\delta Y}{\delta I}}{\frac{\delta X}{\delta I}} = \frac{c_y}{c_x} p_x$$

where I is income measured in units of Y, p_z is the (given) price of X in terms of Y, $c_y = \delta Y/\delta I$ is the marginal propensity to spend on Y, and $c_x = p_z \, \delta X/\delta I$ is the marginal propensity to spend on X. Since $c_x + c_y = 1$,

$$\frac{c_y}{c_x} p_x = \frac{c_y}{1-c_y} p_x = \frac{1-c_x}{c_x} p_x$$

and the ratio may be said to depend on the marginal propensity to spend on imports or on home goods alone. These alternatives are exploited in the derivation of the conditions required for the exceptional cases discussed below.

25

Regardless of how the tariff proceeds are distributed, the quantity of imports demanded is always greater, and the quantity of exports supplied always less, at any point on the tariff-inclusive offer curve than at the corresponding point with the same internal price-ratio on the free-trade offer curve. If the country's free-trade offer curve is of the normal 'elastic' shape, more exports being supplied as well as more imports demanded at a lower price of imports, the quantities of exports supplied and imports demanded at a given external price ratio must be less with a tariff in force than it would be under free trade. [18] Hence with an 'elastic' domestic free-trade offer curve, the tariff must turn the terms of trade in the country's favour. But if the foreign offer curve is also 'elastic,' so that the foreigner will not supply a larger volume of imports to the home country in return for a smaller volume of its exports, the terms of trade cannot turn in the country's favour to the extent required to offset the effect of the tariff in raising the internal price of imports. With elastic demands on both sides, the external price of imports must fall and the internal price rise; so that the price and earned income of the factor used relatively intensively in producing importable goods must rise, and the price and earned income of the factor used relatively intensively in producing exportable goods must fall.

The foregoing conclusions about the effects of the tariff on the external and internal price ratios with 'elastic' offer curves on both sides can be demonstrated by reference to Figure 7. Suppose first that the slope of $C_L C_C'$ represents the free-trade equilibrium price ratio; since the apices of the free-trade triangle for that price ratio must lie on $C_C D_C$ and $C_L D_L$, its hypotenuse must be longer than $C_C' C_L$ or $C_C C_L'$ if $C_C Q$ increases as $C_C C_L$ rotates and shifts to the left, so that the tariff reduces the country's demand for imports and supply of exports at the free-trade equilibrium price below the free-trade equilibrium quantities, and the world-market price of imports must fall to restore international equilibrium. Now suppose that $C_C Q C_L$ is

[18] Exports supplied at the given external price ratio with the tariff must be less than they would be at the corresponding higher internal price ratio under free trade and *a fortiori* less than they would be under free trade at the given external price ratio.

the free-trade international equilibrium trade triangle, and $C_L Z C_C F$ is the foreign offer curve. At the external price ratio with the tariff correspodning to the initial free-trade equilibrium price-ratio equal to the slope of $C_C C_L$, the foreign country's equilibrium trade triangle would have the hypotenuse $C_L Z$, and necessarily be smaller than the domestic equilibrium trade triangle with hypotenuse $C'_C C_L$ or $C_C C'_L$, so that there would be an excess demand for imports and supply of exports in the world market and the external and internal prices of imports would have to be higher to restore equilibrium.

The same conclusions can be demonstrated more simply by means of the conventional offer-curve analysis, as in Figure 8. In the Figure, OH_f and OF are respectively the home and foreign free-trade offer curves, both representing elastic demands for imports; P_f is the free-trade equilibrium point; and the slope of OP_f measures the price of the home country's imports. The tariff shifts the home country's offer curve to OH_t; the arrows connect points on the tariff-inclusive offer curve with the corresponding points on the free-trade offer curve with the same internal price-ratio.[19] At the new equilibrium point with the tariff P_t, the world-market price of imports has fallen to the slope of OP_t, but the internal price of imports has risen to the slope of OP_i.

PART IV. TWO EXCEPTIONAL CASES

If both countries' offer curves are of the elastic demand shape, the effect of a tariff is to lower the external price of imports (improve the country's terms of trade) and raise the internal price of imports, with a consequent increase in domestic production of importables and redistribution of earned income towards the factor used relatively intensively in producing importables. If, however, one or other country's offer curve is of the 'inelastic' shape, this conclusion does not necessarily hold. If the domestic offer curve is 'inelastic,' the demand for imports may increase and the terms of trade turn against the country as

[19] The slopes of the arrows decrease from left to right, because as the price of importables falls a higher ratio of importables to exportables is consumed.

ASPECTS OF THE THEORY OF TARIFFS

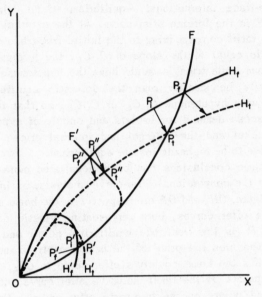

Fig. 8

a result of the tariff. This possibility, which may be termed the
'Lerner case,'[20] is illustrated in Figure 8 by the free-trade offer
curve OH'_f and international equilibrium point P'_f and the tariff-
inclusive offer curve OH'_t and international equilibrium point
P'_t with corresponding internal equilibrium point P'_i; with the
tariff, the external price of imports has risen to the slope of
OP'_t as compared with the slope of OP'_f under free trade. If the
foreign offer curve is 'inelastic,' the terms of trade may improve
so much that the domestic price of imports falls, production of
importables falls, and income is redistributed towards the factor
used relatively intensively in producing exportables. This
possibility, which may be termed 'the Metzler case,'[21] is

[20] See Abba P. Lerner, *loc. cit.*, p. 311 and Figs 4 and 5, p. 313, for
the first rigorous investigation of the conditions required for the imposition of a tariff to have this result.
[21] This case, and the conditions required to produce it, are also to
be found in Lerner, *loc. cit.*, text and footnote pp. 310—11 and Fig. 4;
but its implications for the distribution of income were first developed
by Metzler. See L.A. Metzler, 'Tariffs, the Terms of Trade and the
Distribution of National Income, '*Journal of Political Economy*, Vol. 57
(1949) pp. 1—29.

illustrated in Figure 8 by the foreign offer curve OF', free trade international equilibrium point P''_f, international equilibrium point with tariff P''_t, and corresponding internal equilibrium point P''_i; with the tariff, the internal price of imports has fallen from the slope of OP''_f to the slope of OP''_i. The conditions required for these two exceptional results of the imposition of a tariff to occur in the present model must now be investigated.[22]

[22] As is evident from Fig. 8, and from the conditions developed below, both exceptional results are simultaneously possible only if the free-trade equilibrium is unstable, a case which can be disregarded here. As shown in footnote 17, the ratio of reduction in exports of Y supplied to the increase in imports of X demanded resulting from the tariff is

$$\frac{1-c_x}{c_x}\,p_x,$$

where c_x is the marginal propensity to spend on X and p_x is the given initial price of X. The ratio of the reduction in exports of Y supplied to the increase in imports of X demanded resulting from a reduction in the price of imports is

$$-\frac{dY_t}{dX_t} = \frac{\dfrac{-\delta(p_x X_t)}{\delta p_x}}{\dfrac{\delta X_t}{\delta p_x}} = \frac{1-\eta_x}{\eta_x}\,p_x,$$

where Y_t and X_t are the quantities traded internationally at the initial price ratio, and

$$\eta_x = -\frac{p_x}{X_t}\frac{\delta X_t}{\delta p_x}$$

is the elasticity of the country's demand for imports of X. For the tariff to increase the quantity of imports demanded more than would the corresponding price reduction, the first ratio must be less than the second, which requires $c_x > \eta_x$.

The same result may be established in another way. The tariff proceeds on the initial quantity of imports are

$$\frac{t}{1+t}\,p_x X_t,$$

where t is the proportional tariff rate, and the increase in the quantity of imports demanded due to the spending of these proceeds is

$$c_x\,\frac{t}{1+t}\,X_t.$$

(1) *The Lerner Case: Deterioration of the Terms of Trade*

The Lerner case requires that, starting from a given internal price ratio, the imposition of the tariff would lead to a greater increase in the quantity of imports demanded than would a reduction of the internal price to the external price ratio determined by the tariff rate. The effect of the tariff is determined by the (weighted average) marginal propensity to spend on imports of the tariff recipients; the effect of the price reduction is determined by the elasticity of demand for imports. Comparison of P'_t with P'_f in Figure 8 suggests a conclusion which can be rigorously proved, that the tariff will increase the quantity of imports demanded more than the price reduction will if the marginal propensity to spend on imports of the tariff recipients is greater than the elasticity of demand for imports.

The Lerner case requires that the marginal propensity to spend on imports from the tariff proceeds should exceed the country's elasticity of demand for imports. This is only possible if each factor has a preference for consumption of the good which uses it relatively intensively in production, in the sense that its marginal propensity to consume that good is higher than that of the other factor.

The effect of the tariff on the demand for imports is a pure income-effect, whose magnitude depends on the marginal propensities to spend on imports of the factor owners and on the distribution of the tariff proceeds between them. The corresponding price reduction affects the demand for imports in three ways. In the first place, the economy's income is increased by the income effect of the fall in the price of imports and by the shift of production towards exports and away from imports

Footnote continued from previous page

The reduction in the external price due to the tariff is

$$\frac{t}{1+t}\, p_x,$$

and the increase in quantity of imports this would induce under free trade is

$$\frac{\delta X_t}{\delta p_x} \frac{t}{1+t}\, p_x \;=\; \eta_x \frac{t}{1+t} X_t.$$

For the former increase to exceed the latter requires $c_x > \eta_x$.

induced by the tariff reduction; at the same time income is redistributed away from the factor used relatively intensively in producing imports, so that the income of the factor used relatively intensively in producing exports is raised by more than the total increase in national income; the net effect of these changes on the quantity of imports demanded may be termed the 'income effect' of the reduction in the price of imports.[23] Secondly, the shift of production away from production of importables increases the quantity of imports demanded; and thirdly, the reduction of the price of imports induces substitution of imports for exportables in consumption. Since the second and third effects tend to increase the quantity of imports demanded, the tariff can only increase the quantity of imports demanded by more than would the corresponding price reduction if the (income) effect of the tariff on the quantity of imports demanded exceeds the income effect of the price reduction.

This result is impossible if the factor used relatively intensively in export production has the relatively higher marginal propensity to consume imports. In this case, the maximum increase in the quantity of imports demanded with the tariff occurs when the whole of the tariff proceeds is received by this factor. But with the price reduction corresponding to the tariff, this factor receives not only the whole of the increase in the national income, which exceeds the benefit of the lower price of imports (approximately equal to the tariff proceeds on the initial volume of imports) by the increase in national income due to the shift of production towards imports, but income redistributed from the other factor; both the greater increase in national income due to the production shift and the redistribution of income make the income effect of the price reduction on the demand for imports greater than it would be under the tariff.[24]

[23] This net effect was earlier termed 'the income-redistribution effect'; that description is perhaps misleading, since the effect includes the effects of the increases in income due to lower import prices and the shift of production towards imports.

[24] If the tariff proceeds are spent by the government as a third sector of the economy, and the government's marginal propensity to spend on imports is higher than that of either factor, the Lerner result may occur even if the factor used relatively intensively in export production has the higher marginal propensity to spend on imports.

The condition required for the Lerner case can, however, be fulfilled if the factor used relatively intensively in export production has the relatively lower marginal propensity to consume imports (prefers the goods in whose production it is used relatively intensively). In this case, the minimum increase in quantity of imports demanded with the tariff occurs if the whole proceeds are received by this factor; the larger the share going to the other factor, the larger the increase in the quantity of imports demanded. With the corresponding reduction in the price of imports, the factor used relatively intensively in export production receives the whole of the gain from the lower cost of imports, which cannot increase the quantity of imports demanded by more than the spending of the tariff proceeds would; the increase in the value of national income due to the production shift, which will increase the quantity of imports demanded; and a redistribution of income from the other factor, which will reduce the quantity of imports demanded. In this case, therefore, the income effect of the tariff may exceed the income effect of the corresponding reduction in the price of imports on the quantity of imports demanded, so that the Lerner case is possible.

The foregoing argument is illustrated geometrically in Figure 9. In both parts of the Figure, MN is labour's budget line at the free-trade international price ratio of the same slope, and C_C and C_L are respectively capital's and labour's consumption points at that price ratio. The tariff shifts the external price ratio corresponding to this internal price ratio to that shown by the slope of $C'_C C_L$. Labour's budget line at the internal price ratio equal to the external price ratio produced by the tariff is $M'N'$; C''_C and C''_L are respectively capital's and labour's consumption points with the internal price ratio given by the slope of $M'N'$. Comparing the free trade equilibrium positions at the initial price ratio and that corresponding to the tariff, the movement from C_C to A and from C_L to D corresponds to the income effect of the reduction in price (A and D lying on the income-consumption lines through C_C and C_L respectively and A lying to the left of $M'N'$); AB corresponds to the substitution of importables for exportables in production induced by the price reduction; and BC''_C and DC''_L correspond to the substitution of importables for exportables in the consumption of capital

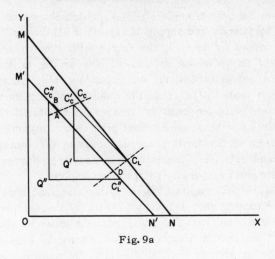

Fig. 9a

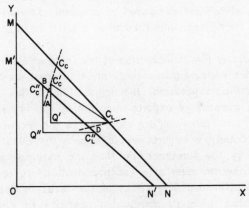

Fig. 9b

and labour induced by the price reduction. $C_C'' Q C_L''$ is the free trade triangle at the internal price ratio equal to the external price ratio produced by the tariff.

In Figure 9A, capital (the factor used relatively intensively in export production) has a higher marginal propensity to spend on imports than labour, as shown by the fact that AC_C has a less steep slope than DC_L. Because AC_C has a less steep slope than DC_L, and C_C'' must lie to the north-west of A and C_L'' to the south-east of D, the free trade triangle $C_C'' Q'' C_L''$ must

33

be greater than the triangle $C'_C Q' C_L$, which shows the country's demand for imports and supply of exports if all the tariff proceeds were received by capital, the factor with the higher marginal propensity to spend on imports. If any of the tariff proceeds were received by labour, the corresponding trade triangle would be smaller than $C'_C Q' C_L$; so the quantity of imports demanded and exports supplied must be less under the tariff than under free trade with the same external price ratio, regardless of the distribution of the tariff proceeds between the factors, if the factor used relatively intensively in export production has the higher marginal propensity to spend on imports.

In Figure 9B, capital has a lower marginal propensity to spend on imports than labour, as shown by the steeper slope of AC_C as compared with DC_L. AD must therefore be shorter than $C'_C C_L$,[25] so that it is possible (as shown in Figure 9B) for $C''_C C''_L$ to be shorter than $C'_C C_L$ and the quantity of exports supplied and imports demanded at a given external price ratio to be less under free trade than when a tariff is in force.

(2) *The Metzler Case*: *Reduction of the Internal Price of Imports*
The Metzler case requires that, starting from an initial free-trade equilibrium position, the imposition of the tariff would reduce the quantity of exports supplied by the home country by more than the corresponding increase in the external price of the home country's exports would reduce the quantity of them demanded by the foreigner, so that the external and internal prices of exports must rise (of imports fall) to restore international equilibrium. The effect of the tariff is determined by the (weighted average) marginal propensity to spend on exportable goods of the tariff recipients; the effect of the increased price of exports on the quantity of them demanded is determined by the elasticity of the foreign demand for them. Consideration of P''_f in Figure 8 suggests the conclusion, which

---

[25] The trade triangle with hypotenuse AD must have a shorter vertical side than $C'_C Q' C_L$, indicating a smaller quantity of exports supplied, but it may nevertheless have a longer horizontal side, indicating a larger quantity of imports demanded, as a consequence of the income effect of a free-trade price reduction as compared with that of the tariff.

can be rigorously proved,[26] that the tariff will decrease the quantity of exports supplied by the home country by more than the corresponding increase in the price of exports will decrease the quantity of exports demanded by the foreigner, if the marginal propensity of the tariff recipients to spend on exportable goods

---

[26] As shown in footnote 17, the ratio of the reduction in exports of Y supplied to the increase in imports of X demanded resulting from the tariff is

$$\frac{c_y}{1 - c_y} p_x,$$

where c_y is the marginal propensity to spend on Y and p_z the given initial price of X. The ratio of the reduction in exports of Y demanded to the increase in imports of X supplied by the foreigner resulting from an increase in the price of exports is

$$-\frac{dY_t}{dX_t} = -\frac{\delta Y_t}{\delta P_y} \bigg/ \frac{\delta(p_y Y_t)}{\delta p_y} = \frac{\eta_y}{1 - \eta_y} p_x,$$

where Y_t and X_t are the quantities initially traded,

$$p_y = \frac{1}{p_x}$$

is the price of Y, and

$$\eta_y = -\frac{p_y}{Y_t} \frac{\delta Y_t}{\delta p_y}$$

is the elasticity of the foreign country's demand for imports of Y. For the tariff to reduce the quantity of exports supplied by more than the corresponding price increase would reduce the quantity of them demanded by the foreigner, the first ratio must exceed the second, which requires $c_y > \eta_y$.

The same result may be established in another way. If the initial quantity of exports were exchanged for imports and duty collected on these imports, the tariff proceeds would be tY_t, where t is the proportional tariff rate; and the reduction in the quantity of exports supplied due to the spending of these proceeds would be $c_y tY_t$. The increase in the external price of exports due to the tariff is tp_y, where $p_y(=1)$ is the given initial price of Y, and the decrease in the quantity of exports demanded abroad that this would induce is

$$-\frac{\delta Y_t}{\delta p_y} t p_y = \eta_y tY_t.$$

For the reduction in quantity supplied to exceed the reduction in quantity demanded requires $c_y > \eta_y$.

For both Lerner and the Metzler cases to be possible simultaneously requires $\eta_x + \eta_y < c_x + c_y = 1$, that is, instability of the initial free trade equilibrium position.

is greater than the elasticity of foreign demand for imports of such goods.

Since the possibility of the Metzler case depends on the relationship between the (weighted-average) marginal propensity to spend on exportable goods of the domestic recipients of the tariff proceeds, and the elasticity of foreign demand for exports, the analysis of the relation between domestic income-distribution and the offer curve does not, as in the Lerner case, shed further light on the conditions required for this case to emerge. It does, however, introduce an additional reason why the elasticity of foreign demand for the home country's exports may be low, apart from the usual one of low substitutability of exports for importable goods in foreign consumption. If foreign factors have a preference for the goods in whose production they are used relatively intensively, in the sense that each factor has a higher marginal propensity to spend on the good which uses it relatively intensively in production than has the other factor, the redistribution of foreign production and incomes brought about by a reduction in the price of the home country's exports will tend to reduce the foreign country's demand for those exports. This adverse redistribution-effect will offset part of the usual income and substitution effects of the price reduction, and may be so strong, that the quantity of the country's exports demanded actually falls as their price falls.

PART V. THE TARIFF AND THE DISTRIBUTION OF INCOME[27]

Except in the Metzler case, the effect of the imposition of a tariff is to raise the internal price of imported goods, so promoting a re-allocation of domestic production towards importable goods and away from exportable goods, and in the process raising the relative price of the factor used relatively intensively in producing the country's import good and lowering that of the factor used relatively intensively in producing the country's export good. The effect of a tariff in the normal case, therefore, is to increase the real earnings of the factor used relatively intensively in the 'protected' industry, and to reduce the real earnings of the factor used relatively intensively in the export industry.

Contrary to the general implication of previous analysis of the problem,[28] however, the effect of the tariff on the 'real wages' of factors is not the end of the story. The effects on the real disposable incomes of factors of the distribution of the proceeds of the tariff collected on the quantity of imports surviving when the tariff is in force must also be taken into account. Since the receipt of any share whatever in the tariff proceeds must increase a factor's real disposable income above its earned income, making allowance for the distribution of the tariff proceeds does not alter the conclusion reached by earlier writers that the factor used relatively intensively in the production of importable goods must enjoy an unambiguous increase in real income as a result of the imposition of the tariff. It does, however, modify the conclusion that the tariff will damage the factor used relatively intensively in the export industry, since that factor may gain more from its share in the tariff proceeds than it loses by the reduction in its real earnings. It is even conceivable that the gain may be so great that the relative share of this factor in the country's income increases, and the relative share of the 'protected' factor decreases.[29]

Such a result is impossible if the foreign offer curve is perfectly elastic, so that the country's terms of trade are fixed

[27] Priority in reaching the central conclusion of this Part belongs to Jagdish Bhagwati; see his 'Protection, Real Wages and Real Incomes,' *Economic Journal*, Vol. LXIX, No. 276 (December 1959) pp. 733–48, esp. pp. 744–48. An earlier writer, S. Venkateswara Rao ('Tariffs, Terms of Trade and the Distribution of National Income,' *The Indian Economic Journal*, Vol. VI, No. 3 (January 1959) pp. 410–13) reaches the same conclusion, that the factor whose rate of earnings is reduced by the tariff may nevertheless enjoy a higher real income under the tariff. But his argument, which runs in terms of the effect of the increase in real income due to the terms-of-trade effect of the tariff on the absolute value of a lower relative share, does not distinguish between earnings and income, and does not recognize that it is not the higher total income of the country as such but the fact that part of it appears as tariff proceeds, a share in which can be added to the lower real earnings of the factor damaged by the tariff, which makes the result possible.

[28] See the articles by Stolper and Samuelson, Metzler, and Lancaster, cited in the first footnote to this chapter.

[29] In the Metzler case, these conclusions apply to the factor used relatively intensively in import production.

and independent of the volume of its trade; for in this case the country as a whole must lose by the distortion of consumption and production away from the optimum conforming with the equalizing of the internal marginal rates of substitution in production and consumption with the marginal rate of transformation of exports into imports through foreign trade, while the 'protected' factor must enjoy a higher real income. This point is easily illustrated by reference to Figure 9; if the slope of $M'N'$ is the fixed external price ratio, at which capital's consumption point is C_C'', and a tariff is imposed which brings the internal price ratio to the slope of MN, the most favourable situation for capital is that in which it receives all the tariff proceeds and has the consumption point C_C', at which point its level of utility is necessarily less than at C_C''.

If, however, the foreign offer curve is not perfectly elastic, so that the tariff secures a terms-of-trade benefit for the country, the damaged factor's share in the tariff proceeds may outweigh its loss of earned income. This will definitely occur when conditions are such that the country is exactly on the borderline between the normal and the Metzler case, with the country's marginal propensity to spend on exportable goods exactly equal to the foreign elasticity of demand for exports, so that real earned incomes of factors are unchanged by the tariff and each factor gains in real disposable income by the amount of its share in the tariff proceeds. The possibility of its occurring in the normal case is illustrated in Figure 10. In the Figure, the slope of MN represents the free-trade equilibrium price, and $C_C Q C_L$ is the free-trade equilibrium trade triangle; with the tariff, the total proceeds of which are assumed to be received by capital, the equilibrium internal price ratio is given by the slope of $M'N'$ and the equilibrium external price ratio by the slope of $C_C' C_L'$. The equilibrium trade triangle with the tariff is $C_C' Q' C_L'$, the quantities of both imports and exports being less than under free trade, representing an 'elastic' foreign offer curve. The point B represents the same consumption of the two goods by capital as C_C, its location having been shifted to match the shift in the origin of capital's indifference curves due to the shift in the production point of the economy induced by the increased internal price of imports. With the income earned at the internal

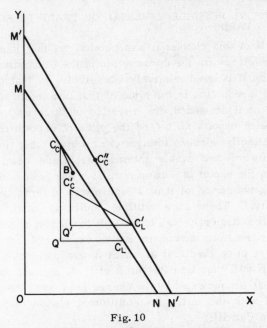

Fig. 10

price ratio associated with the tariff, capital's consumption point would be C_C'', yielding less satisfaction than B, the free-trade consumption point; but thanks to the receipt of the tariff proceeds, capital's actual consumption point is C_C', yielding a higher level of satisfaction than the level B enjoyed under free trade.

The conditions under which the factor whose real earned income falls as a result of the tariff is more than compensated by the receipt of its share of the proceeds of the tariff are obviously more restrictive than those under which both factors gain from the tariff when a socially optimal distribution of income is enforced. In the latter case, the higher earned income of the factor used relatively intensively in the production of importable goods can be tapped for purposes of compensation, whereas in the former case only the tariff proceeds are available for this purpose.[30]

[30] Compensation of the factor whose real earnings are reduced by the tariff for its loss out of the tariff proceeds is clearly impossible in the Lerner case, since the adverse movement of the terms of trade in this case means that both factors together must lose.

39

PART VI. POSSIBLE REVERSAL OF TRADE DIRECTION DUE TO A TARIFF

In Part II of this chapter it was pointed out that if each factor has a preference for the consumption of the commodity in whose production it is used relatively intensively, so that the income effect of a reduction in the price of that commodity reduces the quantity of it demanded, the direction of trade may reverse as the price of imports falls (and the price of exports rises). With an imperfectly elastic foreign offer curve, this implied the possibility of two stable international trade equilibria, one involving the export of a commodity at a low price and the other involving the import of it at a high price, in terms of the other commodity.[31] Where such multiple equilibria exist, the effect of a tariff sufficiently high to prohibit the import of a commodity will be to transform the country into an exporter of that commodity at a lower price than that at which it was previously imported. The tariff will thus turn the terms of trade against the country, when these are reckoned by the change in price of the commodity imported with the tariff, for a different reason than that discussed in Part III.

---

[31] For the same reason, a tariff levied by the foreign country might convert the home country into an importer of the good formerly exported.

Appendix:
An Alternative Derivation of the Transformation Curve and Income Distribution Function

The derivation of the distribution of income in the main text of the chapter has certain pedagogical advantages, in particular emphasizing that a factor's income share is a transformation curve, the position on which is determined by the equilibrium commodity price ratio. But this derivation can be greatly simplified by developing a technique for deriving the transformation curve directly from the contract curve, invented by K.M. Savosnick.[1] This analysis makes use of the accompanying Figure 11.

In the Figure, the sides of the box represent the factor endowments. Isoquants for the two goods are sketched into the box with origins O_x and O_y respectively. Tangencies of isoquants from the two systems form the contract curve $O_x Q O_y$ (not drawn). At Q, the two isoquants show outputs of X_o and Y_o respectively.

The technique for deriving the transformation curve makes use of the fact that, with constant returns to scale, output on any isoquant can be measured by the distance of the isoquant from the origin along any fixed ray through the origin. The diagonal $O_x O_y$ is a common ray for the two isoquant systems, with O_x corresponding to zero output of X and maximum output of Y, and O_y corresponding to zero output of Y and maximum output of X. Taking O as the origin for commodity space, O_x and O_y represent the maximum-Y-production and maximum-X-production termini of the transformation curve (production possibility curve) TT.

The outputs of X and Y corresponding to point Q on the contract curve may be found by following the Y_o — isoquant to its intersection at S with $O_x O_y$, and dropping a perpendicular

[1] K.M. Savosnick, 'The Box Diagram and the Production Possibility Curve', *Ekonemisk Tideskrift*, Vol. LI, No. 3 (September 1958) pp. 183–97.

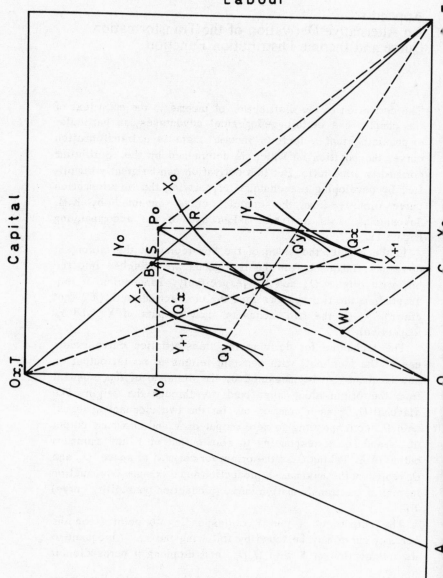

Fig. 11

to the vertical axis to find Y_o; and similarly following the X_o — isoquant to its intersection R with the diagonal and dropping a perpendicular to the horizontal axis to find X_o. The points Y_o and X_o are the coordinates for the production point P_o on the transformation curve corresponding to Q on the contract curve.

The point P_o must obviously be northeast of the diagonal; but this does not suffice to prove the property of strict concavity to the origin O. To prove this, assume factor prices held constant temporarily, and consider equal decreases and increases of production of X about point Q, to X-isoquants X_{-1} and X_{+1} respectively. With constant factor prices, these shifts would involve equal increases and decreases in Y production, to isoquants Y_{+1} and Y_{-1} respectively. But constant factor prices would entail an excess demand for labour when X production decreases, and excess demand for capital when X production increases. Equilibrium with the given factor endowment requires a Y-isoquant tangent to X_{-1} when X decreases, and a Y-isoquant tangent to X_{+1} when X increases. Each isoquant must involve a lower level of Y output than Y_{+1} and Y_{-1} respectively. Thus an increase in X output from X_{-1} to X must involve a smaller reduction in Y output (from something less than Y_{+1} to Y) than an increase in X output from X to X_{+1} (from Y to something less than Y_{-1}). Since this proof holds regardless of the magnitude of the equal changes in X, the transformation curve must be actually concave to the origin.

At the point Q, the factor price ratio is the slope of the common tangent to the isoquants Y_o and X_o. Draw $O_x A$ parallel to the common tangent at Q, to intersect $O_y O$ produced at A. OA then represents the value of labour's contribution to total output, in terms of capital, while capital's contribution in the same terms is the amount of capital itself. Hence AO/AO_y and OO_y/AO_y are the relative shares of labour and capital respectively. Draw OB parallel to AO_x to intersect the diagonal at B, transferring the share ratio to the diagonal. Drop a perpendicular from B to C, so that the shares are represented by OC and CO_y. Finally, draw OP_o (left broken in the diagram to avoid clutter) and $O_y P_o$, and draw CW_l parallel to $O_y P_o$ to intersect OP_o at W_l. OW_l/OP_o is labour's relative share in output, while

W_l itself represents labour's absolute share in terms of quantities of X and Y. It is a reference point fixing the location of labour's budget line, the slope of which is the commodity price ratio given by the tangent to the transformation curve at P_o. It also of course locates capital's budget line with reference to P_o as origin.

Repetition of the construction for different contract curve points Q will trace out the transformation curve and the income distribution locus. It is obvious from the construction that, as production of Y expands and of X falls, the slope of the common tangent at Q becomes steeper, and labour's relative and absolute shares fall, i.e. the successive budget lines for labour must lie inside one another for movements along the contract and transformation curves in the northwestern direction.

2. A Generalized Theory of the Effects of Tariffs on the Terms of Trade*

Traditional analysis of the effect of a tariff on the terms of trade of the protecting country draws a distinction between two cases: (1) where the tariff revenue is spent by the government; and (2) where the tariff revenue is redistributed as an income subsidy to the private sector. In both cases the conclusion reached is that the terms of trade of the protecting country will improve or deteriorate according as the country's elasticity of demand for imports is greater or less than the marginal propensity to consume importables (of the government or the private sector, as the case may be). By splitting the elasticity of demand for imports into the sum of the compensated elasticity of demand for imports and the private sector's marginal propensity to consume importables, it can further be shown (on the usual assumption of convex indifference and transformation curves) that the terms of trade must improve if the private sector spends the tariff revenue; and that, if the government spends the tariff revenue, the terms of trade can only deteriorate if the government's marginal propensity to consume importables exceeds the private sector's marginal propensity to consume importables by more than the private compensated elasticity of demand for imports. Normally, the terms of trade will not improve sufficiently to offset the effect of the tariff in raising the domestic price of importables; but the tariff will reduce the domestic price of importables if the marginal propensity to consume exportables of whichever sector spends the tariff revenue is greater than the foreign elasticity of demand for exportables.

This analysis, however, is founded on four restrictive postulates:

(1) *Initial free trade.* It is assumed that there is no tariff in

Oxford Economic Papers Vol. XIII, No. 3 (October 1961) pp. 225–53.

effect in the initial situation; hence the analysis does not apply to the case of an increase in an existing tariff rate.

(2) *Independence of consumer taste and government expenditure.* Where the government spends the tariff revenue, it is assumed that the amount of government expenditure – either the total, or the amount spent on particular commodities – does not affect the way in which the private sector divides its expenditure between importables and exportables; hence the analysis does not apply to the case of dependence of consumer taste on the amount of government expenditure.

(3) *Aggregation of the private sector.* It is assumed that the private sector can be treated as a homogeneous unit with respect to its demand for imports; this ignores the effects of a change in the domestic price of importables in redistributing real income (a) between consumers with different tastes, and (b) between owners of different collections of factors of production, as well as the influence [in case (2)] of the way in which the redistributed tariff revenue is allocated among private consumers.

(4) *Inelastic supply of factors.* In dealing with the effects of a change in the domestic price of importables on domestic production, it is assumed that the supply of resources is given; hence the analysis does not take account of the effects on import demand of changes in factor supplies consequential on the change in the tariff rate.

In this chapter we generalize the theory of tariffs by examining the effect of an increase in the tariff rate when these restrictive assumptions do not hold.[1] We distinguish three major cases: (1) where the government spends the tariff revenue and private

---

[1] For the traditional analysis, reference may be made to A.P. Lerner, 'The Symmetry Between Import and Export Taxes', *Economica*, N.S., Vol. III, No. 11 (Aug. 1936) pp. 306–13; L. Metzler, 'Tariffs, the Terms of Trade and the Distribution of National Income', *Journal of Political Economy*, Vol. 1VII, No. 1 (Feb. 1949) pp. 1–29; and R.E. Baldwin, 'The Effect of Tariffs on International and Domestic Prices', *Quarterly Journal of Economics*, Vol. 1XXIV, No. 1 (Feb. 1960) pp. 65–78. In a later supplement to his classic paper, *op. cit.*, Lloyd Metzler recognized explicitly the dependence of the analysis developed by him, of the effect of tariffs on domestic prices, on the assumption of initial free trade; see his 'Tariffs, International Demand, and Domestic Prices', *Journal of Political Economy*, Vol. 1VII, No. 4 (Aug. 1949) pp. 345–51.

demand is independent of government expenditure; (2) where the proceeds of the tariff are consumed by the private sector; (3) where the government spends the tariff revenue and the amount of government expenditure influences the private sector's demand for imports. Section I analyses the first two (the traditional) cases, abandoning the restriction of initial free trade. Section II analyses the third case, abandoning the second restriction of independence of private demand and government expenditure. Section III abandons the third restriction and incorporates the effects of disaggregating consumption demand and factor ownership in the analysis of the three cases. Section IV abandons the fourth restriction and extends the analysis to include the effects of variable supplies of factors. These four sections are concerned with the effect of the tariff increase on the terms of trade; in Section V we analyse the effect of the tariff increase on the domestic price of importables.

Throughout the analysis we assume that only two goods are produced and consumed, 'exportables' and 'importables'; in analysing case (3), however, we assume that the amount of government expenditure enters consumers' utility functions as a third consumption good. In dropping restrictions (3) and (4) we assume that income is shared between two individuals, each of whom owns a collection of productive factors and earns an income from the sale of their services; and that each good is produced in a linear homogeneous production function employing two factors, labour and capital, whose earnings are wages and rent respectively, these factors being employed in different ratios in the two industries. Markets for goods and factors are assumed to be perfectly competitive. In analysing the effect of the tariff increase in the various cases, we employ the simplifying device of assuming the conditions for stability in the international market; this permits the effect of the tariff on the terms of trade to be inferred from its effect on the excess demand for imports at the initial terms of trade, and its effect on the domestic price of importables to be inferred from its effect on the excess demand for imports at the initial domestic price of imports.

We employ the following mathematical symbols throughout the chapter; other symbols are defined when they appear in the argument:

47

p, the international price of the importable good in terms of the exportable good (the terms of trade); by choice of units, p is initially made equal to unity;

t, the tariff rate, defined as a proportion of the international price of importables;

π, the domestic price of importables in terms of exportables; $\pi = (1 + t)p$; because p is initially unity $d\pi/dt$ in the mathematical development below is equal to unity;

P, the quantity of importables produced domestically;

Q, the quentity of exportables produced domestically;

Y, the amount of earned income: $Y = \pi P + Q$;

C, the quantity of importables consumed out of private income; private income is equal to earned income where the government spends the tariff revenue [cases (1) and (3)], and to earned income plus tariff proceeds where the latter are redistributed to the private sector [case (2)];

M_1, the quantity of importables imported for private consumption: $M_1 = C - P$;

M_2, the quantity of importables consumed by the government out of tariff revenue; this quantity must obviously be imported, and it simplifies matters to assume that the government buys its importables abroad at the world market price;

M, the total quantity of imports: $M = M_1 + M_2$;

R, the tariff revenue: $R = tpM_1$;

c, the private sector's marginal propensity to spend on importables at the domestic price of importables; the private sector's marginal propensity to consume importables is c/π;

g, the government's marginal propensity to spend tariff revenue on imports at the international price of imports; the government's marginal propensity to consume imports is $g/p = g$;

ξ, the domestic price elasticity of private demand for imports, tariff revenue being held constant where it affects private demand [cases (2) and (3)];

$$\xi = \frac{\pi \delta M_1}{M_1 \delta \pi};$$

η, the price elasticity of private demand for importables, earned income and tariff revenue being held constant;

$$\eta = \frac{\pi \delta C}{C \delta \pi};$$

η', the compensated elasticity of private demand for importables; $\eta' = \eta - c$;

ϵ, the elasticity of domestic supply of importables with given

supplies of factors of production; $\epsilon = \frac{\pi \delta P}{P \delta \pi}$;

ξ', the compensated elasticity of private demand for imports:

$$\xi' = \frac{C}{M_1} \eta' + \frac{P}{M_1} \epsilon = \xi - c.$$

Barred symbols denote initial magnitudes of the variables when these might be confused with the functional relationships that determine them. The main equations in the mathematical argument have been numbered; the formulae derived have also been assigned roman numerals.

I. THE EFFECT OF AN INCREASE IN THE TARIFF ON THE TERMS OF TRADE: CASES (1) AND (2)

An increase in the tariff rate will cause an improvement or a deterioration in the terms of trade according as it gives rise to a negative or a positive world excess demand for importables at the initial international price of imports. Since the quantity of imports supplied by the rest of the world at the initial terms of trade is unchanged by the increase in the tariff, the change in the world excess demand for importables resulting from the tariff increase is equal to the change in the tariff-increasing country's demand for imports. On the usual assumptions that the private sector can be treated as an aggregate and that factor supplies are inelastic, this change, in cases (1) and (2), is the net result of two effects of the tariff increase:

(i) the effect of the increase in the domestic price of importables due to the tariff increase on the quantity of imports privately demanded;

(ii) the effect of the change in the amount of tariff revenue due to the increase in the tariff and the consequential change in the quantity of imports privately demanded under (i) above, on the quantity of imports demanded by the government or the private sector, whichever spends the tariff revenue.

Case (1). The change in the quantity of imports privately demanded is determined by the elasticity of private demand for imports; this change, which we denote by $\delta M_1 / \delta t$ because the tariff also affects private demand for imports in other ways in case (2) and other cases considered below, is:

$$\frac{\delta M_1}{\delta t} = \frac{\delta M_1}{\delta \pi} \frac{d\pi}{dt} = -\frac{\bar{M}_1}{\pi} \xi.$$

The change in the quantity of imports demanded due to the increase in the domestic price of importables is actually the net result of three effects of the increase in the domestic price of importables:

(i) the change in private consumption of importables due to the increase in the price of importables, determined by the price elasticity of private demand for importables; this change is:

$$\frac{\delta C}{\delta \pi} \frac{d\pi}{dt} = -\frac{\bar{C}}{\pi} \eta;$$

(ii) the change in private consumption of importables due to the increase in income earned in domestic production resulting from the increased domestic price of importables, determined [2] by the initial amount of domestic production of importables and the marginal propensity to consume importables; this change is:

$$\frac{\delta C}{\delta Y} \frac{\delta Y}{\delta \pi} \frac{d\pi}{dt} = \frac{c}{\pi} \bar{P};$$

[2] The effect on the value of output of the increase in production of importables (analysed under (iii) above) and the associated reduction in the production of exportables induced by the increase in the domestic price of importables can be ignored, since maximization of the value of output under competition implies that the effect of small departures of production from the equilibrium quantities is of the second order of smalls.

(iii) the increase in domestic production of importables in response to the increase in their domestic price, determined by the elasticity of domestic supply of importables; this change is:

$$\frac{dP}{d\pi}\frac{d\pi}{dt} = \frac{\bar{P}}{\pi}\epsilon.$$

The net result of these three effects is:

$$
\begin{aligned}
\frac{\delta M_1}{\delta t} &= -\frac{\bar{M}_1}{\pi}\left(\frac{\bar{C}}{\bar{M}_1}\eta - \frac{\bar{P}}{\bar{M}_1}c + \frac{\bar{P}}{\bar{M}_1}\epsilon\right) \\
&= -\frac{\bar{M}_1}{\pi}\left(\frac{\bar{C}}{\bar{M}_1}\eta' + \frac{\bar{P}}{\bar{M}_1}\epsilon + c\right) \\
&= -\frac{\bar{M}_1}{\pi}(\xi' + c).
\end{aligned}
\tag{1}
$$

Case (2). (a) Where the government spends the tariff revenue, the change in the quantity of imports it demands will be determined by the change in the tariff revenue from private imports and the government's marginal propensity to consume importables; this change is:

$$\frac{dM_2}{dt} = g\frac{dR}{dt} = g\left(t\frac{\partial M_1}{\partial t} + \bar{M}_1\right) = g\bar{M}_1\left(1 - \frac{t}{\pi}\xi\right). \tag{2a}$$

(b) Where the tariff revenue is redistributed to the private sector the change in the quantity of imports privately demanded will be determined by the change in the tariff revenue and the marginal propensity to consume importables of the private sector; but the change in the tariff revenue in this case is not simply the change in tariff revenue due to the change in private imports analysed under (2) above, but the product of that change and the sum of a series which is determined by the marginal propensity to consume imports of the private sector. The initial change in the tariff revenue due to the increase in the tariff rate and its effect on the quantity of imports privately demanded will change private expenditure on imports by a fraction of itself approximately equal to c, of which c/π will represent a change in the quantity of imports demanded and ct/π a further change in tariff revenue, which will lead to further changes of $c^2 t/\pi^2$ in the quantity of imports demanded and $c^2 t^2/\pi^2$ in tariff revenue, and so on. Hence the total change in redistributed tariff revenue will be:

$$\frac{dR}{dt} = \left(1 + \frac{ct}{\pi} + \frac{c^2 t^2}{\pi^2} + \ldots\right) \frac{\delta R}{\delta t} = \frac{1}{1 + (1 - c)t} \frac{\delta R}{\delta t},$$

where

$$\frac{\partial R}{\partial t} = \frac{\delta}{\delta t}(tM_1) = \bar{M}_1 \left(1 - \frac{t}{\pi} \xi\right);$$

and the change in the quantity of imports demanded due to the effect of the tariff change on the amount of redistributed tariff revenue will be:

$$\frac{\partial C}{\partial R} \frac{dR}{dt} = \frac{c}{\pi} \frac{\pi}{1 + (1 - c)t} \frac{\partial R}{\partial t} = \frac{c\bar{M}_1}{1 + (1 - c)t} \left(1 - \frac{t}{\pi} \xi\right). \quad (2b)$$

In case (1) the total effect of the tariff increase on the world excess demand for importables is [the sum of equations (1) and (2a)]:[3]

$$\frac{dM}{\partial t} = -\frac{\bar{M}_1}{\pi} \xi + g\bar{M}_1 \left(1 - \frac{t}{\pi} \xi\right)$$

$$= \bar{M}_1 \left(g - \frac{1 + gt}{\pi} \xi\right)$$

$$= \bar{M}_1 \left[g - (1 + gt)\frac{c}{\pi} - \frac{1 + gt}{\pi} \xi'\right]. \quad (3)\mathrm{I}$$

If initially there is free trade, this reduces to $dM/dt = M_1 (g - c - \xi')$, which yields the traditional conclusion that world excess demand for importables at the initial world price will be negative and the terms of trade turn in the country's favour unless the government's marginal propensity to consume importables exceeds the private sector's marginal propensity to consume importables by more than the private sector's compensated elasticity of demand for imports. This in turn requires that the government have a stronger marginal preference for

---

[3]This result can be obtained directly by differentiating the basic equation for this case, $M \equiv M_1 + M_2 = M_1(\pi) + M_2(R)$, where $R = tM_1$ and $dM_2/dR = g$.

importables than the private sector (a higher marginal propensity to spend on them at the same price) and that the private compensated elasticity of demand for imports be less than unity (assuming that imports are not inferior in private consumption, and that the government, having no initial revenue, cannot have a marginal propensity to spend on importables greater than unity). *If there is a tariff in effect, it remains true that the government must have a higher marginal propensity to consume importables than the private sector for the terms of trade to deteriorate; but since the tariff makes the real cost of importables to the consumer higher than to the government* (assuming that the latter chooses rationally on the basis of world and not domestic prices), *this does not necessarily imply that the government has the stronger marginal preference for importables* (in the sense defined above). *In the general case, also, the terms of trade can deteriorate even if the private compensated elasticity of demand for imports exceeds unity;* this could occur if the government's marginal propensity to consume importables (though higher than the private) were sufficiently low or the tariff rate sufficiently high to offset a compensated elasticity above unity, or if importables were inferior goods to the government at the income level represented by the initial tariff revenue.

In case (2) the total effect of the tariff increase on the world excess demand for importables is [the sum of equations (1) and (2b)]: [4]

$$\frac{dM}{dt} = -\frac{\overline{M}_1}{\pi}\,\xi + \frac{c\overline{M}_1}{1+(1-c)t}\left(1 - \frac{t}{\pi}\,\xi\right)$$

$$= \frac{\overline{M}_1}{1+(1-c)t}\,(c - \xi)$$

$$= -\frac{\overline{M}_1\,\xi'}{1+(1-c)t}. \tag{4) II}$$

It follows that world excess demand for importables at the initial world price must be negative and the terms of trade must be improved following an increase in the tariff rate; hence *the result*

---

[4]This result can be obtained directly by differentiating the basic equation for this case. $M \equiv M_1 = M_1(\pi, R)$ where $\delta M_1/\delta R = c/1 + t$ and $R = tM_1$.

of a tariff increase in case (2) *is the same, whether the tariff increase is imposed on an initial free-trade situation or on an existing tariff.* This is only what one would expect, since redistribution of tariff proceeds reduces the effect of a tariff increase on the demand for imports to a pure substitution effect.

II. THE EFFECT OF AN INCREASE IN THE TARIFF ON THE TERMS OF TRADE: CASE (3), DEPENDENCE

In the preceding section we have analysed the two traditional cases, (1) where the government spends the tariff revenue, and (2) where the tariff revenue is redistributed to the private sector. In analysing the latter case we have assumed that the tariff proceeds are redistributed in the form of an income subsidy, which is spent by the private sector in the same way as would be an increment in earned income.[5] But it would make no difference to the final result if it were assumed that the tariff proceeds were distributed in kind instead of in cash — that the government used the tariff revenue to purchase some collection of exportables and importables and distributed that collection to the public. For the public would merely adjust its purchases from its earned income to obtain the same total consumption of each good as it would have chosen if the tariff proceeds had been redistributed in cash. A subsidy in kind can only produce a different consumption pattern than a cash subsidy if the amount of a particular good distributed in kind is larger than the total that would have been purchased out of the subsidy-recipient's own income plus the cash subsidy, and this possibility is excluded in the present case by the fact that the amount of goods the government can distribute in kind is restricted by the amount of tariff proceeds it collects.

In analysing the former case we have made the traditional assumption that the behaviour of the private sector is unaffected by the expenditure of the tariff revenue by the government — that private-sector tastes are independent of government consumption. The case of dependence of private tastes on government

[5]This income-subsidy assumption is to be found in J.E. Meade, *A Geometry of International Trade* (London: Allen & Unwin, 1952), Chapter VI. Metzler, *op. cit.*, assumes, however, a reduction in an existing income tax by this amount, which reduces to the same thing.

consumption has recently been examined by Robert Baldwin, who reaches the rather surprising conclusion that the results in the dependence case are the same as in the income-subsidy case. This conclusion is understandable, however, once it is realized that Baldwin identifies the general case of dependence with the special case in which consumers regard government purchases as equivalent to an addition to their own private consumption of the goods concerned. In fact, in his theoretical analysis, Baldwin explicitly treats government consumption as the provision of benefits in kind to consumers, which means that the government in effect is not consuming the tariff proceeds on its own behalf but is redistributing them in kind; and, as we have just argued, this should have the same effect as re-distributing them through income subsidies.[6]

The more interesting general problem of dependence arises when the government uses the tariff proceeds for its own con-sumption, *and* the amount of some or all of the governmental services provided by this consumption influences the relative quantities of commodities purchased by the private sector from its earned income in a way not necessarily identifiable with the influence of a direct governmental subsidy in cash or kind. This is a more realistic case than that traditionally analysed [our case (1)] and a more general case than that analysed by Baldwin. One would expect that an increase in state expenditure on, say, police services would lead to a reduction in the amount of private expenditure on fire-arms, locks and bolts, and body-guards, but not that the effects of the two changes on demand would exactly offset one another, since the government provides services in a different form than they would be privately provided. Similarly the government provides collective goods which would not be privately provided if consumers had the spending of their

[6]R.E. Baldwin, *op. cit.*, especially pp. 69–71. In note 5 to p. 67, Baldwin interprets 'dependence' in the broader sense in which we discuss it: 'However, as long as the consumption by the government furnishes some utility to the private sector, it is possible for this public consumption to change the civilian offer curve of exports for imports.' But in his analysis he gives it the narrow interpretation discussed here. We are indebted to Mr. Baldwin for correspondence and personal discussion which removed a misunderstanding of his argument on our part.

tax contributions, and which influence the pattern of private demand.

Technically, dependence implies that the amount of some or all of the service provided by government enters the utility function of the private sector in a significant way (i.e. its substitute-complement relationship with commodities privately consumed varies between commodities) so that the private sector's demands for goods become functions of the total or of some component of the amount of government consumption. In so far as the composition of governmental services depends on the relative prices of commodities purchased by the government, the equilibrium of the economy will vary with the nature of the dependence of private demands on the amounts of governmental services provided; but for the present analysis, which is concerned with the effect of a tariff increase on the excess demand for importables at the given initial world price of importables and assumes that the government chooses on the basis of this price, private demands can be assumed to depend only on the total amount of governmental expenditure, since this will determine the amounts of the separate types of government service provided.[7]

Dependence means that, in addition to the price effect on private demand for imports and the revenue effect on governmental demand for imports analysed under case (1), the tariff increase will have a dependence effect on private demand for imports through its effect on the amount of government revenue and consumption. This effect will be:

$$\frac{\delta C}{\delta R} \frac{dR}{dt} = \frac{b}{\pi} \left(t \frac{dM_1}{dt} + \bar{M}_1 \right) , \qquad (5)$$

where b, the change in private expenditure on importables associated with a unit change in government expenditure, will be positive or negative according as imports are complementary or substitutary with government expenditure in private consumption. The total change in private demand for imports is

---

[7] Our problem here is analytically similar to that faced by J.R. Hicks in his analysis of the effects of a change in wants, in Chap. XVII, especially pp. 162–4, of *A Revision of Demand Theory* (Oxford: At the Clarendon Press, 1956).

now [the sum of equations (1) and (5)]:

$$\frac{dM_1}{dt} = -\frac{\bar{M}_1}{\pi} \xi + \frac{b}{\pi}\left(t\frac{dM_1}{dt} + \bar{M}_1\right) = \frac{(b - \xi)\bar{M}_1}{1 + (1 - b)t}, \quad (6)$$

and the resulting change in governmental demand for imports is:

$$\frac{dM_2}{dt} = g\left[\frac{t(b - \xi)\bar{M}_1}{1 + (1 - b)t} + \bar{M}_1\right] = \frac{(\pi - t\xi)g}{1 + (1 - b)t}\bar{M}_1; \quad (7)$$

hence the total change in world excess demand for importables is [the sum of equations (6) and (7)]:[8]

$$\frac{dM}{dt} = \frac{\bar{M}_1}{1 + (1 - b)t}[b + g\pi - (1 + gt)\xi]$$

$$= \frac{\bar{M}_1}{1 + (1 - b)t}[b + g\pi - (1 + gt)c - (1 + gt)\xi']. \quad (8)\,\text{III}$$

If initially there is free trade, this formula reduces to $\bar{M}_1(b + g - c - \xi')$. In contrast to the case of independence [case (1) above], *world excess demand for importables at the initial world price can be positive and the terms of trade deteriorate even if the private sector has a higher marginal propensity to consame importables than the government and the private compensated elasticity of demand for imports exceeds unity; this result can occur if government services are sufficiently strongly complementary with importables in private-sector consumption.* The same conclusion holds *a fortiori* for the case of an existing tariff.[9]

[8] This result can be obtained directly by differentiating the basic equation for this case, $M \equiv M_1 + M_2 = M_1(\pi, R) + M_2(R)$, where $\delta M_1/\delta R = b/\pi$, $\delta M_2/\delta R = g$, and $R = tM_1$; it is necessary first to solve for dM_1/dt by differentiating M_1 alone. It should be noted that the stability of equilibrium requires that the denominator in this and similar expressions presented subsequently for cases (2) and (3) must be positive; this is assumed without further comment in the argument of the rest of this article.

[9] It should be noticed that if consumers treat government consumption as equivalent to personal consumption of the commodities concerned (the Baldwin case), with initial free trade $b = c - g$ and the formula is identical with that given earlier for case (2). With a tariff initially in effect the formulae are different because we have assumed that the government does not pay tariff revenue to itself on its imports.

III. THE EFFECT OF AN INCREASE IN THE TARIFF ON THE TERMS OF TRADE: DISAGGREGATION OF THE PRIVATE SECTOR

In the previous two sections we have analysed the effect of an increase in the tariff rate in our three cases on the assumption that the private sector could be regarded as a homogeneous unit. Abandonment of this assumption introduces three complications:

(1) In so far as consumers consume exportables and importables in differing proportions, as a result of either taste or income differences, a change in the domestic price of importables alters the distribution of real income between them.

(2) In so far as consumers own factors of production in different proportions, a change in the domestic price of importables, by altering the relative prices of factors of production, alters the distribution of earned income between them.

(3) Where the tariff proceeds are redistributed to the private sector and the marginal propensities of consumers to consume importables differ, as a result of either taste or income differences, the way in which the tariff proceeds are divided among consumers will influence the effect of redistribution on the demand for importables.

To develop the analysis of the disaggregated case we assume that the private sector consists of two typical consumers, each of whom derives his earned income from the ownership of a collection of factors used in production. We begin with case (1); once the results for this case have been developed, the modifications required for the other cases are minor. The problem in case (1) is to disaggregate the elasticity of private demand for imports.

It has been shown elsewhere by one of the present writers that the income earned by a factor owner at any particular domestic price ratio between exportables and importables can be equated with the sum of the real values of the quantities (one of which may be negative) of the two commodities which would be produced with his factors at that price ratio.[10] Accordingly, let the earned incomes of the two factor owners at the initial domestic price of importables be:

$$Y_1 = \pi P_1 + Q_1 \tag{9a}$$

and

$$Y_2 = \pi P_2 + Q_2, \tag{9b}$$

where Y represents income and P and Q quantities of importables and exportables produced, and subscripts 1 and 2 denote the two individuals. We now write the total private-sector demand for importables as the sum of the demands of the two individuals, each of which depends on the domestic price of importables and the individual's income: [11]

$$C \equiv C_1 + C_2 = C_1(\pi, Y_1) + C_2(\pi, Y_2).$$

Differentiating by π, we obtain: [12]

$$\frac{dC}{d\pi} = \frac{\partial C_1}{\partial Y_1}\bar{P}_1 + \frac{\partial C_1}{\partial \pi} + \frac{\partial C_2}{\partial Y_2}\bar{P}_2 + \frac{\partial C_2}{\partial \pi}$$

$$= \frac{c_1}{\pi}\bar{P}_1 - \frac{\bar{C}_1}{\pi}\eta_1 + \frac{c_2}{\pi}\bar{P}_2 - \frac{\bar{C}_2}{\pi}\eta_2$$

$$= -\frac{\bar{C}_1}{\pi}\eta_1' - \frac{\bar{C}_2}{\pi}\eta_2' - \frac{c_1}{\pi}(\bar{C}_1 - \bar{P}_1) - \frac{c_2}{\pi}(\bar{C}_2 - \bar{P}_2), \tag{10a}$$

where c_1 and c_2 are the marginal propensities to spend on importables of the two individuals, η_1 and η_2 are the price elasticities of their demands for importables from their initial incomes, and $\eta_1'(=\eta_1 - c_1)$ and $\eta_2'(=\eta_2 - c_2)$ are their compensated price elasticities of demand for importables.

The two terms on the right-hand side of the above expression represent the net income effects of the increased price of imports on the demands of the two individuals; the terms in

[10] H.G. Johnson, 'International Trade, Income Distribution, and the Offer Curve', *Manchester School of Economic and Social Studies*, Vol. XXVII, No. 3 (Sept. 1959) pp. 241–60, reprinted in Chapter 1 above.

[11] For the analysis of case (2), demands depend on the sum of earned income and the amount of redistributed tariff proceeds received; but the latter is assumed constant in deriving the elasticities of consumption demand and the elasticity of import demand.

[12] For each individual $\delta Y/\delta\pi = P$, since the effect on the real value of his income of changes in the relative amounts of the two goods produced by his factors induced by the change in π can be neglected for small changes.

parentheses are the net income-losses themselves. Unless the excess of initial consumption over the amount of importables the individual's factors would produce bears the same ratio to the initial amount of income for each individual, the price increase will alter the relative real incomes of the individuals; that individual will gain relatively who initially spent the smaller proportion of his income on importables, factors being owned in equal ratios by the two individuals, or who possesses the higher proportion of factors used relatively intensively in the importable-good industry, initial consumption proportions being equal. If tastes, incomes, or factor-ownership ratios differ considerably, it is even possible that one individual's consumption of importables will be less than the amount of importables produced by his factors, so that that individual gains real income as a result of the increase in the price of imports; this must be true in the extreme case in which each individual owns the whole supply of one factor, since in that case the individual's income will comprise a negative quantity of the good which uses intensively the factor he does not own. If conditions are such that one individual gains real income, and his marginal propensity to spend on importables is higher than that of the other individual, the aggregate income effect on demand for importables may be positive rather than negative; the individual gaining real income must have the higher marginal propensity to spend on importables for this to happen, since the other individual must be consuming both the excess of this individual's production of importables over his consumption and the country's imports from the rest of the world ($\bar{C}_1 - \bar{P}_1 = \bar{M}_1 + \bar{P}_2 - \bar{C}_2$). If the aggregate income effect on demand for imports is positive it may outweigh the negative effects of the compensated elasticities, so that the aggregate effect of an increase in the price of importables is to increase the quantity of imports demanded.

This possibility can be shown by re-writing $dC/d\pi$ in the form

$$\frac{dC}{d\pi} = -\frac{\bar{C}_1}{\pi}\eta_1' - \frac{\bar{C}_2}{\pi}\eta_2' - \left(\frac{c_2}{\pi} - \frac{c_1}{\pi}\right)(\bar{C}_2 - \bar{P}_2) - \frac{c_1}{\pi}\bar{M}_1. \quad (10b)$$

If individual 2 has the higher marginal propensity to consume importables and his factors produce more importables than he consumes, the second-to-last term on the right will be positive. The quantity of importables demanded will increase when the price of importables rises if

$$(c_2 - c_1)(\bar{C}_2 - \bar{P}_2) > \bar{C}_1 \, \eta'_1 + \bar{C}_2 \, \eta'_2 + c_1 \, \bar{M}_1.$$

The total change in private demand for imports resulting from an increase in the domestic price of importables is the difference between the change in consumption demand and the increase in domestic production. Hence the disaggregated elasticity of private demand for imports is:

$$\xi = \left[\frac{\bar{P}}{\bar{M}_1} \, \epsilon + \frac{\bar{C}_1}{\bar{M}_1} \, \eta'_1 + \frac{\bar{C}_2}{\bar{M}_1} \, \eta'_2 + c_1 + (c_2 - c_1) \frac{\bar{C}_2 - \bar{P}_2}{\bar{M}_1} \right]$$

$$= [\xi' + c_1 + (c_2 - c_1) m_2], \tag{11}$$

where $m_2 = (\bar{C}_2 - \bar{P}_2)/\bar{M}_1$ is the proportion of the country's imports consumed, net, by individual 2. If m_2 is negative, individual 2 is a 'net supplier' of importables to the economy. For convenience we shall assume in what follows that individual 2 has the higher marginal propensity to consume importables ($c_2 > c_1$).

The formula for the effect of an increase in the tariff rate in the *disaggregated case* (1) is readily obtained by substituting the expression for the disaggregated elasticity of private demand for imports just derived into the formula [equation (3)] given in Section I above. The resulting formula is:

$$\frac{dM}{dt} = \bar{M}_1 \left[g - (1 + gt)\frac{c_1}{\pi} - \frac{1 + gt}{\pi} (c_2 - c_1) m_2 - \frac{1 + gt}{\pi} \xi' \right].$$

$$\tag{12)IV}$$

In the initial free-trade case this reduces to

$$\frac{dM}{dt} = \bar{M}_1 \, [g - c_1 - (c_2 - c_1) m_2 - \xi'].$$

The chief modification to the preceding analysis of case (1) introduced by disaggregation which emerges from this formula is that *it is not necessary for the government to have a higher marginal propensity to consume importables than the private*

61

sector for the tariff increase to give rise to a positive excess demand for importables in the world market and so necessitate a deterioration in the terms of trade. *Such a deterioration can occur even though the government has a lower marginal propensity to consume importables from an increment of tariff revenue than does either individual from an increment in his income,* if the individual with the higher marginal propensity to consume importables is a net supplier of importables to the economy (m_2 is negative in the above formula). Similarly, even in the case of initial free trade a deterioration of the terms of trade does not require an inelastic compensated private demand for imports.

To obtain the formula for the effect of the tariff increase in the *disaggregated case* (2) from the formula given [equation (4)] for the aggregated case (2) in Section I, it is necessary both to substitute the disaggregated expression for the aggregate elasticity of private demand for imports and to replace the single marginal propensity to consume importables used in analysing the effect of the change in the amount of redistributed tariff proceeds by an average of the marginal propensities of the two individuals, weighted by the proportions in which they share in the redistributed tariff proceeds. The resulting formula is:

$$\frac{dM}{dt} = \frac{\bar{M}_1}{1 + (1 - \bar{c})t} \, (\bar{c} - \xi)$$

$$= \frac{\bar{M}_1}{1 + (1 - \bar{c})t} [(c_2 - c_1)(s_2 - m_2) - \xi'], \qquad (13)\,\text{V}$$

where s_2 is the share of individual 2 in marginal redistributed tariff proceeds and $\bar{c}[= c_1 + s_2(c_2 - c_1)]$ is the weighted average marginal propensity to spend redistributed tariff proceeds on importables. This formula shows that, in contrast to the aggregated case (2), *in the disaggregated case* (2) *the tariff increase does not necessarily produce a negative world excess demand for importables* and turn the terms of trade in the tariff-increasing country's favour. *The reverse is possible if the share in the redistributed tariff proceeds of the individual with the higher marginal propensity to consume importables is larger than the proportion of the initial quantity of imports he consumes.* This will be the case, for example, if tariff proceeds are redistributed in proportion to income and (for reasons discussed above) the quantity of imports he consumes is smaller in relation to his income than is the quantity consumed by the other individual in relation to the latter's income — so that this individual is overcompensated for the income effect of the increased domestic price of importables. It should be noticed also that, since the individual with the higher marginal propensity to consume importables may be a net supplier of importables to the economy (m_2 negative) there may be *no* way of allocating the marginal change in tariff proceeds between the two individuals which would compensate both of them exactly for the income effect of the tariff increase.

To obtain the formula for the effect of the tariff increase in the *disaggregated case* (3) from the formula [equation (8)] given for the aggregated case (3) in Section II above, it is necessary to substitute the disaggregated expression for the elasticity of private demand for importables in that formula and to rewrite the dependence effect as the sum of the dependence effects on the two individuals (which may be of different magnitudes and opposite signs). The resulting formula is:

$$\frac{dM}{dt} = \frac{\bar{M}_1}{1 + (1 - b_1 - b_2)t}$$
$$[b_1 + b_2 + g\pi - (1+gt)c_1 - (1+gt)(c_2 - c_1)m_2 - (1+gt)\xi'].$$

(14) VI

The main modification introduced by disaggregation arises from the possibility that the individual with the higher marginal propensity to consume importables will gain real income from the increase in the domestic price of importables; the nature of this modification has already been discussed in connexion with the disaggregated case (1).

IV. THE EFFECT OF AN INCREASE IN THE TARIFF ON THE TERMS OF TRADE: VARIABLE SUPPLIES OF FACTORS OF PRODUCTION

In the preceding sections we have successively relaxed three of the assumptions of the traditional analysis of the effect of a tariff on the terms of trade — the assumptions of initial free trade, independence of private from government consumption, and homogeneity of the private sector. We must now relax the fourth assumption, constancy of supplies of factors of production. The analysis of the effects of a tariff when factor supplies are variable is the subject of a paper by Murray C. Kemp, which we have been privileged to read and which suggested the inclusion of the present section of this article to us. We gratefully acknowledge his priority, and also our indebtedness to R.W. Jones, who has since produced a broader study of variability of factor supplies in international trade;[13] our own analysis takes a slightly different form from theirs, better adapted to the general purpose of this chapter.

For simplicity of analysis we shall assume that only the quantity of labour is variable. This assumption has some economic justification, inasmuch as we may assume that the quantity of labour available for employment from a given total stock depends on the relative attractiveness at the margin of the real consumption obtainable by offering labour and of the leisure obtained by not offering it, to the owner of labour, while the total stock of capital, having no alternative utility-yielding use, is always available for employment. The real consumption enjoyed with the employment of a given quantity of labour depends on the quantity of labour employed, the quantity of capital owned, the real wage rate and real rent rate measured in terms of exportable goods, and the relative price of importables; but the real wage and real rent rates are linked through the technology of the economy to the relative price of importables, so that the latter determines the former. In cases (2) and (3), though in different ways, real consumption also depends on the amount of tariff revenue.

With leisure as the alternative to labour the quantity of labour supplied will decrease with an increase in the amount of real income that could be enjoyed with the employment of the initial amount of labour, since some (but not all, barring inferiority of

[13]M.C. Kemp, 'Tariffs, Protection, and the Distribution of National Income', and R.W. Jones, 'General Equilibrium with Variable Labor Supply'; these two papers were merged in a joint article, M.C. Kemp and R.W. Jones, 'Variable Labour Supply and the Theory of International Trade; *Journal of Political Economy*, Vol. 70, No. 1 (February 1962) pp. 30—36.

real consumption) of the potential increase in real consumption will be consumed in the form of leisure. The real consumption enjoyable from the employment of the initial amount of labour remaining constant, an increase in the real wage rate will generally, but not always, increase the quantity of labour supplied. Such a 'compensated' increase in the real wage-rate has two effects: it raises the price of labour (the cost of leisure) in terms of goods, and so induces a substitution of labour, and the real consumption it makes possible, for leisure — an increase in the quantity of labour supplied; but it also reduces the relative price of the commodity in whose production labour is used relatively unintensively. If this commodity is substitutary with leisure, the effect is again to induce an increase in the quantity of labour supplied; but if it is complementary with leisure, the effect is to induce a decrease in the quantity of labour supplied, and this effect may be strong enough to outweigh the general tendency to substitute real consumption for leisure, and so reduce the quantity of labour supplied. This possibility we shall describe as one of strong complementarity of leisure and the capital-intensive good in consumption.

With this background, we can proceed to the analysis of the effect of a tariff increase in our three aggregative cases.

The increase in the domestic price of importables resulting from the tariff increase has two effects on the quantity of labour supplied:

(a) The loss of real income due to the increase in the price of importables increases the quantity of labour supplied. The loss of real income due to the increased price of importables is approximately equal to the increased cost of the initial volume of private imports, and the change in the quantity of labour supplied for this reason is therefore:

$$\frac{\partial L}{\partial Y'} \frac{\partial Y'}{\partial \pi} \frac{d\pi}{dt} = (-l)(-\bar{M}_1) = \bar{M}_1 l, \tag{15a}$$

where Y' represents real income and l represents the marginal propensity to consume leisure when potential real income increases; l must be positive and smaller than $1/w$ (w being the real wage-rate) on the assumption that neither leisure nor real consumption is inferior.

(b) The change in the relative price of labour due to the change in the relative price of importables alters the quantity of labour supplied, the direction and extent of the change being determined by the elasticity of the real wage rate with respect to the price of importables and the elasticity of supply of labour with respect to the real wage-rate. The change in the quantity of labour supplied is:

$$\frac{\partial L}{\partial w} \frac{\partial w}{\partial \pi} \frac{d\pi}{dt} = \frac{\bar{L}}{\pi} \lambda e_w, \tag{15b}$$

where $\lambda[= (w/L)\partial L/\partial w]$ is the compensated elasticity of supply of labour, and is positive unless there is strong complementarity between the capital-intensive commodity and leisure, and $e_w[= (\pi/w)\partial w/\partial \pi]$ is the elasticity of the real wage-rate with respect to the price of importables. Since a rise in the price of importables will raise or lower the real wage-rate according as labour is used relatively intensively in the importable-goods or the exportable-goods industry, e_w will be positive or negative according as the importable-goods industry is labour-intensive or capital-intensive.

The change in the quantity of labour initially supplied due to these two effects of the increased domestic price of importables resulting from the tariff increase is therefore:

$$\frac{\partial L}{\partial t} = \frac{\partial L}{\partial \pi} \frac{d\pi}{dt} = \frac{\bar{L}}{\pi} \lambda e_w + \bar{M}_1 l. \tag{16}$$

This change in the quantity of labour supplied due to the increase in the domestic price of importables has two effects on the quantity of imports demanded (in addition to those analysed in Section I):

(i) The change in the quantity of labour supplied changes the amount of income earned by the private sector and so changes the quantity of importables demanded. The change in earned income is approximately equal to the wage rate multiplied by the change in the quantity of labour supplied, and the change in the quantity of imports demanded due to a change in earned income is determined by the marginal propensity to consume importables. Hence the change in the quantity of importables demanded due to the effect of the tariff increase on the domestic price of importables is:

$$\frac{\partial C}{\partial L}\frac{\partial L}{\partial t} = \frac{cw}{\pi}\left(\frac{\bar{L}}{\pi}\lambda e_w + \bar{M}_1 l\right). \qquad (17a)$$

(ii) The change in the quantity of labour supplied changes the amount of importables domestically produced. This change can be deduced from one of the established propositions of the theory of international trade and economic growth, according to which an increase in the quantity of one factor at a given domestic price ratio must be absorbed by transferring both factors out of the industry which uses that factor unintensively into the other industry, where they are combined with the new quantities of the increased factor in the more intensive ratio optimal in that industry; and conversely for a decrease in the quantity of a factor.[14] The changes in the outputs of the two industries, per unit change in the total amount of a factor supplied, are determined by the factor ratios in the two industries and the average output per unit of the factor whose supply is altered in the relevant industry.[15]

---

[14] This proposition is originally due to T.M. Rybczynski, 'Factor Endowment and Relative Commodity Prices', *Economica*, N.S., Vol. XXII, No. 88 (Nov. 1955) pp. 336–41. For a recent statement, see J. Bhagwati and H.G. Johnson, 'Notes on Some Controversies in the Theory of International Trade', *Economic Journal*, Vol. 1XX, No. 277 (Mar. 1960) pp. 74–93, especially p. 82.

[15] Let k_1 and $k_2 (< k_1)$ be the capital:labour ratios in the capital-intensive and labour-intensive industries, and a_1 and a_2 be the average products of labour in those industries. The movement of a unit of labour from the former to the latter industry releases $(k_1 - k_2)$ units of capital, which will permit the employment of an additional $(k_1 - k_2)/k_2$ units of labour in the labour-intensive industry: hence employment of an additional unit of labour in the latter industry requires a transfer of $k_2/(k_1 - k_2)$ labour units (together with the capital employed with them in the capital-intensive industry). Output in the capital-intensive industry, therefore, must fall by $k_2 a_1/(k_1 - k_2)$, and output in the labour-intensive industry rise by $a_2[1 + k_2/(k_1 - k_2)] = k_1 a_2/(k_1 - k_2)$ when the labour supply increases by one unit.

It follows from this principle that the change in the output of importables due to a change in the quantity of labour supplied must be greater absolutely than the change in national income due to the same cause, so that the effect on importable goods production dominates the net effect on imports demanded of a change in the quantity of labour supplied. Also, the change in the domestic output of importable goods due to an increase in the quantity of labour supplied must be of the same sign as the change in the real wage-rate due to an increase in the domestic price of importable goods. If labour is used intensively in importable-goods production, an increase in the domestic price of importables must increase the real wage-rate, and an increase in the quantity of labour must be absorbed by an expansion of production of importables at the expense of exportables; conversely, if labour is used intensively in the production of exportables, an increase in the domestic price of importables must lower the real wage-rate and an increase in the quantity of labour supplied must increase the domestic production of exportables at the expense of importables. Accordingly, the change in the domestic production of importable goods due to the tariff increase is:

$$\frac{\partial P}{\partial L}\frac{\partial L}{\partial t} = \rho\left(\frac{\bar{L}}{\pi}\lambda e_w + \bar{M}_1 l\right), \tag{17b}$$

where ρ, the change in the quantity of importables domestically produced due to an increase in the quantity of labour supplied, must have the same sign as e_w and exceed w in absolute magnitude.[16]

The net change in the quantity of importables demanded by the private sector due to the change in the quantity of labour supplied resulting from the effect of the tariff increase on the real wage-rate is therefore [the difference between (17a) and (17b)]:

$$\frac{\partial M_1}{\partial L}\frac{\partial L}{\partial t} = \left(\frac{cw}{\pi} - \rho\right)\left(\frac{\bar{L}}{\pi}\lambda e_w + \bar{M}_1 l\right). \tag{18}$$

[16] It follows from note 15 that $\rho = k_x a_m/(k_x - k_m)$, where the subscripts x and m refer to the exportable-goods and importable-goods industries respectively.

To allow for variability of the quantity of labour supplied in response to the increase in the domestic price of importables resulting from the tariff increase in deriving the formulae for the effect of the tariff increase on the world excess demand for importables, it is necessary to include the expression just derived in reckoning the effect of the tariff increase on the quantity of importables privately demanded. This entails adding the expression

$$-\frac{\pi}{\bar{M}_1} \frac{\partial M_1}{\partial L} \frac{\partial L}{\partial t} = (\rho \pi - cw)\left(\frac{\bar{L}}{\pi \bar{M}_1} \lambda e_w + l\right), \qquad (19)$$

to the elasticity of private demand for imports in the formulae derived in Sections I and II. In this expression $(\rho \pi - cw)$ must have the same sign as ρ, because ρ exceeds w in absolute magnitude and c, the marginal propensity to consume importables, is assumed to be less than unity and therefore less than π.

In case (1), where the government spends the tariff revenue and the preferences of the private sector are independent of the amount of government expenditure, this is the only adjustment required. In case (2), however, the change in the amount of tariff revenue redistributed due to the tariff increase will alter the real income obtainable with the employment of the initial quantity of labour supplied and so alter the quantity of labour supplied. The change in the amount of importables demanded resulting for this reason from the increase in the tariff rate will be:

$$\frac{\partial M_1}{\partial L} \frac{\partial L}{\partial Y'} \frac{dR}{dt} = \left(\rho - \frac{cw}{\pi}\right) l \frac{dR}{dt}. \qquad (20)$$

In case (3) the quantity of labour supplied will depend on the amount of government services if leisure is substitutary or complementary with government services; in this case the change in tariff revenue due to the tariff increase will change the quantity of imports demanded through its effects on the quantity of labour supplied by the amount

$$\frac{\partial M_1}{\partial L} \frac{\partial L}{\partial R} \frac{dR}{dt} = \left(\frac{cw}{\pi} - \rho\right) \alpha \frac{dR}{dt}, \qquad (21)$$

69

where α is the change in the quantity of labour supplied due to a unit increase in government expenditure, and may be positive or negative.

In the *aggregated case* (1) with variable labour supply, the effect of the tariff increase on the world excess demand for importables is[17] [derived from (3) and (19)]:

$$\frac{dM}{dt} = \bar{M}_1 \left[g - (1+gt)\frac{c}{\pi} - \frac{(1+gt)}{\pi}\xi' - \frac{(1+gt)}{\pi}(\rho\pi - cw)\left(\frac{\bar{L}}{\pi\bar{M}_1}\lambda e_w + l\right) \right].$$

(22) VII

If the elasticity of supply of labour λ is positive, and ρ is also positive, implying that importable-goods production is labour-intensive, the last term within the brackets must be positive, so that all the terms except g have a negative sign, and the traditional conclusion that an adverse movement of the terms of trade requires a governmental marginal propensity to consume importables greater than the private marginal propensity to consume them continues to hold. But if the elasticity of supply of labour λ is positive and ρ is negative, implying that exportable-goods production is labour-intensive, it is possible for the last term to be negative (in spite of the fact that the first half of it must be positive owing to the identity of signs of ρ and e_w), so that the traditional condition is not necessary in this case. If the elasticity of supply of labour λ is negative and ρ is also negative — implying that importables are capital-intensive in production and strongly complementary with leisure in consumption — the last term must be negative, so that the influence of variability of the labour supply is to increase the world excess demand for importables, and the traditional condition is not necessary for the terms of trade to turn against the country. Similarly, if the elasticity of supply of labour λ is negative and ρ is positive — exportables are capital-intensive in production and strongly complementary with leisure in consumption — the last term may be negative on balance, and again

[17] This result is obtained, as explained above, by adding the expression for the effect of the tariff increase, via the labour supply, on the demand for importables to the elasticity of private demand for imports in the formula previously derived for the aggregated case with constant labour supply.

the traditional condition is not necessary for the terms of trade to turn against the country.

In the *aggregated case* (2), with variable labour supply, the effect of the tariff increase on world excess demand for importables is [the sum of (4), (18), and (20)]:

$$\frac{dM_1}{dt} = \frac{\partial M_1}{\partial t} + \left(\frac{cw}{\pi} - \rho\right)\frac{\partial L}{\partial t} + \left(\frac{c}{\pi}\right)\frac{dR}{dt} + \left(\rho - \frac{cw}{\pi}\right)l\frac{dR}{dt}$$

$$= -\frac{M_1}{\pi}\left[\xi + (\rho\pi - cw)\left(\frac{\bar{L}}{\pi\bar{M}_1}\lambda e_w + l\right)\right] + \left[\frac{c}{\pi} + \left(\rho - \frac{cw}{\pi}\right)l\right]\left(\bar{M}_1 + t\frac{dM_1}{dt}\right)$$

$$= \frac{\bar{M}_1}{1 + [1 - c - (\rho\pi - cw)l]t}\left|-\xi' - (\rho\pi - cw)\frac{\bar{L}}{\pi\bar{M}_1}\lambda e_w\right|. \quad (23)\,\text{VIII}$$

Since $(\rho\pi - cw)(\bar{L}/\pi\bar{M}_1)e_w$ must be positive, the tariff increase cannot turn the terms of trade against the country if the supply of labour is positively elastic with respect to the real wage rate (λ is positive). If the supply of labour is negatively elastic (strong complementarity of the capital-intensive commodity, whichever it is, with leisure in consumption) the terms of trade may turn against the country. Thus variability of the labour supply can reverse the traditional conclusion in the exceptional case of a negative elasticity of supply of labour.

In the *aggregated case* (3), with variable labour supply, the change in the amount of imports privately demanded due to the tariff increase is:

$$\frac{dM_1}{dt} = \frac{\partial M_1}{\partial t} + \left(\frac{cw}{\pi} - \rho\right)\left(\frac{\partial L}{\partial t}\right) + \left[\frac{b}{\pi} + \left(\frac{cw}{\pi} - \rho\right)\alpha\right]\frac{dR}{dt}$$

$$= \frac{b - \xi - (\xi\pi - cw)\left[\alpha + \dfrac{\bar{L}}{\pi\bar{M}_1}\lambda e_w + l\right]}{1 + [1 - b + (\rho\pi - cw)\alpha]t}\,\bar{M}_1; \quad (24a)$$

the change in the amount of imports demanded by the government is:

$$\frac{dM_2}{dt} = g\left(\bar{M}_1 + t\frac{dM_1}{dt}\right)$$

$$= \frac{\pi - t\xi - t(\rho\pi - cw)\left(\dfrac{\bar{L}}{\pi\bar{M}_1}\ \lambda e_w + l\right)}{1 + [1 - b + (\rho\pi - cw)a]t}\ g\bar{M}\ ; \qquad (24b)$$

and the change in the total quantity of imports demanded, and the world excess demand for importables, is consequently [the sum of (24a) and (24b)]:

$$\frac{dM}{dt} = \frac{\pi g + b - (1 + gt)\xi' - (1 + gt)c - }{1 + [1 - b + (\rho\pi - cw)a]t}\bar{M}_1.$$

with numerator

$$\pi g + b - (1 + gt)\xi' - (1 + gt)c - (1 + gt)(\rho\pi - cw)\left(\frac{\bar{L}}{\pi\bar{M}_1}\ \lambda e_w + l\right) - (\rho\pi - cw)a$$

$$(25)\text{IX}$$

In the case of initial free trade, which we shall consider for simplicity, this reduces to:

$$\frac{dM}{dt} = \left[g + b - \xi' - c - (\rho\pi - cw)\left(\frac{\bar{L}}{\bar{M}_1}\ \lambda e_w + l + a\right)\right]\bar{M}_1.$$

It follows from this formula that, even with initial free trade, an inverse relation between government expenditure and private demand for importables, and a government marginal propensity to consume importables less than that of the private sector, an increase in the tariff rate can turn the terms of trade against the country. This requires the final term of the foregoing ex-

pression to be negative, which in turn requires $\left(\lambda + \dfrac{l + a}{e_w}\ \dfrac{\bar{M}_1}{\bar{L}}\right)$

to be negative. This is possible in the following cases:

(i) Negative elasticity of supply of labour ($\lambda < 0$), requiring strong complementarity of the capital-intensive good (which may be either commodity) with leisure in consumption; the necessary

condition for the term to be negative in this case is $-\lambda > \dfrac{l + a}{Le_w}\bar{M}_1.$

(ii) Positive elasticity of supply of labour ($\lambda > 0$) and negative elasticity of the wage-rate with respect to the price of importables ($e_w < 0$), which requires the exportable-goods industry to be relatively labour-intensive, together with ($l + \alpha$) positive, which, since l is necessarily positive, is consistent with the quantity of labour supplied either increasing or decreasing as government expenditure increases; the necessary condition for the term to be negative in this case is

$$\frac{l + \alpha}{\lambda} \frac{\bar{M}_1}{\bar{L}} > -e_w.$$

(iii) Positive elasticity of supply of labour ($\lambda > 0$) and positive elasticity of the wage-rate with respect to the price of importables ($e_w > 0$), which requires the importable-goods industry to be labour-intensive, together with ($l + \alpha$) negative, which, since l is necessarily positive, requires that an increase in government expenditure reduce the quantity of labour supplied; the necessary condition for the term to be negative in this case

is $-\alpha > \dfrac{\bar{L} \lambda e_w}{\bar{M}_1} + l.$

To obtain the formulae for the effect of the tariff increase on world excess demand for importables in the *disaggregated cases* it is necessary to introduce appropriately weighted averages of the expressions for the income and substitution effects of the increase in the domestic price of importables due to the tariff increase on the quantity of labour supplied, and of the effects on labour supplied of the change in the tariff revenue due to the tariff increase, for the two individuals. The resulting formulae will not be reproduced here; the general nature of the effects of allowing for differences between members of the private sector can be inferred from the argument of this and the preceding section.

V. THE EFFECT OF AN INCREASE IN THE TARIFF ON THE DOMESTIC PRICE RATIO

The previous sections of this chapter have been concerned with generalizing the theory of the effect of a tariff increase on the terms of trade of the tariff-raising country. In this final

73

section we consider the conditions under which a tariff increase may improve the terms of trade so much that the internal price of importable goods actually falls, a question which is of particular interest in connexion with the effect of the tariff in redistributing income between the owners of factors of production. The traditional analysis concludes (as mentioned in the introduction) that such an improvement requires that the marginal propensity to spend on domestic goods of the government or the private sector, whichever spends the tariff proceeds, must exceed the foreign elasticity of demand for the country's exports (so that, barring inferiority of importables in private or government consumption, that elasticity must be less than unity).

Like the terms of trade problem, this problem can be simplified by considering the effect of the tariff increase on world excess demand for importables at a given price for them; in this case we consider the effect on excess demand at the initial domestic price of importables. World excess demand for importables is symbolized below by $M' \equiv M - M_s$, where M is the quantity of imports demanded by the tariff-imposing country and M_s the quantity of imports supplied by the rest of the world; initially $M' = 0$. The tariff increase will raise or lower the internal price of importables according as it gives rise to an excess demand for or excess supply of importables in the world market at the initial domestic price of importables. We begin with our three aggregated cases, assuming that the private sector can be treated as homogeneous and that factor supplies are constant. The effect of the tariff increase on the world excess demand for importables is then the net resultant of three effects of the tariff increase:

(i) The tariff increase reduces the price offered to foreign suppliers for imports, and so alters the quantity supplied at the initial domestic price ratio. The change in the quantity supplied is

$$\frac{dM_s}{dt} = \frac{dM_s}{dp}\frac{dp}{dt} = \frac{dM_s}{dp}\frac{d}{dt}\left(\frac{\pi}{1+t}\right) = -\frac{\epsilon_f}{\pi}\bar{M}_s = \frac{1-\eta_f}{\pi}\bar{M}, \quad (26)$$

where ϵ_f is the foreign elasticity of supply of imports and η_f is the elasticity of foreign demand for the country's exports. For the quantity of imports supplied to increase when the price offered for them falls, it is necessary for the foreign import demand elasticity to be less than unity. We shall not investigate the determinants of the foreign import demand elasticity; but the analysis of the preceding sections shows that, in addition to the usual possibility of a low demand elasticity due to a low elasticity of substitution between exportables and importables in foreign consumption, the foreign elasticity of demand for imports may be less than unity, and even negative, if the factor used intensively in foreign production of exportables has the higher marginal propensity to consume exportables, or if the supply curve of that factor is backward-rising.

(ii) Where the government spends the tariff proceeds, and allocates expenditure between exportables and importables on the basis of world market prices, the reduction in the world market price increases the quantity of imports it demands from a given tariff revenue. The change in the quantity of imports demanded on this account is

$$\frac{\delta M_2}{\delta p} \frac{dp}{dt} = -\eta_g \bar{M}_2 \frac{d}{dt}\left(\frac{\pi}{1+t}\right) = \frac{\eta_g}{\pi}\bar{M}_2, \qquad (27)$$

where η_g is the elasticity of government demand for imports.

(iii) The increase in the tariff rate increases the tariff proceeds derived from the initial volume of imports and so increases the quantity of imports demanded to an extent which is differently determined in the different cases. The increase in the tariff revenue derived from the initial volume of imports is

$$\frac{\partial R}{\partial t} = \frac{\partial}{\partial t}\left(\frac{t}{1+t}\pi\bar{M}_1\right) = \frac{\bar{M}_1}{\pi}.$$

(a) Where the government spends the tariff revenue and private-sector demand is independent of the level of government activity [case (1)], the increase in the quantity of imports demanded due to the increase in the tariff revenue is:

$$\frac{\partial M_2}{\partial R}\frac{\delta R}{\delta t} = g\frac{\partial R}{\partial t} = \frac{g}{\pi}\bar{M}_1.$$

(b) Where the tariff revenue is redistributed to the private sector [case (2)], the increase in the quantity of imports demanded is

$$\frac{dM_1}{dt} = \frac{\partial M_1}{\partial R}\frac{dR}{dt} = \frac{c}{\pi}\left(\frac{\partial R}{\partial t} + t\,\frac{dM_1}{dt}\right) = \frac{c}{1 + (1-c)t}\,\frac{\bar{M}_1}{\pi}$$

(c) In case (3), where the government spends the tariff revenue and private demand for importables is dependent on the amount of governmental services provided, the tariff increase has a fourth effect, which is most conveniently considered in conjunction with the third. For, in addition to increasing the level of government consumption through increasing the amount of tariff revenue, the increase in the tariff rate, by reducing the price offered to foreign suppliers, both increases the real level and alters the composition of government consumption from the initial amount of tariff revenue. These changes, as well as the increase in tariff revenue, will have a dependence effect on the private demand for importables, which effect will differ according to the precise nature of the dependence of private demand on governmental activity. The latter must accordingly be specified, whereas it could legitimately be ignored in analysing the effect of the tariff increase on the terms of trade. Three cases can be distinguished: (3a) dependence on total real governmental consumption, (3b) dependence on the quantity of importables consumed by the government, and (3c) dependence on the quantity of exportables consumed by the government.

A *general formula for case* (3) which can be adapted to fit these alternative assumptions about the nature of dependence can be derived as follows: define B as the increase in quantity of importables privately demanded when government revenue (expenditure) increases by one unit, and A as the increase in government revenue that would produce the same effect on private demand for importables as the change in whatever aspect of government expenditure influences that demand that results from the tariff increase, tariff revenue being held constant. Then the increase in the quantity of importables privately demanded due to the effect of the tariff increase on governmental consumption is

$$\frac{dM_1}{dt} = \frac{\partial M_1}{\partial R}\left(\frac{dR}{dt} + A\right) = B\left(\frac{\delta R}{\delta t} + t\frac{dM_1}{dt} + A\right) = \frac{B\left(\dfrac{\overline{M}_1}{\pi} + A\right)}{1 - Bt};$$

the increase in the quantity of imports demanded by the government due to the increase in tariff revenue is

$$\frac{dM_2}{dt} = \frac{\delta M_2}{\delta R}\frac{dR}{dt} = g\left(\frac{\delta R}{\delta t} + t\frac{dM_1}{dt}\right) = \frac{g\left(\dfrac{\overline{M}_1}{\pi} + ABt\right)}{1 - Bt}$$

and the total change[18] in the quantity of importables demanded resulting from the effect of the increase in the tariff rate on governmental expenditure and the associated dependence effect on private demand for importables is

$$\frac{dM}{dt} = \frac{(g + B)\dfrac{\overline{M}_1}{\pi} + AB(1 + gt)}{1 - Bt} = \frac{g\overline{M}_1}{\pi} + \frac{(1 + gt)B\left(\dfrac{\overline{M}_1}{\pi} + A\right)}{1 - Bt}. \quad (28)$$

The reduction in the price of imports due to the increase in the tariff (tariff proceeds remaining constant) increases governmental real income by $-\overline{M}_2\, dp/dt = \overline{M}_2/\pi$, increases governmental consumption of importables by $(\delta M_2/\delta p)(dp/dt) = \eta_g(\overline{M}_2/\pi)$, and alters governmental consumption of exportables by $-\delta(p\overline{M}_2)/\delta t = (1 - \eta_g)(\overline{M}_2/\pi)$. Hence the parameter A in the general formula is equal to $\overline{M}_2/\pi$ in case (3a), $(\eta_g/g)(\overline{M}_2/\pi)$ in case (3b), and $[(1 - \eta_g)/(1 - g)](\overline{M}_2/\pi)$ in case (3c). The parameter B in the formula is equal to b_r/π in case (3a), $b_m g/\pi$ in case (3b), and $b_x(1 - g)/\pi$ in case (3c), where the b's are coefficients relating the increase in private expenditure on importables to the increase in real government consumption, government consumption of importables, and government consumption of exportables, which induce it in the three cases. The total changes in the quantity of imports demanded resulting from the effects of the tariff increase under analysis in the three sub-cases are obtained by inserting these values in the

---

[18] This change includes the direct effect of the lower price of imports in increasing government consumption of them from the initial tariff revenue, discussed under (ii) above.

general formula; since the results are rather cumbrous, and are contained in the formulae for the effect of the tariff increase on the excess demand for importables presented below, they are not reproduced here.

In case (1) the total effect of the tariff increase on world excess demand for importables at the initial domestic price of importables is

$$\frac{dM'}{dt} = \frac{dM}{dt} - \frac{dM_s}{dt} = \left(g + \eta_g' \frac{\bar{M}_2}{\bar{M}} - 1 + \eta_f \right) \frac{\bar{M}}{\pi}, \quad (29)X$$

where η_g' is the compensated elasticity of government demand for imports. For this to be negative, representing an excess supply of importables and necessitating a reduction in the world and domestic price of importables to restore equilibrium, requires [19]

$$(1 - g) - \frac{\bar{M}_2}{\bar{M}} \eta_g' > \eta_f.$$

Whether free trade ($\bar{M}_2 = 0$) or a tariff ($\bar{M}_2 > 0$) is initially in force, the internal price of imports can fall only if the government's marginal propensity to spend on exportables $(1 - g)$ exceeds the foreign elasticity of demand for imports (η_f), which in turn requires an inelastic foreign demand for imports unless importables are inferior in government consumption at the pre-existing level of tariff proceeds. Where a tariff is initially in force, an excess of $(1 - g)$ over η_f is a necessary but not a sufficient condition for the internal price of importables to fall.

In case (2) the total effect of the tariff increase on the world excess demand for importables is [20]

---

[19] This result differs from that derived by Metzler in the supplementary paper referred to in note 1, (*op. cit.*, especially equation (7), p. 439). The reason is that Metzler, in dealing with the case, writes governmental demand as a function of the tariff proceeds measured in importable goods, whereas we write it as a function of tariff proceeds measured in exportable goods. On his assumption, $\delta R/\delta t = \delta(tM_1)/\delta t = M_1$, as contrasted with our $\delta R/\delta t = M_1/1 + t$. In dealing with our case (2), Metzler writes private demand as a function of tariff proceeds measured in exportable goods, and obtains a result identical with ours. Metzler's technique for the former case is inferior to ours, since it means that all the income effect of an import price change on government demand falls on the exportable goods.

$$\frac{dM'}{dt} = \left[\frac{c}{1 + (1 - c)t} - 1 + \eta_f \right] \frac{\bar{M}_1}{\pi}. \tag{30)XI}$$

A decrease in the world and domestic price of importables in this case requires

$$(1 - c) > \frac{\eta_f}{\pi - \eta_f t}.$$

This requires the private sector's marginal propensity to spend on exportables $(1 - c)$ to exceed the foreign elasticity of demand for imports when free trade initially prevails, but not when there is a pre-existing tariff; it is always necessary, however, for the foreign demand for imports to be inelastic (barring inferiority of importables).

In case (3) the total effect of the tariff increase on world excess demand for importables is

$$\frac{dM'}{dt} = \left[\frac{b_r(1 + gt)}{1 + (1 - b_r)t} + g + \eta_g' \frac{\bar{M}_2}{\bar{M}} - 1 + \eta_f \right] \frac{\bar{M}}{\pi} \tag{31a)XII}$$

when private demand is influenced by real government consumption;

$$\frac{dM'}{dt} = \left[\frac{\pi + b_m}{1 + (1 - b_m g)t} \left(g \frac{\bar{M}_1}{\bar{M}} + \eta_g \frac{\bar{M}_2}{\bar{M}} \right) - 1 + \eta_f \right] \frac{\bar{M}}{\pi}$$

$$\tag{31b)XIII}$$

when private demand is influenced by governmental consumption of importables; and

$$\frac{dM'}{dt} = \left[\frac{b_x(1 - g) + g\pi}{1 + (1 - b_x + b_x g)t} \frac{\bar{M}_1}{\bar{M}} + \right.$$

$$\left. \frac{b_x(1 + gt) + \pi(1 - b_x)\eta_g}{1 + (1 - b_x + b_x g)t} \frac{\bar{M}_2}{\bar{M}} - 1 + \eta_f \right] \frac{\bar{M}}{\pi} \tag{31c)XIV}$$

[20] Our earlier analysis of this case, presented in J. Bhagwati, 'Protection, Real Wages and Real Incomes', *Economic Journal*, Vol. 1XIX, No. 276 (Dec. 1959) pp. 733–48, p. 746 and explained in note 3 to that page, is erroneous; in the derivation of the excess demand for importables, the changes in quantities of importables demanded and supplied are confused. The formula presented in that paper should be replaced by that presented here.

when private demand is influenced by governmental consumption of exportables.

For simplicity we consider only the case in which private demand is influenced by the level of government consumption [case (3a), equation (31a)]. In this case the tariff increase will lower the domestic price of importables if

$$(1 - g) - \frac{b_r(1 + gt)}{1 + (1 - b_r)t} - \eta'_g \frac{\bar{M}_2}{\bar{M}} > \eta_f. \tag{32}$$

If an increase in government expenditure has the indirect effect of increasing private demand for importables ($b_r > 0$) the tariff can reduce the domestic price of importables only if the government's marginal propensity to spend on exportables is greater than the foreign elasticity of demand for imports, which (barring inferior goods) must be less than unity. [21] But if an increase in government expenditure has the indirect effect of reducing private demand for importables ($b_r < 0$), the tariff can reduce the domestic price of importables even though the government's marginal propensity to spend on exportables is less than the foreign elasticity of demand for imports and even though the latter is greater than unity.

Since the analysis of the effect of a tariff increase on the equilibrium domestic price of importables obtains its results from the effect of the tariff increase on world excess demand at the initial domestic price of importables, *relaxation of the assumption that the private sector can be treated as an aggregate* makes no essential difference to the results: since domestic earned income and its distribution are unchanged if the domestic price of importables is unchanged, disaggregation requires merely the replacement of the aggregate marginal propensity to consume importables by an average of the marginal propensities of the two individuals, weighted by their shares in redistributed tariff proceeds, in case (2), and the replacement of the aggregate dependence coefficient by the sum of the coefficients for the two individuals, in case (3). For the same reason, *variability of the quantity of labour supplied* in response to changes in factor prices will make no difference to the various formulae,

[21] An exception is possible if $b_r > 1 + t/t$.

since the real wage-rate and real rent remain constant by the assumption of a constant internal price of importables. But variability in response to changes in the amount of tariff revenue redistributed will make a difference in case (2) and variability in response to changes in the amount and composition of real government consumption will make a difference in case (3).

In both cases, allowance for variability of the quantity of labour supplied involves introducing another effect of the tariff increase on the world excess demand for importables, the effect of the change in tariff revenue or real government consumption on the quantity of labour supplied and so on the quantity of importables domestically produced and the income available for private expenditure. These effects have already been discussed in connexion with the analysis of the effect of the tariff increase on the terms of trade.

Allowing for variability of the labour supply in response to changes in the amount of tariff revenue redistributed, the total effect of the tariff increase on world excess demand for importables in case (2) is

$$\frac{dM'}{dt} = \left\{ \frac{c + (\pi\rho - cw)l}{1 + [1 - c - (\pi\rho - cw)l]t} - 1 + \eta_f \right\} \frac{\overline{M}_1}{\pi}. \quad (33)\,\text{XV}$$

The corresponding condition for the tariff increase to lower the domestic price of importables is

$$(1 - c) - (\pi\rho - cw)l > \frac{\eta_f}{\pi - \eta_f t}.$$

It follows from this inequality that, even in the case of initial free trade [where the inequality reduces to $(1 - c) - (\rho - cw)l > \eta_f$] it is not necessary for the private marginal propensity to spend on exportables to exceed the foreign elasticity of demand for imports for the tariff to lower the domestic price of importables; since $\pi\rho$ is necessarily greater in absolute value than cw, a reduction of the domestic price of importables with $\eta_f > 1 - c$ requires a negative ρ, which in turn means that labour is used intensively in the exportable-goods industry. If labour is used intensively in the exportable-goods industry, the domestic price of importables can fall even if the foreign demand for imports is elastic.

Allowing for variability of the labour supply in response to change in the amount of real government consumption — the only variant of case (3) we shall consider [22] — the total effect of the tariff increase on world excess demand for importables is

$$\frac{dM'}{dt} = \left\{ \frac{[b_r - (\pi\rho - cw)\,a_r]\,(1 + gt)}{1 + [1 - b_r + (\pi\rho - cw)\,a_r]\,t} + g + \eta'_g\,\frac{\bar{M}_2}{\bar{M}} - 1 + \eta_f \right\} \frac{\bar{M}}{\pi},$$

$$(34)\,XVI$$

where a_r is the change in the quantity of labour supplied due to a unit increase in real government consumption. The corresponding condition for the tariff increase to lower the domestic price of importables is

$$(1 - g) - \frac{b_r - (\pi\rho - cw)\,a_r}{1 + [1 - b_r + (\pi\rho - cw)\,a_r]\,t}\,(1 + gt) - \eta'_g\,\frac{\bar{M}_2}{\bar{M}} > \eta_f.$$

In the initial free-trade case, this reduces to

$$(1 - g) - b_r + (\rho - cw)\,a_r > \eta_f;$$

and it follows from this formula that even if the dependence effect of a change in government revenue is positive, the internal price of importables may fall even though the government's marginal propensity to spend on exportables is less than the foreign elasticity of demand for imports and the latter is greater than unity. This can occur if *either* ρ is positive, implying that labour is used relatively intensively in the importable-goods industry, *and* a_r is positive, implying that the quantity of labour supplied increases when real government consumption increases, *or* ρ is negative, implying that labour is used relatively intensively in the exportable-goods industry, *and* a_r is negative, implying that the quantity of labour supplied decreases as real government consumption increases. Similar modifications apply to the general case in which a tariff is in force in the initial situation.

[22] Since allowing for variability of labour supply requires merely the addition of $(cw - \rho\pi)$, multiplied by the a relating labour supply to whatever aspect of governmental consumption it depends on, to the corresponding b term in the parameter B in the general formula developed above, the interested reader can easily work out the results for the other two variants for himself.

To allow for variability of the quantity of labour supplied in the disaggregated cases (2) and (3) it is necessary merely to replace c, b, $(\rho\pi - cw)l$ and $(\rho\pi - cw)a_r$ by appropriately weighted sums of the corresponding expressions for the two separate individuals. The nature of the resulting modifications in the analysis of the effects of an increase in the tariff rate on the domestic price of importables is evident from the preceding analysis, and will not be developed further here.

3. Tariffs and Economic Development: Some Theoretical Issues*[1]

I. INTRODUCTION

In the course of the past thirty-five years, prevailing opinion among economists regarding the influence of commercial policy on economic development has changed radically. The central tradition of economics, set by the English classical economists, viewed free trade as a potent engine for economic growth, and protection as a policy making for waste of resources and the impediment of economic development. The classical advocacy of free trade evolved out of Adam Smith's attack on mercantilism. On the theoretical side it rested not only on the static theory of comparative advantage developed by Ricardo and Mill, but on a broader sociological recognition of the beneficial effects of exposure to foreign culture and foreign competition in generating the urge for social change and economic improvement. While two exceptions to the case for free trade were early recognised — the terms of trade argument and the infant industry argument — these were not regarded as of great practical importance. Nor did the heretics who advocated protection as a means of promoting the economic development of the relatively backward regions — notably Hamilton in the United States and List in Germany — have any significant influence on the central corpus of economic theory. Towards the end of the nineteenth century, the policies of using protection to promote the industrial growth of the United

* *The Journal of Development Studies*, Vol. I, No. 1 (October 1964) pp. 3–30.

[1] This chapter is a revised version of a lecture delivered at the Universities of Buenos Aires, Cordoba, Cujo, and Chile in the summer of 1963, when I was Visiting Professor at the Instituto Torcuato di Tella in Buenos Aires. It encapsulates propositions discussed in greater detail in several other chapters of this book.

States and Germany attracted the scientific interest of Marshall, and induced Taussig to undertake a major study of the economic effects of the United States tariff; but the results of Taussig's research were at best inconclusive, and both he and Marshall became increasingly sceptical about the efficacy of protection for promoting economic growth. Until the 1930s, free trade was the orthodox position of economists on questions of commercial policy, an orthodoxy based on the principle of comparative advantage and reinforced by the cosmopolitan perspective of the liberal tradition of classical economics.

In the 1930s, however, the orthodoxy of free trade was challenged by a new heterodoxy, associated with the economic problems and theoretical developments of the times. The great depression revived and gave point to mercantilist arguments for tariffs as a means of increasing employment, arguments made respectable by the personal endorsement of J.M. Keynes and sub-Keynesian analysis of 'beggar-my-neighbour' remedies for unemployment. New techniques of analysis and the questioning of the theoretical foundations of welfare propositions in economics revived the terms of trade argument for protection in the form of the 'optimum tariff' theory, a theory more acceptable in the new climate of economic nationalism than it had been in earlier more cosmopolitan times, when Edgeworth had gone so far as to label it 'poison'. Finally, the national aspirations of the new states created by the dissolution of the Austro-Hungarian Empire had stimulated interest in the possibility of promoting industrialization by tariff protection on the German model, and the econmoic philosophy underlying this approach was transfused into the main stream of economic theory through the emigration of many outstanding European scholars induced by the political developments of the 1930s. In addition, European thinking contributed a new argument of the case for protection, the Manoilesco argument, which rests on the existence of a differential between wages in agriculture and wages in industry that is alleged to call for compensation by tariffs on industrial products.

The reconsideration of the case for tariffs evoked by the developments of the 1930s laid the foundations for post-war analysis of the commercial policy aspects of the problem of promoting econmic development in the group of countries, mostly newly

85

independent, that have successively been described as 'backward' 'underdeveloped,' and 'poor'. In the course of theorizing about that problem, not only have traditional arguments for protection been reformulated and sharpened, but the emphasis has shifted to new arguments and new versions of the older arguments. The purpose of this chapter is to review the most important of these arguments and set them in the context of a general theoretical framework, and to outline briefly an analysis of some aspects of tariffs that have heretofore received little theoretical attention, though they are of considerable relevance to the analysis of the effects of protection on economic growth. Specifically, Section II presents a classification of contemporary arguments for protective policies in underdeveloped countries based on a distinction between economic and non-economic arguments for protection. Section III analyses the economic arguments for protection, and shows that the only valid economic argument for protection is the optimum tariff argument, all other arguments, properly interpreted, being arguments for subsidies of one kind or another. Section IV is concerned with the non-economic arguments for protection and shows that whether the tariff is an economically efficient instrument of policy depends on whether the objective of protection is increased domestic production or increased self-sufficiency. Section V carries the analysis of tariffs further, by investigating the requirements of an optimum tariff structure for promoting domestic production. Section VI is concerned with some of the implications for tariff theory of the fact that raw materials and intermediate goods (including capital goods) as well as products for final consumption are traded internationally and subject to tariffs. Section VII dwells briefly on some aspects of the policy of import substitution as a means of economic development.

Throughout the chapter, as in this introduction, the term 'protection' is used synonymously with the term 'tariffs'; the purpose is to confine the term 'protection' to policies that raise domestic prices to both producers and consumers above world prices, as distinct from policies such as subsidization that raise prices only to producers. While the analysis is explicitly conducted in terms of tariffs and subsidies, it should be noted that a variety of other devices such as multiple exchange rates or quota restrictions can be employed to achieve essentially the same effects as tariffs, and similarly tax concessions can be employed to produce the same effects as subsidies.

Finally, it should be noted that while the analysis is concerned primarily with tariffs on industrial products, since economic growth is implicitly or explicitly identified with industrialization in most of the contemporary literature, the analysis applies equally to arguments for the protection of domestic agriculture, such as is practiced particularly in the advanced industrial countries.

II. ARGUMENTS FOR TARIFFS IN UNDERDEVELOPED COUNTRIES

Contemporary arguments for tariffs in underdeveloped countries can be classified into three broad kinds: economic arguments non-economic arguments, and non-arguments.

The economic arguments for protection comprise all those arguments that recommend the tariff as a means of increasing real output or real income above what it otherwise would be. The arguments for protection on these grounds include the traditional infant-industry and terms of trade (optimum tariff) arguments, and certain new arguments based on alleged distortions in the functioning of the economy that prevent competition from achieving the socially optimal allocation of productive resources among economic sectors. Among the new arguments, the most important are those derived from the assumed existence of external economies in manufacturing industry, and those derived from alleged distortions in the labour market which produce a disequilibrium characterized by an excess of the marginal product of labour in industry over its marginal product in agriculture. This last argument, which involves the modern formulation of the concept of 'disguised unemployment' developed in the 1930s and applied somewhat uncritically to analysis of the development problem in the early postwar period, comes in two variants. One of these asserts that labour working on the land under peasant agricultural conditions receives its average product, which exceeds its marginal product by labour's share in the rent of the land, whereas labour in industry is paid its marginal product, so that equalization of wages in the two sectors through mobility of labour leaves labour's marginal product in industry above its marginal product in agriculture. The other asserts that for various reasons — convention, social conscience of employers, trade union action, social welfare legislation — wages in industry are fixed differentially above the wages of comparable labour in agriculture, so that though labour earns its marginal product in both sectors these marginal products are not equalised by labour migration. Both arguments are used to justify industrial protection, protection being recommended to offset the distortion in the labour market; but the difference in the alleged circumstances on which the case for protection is based implies a significant difference in the policies most appropriate for remedying the distortion, as will be shown in Section III.

Non-economic arguments for protection comprise arguments recommending protection as a means of achieving objectives with respect to the structure and composition of output that are desired for their own sake rather than as a means of increasing real income. Much of the argument for protection of industrial activity in underdeveloped countries is of this kind. Industrialization is frequently desired as a matter of national pride and self-respect or as a basis for military and political importance in the world, economic development being identified with industrialization as such rather than with rising real income. Similarly, protection of industry is frequently recommended as a means of promoting national self-sufficiency, self sufficiency being desired for its own sake and identified with economic development. The distinguishing characteristic of non-economic as distinct from economic arguments for protection is that — at least if they are honestly advocated — they involve the willingness to forego potential real income in order to achieve other objectives of national policy. The non-economic arguments for protection may be divided broadly into those that identify economic development with industrialization, and those that identify economic development with self-sufficiency. As will be shown in Section IV, the economic policies appropriate for implementing these two objectives most efficiently are significantly different.

Non-arguments for protection comprise all arguments that purport to, but on logical examination do not, lead to the recommendation of tariffs. Two major types of arguments of this kind figure largely in the contemporary literature and discussion of economic development. One is concerned with the typical dependence of underdeveloped countries on the export of primary products, and argues from an alleged tendency of the terms of trade to turn against such countries or from the variability of the prices of and export earnings from such products to the recommendation of industrial protection. But secularly diminishing comparative advantage is not equivalent to proof of current comparative disadvantage, nor it is self-evident that the competitive adjustment to secularly changing comparative advantage needs to be supplemented by government intervention; analogously, greater variability of earnings in one occupation than in another is not equivalent to lower average earnings in the former than in the latter, and it is not self-evident that competition will attract producers into high-variability low-average-earnings occupations from which they need rescue by government intervention. The other major argument sees balance-of-payments difficulties as an argument for protection aimed at import-substitution. But balance-of-payments difficulties result from inflation or the maintenance of an overvalued exchange rate, for which the appropriate remedies are deflation or devaluation; and there is no argument for protection as a preferable policy in such circumstances that would not hold equally well in the absence of balance-of-payment difficulties.

III. ECONOMIC ARGUMENTS FOR PROTECTION IN UNDER-DEVELOPED COUNTRIES.

The economic analysis of the various arguments for protection as a means of increasing real income can be summarized in two central principles:[2]

(1) Only the optimum tariff argument provides and economic justification for tariffs: all other arguments for protection are arguments for subsidies.

(2) The use of the tariff on the basis of any of the other arguments may make matters worse rather than better, in the sense that

---

[2] For a statement and elaboration of these principles, see J. Bhagwati and V.K. Ramaswami, 'Domestic Distortions, Tariffs and the Theory of Optimum Subsidy,' *Journal of Political Economy*,' Vol. LXXI, No. 1 (February 1963) pp. 44—50; also Chapter 4 above.

whether in these cases the tariff increases or decreases real income depends on the relative magnitudes of various relevant technological and behavior relationships and cannot be determined by *a priori* reasoning.

The first principle is an application of the standard theory of Paretian welfare maximization. According to that analysis, the necessary conditions for a welfare maximum entail equality of the marginal social rates of substitution among goods with the marginal social rates of transformation among them in both domestic production and foreign trade. Where competition does not ensure fulfilment of these conditions, owing to divergences between private and social marginal rates of substitution and transformation, the analysis calls for the imposition of taxes and subsidies at appropriate rates designed to offset any (and all) such divergences. This recommendation has two implications for the economic arguments for protection. First, only where divergences between private and social marginal costs or benefits exist in foreign trade are taxes or subsidies on trade as such required to achieve the social optimum; these cases are precisely those with which the optimum tariff analysis is concerned. Second, divergences between private and social marginal costs or benefits in domestic consumption, production, or factor use require appropriate taxes on consumption, production or factor use, and not taxes or subsidies on international trade, which discriminate between goods according to whether they are of domestic or foreign origin or destination.

The second principle is an application of the modern theory of second best. In one version, that theory demonstrates that if the attainment of a welfare maximum is prevented by the presence of distortions that preclude the fulfilment of the necessary marginal equalities, there is no way of determining *a priori* whether a change to another set of distortions would move the economy closer to or farther away from the welfare maximum. Since the attempt to offset a distortion in the domestic economy by international trade involves eliminating one distortion at the expense of introducing another, it follows directly that use of protection to correct domestic distortion may make the economy worse off rather than better off.

90

The economic effects of the application of tariffs to correct distortions in the domestic economy can be analysed with the assistance of the accompanying diagram (Figure 1). The diagram depicts the demand and supply conditions of a good which is

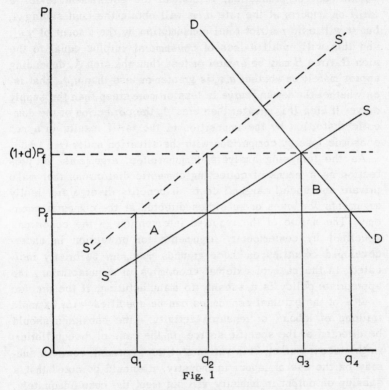

Fig. 1

obtainable through importation at the price p_f, and is produced domestically subject to a distortion which makes the private cost of production and the supply curve in monetary terms $S'S'$ greater than the true domestic supply curve reflecting real costs of production SS by a proportion d of the latter. (It is assumed that this is the only distortion in the economy).

Under free trade and in the absence of government intervention the economy will produce Oq_1 and import q_1q_4 of the good. It could however, replace q_1q_2 of imports by additional domestic production at a saving of real cost equal to the area A, which area represents the reduction of real income below the attainable maximum due to the distortion. In order to achieve this result, the government should give a subsidy on production at the rate d, the proportional excess of the monetary private over the real social cost of production. If instead the government levies a tariff on imports at the rate d, it will obtain the cost saving A, but it will aslo restrict total consumption by the amount of q_3q_4, and this will entail a loss of consumers' surplus equal to the area B. Area B may be greater or less than the area A, depending approximately on whether q_3q_4 is greater or less than q_1q_2, that is, on whether the demand curve is less or more steep than the supply curve. If area B is greater than area A, the correction of the domestic distortion by the imposition of the tariff results in a net economic loss by comparison with the situation under free trade.

As the foregoing analysis demonstrates, arguments for protection as a means of correcting domestic distortions that make private and social marginal costs or benefits diverge are really arguments for taxes or subsidies directed at the domestic economy. The nature of the required intervention in the conditions specified by contemporary arguments for protection in under-developed countries on these grounds may now be briefly indicated. In the case of external economies in manufacturing, the appropriate policy is a subsidy to manufacturing; if the precise source of the external economies can be specified — for example training of labour, or research activity — the subsidies should be directed at the specific source. In the case of disequilibrium in the labour market, both variants of the argument require a subsidy on the use of labour in industry; it should be noted that a subsidy on output in industry will not meet the case adequately, since the need for a higher marginal product of labour in industry than in agriculture will induce employers in industry to choose less labour-intensive techniques than would be socially optimal. In the peasant agriculture variant, labour's participation in the rent of land implies the equivalent of a tax on the use of the co-operant factors in agriculture, and requires in addition to a subsidy on the use of labour in industry a subsidy on the use of other factors in agriculture. In the case of the infant industry argument, it is useful to begin by interpreting this argument as a contention that competition does not allocate investment properly among alternative opportunities: the nursing of an infant industry to viability is an investment of initial development costs for the sake of future profits, and a socially profitable investment opportunity of this kind will not be privately undertaken only if the social rate of return exceeds the private rate of return or if the private rate of discount (interest cost) exceeds the social rate of discount (interest cost). In either case, the appropriate policy calls for subsidization of the interest cost of investment. In any of the three conditions alleged to call for protection, the application of protective policies is certain to produce results worse (in welfare terms) than the application of the appropriate policies just described, and may produce either worse or better results than no intervention at all.

The analysis of the economic arguments for protection presented in this section leads to the conclusion that, except in the case of the optimum tariff argument, the appropriate policy involves a subsidy of one kind or another. The recommendation of subsidies as policy instruments in underdeveloped countries is frequently rejected as unrealistic, on the grounds that such countries lack the capacity to raise adequate revenue to finance such subsidies, and must instead use taxes. This argument is less relevant than it seems, for two reasons: first, the effect of a subsidy on a particular activity can always be obtained by imposing an appropriately designed set of taxes on other goods; and second, given that the state must levy taxes for its own purposes, subsidies can be given in the form of exemption from taxes normally payable. The recommendation of freedom of trade in underdeveloped countries is also frequently objected to on the ground that imports offer the only adimistratively feasible source of tax revenue; this objection, however, is not an argument for protection but rather asserts that fiscal expediency may necessitate violation of the requirements of an efficient competitive system.

IV. NON-ECONOMIC ARGUMENTS FOR PROTECTION

The discussion of non-economic arguments for protection in Section II distinguished between arguments whose objective is increased domestic production, and arguments whose objective is increased self-sufficiency. The economic analysis of these arguments can be summarized very briefly in two propositions:

(1) arguments that define the objective of protection as increased domestic production are arguments for subsidies and not for tariffs: this is so because tariffs impose a consumption cost (loss of consumers' surplus) that contributes nothing to achievement of the objective of protection.

(2) arguments that define the objective of protection as reduced dependence on imports are genuine arguments for tariffs, in the sense that the tariff involves less sacrifice of real income than

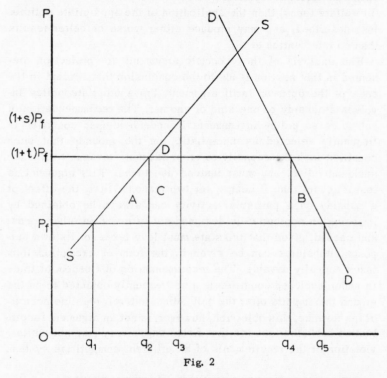

Fig. 2

alternative fiscal methods; the reason is that it is more efficient to reduce imports by both restricting consumption and increasing domestic production than by increasing production or reducing consumption alone,

These propositions may be illustrated by reference to the

accompanying diagram (Figure 2), where DD represents the demand curve, SS the domestic supply curve (there are no distortions between money and real costs in this case), and p_f the price at which imports are obtainable. Under free trade, domestic production would be Oq_1, total consumption Oq_5, and imports q_1q_5. To increase domestic output to the level Oq_2, an excess production cost measured by the area A must be incurred; this result could be secured by the granting of a subsidy on dom-production at the rate t. If instead a tariff were imposed at the rate t, the same effect on domestic production would be secured, but in addition to the excess production cost A the country would incur a consumption cost (loss of consumer's surplus) measured by the area B. Thus the subsidy is more efficient than the tariff in securing an increase in domestic production.

Now consider the situation with the tariff in effect; imports are reduced from q_1q_5 under free trade to q_2q_4 under the tariff, at a cost in real income foregone of $A + B$. The same reduction of imports could be obtained by a production subsidy at the rate s sufficient to increase domestic output to Oq_3, where $q_2q_3 = q_4q_5$; the cost in real income foregone in this case is $A + B + D$. Since $q_2q_3 = q_4q_5$, C is necessarily greater than B and $A + C + D$ greater than $A + B$. The tariff is therefore more efficient than the subsidy in securing a reduction in imports. By a parallel geometrical argument it can be shown that the tariff is more efficient than a third method of restricting imports, taxation of consumption of the commodity regardless of where it is produced. Thus the tariff is the most efficient method of securing a reduction of imports, or increased self-sufficiency. The reason is that the tariff equates the marginal costs of saving imports by increasing production and by decreasing consumption, whereas the two alternative methods do not, because each fixes one of these marginal costs at zero.

V. THE SECOND-BEST OPTIMUM TARIFF STRUCTURE

It has been argued in the preceding section that, if the aim of protection is to increase domestic production of the goods to be protected, protection is an inefficient instrument for the purpose, the same results being obtainable by means of subsidization of production at a lower real cost in terms of foregone income. Supposing, however, that a country is determined to increase the output of a group of industries above what it would be under free trade, and chooses or has to choose protection as its means of achieving this objective. The question then arises, what tariff structure should it employ for this purpose; that is, what should be the relationship among the tariff rates levied on the various items to be protected? The answer to this question defines what may be termed the 'second-best optimum tariff structure,' so called to distinguish it from the optimum tariff structure (which is derived from the Paretian welfare maximization conditions) and to emphasize its origin in the second-best welfare economics. Alternatively, the results may be thought of as a 'scientific' tariff structure, designed to achieve the desired effects on the productive structure at minimum cost.[3]

The usual prescription of economists faced with this question is that the rate of duty should be the same for every item protected This prescription is generally accompanied by the recommendation that the tariff should apply to a wide range of commodities, or to all manufactured goods, and that the rate of duty should be 'low' or 'not too high,' estimates of what is 'reasonable' varying from 10 or 20 to 50 or more per cent.

The logic of the recommendation of a single tariff rate employs the assumption that the cost or waste of protection is the excess of the cost of the protected production over the world price, and the principle that the total cost of protection will be minimized if the marginal cost of protection per value unit of protected output is equal in the protected industries. This logic is illustrated in the accompanying diagram (Figure 3). The diagram depicts the domestic supply curves S_1S_1 and S_2S_2 of two commodities subject to protection, the commodities being measured in units worth £1 at world market prices. At the unequal tariff rates t_1 and t_2, production of the commodities is Oq_{11} and Oq_{21} respectively, and total output of the two together $q_{11}q_{21}$, this total output being achieved at an excess cost over world market prices

---

[3] See my 'The Cost of Protection and the Scientific Tariff,' *Journal of Political Economy*, Vol. LXVIII, No. 4 (August 1960) pp. 327–45, reprinted as Chapter 8 below.

of $A + B + C$. By successively lowering the tariff on commodity 1, and raising the tariff rate on commodity 2 just sufficiently to replace the reduction in output of commodity 1 by an increase in

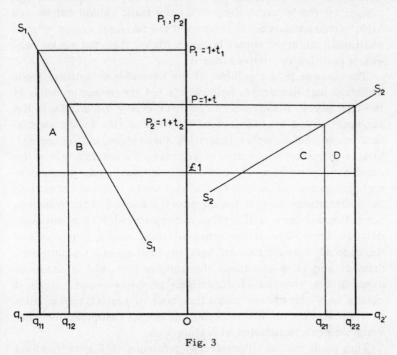

Fig. 3

output of commodity 2, a uniform tariff rate t can be found that generates the same total output as $t_1 t_2$, the excess cost over the world market prices now being $B + C + D$ and the difference from the previous cost $D - A$. Since $q_{11} q_{12}$ is equal to $q_{21} q_{22}$ and and t_1 exceeds t_2, A must exceed D, thus proving that the uniform rate involves a lower total excess cost of protected production than a system of differentiated rates.

A simple extension of this analysis can be used to show that extending protection to a third commodity would permit the same volume of protected production (excess of total output over what would be produced under free trade) to be produced at a lower total excess cost and lower tariff rate, through the replacement of high-excess-cost marginal output in industries 1 and 2 by

97

lower-excess-cost marginal output from industry 3. This is the logic of recommending protection over as wide a range of commodities as possible. Similarly, the fact that the marginal excess cost of protected production is measured by the tariff rate accounts for the recommendation that the tariff should not be 'too high,' since presumably at some point the marginal excess cost of additional protected output becomes higher than the social benefit or gratification derived from it.

The answer to the problem of the second-best optimum tariff structure just discussed, however, is not theoretically valid. In the first place, it assumes the absence of any distortions in the economy of the type discussed in Section III. So far as distortions in the protected industries themselves are concerned, this is in principle a matter of secondary importance, since the recommended uniform rate could be modified to take account of any divergences of private from social costs in these industries; but if distortions exist in the unprotected sectors of the economy, correction for these will involve a complex calculation requiring detailed knowledge of the cross-relations among protected and unprotected commodities in both production and consumption. Second, and more important, the uniform rate rule is incorrect even in the absence of distortions in the economy, since it counts only the excess production cost of protection and fails to take account of the loss of consumers' surplus, the consumption cost, associated with protection.

This point can be illustrated by reference to Figure 4, which reproduces the uniform-rate situation of Figure 3 and introduces the demand curves for the two commodities. With the uniform tariff rate, consumption of the two goods is c_{11} and c_{21}, respectively, and production q_{11} and q_{21} respectively. Assume that the tariff on commodity 2 is simultaneously raised by just enough to replace the lost output of $q_{11}q_{12}$ of commodity 1 (caused by the reduction in the tariff on it) by an equal increase $q_{21}q_{22}$ of commodity 2. The result is an increase in the excess production cost of total protected output, since the area $B + F$, the saving on excess cost of production of commodity 1, must be smaller than the area $C + G$, the increase in excess cost of production of commodity 2. But the change also leads to an increase in tariff revenue and consumers' surplus on consumption of

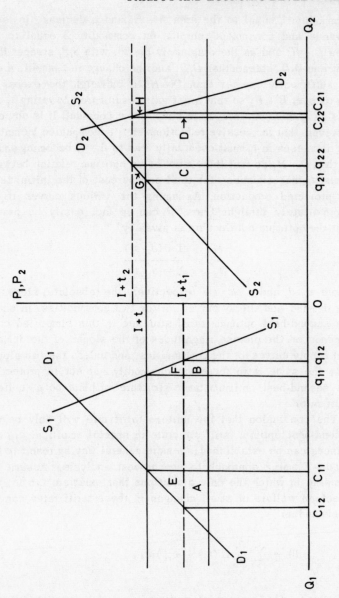

Fig. 4

commodity 1 equal to the area $A + E$, and a decrease in tariff revenue and consumers' surplus on commodity 2 equal to the area $D + H$; and as the diagram is drawn, with S_1S_1 steeper than S_2S_2 and D_2D_2 steeper than D_1D_1 and the change in t_1 small, $A + E$ is sufficiently greater than $D + H$ to outweigh the excess of $C + G$ over $B + F$, so that a net gain results from lowering t_1 and raising t_2 in such a way as to keep output constant. It is obvious however, that successive reductions in t_1 accompanied by matching increases in t_2 must eventually lead to $A + E$ becoming smaller than $D + H$, so that there must be an optimum relation between t_1 and t_2 that minimizes the total excess cost of the initial level of protected production. Assuming the various curves to be approximately straight lines, it can in fact easily be proved that the optimum relationship is given by

$$\frac{t_1}{t_2} = \frac{1 + (d_2/s_2)}{1 + (d_1/s_1)} ,$$

where d_1 d_2 and s_1, s_1 are respectively the (absolute) slopes of the demand and supply curves for the two commodities. In short, the second-best optimum tariff structure in this simplified case depends on the precise magnitudes of the slopes of the demand and supply curves for the commodities, and unless the two slopes bear the same ratio for every commodity subject to protection the second-best optimum tariff structure will not be a uniform tariff rate.

The conclusion that the uniform tariff rate will only be the second-best optimal tariff structure in special empirical circumstances can be established in a more general way by resort to the Meade—Fleming approach to second-best analysis. [4] Assume an economy in which the only distortions that exist are tariffs; the effect on welfare of small changes in these tariff rates can be expressed as

$$dW = \sum_{i=1}^{n} \sum_{j=1}^{n} t_j \left(x_{ji} - c_{ji} \right) dt_i , \tag{1}$$

[4] J.E. Meade, *The Theory of International Economic Policy*, Vol. II: *Trade and Welfare* (London, 1955).

where t_i is the tariff rate on commodity i, and x_{ji} and c_{ji} are the partial derivatives of the quantities of commodity j produced and consumed with respect to the price of commodity i. Assume further that tariff changes are constrained by the condition that the total output of a subset k of the commodities is to be kept constant and consider changes in two tariff rates t_f and t_g that satisfy this condition, so that

$$\sum_{j=1}^{k} x_{jf} dt_f = \sum_{j=1}^{k} x_{jg} dt_g. \tag{2}$$

The effect on welfare is

$$dW = \sum_{j=1}^{k} t_j (x_{jf} dt_f - x_{jg} dt_g) - \sum_{j=1}^{k} t_j (c_{jf} dt_f - c_{jg} dt_g)$$

$$+ \sum_{j=k+1}^{n} t_j (x_{jf} dt_f - x_{jg} dt_g) - \sum_{j=k+1}^{n} t_j (c_{jf} dt_f - c_{jg} dt_g). \tag{3}$$

The second-best optimum tariff structure is the set of tariff rates t_j that equates dW to zero for any dt_f, dt_g. If the tariff rates on the k commodities are all equal to t, the first term in equation (3) becomes equal to

$$t \left(\sum_{j=1}^{k} x_{jf} dt_f - \sum_{j=1}^{k} x_{jg} dt_g \right)$$

and vanishes; but the other three terms will in general not vanish The last two terms will vanish if the tariffs on goods $k + l$ to n are set equal to zero (i.e., the tariff is imposed only on the goods desired to be protected); but there is no reason to expect that zero rates on these goods are implied by the second-best optimum tariff structure, and in any case the second term would only be equal to zero by accident. In other words, the second-best optimum tariff structure will in general involve both differentiated rates on the goods whose production it is desired to encourage, and tariffs (or possibly subsidies, depending on the nature of the cross-effects) on other goods as well.

101

The recommendation of a uniform tariff rate on commodities whose production it is desired to protect therefore has no theoretical validity. To put this conclusion another way, the recommendation must assume both that distortions in the economy causing divergences between private and social marginal cost do not exist, or can be safely ignored, or are unknowable and on the principle of equal ignorance may be expected to cancel out, and that the consumption cost of protection can be ignored or on the same principle of equal ignorance can be expected to cancel out. Further, for consistency it must comprise all imports, since there are no grounds for believing that a uniform tariff on the imports it is desired to replace and a zero tariff on the remainder constitutes the most efficient tariff structure for encouraging domestic production of the desired commodities.

In conclusion, it may be observed that the uniform rate rule makes rather more sense as a guide for a protectionist policy aimed at increasing self-sufficiency. For in this case, as can be shown by a simple extension of the foregoing analysis, if there are no distortions apart from the tariff structure a uniform tariff rate applied to all importable goods will equate the marginal costs of import-saving (by increased production or reduced consumption) and so minimize the total excess cost of import-saving.

VI. SOME ASPECTS OF DIFFERENTIATED TARIFF STRUCTURES

Most of the extant theory of commercial policy, including the theory employed in the analysis of the preceding Sections, is concerned implicitly with tariffs levied on commodities destined for final consumption. In actuality, however, much international trade consists of the exchange of raw materials, semi-finished goods, and capital goods for utilization in the production of finished goods in the importing country; moreover, the rates of duty that make up tariff structures are usually differentiated according to the stage of production or place in the production process of the dutiable goods, as well as being differentiated among goods at the same stage of production. In particular, tariff rates are typically 'cascaded,' the rate increasing from the raw material to the semi-fabricated and from the semi-fabricated to the fabricated stages.

The fact that traded goods may be either inputs or outputs in the importing country's productive system means that a particular tariff may either tax or subsidize domestic production, depending on whether the tariff applies to an input or an output, and makes it necessary to distinguish between the protection accorded to *commodities*, and the protection accorded to *the processes of production* that produce those commodities, by a given tariff structure. The latter may differ markedly from the former, and the rate of protection accorded, or the excess cost of protected production allowed, by the tariff structure to a particular process of production be very different from that indicated by the tariff rate on the commodity it produces. This Section presents a simple mathematical analysis of the relation between the tariff rates on commodities and the degree of protection accorded to processes of production — the rate of protection of value added, as it is sometime termed — incorporated in the tariff structure, and comments on some of the implication for economic development of tariff structures in which tariff rates are differentiated by production stages.

For purposes of analysis, assume that the productive system is characterized by an input-output matrix of the usual type; let a_{ji} be the input coefficient for the jth commodity in the ith production process, and let v_i be the coefficient of value added (or of 'original factors' used) in that process, output being measured in unit values in world currency and the input coefficients being measured in values at world market prices, so that

$$\sum_{j=1}^{n} a_{ji} + v_i = 1,$$

where the input coefficients pertain to the technology employed in the world outside the country whose tariff structure is to be analyzed. Let the tariff structure of the country in question be represented by t_i, $i = 1 \ldots n$; if the country is to take part in trade, at least one of the t_i must be zero, or inoperative (effectively zero) because the relevant commodity is exported. Let τ_i represent the implicit rate of protection of value added or original factors used in the ith industry inherent in the tariff structure t_i, defined as the proportion by which the tariff structure allows

103

the domestic cost of value added or value of original factors used in producing commodity i to exceed the foreign cost or value v_i. The tariff structure allows the domestic price of the ith commodity to be $1 + t_i$, whereas its cost of production will be

$$\sum_{j=1}^{n} (1 + t_j) a_{ji} + (1 + \tau_i) v_i.$$

Equating price and cost to obtain the implicit rate of protection yields the formula

$$\tau_i = \frac{t_i - \sum_{j=1}^{n} a_{ji} t_j}{v_i}$$

It is evident from the formula that the implicit rate of protection on a particular productive process will be equal to the explicit rate of protection on the commodity it produces only if the weighted average tariff rate on the inputs it uses

$$\left(\sum_{j=1}^{n} a_{ji} t_j \ \Big/ \ \sum_{j=1}^{n} a_{ji} \right)$$

is equal to the tariff rate on the commodity it produces. If the weighted average tariff rate on inputs is lower than the tariff rate on the output the implicit rate of protection exceeds the commodity tariff rate.[5] If the weighted average tariff rate on inputs is higher than the tariff rate on the output, the implicit rate of protection is lower than the commodity tariff rate, and may even be negative; that is, the tariff structure may tax rather

[5] Even if the tariff rate on all imports is the same, implicit rates of protection will differ if the protected industries use inputs of exportable goods to different extents. This fact provides another reason why the uniform rate rule discussed in the preceding Section is unlikely to be optimal.

than subsidize the production of certain commodities.[6]

The most obvious examples of this last possibility are export industries, which by definition are not protected but may use inputs subject to protection, and so be taxed by the tariff structure. This point has some relevance to the difficulties typically encountered by developing countries in expanding their traditional exports sufficiently to pay for the imports required for development; the heavily protective policies frequently used to promote development may tax the inputs of the export industries sufficiently severely to prevent their growth. In addition, since increasing productivity in agriculture hinges on increasing use of manufactured inputs, and taxation of such inputs discourages their use, protection may be a direct deterrent to agricultural progress. Protection may indeed produce a vicious circle of self-justifying policy measures, in which the planners start from the assumption that agriculture is incorrigibly backward, adopt a policy of heavy industrial protectionism to promote development, and by doing so throttle the development of agriculture and so provide evidence in support of the assumption of incorrigible

[6] These two propositions are exemplified by the following extreme examples of divergences between the tariff rates and the implicit rate of protection in the U.S. tariff schedule, taken from estimates prepared by Giorgio Basevi in connection with his doctoral study of the U.S. tariff and reproduced with his permission:

S.I.C. No.	Industry Description	Tariff Rate(%)	Implicit Rate of Protection(%)	
			(a)	(b)
2011	Meat packing	3·8	− 31·9	− 30·9
2823	Plastic materials	17·1	− 30·4	− 30·3
3111	Leather tanning and finishing	11·3	− 34·2	− 32·6
2561	Screens, shades and blinds	50·0	+ 189·0	+ 225·8
3491	Metal barrels, drums, and pails	35·0	+ 107·1	+ 115·3
3871	Watches and clocks	39·3	+ 88·1	+ 102·9

Note: The input-output data used in the estimates included a residual category of 'other material inputs' of unspecified origin; estimate (a) applies the average tariff rate collected on total imports (5·1 per cent) to these inputs, estimate (b) used a zero tariff rate. See also Table I, Chapter 12 below.

agricultural backwardness from which their faith in industrialization is derived.

While export industries are the most obvious examples of industries taxed by a protective tariff structure, any tariff structure containing differentiated rates may involve such taxation of particular industries. This point also has relevance for underdeveloped countries, which usually go in for extensive protection of industrial activities of all kinds, from materials production through semi-fabrication to final production processes, and implement this policy not only by tariffs but by exchange controls, import licensing, prohibition of imports of 'non-essentials,' and bargains with foreign-owned companies or legislation making protection conditional on the use of domestically-produced components and materials. The effort to protect activities that produce inputs for other protected activities may use up all or more than all of the protection accorded to the latter, so that in spite of apparently heavy protection (as measured by the tariff rates on the commodities produced) these industries have difficulty in surviving and growing (because the implicit rate of protection they enjoy is low or negative). It is in this sense that protection may said to 'cancel itself out.' [7]

The cases just discussed are ones in which the tariff structure, by imposing higher rates on inputs than on the finished product, reduces or eliminates the implicit protection accorded to the production process or subjects it to a net tax. Where the tariff on inputs is lower than the tariff rate on the output, the effect is to raise the implicit rate of protection on the process above the tariff rate on the commodity produced by it. This fact, in conjunction with the typical structure of tariff rates according to which tariff rates rise with stage of production, has important implications for world trade and economic development.

In the first place, the prevalence of such tariff structures in the advanced countries implies that the advanced countries grant much heavier protection to their manufacturing industries than their tariff rates by themselves suggest. The effect of

[7] Another way in which protection may cancel itself out is that wages in the protected industries may rise, under the shelter of the tariff, sufficiently to offset the competitive advantage of the tariff.

'cascading' may be quite substantial: for example, suppose that materials constitute 50 per cent of the value of final output, and that final output is protected by a tariff rate of 30 per cent while materials enter free of duty; then the implicit rate of protection of value added will be 60 per cent, or double the tariff rate on the output. With a material content of 75 per cent, the implicit rate of protection would be 120 per cent, or four times the tariff rate on the output. The effect of implicit rates of protection of value added that rise sharply with stage of production is obviously to create a strong bias towards confining world trade as a whole predominantly to raw materials and semi-finished goods, and world trade in manufactures to capital goods and goods whose technological superiority or luxury nature enables them to overcome high protective barriers. Moreover, the pattern of trade fostered by such differentiated tariff structures itself disguises the protectiveness of those tariff structures, by giving a heavy weight in the conventional measurements of protection – tariff rates weighted by values of goods traded, or total duties collected divided by value of imports – to the very items whose entry at low or zero rates increases the protection afforded by the tariff structure to the higher stages of production. It is even possible for a country to increase the real protectiveness of its tariff structure while simultaneoulsy reducing the degree of protectiveness as conventionally measured, by lowering or eliminating duties on imported inputs.

From the point of view of countries seeking to develop and industrialize, the heavy protection of final production processes implicit in the tariff structures of the advanced countries constitutes a major barrier to success. For it neutralizes part or all of the advantage of low wage rates that these countries possess, thereby debarring them from achieving the economies of scale and specialization that access to rich markets would permit, and forcing them if they insist on industrializing, to do so within the confines of their domestic markets, with all the disadvantages of small scale that that entails. That this can be a major barrier is illustrated by the following hypothetical example; suppose that in the advanced countries 50 per cent of the cost of a product is materials, 25 per cent capital charges, and 25 per cent labour cost, and that the tariff on the product is at the rate of 25 per cent. If the materials were available to the underdeveloped countries at the same prices and capital were freely mobile, the underdeveloped countries would have to have labour costs amounting to only 20 per cent of labour costs in the advanced countries for them to be able to land imports at the domestic market price in the advanced countries.[8] In view of the potential magnitude of the barrier to the industrialization of the underdeveloped countries inherent in the differentiated tariff structures of the advanced countries, it is somewhat surprising that the underdeveloped countries have devoted so much attention to the level and variability of the prices at which the of the prices at which the advanced countries buy their primary products, instead of to the tariff differentiation that keeps them dependent on the sale of such products for their earning of foreign exchange and deprives them of access to the large markets necessary for efficient industrialization.

In the second place, the underdeveloped countries in their own protective policies tend to follow the model of the advanced countries in differentiating their tariff rates and other protective devices according to stage of production. To the extent that they do this, the excess cost of the domestic production achieved by protection may be substantially higher than appears from the tariff rates on commodities or from the excess of the domestic price over the foreign price, and far higher than can be easily justified by presumed external economies, distorted wage rates, inelasticity of the demand for traditional exports, or *de facto* overvaluation of the currency.

Again taking a hypothetical illustrative example, suppose that the domestic price of the finished product is double the foreign price — an excess not outside the range of actual experience — and that 25 per cent of the total domestic cost consists of materials allowed entry duty-free; then the country will be paying three times as much for the working-up of the materials domestically as it would have to pay to have the working-up done abroad and incorporated in imports of the finished product. Such an arrangement would only be economically advantageous if the

[8]Let a = the ratio of underdeveloped to advanced country labour costs necessary for the former to compete in the latter's domestic market; then $(50 + 25 + a \cdot 25)(1 \cdot 25) = 50 + 25 + 25$, whence $a = \cdot 2$.

alternative opportunity cost of the domestic factors used were less than one-third of their money earnings, or if reallocation of them to export industries would increase foreign exchange earnings by less than one-third of their value. Moreover, given the complex interaction of tariff rates in determining the implicit rates of protection accorded to different industries, these rates may vary substantially from industry to industry, with no rational justification in terms of varying values of these industries to the economic development of the country. In other words, the implicit rates of protection may depart widely from the requirements of a second-best optimum tariff structure.

VII. SOME OBSERVATIONS ON IMPORT SUBSTITUTION AND ECONOMIC DEVELOPMENT

Countries seeking to promote their own economic development generally employ tariffs and other trade barriers to encourage the establishment of domestic production of substitutes for imports. The attractions of a policy of import substitution are appealing — the existence of imports indicates the presence of a market for the product — especially when the country is in chronic balance-of-payments difficulties. Yet the results are commonly disappointing. Whereas the purpose of protection is to promote the development of locally owned and operated enterprises, it tends instead to encourage the establishment of subsidiaries or affiliates of foreign enterprises, generally the large international companies with headquarters in the United States or Europe, and so give rise to political anxieties about foreign 'control' and 'domination' of the economy. Moreover, whether the enterprises are domestically or foreign owned, their methods of operation prove objectionable in a variety of ways to those ambitious for economic development. Protected enterprises are frequently criticized for duplicating the market structure and marketing methods of the advanced countries — high distributive margins, heavy advertizing, extensive product differentiation, rapid product changes, and so on; for using a technology that is backward by comparison with that of the advanced countries — for example, relying on second-hand or antiquated equipment; for using techniques adopted from the advanced countries and therefore inappropriate to the relative factor availabilities in the domestic economy; for failing to

109

develop export markets; and for continuing reliance on extensive use of imported parts and machinery.

These subjects of criticism, far from being the demonstrations of the wilful perversity of capitalism that they are often alleged to be, are the natural economic consequences of pursuing economic development by a policy of import substitution implemented by protection. Goods are initially imported rather than produced domestically because the foreign producer possesses comparative advantages sufficiently strong to overcome the natural barriers to international trade imposed by transportation and communication costs; in the modern industrial world, these advantages generally stem from access to a large domestic market, which permits the exploitation of economies of scale and of specialization and fosters product improvement through research and development expenditure. The use of protection to promote substitution of local for foreign production does nothing to reduce the comparitive disadvantage of local as contrasted with foreign entrepreneurship, and its main effect is therefore likely to be to induce the foreign firms to set up local production facilities to satisfy the demand previously satisfied by exports from their home country, rather than to create a domestically owned and operated industry capable of competing successfully with its foreign rivals. Where domestic ownership is insisted on, it is still likely to be most economical for the local entrepreneurs to come to an arrangement with the foreign firms that in the absence of the import-substitution policy would supply the market, to obtain access to the production and management methods the latter command. Hence the economic policy of import-substitution almost inevitably creates the political problem of foreign 'control' of the economy.

Given that the policy of import-substitution by protection involves forcing industry to move from an economic to an uneconomic location, the methods of operation of the transplanted industries are likely to be objectionable to development enthusiasts on the various grounds previously mentioned. For, quite apart from any psychological and political implications of the fact that foreign enterprises are simultaneously coerced and bribed by protection to establish facilities that they otherwise would not establish, and so may feel no obligation to do more than the minimum necessary to satisfy the policy-makers of the developing country, there are strong economic reasons for adopting these methods of operation. The production and marketing methods of the advanced countries are known and familiar, and hence cost little to apply elsewhere, whereas the invention of new techniques of production and marketing adapted to the small markets, low income levels, and cheap but poorly trained labour of the underdeveloped countries would require an expensive investment in research that might not justify its cost. In other words, it is likely to be more efficient to adapt methods inappropriate to local conditions as far as possible than to invest in the development of the methods most appropriate to local conditions. Similarly, the use of second-hand equipment may be more efficient than either using up-to-date equipment designed for a higher-wage and larger-scale and more specialized economy, or designing and building new equipment tailored to the scale and factor prices of the underdeveloped economy. Again, given that the import-substitute industries are established to supply an existing market they are unlikely to become exporters, since the existing market typically demands small quantities of a large variery of goods whereas successful exporting for a small country typically demands concentration on quantity production of a limited range of standard lines. And given that the efficiency of industry in advanced countries frequently rests on tight control over the quality of material inputs and components and on the use of carefully designed precision machinery, it is likely to be relatively inexpensive to transplant the assembly or fabricating processes and relatively expensive to transplant the production of the materials and components themselves and of the machinery used in the process, so that industries transplanted by import-substitution policies are likely to remain dependent on extensive imports of materials, components, and machinery.

All this suggests that a policy of import-substitution is unlikely to transform an underdeveloped country into a major industrial power, competitive in the world market for manufactured products. Instead, such a policy is likely to transform it into a miniature replica of the economies of the advanced countries, though less efficient and technologically laggard to an extent depending on the size of the domestic market and the degree of

111

protection employed.

From the point of view of the economic welfare of the under-developed country this result may nevertheless constitute an improvement, at least in the longer run, especially if the policy of import-substitution attracts substantial amounts of foreign direct investment. For though the substitution of domestic pro-duction for imports entails an increase in cost and therefore a reduction in real income, the country may subsequently benefit from the resulting opportunity to learn modern industrial methods and participate directly in the progress of technology in the advanced countries. This expectation, in one form or another, is of course the motivation of import-substitution as a development policy and the justification usually offered for it. [9]

The attraction of foreign direct investment may be particularly beneficial in this regard for two reasons. First, under the usual double-taxation agreements the country in which investment occurs receives the first slice of profits taxation, so that foreign direct investment in an underdeveloped country enables that country to tax the capitalists of the advanced countries at the expense of the latter's own Treasuries; this is a tangible and important benefit derived by the receiving country from foreign direct investment quite apart form the benefits accruing through increased scale, improved technology, and increased competition in the domestic economy, Second, affiliation with an international parent company gives the local enterprise access to the research and development carried on by the parent and other affiliates, and so provide a flow of productivity-improving knowledge at relatively low cost to the country. [10]

It is not true, however, that a policy of import-substitution will

---

[9] By direct participation is meant participation as producers, earning higher incomes as a result of technical progress, in contrast to partici-pation as consumers, enjoying higher quality and (or) lower prices of commodities as a result of technical progress. It is sometimes over-looked that underdeveloped countries dependent on imports of manufac-tured goods benefit from progress in the latter way without having to bear the research and development costs of progress.

[10] For analysis of the gains from foreign investment in the Canadian case, see the Foreword to my *The Canadian Quandary* (Toronto, 1963).

112

necessarily prove beneficial in the long run, by giving the country a share in technical progress in the industries involved. It is, on the contrary, possible for a country to be made worse off by technical progress in its import-competing sector, because the reduction in the cost of currently-produced import-substitutes is more than outweighed by a consequent further replacement of imports by higher-cost domestic substitutes. This possibility is illustrated in Figure 5, where the supply curve is to be thought of as a supply curve of import substitutes and the policy of

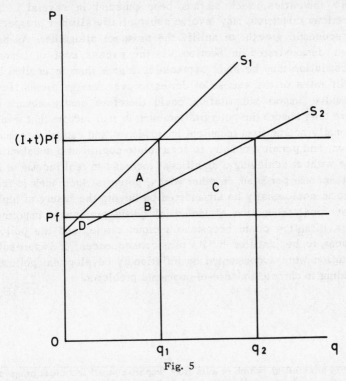

Fig. 5

import substitution is represented by a tariff at the rate t imposed on imports available at the world price p_f. Prior to the technical change the supply curve of import substitutes is S_1S_1 and the excess production cost imposed by the import-substitution policy is the area $A + B$. Technical change shifts the supply curve to S_2S_2, involving an excess production cost of import-substitution

113

of $B + C$; as the diagram is drawn, C is greater than A by more than the area D (the increase in domestic producers' surplus at the free-trade price), so that technical progress in the import-substitution sector results in a net loss to the country. [11]

The foregoing analysis relates to import-substitution considered as a once-for-all measure, exemplified for example by the introduction of a protective tariff. A policy of progressive import substitution which seeks continually to expand the size of the import-competing sector by granting protection to more and more industries, such as has been pursued in several Latin American countries, may involve substantially slimmer prospects of economic growth, or nullify the prospect altogether. As has been demonstrated in Section VI, the excess cost of import-substitution may be high, appreciably higher than in implied by tariff rates or the excess of domestic over foreign prices. Progressive import substitution could therefore easily absorb or more than absorb the potential increase in real income that would normally accrue from technical improvement and capital accumulation, and permit a country to accumulate capital at a substantial rate without achieving a significant increase in real income or in real income per head. In other words, potential increases in real income could easily be squandered on buying the luxury of high-cost local production of industrial goods previously imported. This situation could become a vicious circle, and the policy appear to be justified by its own consequences, if import-substitution were accompanied by inflationary development policies leading to chronic balance-of-payments problems.

[11] This possibility, which results from 'import-biased' technical progress in the presence of a tariff, is to be distinguished from the standard proposition originated by J.R. Hicks ('An Inaugural Lecture,' *Oxford Economic Papers*, Vol 5, No. 2 (June 1953) pp. 117–35, reprinted in *Essays in World Economics*) that 'import-biased' technical progress under free trade conditions benefits a country by turning the terms in its favour. A full analysis of the effects of 'import-biased' progress would require weighing the import-substitution and terms-of-trade effects against one another.

PART II:
Tariffs and Distortions

4. Optimal Trade Intervention in the Presence of Domestic Distortions*

I. INTRODUCTION

In the period since the war, the concern of economists with the problems of the underdeveloped countries and the formulation of policies to stimulate economic development has led to renewed interest in the economic arguments for protection. I use the description 'economic arguments' to distinguish arguments that recommend protection as a means of increasing real income or economic welfare from arguments that recommend protection as a means of achieving such essentially non-economic objectives as increasing self-sufficiency for political and military reasons, diversifying the economy to provide a richer way of life for the citizenry and so strengthening national identity, or preserving a valued traditional way of life. In the first place, writers on economic development have taken over and made considerable use of the theory of the optimum tariff, originated by Bickerdike and revived in the 1940s and early 1950s as a by-product of the contemporary debate over the legitimacy of welfare propositions in economics. Secondly, writers in the

* Reprinted from Baldwin *et al*, *Trade, Growth and the Balance of Payments*: *Essays in Honor of Gottfried Haberler* (Chicago: Rand-McNally Co., 1965) pp. 3—34. The chapter represents a condensation of analysis developed in lectures and writings over a period of years. The organization of the argument around the two central propositions of the chapter, however, is derived from discussion with Jagdish Bhagwati, and particularly from an early reading of his brilliant joint article with V.K. Ramaswami, 'Domestic Distortions, Tariffs and the Theory of Optimum Subsidy', *Journal of Political Economy*, Vol. LXXI, No. 1 (February 1963) pp. 44—50. To these two authors belongs the credit for reducing a mass of *ad hoc* arguments concerning tariffs to a simple application of second-best welfare theory. This chapter extends their analysis to some arguments for protection not considered by them, elaborates more fully on the infant industry argument, and adds to their results two propositions about non-economic arguments for protection. I should like also to acknowledge a debt to Erling Olsen, whose comments on an earlier draft prompted improvements in the presentation of the factor-price rigidity case.

117

economic development area have laid considerable stress on the traditional 'external economies' and 'infant industry' arguments for protection; in recent years they have also developed new, or at least heretofore not much emphasized, arguments for protection based on the alleged fact that in underdeveloped countries wages in manufacturing exceed the opportunity cost of labour in the economy – the marginal productivity of labour in the agricultural sector. Two distinct reasons for the alleged discrepancy between industrial wage rates and the opportunity costs of labour are advanced, it not always being recognized that they are distinct. One, which can be associated with the name of Arthur Lewis,[1] is that industrial wages are related to earnings in the agricultural sector, and that these earnings are determined by the average product of labour, which exceeds the marginal product of labour because agricultural labour has familial or traditional claims on the rent of land. The other reason, associated with the name of Everett Hagen[2] but equally attributable to Lewis,[3] is that the industrial wage rate exceeds the agricultural wage rate by a margin larger than can be explained by the economic costs of urban life:[4] this difference Hagen associates with the dynamic need for a growing economy to transfer labour from agriculture to industry, although it can also be explained by social influences on industrial wage determination.

The theory of the optimum tariff rests on the proposition that if a country possesses monopolistic or monopsonistic power in world markets, world market prices for its exports and imports

---

[1] W. Arthur Lewis, 'Economic Development with Unlimited Supplies of Labour', *Manchester School of Economic and Social Studies*, Vol. XXII, No. 2 (May 1954) pp. 139–91, and 'Unlimited Labour: Further Notes', *Manchester School of Economic and Social Studies*, Vol. XXVI, No. 1 (January 1958) pp. 1–32.

[2] Everett E. Hagen, 'An Economic Justification of Protectionism', *Quarterly Journal of Economics*, Vol. LXXII, No. 4 (November 1958) pp. 496–514.

[3] 'Economic Development...', pp. 150–51.

[4] Hagen (*op. cit.*, p. 496, n. 2) traces the origins of the argument to Jacob Viner's review of M. Manoilesco's *The Theory of Protection and International Trade* (London: P.S. King, 1931), in the *Journal of Political Economy*, Vol. XI, No. 1 (February 1932) pp. 121–25.

will not correspond to the marginal national revenue from its exports or marginal national cost of its imports, and asserts that by appropriately chosen export and import duties — taxes on trade — the country can equate the relative prices of goods to domestic producers and consumers with their relative opportunity costs in international trade. In other words, the theory of the optimum tariff rests on the existence of a distortion in international markets, viewed from the national standpoint, such that market prices diverge from opportunity costs, and the optimum tariff is recommended as a means of off setting this distortion. The other economic arguments for protection, with which this chapter is concerned, rest on the presence of distortions in the domestic economy, which create a divergence between domestic prices and domestic opportunity costs; in these arguments, protection is recommended as a means of offsetting the distortions that prevent domestic prices from reflecting domestic opportunity costs.

The purpose of this chapter is to explain and elaborate on two propositions concerning arguments for protection derived from the existence or alleged existence of domestic distortions. The first proposition is that such distortions do not logically lead to the recommendation of protection, in the sense of taxes on international trade; instead, they lead to the recommendation of other forms of government intervention which do not discriminate between domestic and international trade and which differ according to the nature of the distortion they are intended to correct. The second proposition is that if protection is adopted as a means of correcting domestic distortions, not only will the result be that economic welfare will fall short of the maximum obtainable, but economic welfare may even be reduced below what it would be under a policy of free trade. These two propositions can be combined in the proposition that the only valid argument for protection as a means of maximizing economic welfare is the optimum tariff argument; all other arguments for protection of this kind are in principle arguments for some form of government intervention in the domestic economy, and lead to the recommendation of protection only when supported both by practical considerations that render the appropriate form of intervention infeasible, and empirical evidence that protection will in fact increase economic welfare.

In this connection, there is a third proposition implicit in the two just stated, namely that if domestic distortions exist, and if for some reason the use of the appropriate government policies for dealing with them (policies non-discriminatory as between domestic and international trade) is precluded, it will in general be possible to improve on the level of welfare attainable under free trade by the imposition of a tax or subsidy at some rate on international trade; but the welfare-maximizing rate of tax or subsidy will not except in special cases correspond to the rate of the domestic distortion. This proposition stems from the simple consideration that a marginal departure from free trade conditions will impose a negligible consumption (or in some cases production) loss on the community, but will produce a non-negligible welfare gain if it moves the economy marginally from a distorted towards a Pareto-optimal equilibrium position. The proposition has excited some controversy since the present analysis first appeared, but will not be developed further here, as it assumes a restriction on the policy alternatives available to government not assumed in the ensuing analysis.[5]

The reader should note that the proposition in question assumes continuous variation of resource allocation as a function of prices. In certain cases, including some of those analysed below under 'Factor immobility and price rigidity' and the infant-industry argument, there is an 'all-or-nothing' choice between free trade and a tariff at a rate sufficient to offset the assumed distortion.

II. DEFINITIONS AND ASSUMPTIONS

As a preliminary to the development of the main theme, it is necessary to comment briefly on certain aspects of the setting of the problem and the definition of terms.

[5] See Kemp, M.C., and Negishi, Takashi, 'Domestic Distortions, Tariffs and the Theory of Optimum Subsidy, *The Journal of Political Economy.* Vol. 77, No. 6 (December 1969) pp. 1011—13; Also Bhagwati, J., *Trade, Tariffs and Growth* (Cambridge: M.I.T. Press, 1969), Chapter 11, 'Domestic Distortions, Tariffs and the Theory of Optimum Subsidy', especially 'postscript', pp. 306—07.

In the first place, it is necessary to define the word 'protection'. Economists generally use this word in a very loose sense, which carries the connotation of a tariff on imports but also lends itself to extension to any policy that raises the price received by domestic producers of an importable commodity above the world market price. Not only can the effect of a tariff be achieved in the modern world by other devices, such as import restrictions, exchange controls, and multiple exchange rates — devices which may achieve the effect of raising the domestic relative price of importable goods above their relative price in the world market by operating to restrict exports as well as to restrict imports — but the domestic relative price received by producers of importable goods can be raised above the world price by two quite different means — by raising the domestic price to both producers and consumers above the world price, through tariffs or equivalent devices, and by raising the domestic price to producers only above the world price, while leaving consumers free to buy at world prices, through subsidies on production or equivalent taxation of production of alternative products. These two means of raising prices to domestic producers above world prices differ sharply in their economic implications, as will appear from what follows, and the confusion of them in the loose usage of the term 'protection' has been responsible for serious analytical errors in the literature. In this chapter, I confine the term 'protection' to policies that create a divergence between the relative prices of commodities to domestic consumers and producers, and their relative prices in world markets. This usage does not preclude anyone who wishes to describe policies of subsidizing domestic production by one means or another as protection from doing so, and interpreting my analysis as showing that protection by subsidies is economically desirable in certain cases of domestic distortion, provided that he clearly distinguishes protection by subsidy from protection by tariff. It is perhaps worth noting in passing — though this is not part of the subject of this chapter — that the identification of protection with the tariff is a potent source of confusion in other contexts than the relation of protection to economic welfare; for example, the degree of protection afforded to a particular industry by a tariff structure depends not only on the tariff rate on its product but on the tariffs and other taxes levied or subsidies paid both on its inputs and on the other goods that could be produced by the resources it uses;[6] and these complications include the effects of over-valuation or undervaluation of the exchange rate.

Secondly, it is necessary to be precise about the meaning attached to an improvement or deterioration in economic welfare. Disagreement on this question was the foundation of the classic debate between Gottfried Haberler and Thomas Balogh that followed on Haberler's attempt to analyse the issues discussed in this chapter with the assistance of a criterion of improvement in welfare that has subsequently been shown to be objectionable.[7] This chapter employs the concept of welfare in the modern sense of potential welfare, and regards a change in the econ-omic environment as producing a potential improvement in econ-omic welfare if, in the new environment, everyone could be made better off – in the usual sense of enjoying a higher consumption of goods and services – than in the old environment, if income were distributed in accordance with any social welfare function applied consistently in the new and the old environment. This approach permits the use of community indifference curves to represent the potential welfare of the community. One might indeed go further and maintain that the assumption that some social welfare function exists and is implemented is essential to any rational discussion of national economic policy.

Thirdly, it is assumed in this chapter, in accordance with the conventions of theoretical analysis of these problems, that government intervention is a costless operation: in other words, there is no cost attached to the choice between a tax and a

[6] For an analysis of the protective incidence of a particular tariff structure, see my ' The Bladen Plan for Increased Protection of the Canadian Automotive Industry', *Canadian Journal of Economics and Political Science*, Vol. XXIX, No. 2 (May 1963) pp. 212–38, reprinted in part as Chapter 11 below.

[7] Haberler, 'Some Problems in the Pure Theory of International Trade', *Economic Journal*, Vol. LX, No. 2 (June 1950) pp. 223–40; Balogh, 'Welfare and Freer Trade – A Reply', *Economic Journal*, Vol. LXI, No. 241 (March 1951) pp. 72–82; Haberler, 'Welfare and Freer Trade – A Rejoinder', *Economic Journal*, Vol. LXI, No. 244 (December 1951) pp. 777–84.

subsidy. This assumption ignores the empirical consideration, frequently introduced into arguments about protection, that poor countries have considerably greater difficulty in levying taxes to finance subsidies than they have in levying tariffs on imports. This consideration is of practical rather than theoretical consequence, and to constitute a case for tariffs requires supplementation by empirical measurement of both the relative administrative costs and the economic effects of the alternative methods of promoting favoured industries — as has already been mentioned. Its relevance to practical policy-making is probably less than is frequently assumed, since on the one hand the intent of a protective tariff is not to yield revenue, and on the other hand the effect of a subsidy on one type of production can be achieved by taxes levied on alternative lines of production. The assumption also ignores the possibility that the income or other taxes levied to finance subsidies to production may have a distorting effect on the supply or allocation of resources. Abandonment of this assumption would also lead to the necessity of empirical assessment of the relative economic costs of alternative methods of promoting favoured industries.

Finally, something should be said about the bearing of theoretical analysis of the arguments for protection on practical policy-making and the assessment of actual tariff systems. The demonstration that in certain carefully defined circumstances a tariff levied at a theoretically specified rate would make a country better off than it would be under free trade is not — contrary to the implication of many economic writings on protection — equivalent to a demonstration that past or present tariffs have in fact made the nations imposing them better off than they would have been under free trade, or a justification of whatever tariffs legislators might choose to adopt. Modern economic analysis of the cases in which a tariff or other governmental intervention in the price system would improve economic welfare, in other words, does not constitute a defence of indiscriminate protectionism and a rejection of the market mechanism; rather, it points to a number of respects in which the market mechanism fails to work as it should, and indicates remedies designed to make the market function properly. The usefulness of the exercise depends

123

precisely on the assumption that legislators do not normally known what makes for improvement of economic welfare, and would be prepared to act on better information if it could be provided. If economists did not customarily accept this assumption, their work on economic policy would have to be oriented entirely differently; in particular, research on commercial policy would — depending on the theory of government adopted — be concerned with inferring from actual tariff structures either the divergences between social and private costs and benefits discovered by the collective wisdom of the legislators to exist in the economy, or the political power of various economic groups in the community, as measured by their capacity to extort transfers of income from their fellow-citizens.

III. THE TWO PROPOSITIONS

With the preliminary definitions, assumptions, and observations established, I turn to the main theme of this chapter, the two propositions concerning optimal government intervention in the presence of domestic distortions. The first proposition, that the correction of such distortions does not require intervention in the form of taxes on international trade (taxes here include negative taxes or subsidies), follows directly from the well-known first-order marginal conditions of Pareto optimality. These conditions specify that the marginal rate of substitution between goods in consumption should be equal to the marginal rate of transformation between goods in production, and in an open economy include transformation through international exchange as well as transformation through domestic production. It follows that any distortion that prevents market prices from corresponding to marginal social rates of substitution or transformation should be corrected by a tax, a subsidy, or a combination of taxes and subsidies that restores the necessary marginal equalities; for simplicity, it is convenient to consider the simplest remedy, a tax or subsidy imposed at the point where the distortion occurs. Where there is a distortion in foreign markets, owing to imperfectly elastic foreign demand or supply, Pareto optimality requires the imposition of taxes on trade designed to equate the domestic price ratios facing producers and consumers with the marginal rates of transformation between commodities in international trade — that is, the imposition of the optimum tariff structure.[8] In the case of domestic distortions, Pareto optimality requires the imposition of taxes or subsidies on consumption, production, or factor supply, as the situation requires.

Where externalities in consumption make social marginal rates of substitution diverge from private, taxes or subsidies on consumption are required; where external economies in production exist, or where monopolistic influences raise prices above marginal costs, marginal subsidies on production are required, and where external diseconomies are present, marginal taxes on production are required; and where the price of a factor in a particular occupation exceeds its price in other occupations by more than can be accounted for by the nonpecuniary disadvantages of that occupation, a subsidy on the use of that factor in that occupation is required. The point of central im-importance is that the correction of domestic distortions requires a tax or subsidy on either domestic consumption or domestic production or domestic factor use, not on international trade.

The imposition of any tax or subsidy on international trade, other than what is indicated by the optimum tariff analysis, for the purpose of correcting a domestic distortion, itself introduces an inequality between either the marginal rate of substitution in domestic consumption or the marginal rate of transformation in domestic production and the marginal rate of transformation in foreign trade, and so constitutes a violation of Pareto optimality. A tax on luxury imports, for example, designed to discourage an undesirable demonstration effect and therefore to correct an external diseconomy of consumption, permits the marginal rate of transformation of domestic resources into the importable good in question to exceed the marginal rate of

---

[8] It should perhaps be emphasized that the welfare being maximized is the national welfare, and the distortions in question are distortions only from the national point of view. Also, tariff retaliation by other countries does not necessarily prevent a country from gaining by the imposition of an optimum tariff structure; see my 'Optimum Tariffs and Retaliation', *Review of Economic Studies*, Vol. XXII (2), No. 55 (1953–54) pp. 142–53, reprinted in H.G. Johnson, *International Trade and Economic Growth* (London: George Allen & Unwin, 1958) Chapter II.

transformation through foreign trade. A tax on imports or subsidy to exports of goods subject to external economies or monopolistic pricing in domestic production, designed to offset these distortions, makes the relative marginal cost of these goods to consumers higher than their marginal cost to the economy. Since the offsetting of domestic distortions by taxes or subsidies on trade necessarily removes one distortion at the expense of introducing another, interventions in international trade introduced for this purpose cannot lead to a situation of Pareto optimality. Consequently, tariffs and other trade interventions justified on grounds of the existence of domestic distortions cannot lead to the maximization of real income. The only forms of intervention that can do so are interventions that offset the existing distortions without introducing new distortions; such interventions are confined to taxes and subsidies on domestic consumption, production, or factor use.

The second proposition, that taxes or subsidies on international trade designed to offset domestic distortions will not necessarily increase economic welfare by comparison with the free trade situation, is a direct application of the theory of second best developed by Meade, Lipsey and Lancaster, and others.[9] One implication of that theory is that it is impossible to predict on *a priori* grounds — that is, without comprehensive empirical information on the tastes and technology of the economy — whether the substitution of one violation of the Pareto optimality conditions for another will worsen or improve economic welfare. Since the use of intervention in trade to offset domestic distortions necessarily involves precisely this kind of substitution, it is impossible to say whether the result will be an improvement in welfare or not. For example, in the consumption externality case mentioned above, free-trade produces the result $MRT_d = MRT_f > MRS$; and an import tariff produces the result $MRT_d > MRT_f = MRS$. In the case of external economies in production or monopolistic pricing, free trade produces the result $MRT_d < MRT_f = MRS$, and an import tariff produces the

[9] See J.E. Meade, *Trade and Welfare* (London: Oxford University Press, 1955), and R.G. Lipsey and K. Lancaster, 'The General Theory of the Second Best', *Review of Economic Studies*, Vol. XXIV, No. 63 (1956—57) pp. 11—32.

result $MRT_d = MRT_f < MRS$. In the case of a distortion in the market for factors, there are additional violations of the Pareto optimality conditions in the factor markets under both free trade and protection.[10]

The remainder of this chapter is concerned with illustrating these propositions by reference to various arguments for protection. For this purpose, it is convenient to follow the general outline of Haberler's classic article,[11] modified to include fuller treatment of the arguments emphasized in the recent literature on underdeveloped countries, and to divide the arguments for protection into four groups. These are: arguments derived from immobility of factors and downward rigidity of factor prices; arguments derived from distortions in commodity markets; arguments derived from distortions in factor markets; and the infant industry argument. The first class of argument, to which Haberler devoted considerable space, grew out of the unemployment problem of the 1930s and the associated revival of protectionism. The second includes both the classical problems of external economies and diseconomies, and the problem of monopolistic distortions to which considerable attention was devoted in the 1930s following the development of the theory of monopolistic (imperfect) competition. The third involves the essential elements of the new case for protection developed on the basis of the disequilibrium in the labour market alleged to be characteristic of underdeveloped countries. The fourth is, of course, the orthodox accepted exception to the case for free trade.

IV. THE STANDARD TRADE MODEL

To provide a frame of reference for the analysis of these arguments, it is convenient to use the standard model of international trade. This model simplifies the problem by assuming that the

---

[10] MRS symbolizes marginal rate of substitution in domestic consumption, MRT_d marginal rate of transformation in domestic production, MRT_f marginal rate of transformation in foreign trade; all of these are defined in terms of the amount of the export good given up in exchange for a unit increment of the import good.

[11] 'Some Problems...', pp. 223–40.

economy produces two commodities only, by employing only two factors of production, the available quantities of which are assumed to be given; the production functions for the two commodities are assumed to be subject to constant returns to scale, an assumption which eliminates externalities in production; and perfect competition is assumed in the commodity and factor markets, which assumption includes perfect flexibility of prices and mobility of factors between industries. These assumptions permit the production conditions of the economy to be summarized in a community transformation curve between the two commodities, such that at any exchange ratio between the commodities production will be represented by the point on the transformation curve at which the slope of that curve is equal to the exchange ratio. On the demand side, factor owners are assumed to be indifferent between occupations — utility depends only on the quantities of goods consumed — and consumers' welfare is assumed to depend only on personal consumption, which assumption eliminates externalities in consumption. (Such consumption externalities are ignored in the remainder of this chapter, since they have not been advanced as an important argument for protection, and the relevant analysis follows directly from the proposition already presented, and from analogy with the cases of production distortion dealt with below.) The individual tastes and distribution of income that determine the demand for the two commodities are assumed to be summarizable in a set of community indifference curves, such that for any given income and exchange ratio the consumption of the two commodities will be that which places the community on the highest attainable indifference curve. Since in a competitive economy the distribution of income depends on the distribution of factor ownership and varies with factor prices, the set of community indifference curves has to be interpreted as embodying either the concept of potential welfare employed in modern welfare economies, or the expression of a particular social welfare function in a particular invariant distribution of income among the members of the community. The conclusions concerning the effects of alternative types of government intervention on economic welfare derived below are to be interpreted as referring to welfare in either of these two senses. Since the concern of the paper is with government intervention in the presence of domestic distortions, it is convenient to exclude distortions in foreign markets by assuming that the opportunity to trade internationally consists in the opportunity to exchange goods in the world market at an exchange ratio different from that which would rule in the economy in the absence of the opportunity to trade, which international

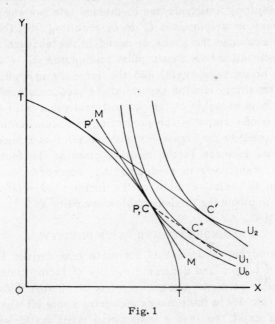

Fig. 1

exchange ratio is assumed to be independent of the direction or magnitude of the trade of the country under analysis. The two commodities will be referred to as X and Y, and it is assumed throughout that the country's true comparative advantage lies in Y, in the sense that the comparative cost of Y in the absence of the opportunity to trade is lower than the comparative cost of Y embodied in the international exchange ratio.

This standard model of international trade is represented in the accompanying Figure 1, where TT is the transformation curve and U_0, U_1, U_2, are the community indifference curves. In the absence of the opportunity to trade, the community would produce and consume at P, C, the closed-economy exchange ratio between the goods being represented by the slope of the common tangent MM to the transformation and indifference curves at that point. The opportunity to trade (represented by the slope $P'C'$) allows the economy to increase its welfare from U_0 to U_2, by shifting from production and consumption at P, C to production at P' and consumption at C'. The gain in welfare resulting from trade can be divided into two components: the increase in welfare from U_0 to U_1 resulting from the opportunity to exchange the goods produced in the absence of trade for the more attractive consumption combination C'' — the consumption or exchange gain; and the increase in welfare from U_1 to U_2 resulting from the opportunity to produce a combination of goods more valuable at the international price ratio than the closed economy output — the production or specialization gain. The adjustment to the higher international price of Y necessarily involves an increase in the relative price of the factor used relatively intensively in producing that commodity, and a reduction in the relative price of the factor used relatively intensively in producing the importable commodity X.

V. FACTOR IMMOBILITY AND PRICE RIGIDITY

For the analysis of arguments for protection derived from immobility of factors and downward rigidity of factor prices, it is convenient to pose the problem in terms of whether the opening of the opportunity to trade makes a country worse off when these conditions exist, so that a prohibitive tariff would secure a higher level of welfare than could be attained under free trade, even though in reality the argument for protection on these grounds usually arises when trade is already established and the international price of imports suddenly falls. The difference of assumptions merely simplifies the problem without altering the conclusions.

As Haberler has shown, there is a fundamental difference between the effects of immobility of factors, combined with flexibility of factor prices, and of downward rigidity of factor prices, whether combined with immobility or not. As the analysis of the standard model of trade shows, the country would enjoy a consumption or exchange gain from trade even if production remained at the closed-economy equilibrium point. Production would remain at that point if factors were completely immobile but their prices were perfectly flexible; if factors were partially mobile, production would shift to some point within the transformation curve but necessarily entailing a higher value of production at world market prices, that is, yielding some production or specialization gain. It follows that so long as factor prices are flexible, immobility of factors cannot prevent the country from being better off under free trade that with protection. The fundamental reason for this is that immobility does not by itself entail a distortion of the first-order conditions of Pareto optimality. So long as factor prices are flexible, and immobility is taken as an immutable fact of life (more is said on this point below), factor prices will reflect the alternative opportunity costs of factors to the economy; hence there is no domestic distortion to be offset by protection, and protection will simply introduce a distortion of the marginal conditions for optimality in foreign trade.

Downward rigidity of factor prices does introduce a distortion, if (as Haberler has carefully pointed out) such rigidity does not reflect a perfectly elastic supply of the factor in question (derived, for example, from an infinite elasticity of substitution between leisure and consumption) but instead reflects institutional limitations on voluntary choice (imposed, for example, by conventional pricing of labour services or collective bargaining). [12] Analysis of the effects of downward rigidity of factor prices requires definition of the terms in which factor prices are rigid downwards, since factor prices may be rigid in terms of one commodity or the other or of the utility level enjoyed, and consideration of various possible combinations of downward price rigidity and immobility.

If factor prices are rigid in terms of X and both factors are immobile, production will remain where it was in the absence

[12] It should be noted that, for analysis with the techniques of trade theory, factor prices must be assumed to be rigid in real terms; if factor prices are rigid in money terms ('money illusion' of the Keynesian type is present), full employment can always be secured by devaluation coupled with an appropriate domestic fiscal-monetary policy. This point is not made explicit in Haberler's analysis; cf. 'Some Problems...', pp. 227—31.

of trade (at point P in Figure 2). The result will be the same as with factor price flexibility, since the marginal productivities of the factors in the X industry in terms of X are unchanged, while the marginal productivities of the factors in the Y industry are unchanged in terms of Y but greater in terms of X, because

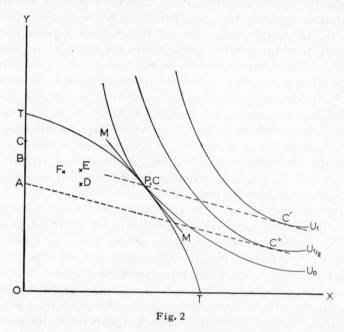

Fig. 2

the price of X in terms of Y has fallen as a result of trade. If both factor prices are rigid in terms of Y or of constant-utility combinations of X and Y, and both factors are immobile, production of X will cease, and both factors used in producing X will become wholly unemployed (the economy will produce at point A in Figure 2, level with P, C). This result follows from the fact that the marginal productivities of the factors in the X industry will be unchanged in terms of X but lower in terms of Y or any combination of X and Y, because the price of X in terms of Y has decreased as a result of trade. Since the value of each factor's marginal product is now below its price when the factors are combined in the ratio optimal at these factor prices, and since neither factor price can fall to induce factor

132

substitution and raise the marginal productivity of the other factor, the cost of production of X must exceed its price at any positive level of output.

If both factor prices are rigid (in terms of X or of Y or of a constant-utility combination of X and Y), and both factors are perfectly mobile, production of X will cease and factors will be transferred into production of Y. Some of the factor used intensively in producing X must, however, become unemployed, so that production of Y will be less than the maximum possible production shown by the transformation curve, since full employment of both factors necessitates a reduction of the price of that factor in terms of both commodities, according to the well-known Stolper-Samuelson analysis.[13] The amount of unemployment of the factor in question will be greater, and the increase in production of Y less, if factor prices are rigid in terms of Y than if they are rigid in terms of X, since a given factor price expressed in Y now buys more X, and the marginal productivity of the surplus factor in the Y industry can fall if factor prices are rigid in terms of X but not if they are rigid in terms of Y. (The extremes are represented for illustrative purposes by points B and C in Figure 2: if factor prices are rigid in terms of utility, production of Y will fall somewhere between these points.)

If both factors are immobile but the price of one of them is flexible, whereas the price of the other is rigid in terms of Y or of a constant-utility combination of X and Y, production of X will not cease altogether, instead, enough of the rigid-priced factor in that industry will become unemployed to lower its ratio to the other factor to what is consistent with its rigid price. Obviously, the unemployment of that factor and the decrease in production of X will be greater if that factor's price is rigid in terms of Y than if it is rigid in terms of a constant-utility combination of X and Y, and in the latter case will be less the less important is Y in the factor's consumption. (This case is represented in Figure 2 by the single point D, in the same horizontal line as A and P, C.) If one of the factors is mobile, and its price is rigid in terms of X or of a constant-utility

13 W.F. Stolper and P.A. Samuelson, 'Protection and Real Wages', *Review of Economic Studies*, Vol. IX (November 1941) pp. 58–73, reprinted in *Readings in the Theory of International Trade* (Philadelphia: The Blakiston Co., 1949).

combination of X and Y, whereas the other factor is immobile and flexible-priced, some of the rigid-priced factor will transfer to the Y industry, increasing output there. The transfer will proceed to the point where its effect in raising the ratio of the mobile factor to the other in the Y industry lowers the marginal productivity of the mobile factor in the Y industry to the level set by its price-rigidity. (This case is represented by point E in Figure 2; E may be vertically above D as in the diagram or to the left of it, and must correspond to a higher value of output at world prices than D.) If one of the factors is mobile and flexible-priced, whereas the other factor is immobile and its price is rigid in terms of X or of Y or of a constant-utility combination of X and Y, production of Y will increase and of X decrease as compared with the case of immobility of both factors; production of X may or may not cease entirely depending on the elasticities of substitution between the factors in the two industries and on the terms in which the immobile factor's price is rigid. (This case is represented by point F in the diagram, and may or may not correspond to a higher value of output than at D.)

Whatever the combination of factor immobility and factor price rigidity assumed, production will be altered to some point in the interior of the transformation curve corresponding to production of less X and possibly no more Y than in the closed-economy equilibrium (except for the extreme case of complete immobility and factor price rigidity in terms of X already noted). This does not, however, necessarily imply that free trade makes the country worse off than it would be under the self-sufficiency obtainable by a prohibitive tariff. It may, or it may not. Figure 2 illustrates the possibility of the country's being better off with free trade than with a prohibitive tariff even in the extreme case in which production of X ceases altogether, with no consequent increase in the production of Y, owing to a combination of complete factor immobility with factor price rigidity. In this case, as the diagram shows, the country could be made still better off than under free trade by subsidizing production of the initial output of X sufficiently to permit the factors being paid the minimum prices they demand, but trading at the international exchange ratio. In the less extreme cases, more complex forms of subsidy may be necessary to achieve the output combination that has the highest value at the international exchange ratio attainable under the relevant restrictions on factor mobility.

VI. DISTORTIONS IN THE COMMODITY MARKET

The second group of arguments for protection to be discussed comprises arguments derived from the existence of distortions in the markets for commodities that have the effect of raising the market price of the commodity in which the country has a comparative advantage above its alternative opportunity cost. One possibility is the presence of monopoly or oligopoly conditions in the production of the good, which have the effect of raising the price to consumers above the marginal cost of production. Another is the presence of external economies or diseconomies, which make marginal cost as it appears to producers differ from marginal social cost. The marginal social cost of increased output of a particular commodity may be lower than the marginal private cost because expansion of the industry producing it yields economies of scale external to the individual firm, or because contraction of the industry from which this industry draws its factors of production lowers costs of production in the former because that industry is subject to diseconomies of scale, or because expansion of the one industry lowers the cost of production of the other through any one of a variety of effects.

The result of either type of distortion, in terms of the simple model of international trade; is that the market price ratio at which a particular combination of X and Y will be produced will be less steep than the slope of the transformation curve, reflecting the assumption that the relative price of Y (the good in which the country is assumed to have a comparative advantage) exceeds its social opportunity cost. In the absence of the opportunity to trade, the country will therefore in equilibrium produce more X and less Y than would be socially optimal; the closed-economy equilibrium is represented in Figure 3 by the point P, C, the slope of MM corresponding to the market price ratio and that of RR to the true comparative cost ratio. The opening of the opportunity to trade at an international price

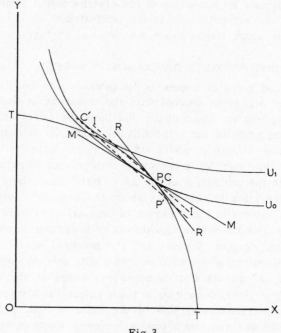

Fig. 3

ratio at which the country's true comparative advantage lies in Y has two alternative possible results, according to the relation between the international price ratio and the closed-economy market price ratio: this relation may indicate either an apparent comparative advantage in X, in which case the country specializes in the wrong direction, or an apparent comparative advantage in Y corresponding to the country's true comparative advantage, in which case the country specializes in the right direction but to a suboptimal extent.

The first case is represented in Figure 3 by the international price ratio II, which leads the country to the production equilibrium P' and the consumption equilibrium C', involving the export of X, in which the country is at a true comparative disadvantage. The point P' necessarily represents a lower value of output at the international price ratio than the closed-economy production point P; but C' may lie on either a lower indifference curve than the closed-economy consumption point

136

C, or a higher one, the latter possibility being illustrated in the diagram. In other words, trade leads to a production loss and a consumption gain, and the latter may or may not offset the former.

The argument for protection in this case is that the country will gain by imposing a tariff on imports to raise their price to consumers above the world price, compensating for the distortion that makes the apparent cost of domestically produced importables exceed their true social cost. (Alternatively, the country could levy a tax on exports to compensate for the distortion that makes their true social cost exceed their apparent cost.) Since the country's true comparative advantage lies in the good it imports, the imposition of an import tariff (or an export duty) at a rate just sufficient to compensate for the distortion would effect a return to self-sufficiency at the production and consumption equilibrium P, C, since a tax on trade cannot reverse the direction of trade. The effect of the tariff would be to increase the value of the country's output at the international price ratio, but, as the diagram exemplifies, the resulting pattern of consumption might yield a lower level of economic welfare than would be attained in the absence of protection. In short, the imposition of the tariff to correct the distortion of domestic prices from opportunity costs achieves a production gain at the expense of a consumption loss, and the net effect may be a gain or a loss, by comparison with free trade. Thus free trade in the wrong direction may be superior to protection designed to correct a distortion of domestic market prices; which policy is actually superior depends on the magnitudes of the distortion of domestic prices from opportunity costs and the difference between the closed-economy exchange ratio and the international exchange ratio, and the shape of the community's preference system.[14]

The second case is illustrated in Figure 4, where at the international price ratio II the country's apparent comparative advantage lies in the commodity in which it has a true comparative advantage, and the opportunity to trade leads to the

[14] Bhagwati and Ramaswami (*op. cit.*, p. 49) use this demonstration to show that Hagen's analysis errs in concluding that self-sufficiency is necessarily better than free trade in this case.

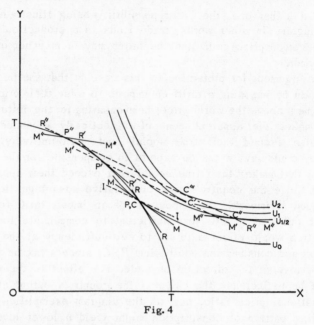

Fig. 4

production equilibrium P' and consumption equilibrium C', involving the export of commodity Y. P' necessarily represents a higher value of national output at the international exchange ratio than the closed-economy production point P, so that the country enjoys both a consumption gain and a production gain from trade; but the volume of international trade falls short of the optimum level, owing to the excess of the price of Y over its comparative cost.

In this case, the arguments for intervention in international trade to correct the distortion of domestic prices would indicate an export subsidy on Y (or import subsidy on X). The same policy might be recommended to overcome the inability of the tariff to promote exports in the circumstances of the case previously considered. (In either case, to be effectively a subsidy on trade rather than on production, the export subsidy would have to be accompanied by measures preventing reimportation.) The introduction of such a subsidy at a rate just sufficient to offset the distortion would lead to the production equilibrium P'' and consumption equilibrium C'' shown in Figure 4, the new domestic price ratio being represented by $M''M''$. The subsidy would necessarily raise the value of output at the international exchange ratio above what it would be under free trade, but, as the diagram illustrates, it might nevertheless lead to a consumption pattern yielding a lower level of welfare than that enjoyed under free trade, owing to the consumption loss induced by the effect of the subsidy in raising the domestic relative price of the exported good Y above the world market price. In order to achieve the maximum attainable economic welfare (C'' in Figure 4), the country should subsidize production of Y (or tax production of X) at a rate sufficient to compensate for the domestic distortion, without discriminating between domestic and foreign consumers by a tax (in the first case) or subsidy (in the second case) on international trade.[15]

One further comment on arguments for governmental intervention derived from distortions in domestic commodity markets is worth making. The foregoing analysis lumps together distortions originating in external economies and diseconomies, and distortions originating in imperfectly competitive market organization; and it assumes that the distortions are independent of the governmental intervention, so that intervention can be designed to offset them. This assumption is legitimate for the first type of distortion, but of doubtful validity for the second. Monopolistic practices are generally intimately interrelated with commercial policy, and there is reason to believe that producers often collude to exploit the profit opportunities created by protection. Where this is so, the attempt to offset monopolistic distortions by protective interventions in trade (taxes or subsidies on trade) may well be offset by increased distortions, so that intervention generates a consumption loss without a countervailing production gain; the same reaction could render nugatory the attempt to employ optimal intervention in the form of production taxes or subsidies. In these circumstances, the only effective means of achieving maximum economic welfare would be a direct attack on the source of the distortion, through trust-bursting policies, although it is

[15] Bhagwati and Ramaswami (*op. cit.*, p. 47) use this demonstration to show that Haberler was wrong to recommend an export or import subsidy in this case:

worth noting that genuine free trade may be the most effective policy for controlling monopoly.

VII. DISTORTIONS IN THE FACTOR MARKET

The third group of arguments for protection comprises arguments derived from the existence of distortions in the markets for factors that, by raising the price of a factor used in producing the commodity in which the country has a comparative advantage above the factor's marginal productivity in the rest of the economy, raises the private cost of production of the commodity above its alternative opportunity cost. As mentioned, two reasons for such a distortion are commonly advanced in the literature on economic development, both of which pertain to a distortion in the labour market and are used to favour protection of industry — that earnings of labour in agriculture exceed the marginal productivity of labour there, so that the industrial wage must exceed the alternative opportunity cost of labour, and that industrial wages exceed wages in agriculture by a margin greater than can be accounted for by the disutility or higher cost of urban life.

The effect of such distortions in factor markets is twofold: first, they make the allocation of factors between industries inefficient, so that production is below the maximum attainable — in terms of the model of international trade, the transformation curve is pulled in toward the origin, except at the extreme points of specialization on one or the other commodity. Second, they will normally cause the market exchange ratio between the commodities to differ from the social opportunity cost ratio, the only exception occurring when a distortion in the market for one factor is exactly offset by an opposite distortion in the market for the others. In particular, if the marginal productivity of one particular factor in one industry must exceed its marginal productivity in the other, the price of the commodity produced by the former industry must exceed its opportunity cost. Consequently, in this case the country's economic welfare will be below the maximum attainable, both in the absence of the opportunity to trade and under free trade, for two reasons: first, the country will be on a transformation curve inferior to the transformation curve that would be available to it in the absence of the distortion in the factor market; and second, owing to the discrepancy between private costs of production and social costs in the commodity market resulting from the distortion in the factor market, the country will choose a suboptimal position on the restricted transformation curve available to it.

Given the existence of a distortion in the market for a factor requiring its marginal productivity to be higher in the industry in which the country has a comparative advantage, the opportunity to trade may have either of the two consequences analysed in connection with distortions in the commodity markets; and, as demonstrated in that analysis, the protectionist policy of remedying the effects of the distortion by an export or import duty (if the country specializes on the commodity in which it has a comparative disadvantage) or an export or import subsidy (if the country specializes on the commodity in which it has a comparative advantage) may make the country either worse off or better off than it would be under free trade. A policy of subsidization of production of the commodity overpriced by the distortion, or of taxation of production of the other commodity, would maximize the economic welfare attainable from the restricted transformation curve. The important point, however, is that all of these policies aimed at offsetting the distortion by operating on the prices received by producers of commodities would leave the country on a transformation curve restricted by the inefficiency of factor use induced by the factor market distortion. This particular cause of suboptimal economic welfare could be eliminated in four different ways — by a tax on the use in one industry or subsidy on the use in the other of either factor, the rate of tax or subsidy being chosen to exactly offset the distortion. But only two of these — a subsidy on the use of the factor subject to distortion in the industry in which its marginal productivity is required to be higher, or a tax on its use in the other industry — would simultaneously eliminate the associated distortion of commodity prices from opportunity costs, the other two accentuating the distortion in the commodity market. Thus the attainment of maximum economic welfare in this case requires subsidization or taxation of the use of the factor subject to distortion; taxation or subsidization of commodity

141

production can maximize welfare subject to the inefficiency of factor use but cannot correct that inefficiency; taxation or subsidization of commodity trade not only fails to eliminate inefficiency in factor allocation but may even reduce welfare, given the inefficiency of factor allocation, below what it would be under free trade.

The foregoing argument has accepted the validity of the contention that in underdeveloped countries there is a distortion in the labour market such that the marginal productivity of labour in industry must be higher than the marginal productivity of labour in agriculture (the alternative opportunity cost of labour). Before leaving this group of arguments for protection, it is appropriate to express some doubts about the validity of this contention and its implications for economic policy. As already mentioned, there are two separate arguments supporting this contention — that industrial wages exceed agricultural wages, and that industrial wages are comparable to agricultural earnings but that the latter exceed the marginal productivity of labour in agriculture because agricultural workers claim a share of agricultural rent.

So far as the first argument is concerned, the mere fact that industrial wages exceed agricultural wages is not sufficient to prove a distortion, since the difference may be accounted for by the higher costs or disutility of urban living, the greater skill or stamina required of urban industrial labour, or the economic cost of migration, factors which necessitate compensation in the form of a higher industrial than agricultural wage if allocation of the labour force is to be efficient. An attempt to iron out wage differences due to these factors would involve misallocation of labour. There are, however, two plausible reasons for believing that observed industrial-agricultural wage differences may entail a genuine distortion.[16] The first is that frequently in underdeveloped countries either trade union organization or social legislation and popular sentiment impose industrial wage levels well above the alternative opportunity cost of labour; this possibility is substantiated by the evidence of persistent large-scale urban unemployment, and by the fact that wage levels tend to increase with size of establishment. Insofar as trade union organization or political pressure forces industry to pay wages above the alternative opportunity cost of labour, however, any attempt to remedy the distortion by subsidization of the use of labour or by protection might be frustrated by the exaction of still higher wages. The second reason is suggested by an interpretation of migration from rural to urban employment as an investment in the formation of human capital, the investment involving both a transportation and an education cost; insofar as the market for capital to finance investment in human beings is imperfect, the marginal rate of return on such investment may be far higher than the social opportunity cost of capital to the economy.

So far as the second reason for distortion is concerned — the excess of agricultural earnings over the marginal productivity of agricultural labour — since this implies that the private return on capital invested in agriculture is less than the social return, the distortion in the labour market may be more than offset by an opposite distortion in the capital market, so that rather than indicating the desirability of subsidization of the use of labour in industry, this argument may in fact indicate the desirability of. subsidization of the use of capital in agriculture.

VIII. THE INFANT INDUSTRY ARGUMENT

The fourth type of argument for protection to be considered is the infant industry argument. Although this argument is frequently confused, at least in description, with the 'external economies' argument, the two are logically distinct. The external

16 Bhagwati and Ramaswami (*ibid.*) list eight reasons for the existence of a wage differential between the rural and urban sectors, of which four are economic and four (one of which is Hagen's) may involve genuine distortions. They agree with the earlier analysis of A. Fishlow and P. David ('Optimal Resource Allocation in an Imperfect Market Setting', *Journal of Political Economy*, Vol. LXIX, No. 6 [December 1961] pp. 529—46) in regarding Hagen's 'dynamic' argument for the existence of a distortion as an illegitimate superimposition of dynamic considerations on static analysis. The same point has been made by P.B. Kenen ('Development, Mobility, and the Case for Tariffs', *Kyklos*, Vol. XVI, No. 2 [1963] pp. 321—24). Fishlow and David's other reasons correspond approximately with those discussed here, although they introduce the interesting case of factory legislation preventing the younger members of the family from working; they do not, however, raise the possibility that there may be a distortion of investment in migration of human capital.

economies argument is static, in the sense that the assumed distortion due to external economies or diseconomies is by implication a permanent characteristic of the technology of production that would require correction by government intervention of a permanent kind. The infant industry argument, by contrast, is explicitly dynamic, or more accurately an argument for temporary intervention to correct a transient distortion, the justification for protection being assumed to disappear with the passage of time.

The infant industry argument bases the case for temporary protection on the assertion that the industry in question (or, more commonly in the literature on economic development, manufacturing in general) would eventually be able to compete on equal terms with foreign producers in the domestic or world market if it were given temporary tariff protection to enable it to establish itself, but would be unable to establish itself against free competition from established foreign producers owing to the temporary excessive costs it would have to incur in the initial stages. Since the incurring of costs for a limited period in return for future benefits is a type of investment, the infant industry argument is essentially an assertion that free competition would produce a socially inefficient allocation of investment resources. For the argument to be valid, it is not sufficient to demonstrate that present costs, in the form of losses on production in the infancy of the industry, must be incurred for the sake of future benefits in the form of higher income than would otherwise be earned. For if the higher income accrues to those who incur the costs, and the capital market functions efficiently, the investment will be privately undertaken unless the rate of return on it is below the rate of return available on alternative investments, in which case the investment would be socially as well as privately unprofitable. To provide an argument for government intervention, it must be demonstrated either that the social rate of return exceeds the private rate of return on the investment, or that the private rate of return necessary to induce the investment exceeds the private and social rates of return available on alternative investment, by a wide enough margin to make a socially profitable investment privately unprofitable.

144

The social rate of return on investment in an infant industry may exceed the private rate of return for a variety of reasons, of which two may be of particular relevance to the problems of underdeveloped countries.[17] One relates to the fact that, once created, the product of investment in the acquisition of knowledge, unlike the product of material investments, can be enjoyed by additional users without additional cost of production. In other words, once knowledge of production technique is acquired, it can be applied by others than those who have assumed the cost of acquiring it; the social benefit at least potentially exceeds the private benefit of investment in learning industrial production techniques, and the social use of the results of such learning may even reduce the private reward for undertaking the investment. Where the social benefits of the learning process exceed the private benefits, the most appropriate governmental policy would be to subsidize the learning process itself, through such techniques as financing or sponsoring pilot enterprises on condition that the experience acquired and techniques developed be made available to all would-be producers. The other reason why the social benefit may exceed the private hinges on the facts that much of the technique of production is embodied in the skill of the labour force, and that the institutions of the labour market give the worker the property rights in any skills he acquires at the employer's expense. Consequently, the private rate of return to the employer on the investment in on-the-job training may be lower than the social rate of return, because the trained worker may be hired away by a competiror. The appropriate policy in this case would entail the government either financing on-the-job training or establishing institutions enabling labour to finance its own training out of the higher fature income resulting from training.[18] In either of the two cases just described, a subsidy

17 M.C. Kemp, 'The Mill-Bastable Infant Industry Dogma', *Journal of Politica Economy*, Vol. LXVIII, No. 1 (February 1960) pp. 65—67.

18 The analysis here is incomplete, since in certain circumstances competition would lead to the workers bearing the cost of the non-specific part of the training received on the job through lower initial wages. On this point see Gary S. Becker, 'Investment in Human Capital: A Theoretical Analysis', *Journal of Political Economy*, Vol. LXX, No. 5, Part II, Supplement (October 1962) pp. 9—49, esp. pp. 10—25.

on production or on investment in the infant industry would in principle be economically inefficient, since neither type of subsidy would necessarily stimulate the type of investment in knowledge subject to an excess of social over private return.

The private rate of return necessary to induce investment in infant industries may also exceed the private and social rates of return on alternative investments for a variety of reasons. Entrepreneurs may be excessively pessimistic about the prospects of success, or unwilling to take chances; in this case the most appropriate policy would involve publication of expert estimates of the prospects for the industries in question. Alternatively, imperfections in the capital market may make the cost of finance for investment in new industries excessively high, especially if these industries require an initially large scale for economical production by the firm; in this case, subsidization of provision of capital would be the appropriate policy.

Whatever the distortion in the allocation of investment capital used to support the infant industry argument for protection, it is apparent from the general principles governing optimal governmental intervention in the presence of domestic distortions that the optimal policy entails some sort of subsidy to the infant industries, rather than protection. Where infant industry distortions exist, protection justified by their presence may have the effect of reducing economic welfare rather than raising it. The reason is that protection increases the social cost of the investment in the learning process of the infant industry, by adding to the cost of a transitional subsidy the consumption cost of protection; the additional cost may be sufficient to reduce the social rate of return on the investment below the social rate of return on alternative investments.

It has been mentioned above that, for the infant industry argument to justify government intervention, investment in the learning process of the infant industry must be socially profitable. This requirement implies that the customary formulations of both the infant industry argument and the most potent argument used against it are seriously defective. The customary formulation argues that there is a case for protection on infant industry grounds if the industry could eventually compete in the domestic or world market without protection. This argument is invalid because protection involves a present cost which can only be justified economically by an increase in future income above what it would otherwise be; and a necessary condition for this is that the infant industries should eventually be able to compete while paying higher returns to the factors they employ than those factors would have enjoyed if the infant industries had not been assisted to maturity by protection. The most potent argument against infant industry protection is that the infant industries in fact never grow up, but instead continue to require protection. The argument overlooks the possibility that, although the continuance of protection is a political fact, it is not always an economic necessity: protection may be continued even though intramarginal firms or units of production do not require it, and the country may gain from infant industry protection even though such protection continues indefinitely. The possibility of such a gain is illustrated in Figure 5, where

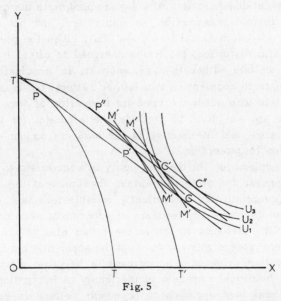

Fig. 5

as a result of infant industry protection the transformation curve shifts outwards from TT to TT', and the community as a consequence enjoys the welfare level U_2 in place of the welfare level U_1 in the long run. If the cost of protection, in terms of a lower welfare level in the period of transition from TT to TT', is low enough, the increase in welfare from U_1 to U_2 great enough, and the social rate of return required to justify the investment low enough, the eventual welfare level U_2 may be superior to the eventual welfare level U_1, even though U_2 is inferior to the welfare level U_3 that could be enjoyed if the infant industry tariff were removed once it had served its purpose.

IX.   CONCLUSION: NON-ECONOMIC ARGUMENTS FOR PROTECTION

This chapter has been concerned with elaborating on two propositions concerning arguments for protection based on the alleged existence of domestic distortions creating a divergence between marginal private and marginal social benefits or costs. These are that welfare maximization requires a correction of the relevant domestic distortion by an appropriate tax or subsidy on production, consumption, or factor use, and not a tax or subsidy on international trade; and that, given the presence of a domestic distortion, protection designed to offset it may decrease welfare rather than increase it. In conclusion, it is appropriate to comment on two further matters, the reasons why economists who admit the need for correction of domestic distortions are so prone to concede the argument for tariffs in these cases, and the bearing of the analysis on non-economic arguments for protection.

The explanation for the propensity of economists to concede the argument for protection rather than present the case for more appropriate and theoretically reliable remedies seems to lie in two factors — the tendency of economists when confronted with policy problems to ignore the rather elusive principle of consumers' sovereignty and to adopt the apparently but illusively firmer welfare criterion of an increase in the value of production, and the historical emphasis of the theory of international trade on the real cost approach to economic welfare as contrasted with the opportunity cost approach, an emphasis ultimately derived from the labour theory of value. The latter emphasis has been a major source of weakness in the theoretical analysis of contemporary international trade problems, both in connection with the theory of tariffs and in connection with the more recently evolved theory of customs unions and discriminatory tariff reduction.

While this chapter has concentrated on the economic arguments for protection − specifically, on arguments for protection as a means of correcting domestic distortions leading to inequalities between marginal social and marginal private costs or benefits − the analysis does have some important implications for what have been described in the introduction as non-economic arguments for protection.[19] Such arguments stress the non-economic value of changes in production and consumption or resource allocation patterns achieved by protection. Conceptually, they can be divided into arguments that stress the non-economic value of increased *domestic production* of, and arguments that stress the non-economic value of increased *self-sufficiency* in (a reduced volume of imports of) certain types of commodities that under free trade would be imported. The argument of this chapter has shown that where domestic distortions make the production of a commodity lower than it should be, optimal government intervention entails subsidization of production rather than interferences with international trade. The same conclusion can be shown to hold for non-economic arguments based on the desirability of larger domestic production, such as the national identity and way-of-life arguments mentioned above. On the other hand, it can be shown that for non-economic arguments based on the desirability of a smaller volume of imports, the method of tariff protection is superior to the method of subsidization. The reason is that in the first case an increase of domestic production achieved by protection,

[19] This paragraph was prompted by the existence of an apparent conflict in the literature on protection. W.M. Corden ('Tariffs, Subsidies and the Terms of Trade', *Economica*, Vol. XXIV, No. 3 [August 1957], pp. 235−42) shows that the most efficient (least-cost) method of protection is by a subsidy (when the terms of trade are fixed) or by an optimum tariff and a production subsidy (when the terms of trade are variable). J.H. Young (*Canadian Commercial Policy* [Ottawa: Royal Commission on Canada's Economic Prospects, 1957]) shows that protection by tariff costs less than protection by subsidy. As shown below, both are right. The explanation is that Corden takes the object of protection to be to increase domestic production, whereas Young takes the object to be to replace imports by domestic production.

as contrasted with an increase achieved by subsidization, involves an additional cost in the form of a consumption
loss. In the second case, however, the reduction in consumption
achieved by the tariff is to be regarded as a gain, since it also
contributes to the reduction of imports; and since at the margin
the production loss from subsidizing production is proportional
to the rate of subsidy, and the consumption loss from taxing
consumption is proportional to the rate of tax, it follows that a
given reduction in imports can be achieved more efficiently by
means of the tariff, which subsidizes production and taxes
consumption at the same rate, than by means of a production
subsidy alone, which subsidy would necessarily be at a higher
rate than the required tariff rate.

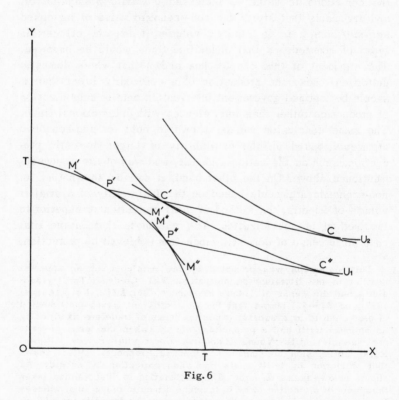

Fig. 6

These propositions are illustrated in Figure 6, where P' represents the production point and C' the consumption point achieved by the imposition of a tariff that distorts the domestic exchange ratio and transformation ratio from the international exchange ratio $P'C'$ to $M'M'$. It is obvious that the country could reach the consumption point C and the associated higher welfare level U_2, while keeping domestic production at the same level P', by replacing the tariff by a subsidy on production of X (or a tax on production of Y). If, however, the object of policy is not the domestic production pattern shown by P' but the restriction of international trade to the level represented by the distance $P'C'$, achievement of this object by means of subsidization of domestic production necessarily involves a greater loss of welfare than achievement of it by means of tariff protection. To appreciate this, consider the production subsidy represented by the domestic price ratio $M''M''$, which combined with free trade places the country on the indifference curve U_1 reached with the tariff. It follows from the tangencies of the transformation curve and the indifference curve U_1 to the tariff-distorted domestic exchange ratio at P' and C' that the distance between the production point P'' and consumption point C'' achieved with a subsidy welfare-indifferent to the tariff is greater than that between the production point P' and consumption point C' achieved with the tariff. In short, for a given welfare loss, trade is restricted less by a production subsidy than by a tariff; therefore, the achievement of a given restriction of trade requires a smaller welfare loss if trade is restricted by a tariff than if trade is restricted by a production subsidy.

5. Factor Market Distortions and the Shape of the Transformation Curve*

General equilibrium theorists customarily assume that factor and goods markets are characterized by perfect competition. Recently, however, an interest has developed in the economic effects of distortions in factor markets, such that the price of a factor's services is higher in one sector of the economy than it is in another. Such distortions may be the result of taxation, specifically of corporate income taxation which raises the cost of capital in the corporate sector above its cost in the non-corporate sector (see Harberger[5]); of existence of a differential between wages in the industrial and the subsistence sector of an underdeveloped country (see Hagen[4]); of the effect of unionization in raising union wages above comparable non-union wages (see Mieszkowski and Johnson[9]); or of a variety of factors (see Fishlow and David[3]). In the course of the examination of the effects of such distortions on economic efficiency, income distribution, and economic welfare, it has been remarked that such distortions may alter the shape of the transformation curve, making it concave instead of convex outward,[1] i.e., convex instead of concave to

* *Econometrica*, Vol. 34, No. 3 (July 1966) pp. 686—98.

[1] The terms 'concavity' and 'convexity' in this chapter have to be interpreted as meaning that the transformation curve lies inside or outside respectively of the chord joining its end points, and not in the strict mathematical sense of the term, which refers to the curvature of the curve in the neighbourhood of a point on it. This should be evident from the context. M.C. Kemp and H. Herberg have subsequently shown that the curvature of a part of the transformation curve cannot be inferred from its situation relative to the chord joining its end points, so that if the terms 'concavity' and 'convexity' are given their strict mathematical meanings, the last sentence of the second-last paragraph and the third- and second-last sentences of the final paragraph of Section I below are incorrect. See M.C. Kemp and H. Herberg 'Factor Market Distortions, the Shape of the Locus of Competitive Outputs, and the Relation Between Product Prices and Equilibrium Outputs', University of Southampton Discussion Paper in Econometrics No. 6908, to be published in a volume of essays in honour of C.P. Kindleberger.

the origin (see Fishlow and David[3, p. 541, n. 29]; and Bhagwati and Ramaswami[1, p. 48, n. 15]). No systematic examination of the conditions required for this interesting possibility to occur has, however, been undertaken. This chapter presents such an examination for the two-commodity, two-factor, constant-returns to scale model customarily employed in the theory of international trade. Section I presents a geometrical examination and exposition of the two alternative conditions under which the transformation curve can become concave outward, utilizing a technique of geometrical analysis invented by K.M. Savosnick[10]. While geometry may seem a childish tool in this day and age, it has the great advantage in this case of simplicity in establishing results that can be established algebraically only by much greater effort, as will be apparent from the subsequent sections. Section II presents essentially the same analysis in algebraic terms, for this purpose simplifying the problem by restricting the two production functions to the Cobb-Douglas form. The algebraic analysis indicates that, while in one of the cases of distortion previously considered, the transformation curve must be either concave or convex throughout; in the other the possibility emerges that the transformation curve will be concave at one end and convex at the other, or more generally may change from one shape to the other as the production point moves along it. To investigate these possibilities, a computer program was set up to compute and chart the transformation curve for various assumed values of the exponents of the production functions and of the degree of factor market distortion.

I. THE POSSIBILITY OF CONCAVITY OF THE TRANSFORMATION CURVE: GEOMETRICAL ANALYSIS[2]

Figure 1 depicts the familiar Edgeworth-Bowley, two-commodity, two-factor, contract box; in the construction, commodity X is assumed to be labour intensive, and commodity Y capital intensive, both being subject to constant returns to scale, and labour

---

[2] The use of the Savosnick technique in this context was suggested to me by Duncan McCrae of Cambridge University in a discussion in February 1964. McCrae also demonstrated to me that the first type of distortion discussed below must, if the distortion is large enough, make the transformation curve concave outward. The analysis of the second type of distortion is my own extension of McCrae's analysis.

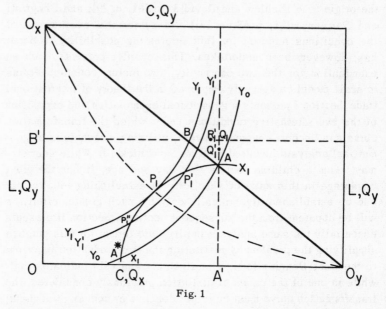

Fig. 1

forms the vertical and capital the horizontal sides of the box. The contract curve is defined in the absence of distortions by the tangency of isoquants for the two goods; by the assumption about factor intensities and the construction of the box, it must lie southwest of the diagonal of the box.

Using the Savosnick technique, units of output can be so defined that the quantities of the two outputs can be measured by the distances from their respective origins cut off on the diagonal O_xO_y by the isoquants X_1X_1 and Y_1Y_1, i.e., O_xA of X and O_yB of Y; and these measurements can be transferred to the sides of the box by dropping perpendiculars to them, AA' and BB'. Thus OA' represents the quantity X_1 of X, and OB' the quantity Y_1 of Y, produced at P_1; and Q_1 represents the point on the transformation curve corresponding to P_1, the transformation curve being drawn with reference to the origin O, and quantities of X being measured horizontally to the right of O and quantities of Y being measured vertically from O. It is obvious from the construction that all points on the transformation curve must be to the northeast of the diagonal O_xO_y, giving outward convexity in

154

the large, and it can be shown geometrically that the transformation curve is strictly convex outwards (see for example Black[2], Worswick[11]).

Now the slopes of the production isoquants at any point, with reference to the OO_x side of the box, are equal to $-dC/dL = P_l/P_c$ (the price of labour in terms of capital). A distortion is defined as a departure from factor market perfection such that

$$\left(\frac{P_l}{P_c}\right)_y = \frac{1}{\gamma}\left(\frac{P_l}{P_c}\right)_x, \text{ where } \gamma \neq 1.$$

There are two possible types of distortion to consider

$$\gamma > 1, \text{ i.e., } \left(\frac{P_l}{P_c}\right)_y < \left(\frac{P_l}{P_c}\right)_x; \tag{1}$$

the relative price of labour is lower in industry Y (the capital-intensive industry) than in industry X (the labour-intensive industry). In this case, the distortion raises the price of a factor in the industry that uses it intensively, relative to its price in the other industry.

$$\gamma < 1, \text{ i.e., } \left(\frac{P_l}{P_c}\right)_y > \left(\frac{P_l}{P_c}\right)_x; \tag{2}$$

the relative price of labour is higher in industry Y (the capital-intensive industry) than in industry X (the labour-intensive industry). In this case, the distortion lowers the price of a factor in the industry that uses it intensively, relative to its price in the other industry.

Consider first a distortion of type (1). If the output of X is kept constant, equilibrium in the factor markets subject to the distortion requires an allocation of the factors between the industries such as that represented by P_1', with the slope of the $Y_1'Y_1'$ isoquant at that point (referred to the vertical) being less than the slope of the X_1X_1 isoquant at that point in the ratio of the distortion, and with a lower output of Y, the corresponding point on the distorted transformation curve being Q_1'. Similarly, if the output of Y were held constant, the distorted equilibrium would involve a lower output of X and a corresponding point on the distorted transformation curve such as R_1'. Thus the distortion in the factor market pulls the transformation curve in towards the diagonal (except at O_x and O_y, where the distortion cannot affect the allocation of factors between the industries because they are all employed in one or the other industry).

It is evident that as the degree of distortion is increased, the transformation curve is pulled further in towards the diagonal. When the distortion becomes equal to the ratio of the slopes of X_1X_1 and Y_0Y_0 at A, P_1' and Q_1' coincide at A, and the transformation curve for that distortion becomes contiguous with the diagonal. This is so because the constant returns to scale property implies that the slopes of all members of the set of X-isoquants along the diagonal are equal, and the same is true of the Y-isoquants; hence a degree of distortion that places one point of the contract curve on the diagonal will do so for all points of the contract curve, and therefore for all points of the corresponding transformation curve. Further, it may be noticed that this degree of distortion is that which makes the factor intensities of the two industries equal. Finally, any greater degree of distortion would shift P_1' to the northeast of the diagonal, and Q_1' to the southwest, interchanging their respective locations. This would be true for all points on the contract curve and the transformation curve, by extension of the reasoning just presented, so that the transformation curve would be uniformly outwardly concave in the large if the degree of distortion were great enough to reverse the relative factor intensities of the two industries.

Now consider a distortion of type (2). If the output of X is kept constant, equilibrium in the factor markets subject to the distortion requires an allocation of the factors between the industries such as that represented by P_1'', with the slope of the $Y_1'Y_1'$ isoquant at that point being steeper (referred to the vertical) than the slope of the X_1X_1 isoquant at that point in the ratio of the distortion, and with a lower output of Y, the corresponding point on the distorted transformation curve again being Q_1'. Similarly, keeping the output of Y constant would involve a lower output of X and a corresponding point on the distorted transformation curve such as R_1', though (as will appear) there is no reason to identify R_1' with the R_1' of the previous case, even though the distortion is such as to yield the same Q_1'. Again, as the degree of distortion is increased, Q'_1 shifts towards the diagonal, and if the distortion becomes great enough Q'_1 will cross the diagonal into the southwest part of the box, implying local concavity outwards of the distorted transformation curve. (The dividing line between convexity and concavity is the distortion producing the contract curve point A^*.) In this case, however, a distortion that will produce local concavity will not necessarily produce concavity of the whole transformation curve, because unlike the case of distortions of type (1), the contract curve does not move to the northeast half of the box, but remains in the southwest section; hence the locations of the corresponding points on the transformation curve relative to the diagonal depend on the shapes of the isoquants, and not merely on the degree of distortion.

II. THE POSSIBILITY OF CONCAVITY OF THE TRANSFORMATION CURVE: COBB-DOUGLAS PRODUCTION FUNCTIONS

Assume two Cobb-Douglas production functions

$$X = L_x R_x^{1-\alpha},$$
$$Y = L_y R_y^{1-\beta},$$

where L represents labour employed and $R = K/L$ is the capital : labour ratio in the relevant industry, and $\alpha > \beta$ by assumption, so that X is relatively labour intensive. Factor supplies are assumed to be fixed.

$$L_x R_x + L_y R_y = \bar{K},$$
$$L_x + L_y = \bar{L},$$

where $\bar{K}$ and $\bar{L}$ are the fixed endowments of capital and labour. These equations reduce to

$$lR_x + (1-l)R_y = R,$$

where l is the proportion of the labour endowment allocated to the X industry. The marginal productivities of the factors are

$$X_L = \alpha R_x^{1-\alpha},$$
$$X_K = (1-\alpha)R_x^{-\alpha},$$

$$Y_L = \beta R_y^{1-\beta},$$
$$Y_K = (1 - \beta)R_y^{-\beta}.$$

Under competitive conditions, the equilibrium condition in the factor markets would entail $X_L/Y_L = X_K/Y_K = p$, where p is the price of Y in terms of X. Instead, we assume a distortion in the labour market such that $X_L = \gamma p Y_L$, or $X_L/Y_L = \gamma X_K/Y_K$; substituting the values of the marginal productivities, this yields

$$\frac{\alpha}{1 - \alpha} R_x = \gamma \frac{\beta}{1 - \beta} R_y.$$

Using this result and the endowment constraint, and for simplicity writing

$$\frac{\alpha}{1 - \alpha} = a, \quad \frac{\beta}{1 - \beta} = b,$$

we obtain

$$R_x = \frac{\gamma b R}{a + (\gamma b - a)l},$$

$$R_y = \frac{aR}{a + (\gamma b - a)l}.$$

We now for simplicity convert the production functions into functions for output per head by using $x = X/L$, $y = Y/L$, and use the preceding results to express outputs of the two goods per head as functions of the parameters and l, as follows:

$$x = l\left[\frac{\gamma b R}{a + (\gamma b - a)l}\right]^{1-\alpha},$$

$$y = (1 - l)\left[\frac{aR}{a + (\gamma b - a)l}\right]^{1-\beta}.$$

Differentiating, we obtain

$$\frac{dx}{dl} = \left[\frac{\gamma b R}{a + (\gamma b - a)l}\right]^{1-\alpha}\left[\frac{a + \alpha l(\gamma b - a)}{a + (\gamma b - a)l}\right],$$

$$\frac{dy}{dl} = -\left[\frac{aR}{a + (\gamma b - a)l}\right]^{1-\beta}\left[\frac{\gamma b - (1 - l)\beta(\gamma b - a)}{a + (\gamma b - a)l}\right],$$

whence

$$-\frac{dx}{dy} = (\gamma bR)^{1-\alpha}(aR)^{\beta-1}[a + (\gamma b - a)l]^{\alpha-\beta} \frac{a + \alpha l(\gamma b - a)}{a + (\gamma b - a)(1 - \beta + \beta l)}.$$

Differentiating this with respect to l to obtain the curvature of the transformation curve, we obtain

$$\frac{d}{dl}\left(-\frac{dx}{dy}\right) = \left\{(\gamma bR)^{1-\alpha}(aR)^{\beta-1} \frac{[a + (\gamma b - a)l]^{\alpha-\beta}}{a + (\gamma b - a)(1 - \beta + \beta l)}\right\} \times$$

$$(\gamma b - a)\left\{\frac{(\alpha - \beta)[a + \alpha l(\gamma b - a)]}{a + (\gamma b - a)l}\right.$$

$$\left. + \frac{\alpha[a + (\gamma b - a)(1 - \beta + \beta l)] - \beta[a + \alpha l(\gamma b - a)]}{a + (\gamma b - a)(1 - \beta + \beta l)}\right\}.$$

The transformation curve will have the normal convex shape if this derivative is negative, i.e., if the sacrifice of X required to obtain an extra unit of Y is smaller, the larger the proportion of the labour force in the X industry; conversely, the transformation curve will be concave if this derivative is positive.

Since the first term in braces is necessarily positive (as may be seen by simplifying the numerator and denominator of the fraction it contains), the sign depends on the sign of the remainder, which can be rewritten as

$$(\gamma b - a)\left\{\frac{(\alpha - \beta)[a + \alpha l(\gamma b - a)]}{a + (\gamma b - a)l} + \frac{(\alpha - \beta)a + (\gamma b - a)\alpha(1 - \beta)}{a + (\gamma b - a)(1 - \beta + \beta l)}\right\}$$

$$= (\gamma b - a)\left\{2(\alpha - \beta) - \frac{(1 - \alpha)(\alpha - \beta)(\gamma b - a)l}{a + (\gamma b - a)l}\right.$$

$$\left. + \frac{\beta(\gamma b - a)(1 - \beta - \alpha l + \beta l)}{a + (\gamma b - a)(1 - \beta + \beta l)}\right\}$$

This expression will necessarily be positive, and the transformation curve concave throughout, if $\gamma b - a > 0$, i.e., $\gamma > \alpha(1 - \beta)/\beta(1 - \alpha)$, which necessarily requires $\gamma > 1$, i.e., a distortion of type (1). Also, fulfillment of this condition entails $R_x > R_y$, that is, reversal of the factor intensities that would prevail in the absence of the distortion.

The expression may also be positive if $(\gamma b - a)$ is negative

159

and the expression in braces is also negative. Since the first term and the denominator of the second term in the first variant of that expression given above are necessarily positive, a necessary but not sufficient condition for concavity of this mathematical type is that the numerator of the second term be negative. On simplification, this necessary condition reduces to $\gamma < 1$, i.e., the distortion must accentuate the difference in factor intensities that would exist in the absence of distortion and hence must be a distortion of type (2).

Since the expression in braces just referred to is a complex one involving both the exponents of the production functions and the variable l, the possibility exists in this second case both that concavity of the transformation curve may be precluded by the specification of the exponents of the production functions and that the transformation curve may be concave for some range of values of l but not for all.

The first possibility, however, can be shown to be non-existent, in the sense that sufficient distortion will always produce concavity over some range, by substituting the limiting value $\gamma = 0$ into the expression in braces, which then reduces to

$$\frac{(\alpha - \beta)(1 - \alpha l) - (1 - \alpha)}{1 - l} ;$$

this expression can always be made negative by a sufficiently high value of l.[3] The argument implicitly confirms the reality of the second possibility, that concavity may hold only over a range.

The second possibility may be demonstrated by calculating the conditions on γ under which the expression in braces will be negative, and the transformation curve concave for the extreme values $l = 0$ and $l = 1$. For $l = 0$ the expression will be negative for

$$\gamma < \frac{\alpha}{1 - \alpha} \cdot \frac{1 - 2\alpha + \beta}{2\alpha - \beta} ;$$

for $l = 1$ it will be negative for

---

[3] I am grateful to an *Econometrica* referee for detecting an error in the original argument.

$$\gamma < \frac{1 - \beta}{\beta} \cdot \frac{2\beta - \alpha}{1 + \alpha - 2\beta}.$$

For the first of these conditions to be consistent with a positive γ requires the inequality $1 + \beta > 2\alpha$; for the second to be consistent with a positive γ requires the inequality $2\beta > \alpha$.

Pairs of values of α and β obviously exist that will satisfy one of these constraints but not the other, so that the transformation curve will be concave at one extreme and convex at the other for any γ satisfying the nonnegative constraint. Even if both constraints are meaningful, however, the value of γ required for concavity will generally be different at one extreme than at the other, and for values of γ not satisfying both constraints the transformation curve must be concave at one end and convex at the other. Finally, it is possible that the transformation curve may be convex outwards at both ends yet concave in the middle.

III. CONCAVITY OF THE TRANSFORMATION CURVE: COMPUTATIONS

In order to investigate further the possibility of concavity of the transformation curve with distortions of the second type, a computer program was set up to compute and chart the transformation curve for values of β ranging from $0 \cdot 1$ to $0 \cdot 8$, values of α ranging from $\beta + 0 \cdot 1$ to $0 \cdot 9$, and values of γ ranging downwards from $1 \cdot 0$ down to $0 \cdot 1$.[4] For purposes of computation l was assigned values of $0 \cdot 000$, $0 \cdot 025$, $0 \cdot 050$, ... $0 \cdot 975$, $1 \cdot 000$; this had the somewhat unfortunate effect, understandable in terms of the logic of Figure 1, of giving a far better representation of the transformation curve in the neighbourhood of specialization or nearly complete specialization on Y than in the neighbourhood of specialization on X (as the equilibrium point moves along the contract curve from specialization on Y to specialization on X, the reduction in the proportion of the labour force associated with a given decrease in the quantity of Y produced increases steadily).

Some of the results of the computations are presented in Charts 1–6, which have been selected for presentation on the

---

[4] I am grateful to my colleague Herbert Grubel for discovering the existence of the charting technique and assuming responsibility for the computations.

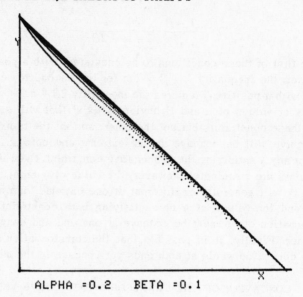

ALPHA =0.2   BETA =0.1

ALPHA =0.5   BETA =0.1

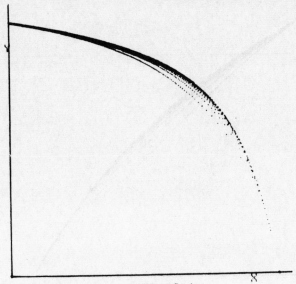

ALPHA =0.9   BETA =0.1

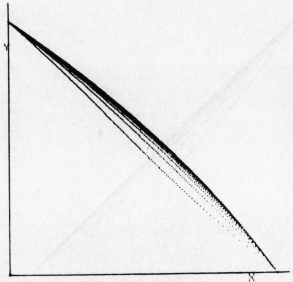

ALPHA =0.8   BETA =0.4

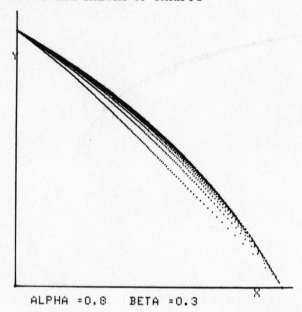

ALPHA =0.8   BETA =0.3

ALPHA =0.6   BETA =0.5

basis of their representativeness and interest. Charts 1–3 depict the consequences of distortions on output with $\beta = 0\cdot1$ and successively higher values of α. Charts 4–6 illustrate various possible shapes of the transformation curve in the presence of distortions, for other values of β and α. It should be recorded that the values of α and β are such that, for a sufficiently high degree of distortion, the transformation curve must be concave at the Y end and convex at the X end for Charts 1 and 2, and concave at both ends for Chart 6. In each case, the degree of distortion increases as the curve bends inwards towards the origin.

Charts 1–3 show that for values of α close to β, and a sufficiently high degree of distortion, the transformation curve is concave at the upper end (towards the Y end) and convex at the lower end (towards the X end); but that as α increases relative to β, the concave range shifts down the transformation curve away from the Y end, becomes less pronounced, and eventually disappears. Charts 4 and 5 illustrate the possibility of concavity in the middle range of the transformation curve. Chart 6 illustrates the case of concavity throughout (for all but very minor degrees of distortion).

Aside from illustrating the possible effects of factor market distortion on the shape of the transformation curve, these charts have two other interesting characteristics. The first, which is incidental to the main purpose of this chapter and comes as rather a surprise, concerns the shape of the transformation curve in the absence of distortions. International trade theorists, including the present writer, have been accustomed to draw the transformation curve with a very marked convexity, and to base on this convexity a number of propositions about the effects of trade on production patterns, specialization, and the functional distribution of income. Yet, as Charts 1, 2, 4, and 5 show, even quite marked differences in the relative labour intensity of the two industries (extending to a five-fold difference in the case of Chart 2 and a two-and-two-thirds-fold difference in the case of Chart 4) are insufficient to make the transformation curve depart markedly from a straight line; only in Chart 3, which represents the extreme of difference in factor intensity, does the transformation curve in the absence of distortions approach

165

the shape typically assumed in writings on international trade theory. It may be, therefore, that the constant cost assumptions of Ricardo, Graham, and the Leontief model are quite reasonable approximations for most practical purposes, and that the effort that has been devoted to refining the Heckscher-Ohlin model and investigating its complexities has been concerned with phenomena of trivial practical importance.

The second concerns the magnitude of the loss from the inefficiency created by distortions in factor markets. The most extreme case of loss of production from such distortions is that represented by Chart 6, where the exponents of the production functions are very close together. But even in Chart 6, the degree of distortion necessary to produce a departure of the transformation curve from its non-distorted position that is visible to the naked eye is that corresponding to $\gamma = 0\cdot50$ (a 100 per cent differential in wages between the two sectors) and in most cases the required value of γ is $0\cdot40$ or even $0\cdot30$ (differentials of 150 and 233-1/3 per cent respectively). Differentials of this magnitude probably represent the limit of the distortions likely to be encountered in practice: the U.S. corporate income tax creates a differential of approximately 100 per cent between the gross returns to capital in the corporate as compared with the non-corporate sector; figures of 33-1/3 to 40 per cent have been cited for the industrial sector-subsistence sector wage differential in the developing countries (Hagen[4], Lewis[7]); and the union-non-union wage differential has been estimated at 15 per cent for recent years (Lewis[8, p. 222]). Of course, the total economic loss from factor market distortions can only be evaluated by taking into account, in addition to the inefficiency of production, the distortion of consumer choices due to the effect of the factor market distortion in producing a divergence of private from social opportunity costs in consumption. But the total loss has also been shown to be small even for quite substantial distortions (see Fishlow and David[3], Harberger[6]). The proper conclusion to be drawn, however, is not that factor market distortions are too unimportant to be worth the attention of economists, but rather that neither their existence nor their elimination is likely to be a strategic determinant of the level of national well-being.

REFERENCES

[1] BHAGWATI, J., and RAMASWAMI, V.K.: 'Domestic Distortions, Tariffs and the Theory of Optimum Subsidy,' *Journal of Political Economy*, Vol. LXXI, No. 1 (February 1963) pp. 44–50.

[2] BLACK, J.: 'A Formal Proof of the Concavity of the Production Possibility Function,' *Economic Journal*, Vol. LXVII, No. 265 (March 1957) pp. 133–35.

[3] FISHLOW, A., and DAVID, P.: 'Optimal Resource Allocation in an Imperfect Market Setting,' *Journal of Political Economy*, Vol. LXIX, No. 6 (December 1961) pp. 529–46.

[4] HAGEN, E.E.: 'An Economic Justification of Protectionism,' *Quarterly Journal of Economics*, Vol. LXXII, No. 4 (November 1958) pp. 496–514.

[5] HARBERGER, ARNOLD C.: 'The Incidence of the Corporation Income Tax,' *Journal of Political Economy*, Vol. LXX, No. 3 (June 1962) pp. 215–40.

[6] HARBERGER, ARNOLD C.: 'The Fundamentals of Economic Progress in Underdeveloped Countries: Using the Resources at Hand More Effectively,' *American Economic Review*, Vol. XLIX, No. 2 (May 1959) pp. 134–46.

[7] LEWIS, A.: 'Economic Development with Unlimited Supplies of Labour,' *The Manchester School of Economic and Social Studies*, Vol. XXII, No. 2 (May 1954) pp. 139–91.

[8] LEWIS, H.G.: *Unionism and Relative Wages in the United States, An Empirical Inquiry* (Chicago: University of Chicago University of Chicago Press, 1963).

[9] MIESZKOWSKI, P. and JOHNSON, H.G.: 'The Economic Effects of Unionization: A General Equilibrium Analysis,' *Quarterly Journal of Economics*, Vol. XXXIV, No. 4 (November 1970), pp. 539–61.

[10] SAVOSNICK, K.M.: 'The Box Diagram and the Production Possibility Curve,' *Ekonomisk Tidsskrift*, Vol. LI (September 1958) pp. 183–97.

[11] WORSWICK, D.: 'The Convexity of the Production Possibility Function,' *Economic Journal*, Vol. LXVII, No. 268 (December 1957) pp. 748–50.

6. The Gain from Exploiting Monopoly or Monopsony Power in International Trade*

The 'optimum tariff' argument for protection, and the prospective gains for a country to be had by exploiting it, play a large part in the literature of trade policy for economic development. There is a widespread impression in this literature that the potential gains available to under-developed countries from this source are substantial. This Note investigates the problem, using some very simple models of the welfare derivable from trade, selected because they are capable of yielding quantitative results. Its purpose is to call attention to the generally neglected points that while the optimum tariff rate varies inversely with the elasticity of demand for exports or supply of imports, and may be surprisingly high when the relevant elasticity is low, the gain in real income derivable from applying the optimum tariff depends on certain 'structural' characteristics of the tariff-imposing country, which may be such as make the resulting gain relatively small by comparison with the level of welfare enjoyed under free trade. In the first place, the gain depends on the nature of the domestic preference system, and especially on the elasticities of substitution between imports and exports in domestic consumption – and production – and will tend to be low when those elasticities are low, as they are generally presumed to be for less-developed countries. In the second place, the gain depends on the magnitude of the free-trade ratio of imports to national income, and will tend to be lower the lower that ratio; and while this ratio may be assumed to be generally higher for less developed than for developed countries, its influence on the order of magnitude of the gain from optimum tariff policy is a relevant consideration.

Throughout it is assumed that the economy contemplating imposing an optimum tariff is completely specialized in producing a fixed amount of $\bar{X}$ of its exportable good, which it exports in return for its import good Y. This assumption is not

* *Economica*, N.S. Vol. XXXV, No. 138 (May 1968) pp. 151–56.

as restrictive as it may seem, since $\bar{X}$ may be taken as a measure of the economy's total productive capacity, and the possibility of substituting for imports through domestic production absorbed into the magnitude of the elasticity of substitution in consumption. It is also assumed that the preference system of the country is homothetic — goods would be consumed in the same ratios at the same relative prices regardless of income level, i.e. the income elasticity of demand for each is unity — and that the marginal utility of income is constant. A little mental experimentation with the usual optimum-tariff geometry will show that the former assumption will overstate the gains from an optimum tariff policy if, as it seems reasonable to assume for underdeveloped countries, the income elasticity of demand for imports is greater than unity — imports are a luxury good. It is also obvious that the latter assumption will overstate the relative real income from an optimum tariff policy if the marginal utility of income is declining.

For convenience of mathematical analysis, it is assumed that the country in question has monopsony power in the world market, measured by the elasticity of foreign supply, ϵ, of its imports; the results are, however, easily converted into an analysis of the exploitation of monopoly power, measured by the elasticity of foreign demand, η, for its exports, through the familiar rule that in a two-good model $\epsilon = \eta - 1$.

At the outset, it is apparent on a little reflection that if there is no elasticity of substitution between exports and imports in consumption, the two being consumed in fixed proportions, no gain whatsoever will accrue to a country from imposing the optimum tariff, except in the extreme case where the foreign demand for its exports is of less than unit elasticity (the foreign supply curve of its imports backward-bending). The reason is that to be better off the country must consume more imports along with more exportables, whereas, under normal assumptions about the conditions facing a country in world markets, fewer and not more imports will be supplied at a lower price. The imposition of the optimum tariff will therefore merely raise the domestic price of imports, leaving quantities traded and the country's terms of trade unchanged, with no effect on its welfare.

The possibility of gain from an optimum tariff policy therefore depends on the possibility of substituting exports for imports in consumption; and it is apparent that the magnitude of the potential gain will be greater, the greater the elasticity of substitution.

Now, to appreciate the influence of the free-trade ratio of imports to national income, assume that the elasticity of substitution is infinite at the free-trade price ratio. Specifically, choosing units so that under free trade X and Y exchange one for one in world trade, assume that the country's utility function is $U = \bar{X} - X + Y$, where X represents exports, $\bar{X} - X$ consumption of exportables, and Y consumption of importables. Under free trade, $X = Y$ and $U_{ft} = \bar{X}$.

Let the supply function of imports be $Y = \bar{Y}\pi^{\epsilon}$, where $\bar{Y}$ is the quantity of Y supplied under free trade and π is the price paid the foreign supplier. Since the domestic price ratio must be unity by the assumption of infinite domestic elasticity of substitution, the price received by the foreign supplier must be $\pi = 1/(1 + t)$, where t is the rate of tariff (not necessarily the optimum tariff) imposed by the importing country; at this price, the quantity of Y supplied will be

$$Y = \bar{Y}\left(\frac{1}{1 + t}\right)^{\epsilon},$$

and its cost in terms of X will be

$$X = \pi Y = \bar{Y}\left(\frac{1}{1 + t}\right)^{\epsilon + 1}.$$

Thus the welfare enjoyed by the tariff-imposing country, as a function of the tariff, will be

$$U_t = \bar{X} - \bar{Y}\left(\frac{1}{1 + t}\right)^{\epsilon + 1} + \bar{Y}\left(\frac{1}{1 + t}\right)^{\epsilon} = \bar{X} + \bar{Y}\left(\frac{1}{1 + t}\right)^{\epsilon} \frac{t}{1 + t}.$$

It is easily shown that this expression is maximized when $t = 1/\epsilon$, which is the usual formula for the optimum tariff.[1]

When the optimum tariff is imposed, the level of welfare achieved is

$$U_{ot} = \bar{X} + \bar{Y}\left(\frac{\epsilon}{\epsilon + 1}\right)^{\epsilon} \cdot \frac{1}{\epsilon + 1},$$

and the relative increase in welfare over the free-trade level is

$$\frac{U_{ot}}{U_{ft}} - 1 = \frac{\overline{Y}}{\overline{X}} \cdot \frac{\epsilon^\epsilon}{(\epsilon + 1)^{\epsilon+1}}.$$

From this formula it is obvious that the relative welfare gain will be smaller the smaller the free-trade ratio of imports to national income, and must always be smaller than that share. It is also obvious, and can be rigorously established,[2] that the relative gain will be a smaller fraction of the free-trade import ratio the greater the elasticity of supply of imports (elasticity of demand for exports). As two examples, suppose, first, that the elasticity of supply of imports is unity (elasticity of demand for exports, two), indicating an optimum tariff of 100 per cent: the relative welfare gain would then be one quarter of the free-trade import ratio; suppose, second, that the elasticity of supply of imports is two (elasticity of demand for exports, three), indicating an optimum tariff of 50 per cent: the relative welfare gain would then be 0·148 of the free-trade import ratio.

The foregoing model of perfect elasticity of substitution between exports and imports sets an outside limit to the relative gain from an optimum tariff policy. This limit might be approached by a large highly-diversified economy, but for the majority of countries imperfect substitutability must be assumed. To investigate the joint influence of the elasticity of substitution and the free-trade import ratio, it would be most instructive to use the constant-elasticity-of-substitution utility function, which permits the elasticity of substitution to vary between

[1] $$\frac{d}{dt}\left[\frac{t}{(1 + t)^{\epsilon+1}}\right] = \frac{(1 + t)^{\epsilon+1} - (\epsilon + 1)t(1 + t)^\epsilon}{(1 + t)^{2\epsilon+2}} = \frac{1 - \epsilon t}{(1 + t)^{\epsilon+2}};$$

this is zero when $t = 1/\epsilon$. It is obvious by inspection that the second-order conditions are fulfilled.

[2] Let

$$\partial = \epsilon^\epsilon/(\epsilon + 1)^{\epsilon+1}; \quad \log\partial = \epsilon \log\epsilon - (\epsilon + 1)\log(\epsilon + 1)$$

$$\frac{d\log\partial}{d\epsilon} = \log\epsilon + \frac{\epsilon}{\epsilon} - \log(\epsilon + 1) - \frac{\epsilon + 1}{\epsilon + 1} = \log\epsilon - \log(\epsilon + 1) < 0.$$

Hence ∂ decreases as ϵ increases.

zero and infinity.[3] Unfortunately, it is not possible using this function to derive an explicit solution for the relative welfare gain from an optimum tariff policy by ordinary algebraic methods; consequently a Cobb-Douglas utility function, which entails a unit elasticity of substitution, has been employed to represent the intermediate case between the two extreme cases just analysed.

Let the utility function be $U = X^{\alpha} Y^{1-\alpha}$, the marginal utilities of the two goods being $U_x = \alpha(U/X)$ and $U_y = (1-\alpha)(U/Y)$, and the marginal rate of substitution between X and Y being

$$\frac{U_y}{U_x} = \frac{1-\alpha}{\alpha} \cdot \frac{X}{Y}.$$

Let p be the domestic price of imports of Y, π the foreign price, and t the tariff (not necessarily the optimum tariff) levied by the country, so that $p = (1+t)\pi$. Given the tariff, the country maximizes welfare by setting

$$\frac{U_y}{U_x} = \frac{1-\alpha}{\alpha} \cdot \frac{X}{Y} = p = (1+t)\pi, \text{ whence } \frac{X}{\pi Y} = \frac{\alpha}{1-\alpha}(1+t).$$

Substituting in this equation the budget constraint of the country, $\overline{X} = X + \pi Y$ or $X = \overline{X} - \pi Y$, yields

$$Y = \frac{1}{\pi} \cdot \frac{(1-\alpha)}{1+\alpha t}\overline{X}; \quad X = \frac{\alpha(1+t)}{1+\alpha t}\overline{X}.$$

Now let the supply of imports be $Y = (1-\alpha)\overline{X}\pi^{\epsilon}$, where the constant term $(1-\alpha)\overline{X}$ is chosen so that the free-trade price of imports will be unity. Solving for the equilibrium world price of imports in the presence of the tariff by equating quantities demanded and supplied yields

$$\pi = \left(\frac{1}{1+\alpha t}\right)^{1/(\epsilon+1)}.$$

The level of welfare achieved with the tariff can be obtained, by substitution in the utility function, as

[3] For an application of this function to problems of protection and its welfare effects, see Harry G. Johnson, 'The Costs of Protection and Self-Sufficiency'. *Quarterly Journal of Economics*, Vol. LXXIX (1965) pp. 356–72, Chapter 9 below.

$$U_t = (1 + t)^\alpha (1 + \alpha t)^{-(\epsilon + \alpha)/(\epsilon + 1)} \; \alpha^\alpha (1 - \alpha)^{1 - \alpha} \, \overline{X}.$$

This function can be shown to reach a maximum when $t = 1/\epsilon$, the formula for the optimum tariff.[4]

Substituting the values of the optimum tariff and $t = 0$ for free trade, dividing, and subtracting unity yields the relative welfare gain from the optimum tariff policy as compared with free trade.

$$\frac{U_{ot}}{U_{ft}} - 1 = \left(\frac{\epsilon + 1}{\epsilon}\right)^\alpha \bigg/ \left(\frac{\epsilon + \alpha}{\epsilon}\right)^{(\epsilon + \alpha)/(\epsilon + 1)} - 1.$$

Here, α is the share of the exportable good in free-trade consumption, the share of imports being $1 - \alpha$. To bring out the influence of the free-trade import share, the formula may be re-written as

$$\frac{U_{ot}}{U_{ft}} - 1 = \frac{\epsilon + 1}{\epsilon} \left(\frac{\epsilon}{\epsilon + 1}\right)^{1 - \alpha} \bigg/ \left(\frac{\epsilon + 1}{\epsilon} - \frac{1 - \alpha}{\epsilon}\right)^{1 - (1 - \alpha)/(\epsilon + 1)} - 1,$$

or, in terms of the elasticity of demand for the country's exports, as

$$\frac{U_{ot}}{U_{ft}} - 1 = \frac{\eta}{\eta - 1} \left(\frac{\eta - 1}{\eta}\right)^{1 - \alpha} \bigg/ \left[\frac{\eta - (1 - \alpha)}{\eta - 1}\right]^{1 - (1 - \alpha)/\eta} - 1.$$

Differentiation of the first expression given above for $U_{ot}/U_{ft} - 1$ yields the results:

$$\frac{\partial}{\partial \epsilon} \left(\frac{U_{ot}}{U_{ft}} - 1\right) = -\frac{U_{ot}}{U_{ft}} \cdot \frac{1 - \alpha}{(\epsilon + 1)^2} \log \frac{\epsilon + \alpha}{\epsilon};$$

$$\frac{\partial}{\partial \alpha} \left(\frac{U_{ot}}{U_{ft}} - 1\right) = \frac{U_{ot}}{U_{ft}} \left(\log \frac{\epsilon + 1}{\epsilon} - \frac{1}{\epsilon + 1} \log \frac{\epsilon + \alpha}{\epsilon} - \frac{1}{\epsilon + 1}\right).$$

The former expression shows that the gain from an optimum tariff policy must diminish as the elasticity of supply of imports (demand for exports) increases.

[4] $$\frac{\partial}{\partial t} \left[\frac{(1 + t)^\alpha}{(1 + \alpha t)^{(\epsilon + \alpha)/(\epsilon + 1)}}\right] =$$

$$= \frac{\alpha(1 - \alpha)(1 + t)^{\alpha - 1}(1 + \alpha t)^{(\alpha - 1)/(\epsilon + 1)}(1 - \epsilon t)}{(1 + \alpha t)^{2(\epsilon + \alpha)/(\epsilon + 1)}};$$

which vanishes when $t = 1/\epsilon$. The second-order conditions for a maximum can be seen to be fulfilled by inspection.

173

The sign of the second expression depends on the magnitude of α, and is positive or negative according as $[(\epsilon + 1)/\epsilon]^{\epsilon+1} \gtrless [(\epsilon + \alpha)/\epsilon]e$. For large enough α the sign must be negative, since as α approaches unity the inequality approximates $1 + 1/\epsilon \gtrless e^{1/\epsilon}$, and by Taylor's expansion $e^{1/\epsilon} = 1 + (1/\epsilon) + (1/2!)(1/\epsilon^2) + \ldots > 1 + (1/\epsilon)$.

For small enough α the sign must be positive, since as α approaches zero the inequality approaches

$$\log \left(1 + \frac{1}{\epsilon}\right) \gtrless \frac{1}{\epsilon + 1}, \text{ or } \log \frac{\epsilon + 1}{\epsilon} - \frac{1}{\epsilon + 1} \gtrless 0;$$

as ϵ approaches zero the left-hand side of this inequality approaches plus infinity, and as ϵ approaches infinity the left-hand side of the inequality approaches zero; and since the derivative of the left-hand side of the inequality with respect to ϵ is $-1/\epsilon(\epsilon + 1)^2 < 0$, the expression must always lie between zero and plus infinity, implying a positive sign for $\partial/\partial\alpha(U_{ot}/U_{ft} - 1)$.[5]

The economic implication is that, for a given elasticity of foreign demand for exports or supply of imports, the gain from an optimum tariff policy will first rise and then decline as the import ratio increases. It can be rigorously proved, however, that regardless of the magnitude of the elasticity of foreign demand (supply), the import ratio will have to exceed one half before the point of maximum gain is reached.[6] Since it may

---

[5] I am grateful to Franklin M. Fisher for providing the mathematical analysis of this and the preceding paragraph.

[6] $\dfrac{\partial}{\partial\alpha}\left(\dfrac{U_{ot}}{U_{ft}} - 1\right)$ turns from positive to negative when

$$\log \frac{\epsilon + 1}{\epsilon} - \frac{1}{\epsilon + 1} \log \frac{\epsilon + \alpha}{\epsilon} - \frac{1}{\epsilon + 1} = 0. \quad (1)$$

Implicit differentiation of this expression yields

$$\frac{\partial\alpha}{\partial\epsilon} = (\epsilon + \alpha) \log \frac{\epsilon + 1}{\epsilon} - 1. \quad (2)$$

Setting this derivative equal to zero defines a stationary value of α. Moreover, repeated differentiation, holding $\partial\alpha/\partial\epsilon$ at zero, yields

reasonably be assumed as an empirical generalization that import ratios are less than one half, it is reasonable to conclude that for practically relevant cases the potential gain from an optimum tariff policy will be greater the higher the import ratio.

Table 1 shows the value of this relative welfare gain, for ranges of selected values for the free-trade import share $(1 - \alpha)$ and the elasticity of foreign demand for the country's exports (η). It is evident from the Table that the gains from an optimum tariff policy will be relatively small unless the import ratio is large or the demand elasticity small.[7]

Footnote 6 *continued*

$$\frac{\partial^2 \alpha}{\partial \epsilon^2} = \log \frac{\epsilon + 1}{\epsilon} - \frac{1}{\epsilon + 1} - \frac{\alpha}{\epsilon(\epsilon + 1)}. \tag{3}$$

On substitution from equation (1) above this becomes

$$\frac{\partial^2 \alpha}{\partial \epsilon^2} = \frac{1}{\epsilon + 1} \left[\log \left(1 - \frac{\alpha}{\epsilon} \right) - \frac{\alpha}{\epsilon} \right];$$

this must be negative, indicating a maximum value of α, because on exponentiation the bracket expression becomes $1 + \alpha/\epsilon - \epsilon^{\alpha/\epsilon} < 0$ (for proof see text above).

For the implicit value of ϵ that maximizes α,

$$\alpha = \frac{1}{\log[(\epsilon + 1)/\epsilon]} - \epsilon.$$

The value of α will be less than ½ if

$$F(\epsilon) = (\epsilon + \tfrac{1}{2}) \log[(\epsilon + 1)/\epsilon] > 1.$$

Now

$$F'(\epsilon) = \log \frac{\epsilon + 1}{\epsilon} - \frac{\epsilon + \tfrac{1}{2}}{\epsilon(\epsilon + 1)} \text{ and } F''(\epsilon) = \frac{1}{2\epsilon^2(\epsilon + 1)^2} > 0,$$

so that $F(\epsilon)$ is minimized at the value of ϵ for which $F'(\epsilon) = 0$. At that value of ϵ,

$$F(\epsilon) = \frac{(\epsilon + \tfrac{1}{2})^2}{\epsilon(\epsilon + 1)} > 1. \text{ QED.}$$

(I am again indebted to Franklin M. Fisher for furnishing this proof; I am also indebted to Brendan Horton for assistance with the mathematics of the preceding paragraph.)

Iterative computations of α for values of ϵ to one decimal point, using five-figure logarithms, indicate that α attains a maximum of 0·4927 at $\epsilon = 3·6$.

TABLE 1. *Relative Welfare Gain from Optimum Tariff Policies* (%)

Elasticity of Demand	Optimum Tariff (%) $t = \dfrac{100}{\eta - 1}$	Free-Trade Import Share									
		0·05	0·10	0·15	0·20	0·25	0·30	0·35	0·40	0·45	0·50
1·10	1000	3·4	6·7	9·9	12·8	15·3	18·1	20·3	22·8	23·7	24·8
1·20	500	2·6	5·1	7·4	9·6	11·7	13·5	15·0	16·3	17·3	18·0
1·30	333⅓	2·1	4·1	6·0	7·6	9·2	10·6	11·7	12·6	13·4	13·8
1·40	250	1·8	3·4	4·9	6·3	7·5	8·6	9·5	10·2	10·7	11·1
1·50	200	1·5	2·8	3·8	5·2	6·2	7·1	7·8	8·4	8·9	9·1
1·75	133⅓	0·9	1·8	2·5	3·4	4·1	4·7	5·2	5·6	5·8	6·1
2·00	100	0·7	1·4	2·0	2·6	3·1	3·4	3·8	4·1	4·3	4·4
2·25	80	0·6	1·1	1·5	2·0	2·3	2·6	2·9	3·1	3·2	3·3
2·50	66⅔	0·5	0·9	1·2	1·6	1·8	2·1	2·3	2·4	2·5	2·6
2·75	57⅐	0·4	0·7	1·0	1·3	1·5	1·7	1·8	1·9	2·0	2·1
3·00	50	0·3	0·6	0·8	1·0	1·2	1·4	1·5	1·6	1·7	1·7
3·50	40	0·2	0·4	0·6	0·7	0·9	1·0	1·1	1·1	1·2	1·2
4·00	33⅓	0·2	0·3	0·4	0·6	0·7	0·7	0·8	0·9	0·9	0·9
4·50	28⁴⁄₇	0·1	0·2	0·3	0·4	0·5	0·6	0·6	0·7	0·7	0·7
5·00	20	0·1	0·2	0·3	0·4	0·4	0·5	0·5	0·5	0·6	0·5

One final observation is worth making. The optimum tariff argument is frequently applied to the recommendation of trade policies for development as if the less developed countries were starting from a free-trade position. This is almost invariably not the case, and it is quite possible, and often probable, that tariffs are initially above and not below their optimum level from the point of view of maximizing the gain from exploiting monopoly or monopsony power.

[7] I am grateful to Paul Wiedemann for providing the calculations necessary to make up Table 1.

7. Two Notes on Tariffs, Distortions and Growth*

I. THE POSSIBILITY OF INCOME LOSSES FROM INCREASED EFFICIENCY OR FACTOR ACCUMULATION IN THE PRESENCE OF TARIFFS [1]

The adoption of more efficient technology and the accumulation of factors of production are generally assumed to increase the real income available to an economy. But when a country is following a protective policy improved efficiency in the protected industry or accumulation of the factor used intensively in that industry will actually reduce the country's real income, over a range of change set by the degree of protection. This possibility of income-reducing growth is relevant to the fact that countries industrialising by means of protectionist and import-substitution policies are frequently dissatisfied with the results. This note presents a formal demonstration of the possibility, in terms of the standard Heckscher-Ohlin model of international trade.

Figure 1 depicts production and consumption equilibrium with the initial technology and factor supplies and the tariff. TT' is the transformation curve, deduced from the standard box-diagram, II is the international price ratio, MM and $M'M'$ are the internal price ratio, which differs from the international price ratio to an extent determined by the rate of protection of Y, and P and C are the production and consumption equilibrium points.

* *The Economic Journal*, Vol. LXXVII, No. 305 (March 1967) pp. 151—54 and Vol. LXXX, No. 320 (December 1970) pp. 990—92. I am indebted to a forth-coming comment by Trent Bertrand and Frank Flatters, which analyses the precise conditions for immiserization to occur with capital accumulation, for some clarification of the text.

[1] This possibility was first pointed out to the author by J.H. Dales, of the University of Toronto, who developed it in connection with his study of the effects of the Canadian 'National Policy' of industrial protection. The formal demonstration presented here was provoked by the disbelief of H.S. Houthakker.

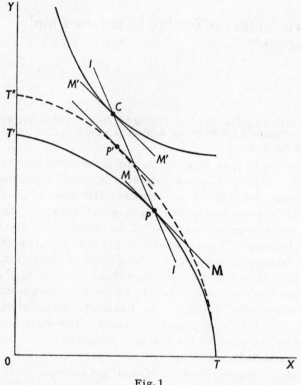

Fig. 1

Now suppose that neutral technical progress occurs in the protected Y industry, and in that industry only. As a result, the transformation curve will shift outward except at point T (where no Y is produced) to TT''; and the new equilibrium production point P' must lie to the northwest of P.[2] P' may lie either to the left or to the right of II, depending on the tariff rate, the extent of the technical improvement, and the elasticities of substitution between the factors in the two production functions. The new utility level of the country is given by the community indifference curve that intersects a new II curve through P' with

[2] For proof, see Harry G. Johnson, 'International Trade and Economic Growth — A Supplementary Analysis,' *Arthaniti*, Vol. V, pp. 1–13. The same result will follow from non-neutral technical progress in the protected industry, unless it is sufficiently strongly biased towards saving the factor used intensively in the export industry.

178

a slope equal to that of $M'M'$. It is obvious, on the usual assumption that neither good is inferior, that the new utility level will be higher if P' lies to the right of II, and lower if P' lies to the left of II. In the latter case the country is made worse off by technical progress in its protected industry. Moreover, it is obvious that for a small enough degree of technical progress in that industry the country must be made worse off, while with a large enough degree of progress it must be made better off, by technical improvement, through the outward movement of the transformation curve.

If, instead of neutral technical progress in the protected industry, there were an increase in the stock of the factor used intensively in producing the protected product, the transformation curve would shift outward throughout its length, but (by the Rybczynski Theorem) the new equilibrium production point P' would in this case also have to be to the northwest of P, again entailing the possibility of loss or gain of real income, and in the case of possible loss the necessity of loss if the factor increment is small enough, and the necessity of gain if the factor increment exceeds some initial minimum quantity, because with sufficient factor accumulation the country must become self-sufficient and eventually reverse its trade pattern.

The analytical results just presented may be understood in the light of the following considerations. Technical progress increases efficiency and therefore potential output per head; but it also shifts resources towards the industry in which progress occurs. If this is the export industry there is an additional gain from the reduction of waste implicit in the excess cost of protected production: but if it is the import-substitute industry there is an offsetting loss from increased waste through the excess cost of additional protected production, which may more than absorb the increase in potential output per head. Similarly, an increase in the supply of a factor increases potential real output, but also reallocates production towards the industry using that factor intensively; and if that industry is protected and so wastes resources through excess production costs, the shift again involves increased waste of resources, which may more than absorb the increase in potential output per head.

It is an interesting reflection on policy that protectionists usually demand increased protection when comparative advantage shifts against the protected industries, in effect claiming that part of the increased productive potential inherent in such a shift should be spent on the increased support of these industries.

In conclusion, it should be noted that the possibility of income-reducing growth demonstrated here is quite different from the possibility of 'immiserizing growth' developed by Jagdish Bhagwati.[3] The latter is associated with the adverse effects of growth on the terms of trade when growth increases the country's supply of exports; the former is associated with the presence of protection, under conditions in which any terms-of-trade effects of growth are excluded by assumption, and growth reduces the demand for imports.

II. A NOTE ON DISTORTIONS AND THE RATE OF GROWTH OF AN OPEN ECONOMY

In an earlier note,[4] I showed that in the presence of a tariff factor accumulation or technical progress of a biased kind could reduce rather than increase a country's real income, thus developing a case of 'immiserizing growth' parallel to Bhagwati's classic case of immiserizing growth based on adverse terms-of-trade effects. Subsequently, Bhagwati has generalized the analysis to show that the presence of any kind of distortion in the domestic or the foreign market (the latter being the terms-of-trade case) may lead to growth being immiserizing.[5] Bhagwati's generalization suggests a stronger hypothesis: that if the causes of growth were biased towards augmenting production of the commodity favoured by the distortion, the rate of growth of real output at world market prices would be less than it would be in the absence of the distortion, and conversely. This hypothesis turns out to be incorrect: real growth may be either faster or slower in the presence of a distortion than it would be in the

[3] Jagdish Bhagwati, 'Immiserizing Growth: A Geometrical Note,' *Review of Economic Studies*, Vol. XXV, No. 3 (June 1958) pp. 201—5.

[4] *The Economic Journal*, March 1967, reprinted as the first part of this chapter.

[5] Jagdish Bhagwati, 'Distortions and Immiserising Growth: A Generalization,' *The Review of Economic Studies*, Vol. XXXV(4), No. 104 (October 1968) pp. 481—5.

absence of any distortion. This note presents the mathematical proof.

For simplicity, we assume that commodity quantities are so measured that commodities exchange one-for-one at world market prices, and that factor quantities are so measured that, in the absence of distortions, their values would be unity in terms of commodities. Denoting production of the two commodities by X and Y respectively, factor endowments by K and L, and capital-output and labour-output coefficients in the respective industries by k_x, k_y, l_x, l_y, output quantities under any circumstances will be determined by the resource constraints

$$k_x X + k_y Y = K \qquad (1)$$

and

$$l_x X + l_y Y = L, \qquad (2)$$

whence

$$X = \frac{K l_y - L k_y}{k_x l_y - l_x k_y}, \qquad (3)$$

$$Y = \frac{k_x L - l_x K}{k_x l_y - l_x k_y}, \qquad (4)$$

$$M = X + Y = \frac{K(l_y - l_x) + L(k_x - k_y)}{k_x l_y - l_x k_y}, \qquad (5)$$

$$\frac{dM}{dt} = \frac{K r_k(l_y - l_x) + L r_l(k_x - k_y)}{k_x l_y - l_x k_y} \qquad (6)$$

where

$$r_k = \frac{1}{K} \cdot \frac{dK}{dt} \text{ and } r_l = \frac{1}{L} \cdot \frac{dL}{dt},$$

$$g = \frac{1}{M} \cdot \frac{dM}{dt} = \frac{R r_k(l_y - l_x) + r_l(k_x - k_y)}{R(l_y - l_x) + (k_x - k_y)} \qquad (7)$$

where

$$R = \frac{K}{L}.$$

Let p represent the introduction of any distortion favouring the production of X (for concreteness, p may be thought of as representing a tariff which raises the domestic price of X to

181

producers above the world market price of unity). Then the numerator of $\frac{dg}{dp}$ is

$$[R(l_y - l_x) + (k_x - k_y)] \left[Rr_k \left(\frac{dl_y}{dp} - \frac{dl_x}{dp} \right) + r_l \left(\frac{dk_x}{dp} - \frac{dk_y}{dp} \right) \right]$$

$$- [Rr_k(l_y - l_x) + r_l(k_x - k_y)] \left[R \left(\frac{dl_y}{dp} - \frac{dl_x}{dp} \right) + \left(\frac{dk_x}{dp} - \frac{dk_y}{dp} \right) \right]$$

$$= R(r_k - r_l) \left[(k_x - k_y) \left(\frac{dl_y}{dp} - \frac{dl_x}{dp} \right) - (l_y - l_x) \left(\frac{dk_x}{dp} - \frac{dk_y}{dp} \right) \right]. \quad (8)$$

Using the fact that, in the absence of distortions, $k_x + l_x = l = k_y + l_y$, this becomes

$$R(r_k - r_l)(k_x - k_y) \left[\left(\frac{dl_y}{dp} + \frac{dk_y}{dp} \right) - \left(\frac{dl_x}{dp} + \frac{dk_x}{dp} \right) \right]. \quad (9)$$

This expression verifies the point that if both factors are accumulating at the same rate (growth is 'neutral' or 'unbiased') distortions will not affect the growth rate (though they will affect the level of output achieved at any time).

The question at issue, however, is whether anything can be said about the influence of distortions on the growth rate when factor accumulation is biased towards one of the factors. Concretely, if the expression in square brackets in equation (9) could be proved negative, it would follow that a distortion favouring production of X would imply a growth rate lower than the non-distortion growth rate if factor accumulation were biased towards the factor used intensively in producing X, and higher than that rate if factor accumulation were biased towards the factor used intensively in producing Y. (The product of the two other terms is positive in the first case and negative in the second.)

Unfortunately the expression in square brackets cannot be given a definite sign; its sign will depend on the specification of the production functions for the two goods and of the distortion. The two terms in the square brackets represent the changes in costs of production of the two goods, evaluated at non-distorted factor prices, consequent on changes in factor utilization ratios induced by the distortion. Elementary index number theory indicates that these must be non-negative; hence the overall sign of the expression depends on their numerical values.

It may be interesting to record the results of a computer calculation using Cobb-Douglas production functions, and assuming a faster rate of increase of capital than of labour and an endowment ratio of unity. Where the capital coefficients for the two industries summed to unity, the rate of growth fell from the non-distorted growth rate as the magnitude of distortion favouring the capital-intensive industry increased, and rose as the magnitude of distortion favouring the labour-intensive industry increased. But when the capital coefficients summed to less than unity, the rate of growth generally rose with the degree of distortion in both directions, and when the capital coefficients summed to more than unity the rate of growth generally varied inversely with the degree of distortion in both directions. (But there were some departures from this pattern for certain values of the Cobb-Douglas coefficients.)

In conclusion, it should be remarked that while the algebra above deals only with factor accumulation, it can readily be extended to cover technical progress, which can be interpreted as equivalent to increasing available factor supplies with given production functions. Also, while the problem considered concerns an open economy, the results clearly apply also to growth in a closed economy. But analysis of the closed economy would involve much more complex mathematics, since the 'small country' assumption used here — that the world price ratio is given — implies that the international price ratio and the distortion fix the domestic commodity and factor price ratios and the factor utilization coefficients, which do not change over time, so long as the country remains incompletely specialized.

PART III:
The Cost of Protection

8. The Cost of Protection and the Scientific Tariff*

INTRODUCTION

The proposition that freedom of trade is on the whole economically more beneficial than protection is one of the most fundamental propositions economic theory has to offer for the guidance of economic policy. Broadly speaking, the proposition stands on two legs: the static argument that interference with freedom of trade worsens the allocation of national and world resources and so reduces realized output below potential output and the dynamic argument that economic liberty and freedom of competition, national and international, provides the most favourable environment for economic growth. Both arguments have been challenged by respectable counterarguments: that there are important cases in which free competition produces non-optimal results, for which a tariff may be an appropriate corrective, and that the tariff may be a potent means of accelerating economic growth.

The arguments of both types on the issue of free trade versus protection are of long historical standing. Their formulation has evolved along with the progress of economic theory and has been greatly sophisticated in recent years as a result of the development of the theories of monopolistic competition and of employment in the 1930's and of modern welfare economics. But the intellectual effort which has gone into the elaboration and refinement of arguments about the harmful or beneficial effects of tariffs has been accompanied by almost no effort to assess the magnitude, or even the existence, of the effects which theoretical analysis shows to be possible.

Admittedly, the determination and measurement of the effects of alternative commercial policy systems on economic growth seems to be beyond the range of contemporary economic science, even in principle, and it is understandable that in this field

* *The Journal of Political Economy*, Vol. LXVIII, No. 4 (August 1960) pp. 327—45.

economists have stuck to argument from historical examples or from assumptions about entrepreneurial behaviour, methods that can lead to any desired conclusions. But the general lines of the conceptual framework required for measuring the static effects of protection on national income have been familiar for a long time, ever since Marshall invented the twin concepts of consumers' and producers' surplus; and that framework has been applied, first by Barone[1] and subsequently by many textbook writers, to demonstrate both the loss from protection and the possibility of national gain from exploiting the foreigner. Nevertheless, there have been only two major attempts to measure the economic effects of a particular country's commercial policy. The first was made by the committee of inquiry into the Australian tariff of 1927–29 (the 'Brigden committee'), which calculated the excess costs of protected production;[2] the defects of this concept as a measure of the cost of protection are set out in Jacob Viner's review of the committee's report and have recently been explored afresh by W.M. Corden.[3] The second is contained in the recently published study, *Canadian Commercial Policy*, by J.H. Young, one of the staff studies prepared for the Royal Commission on Canada's Economic Prospects.[4] Young does not attempt to measure the economic cost of the Canadian tariff but instead measures the 'cash cost,' which is the excess of the cost of Canadian consumption at internal prices over the cost at world market prices and is essentially the same as the

[1] See Enrico Barone, *Principi di economia politica* (Rome: Athanaeum, 1913) Part III, esp. secs. 88–90, pp. 117–21.

[2] J.R. Brigden, D.B. Copland, E.C. Dyason, L.F. Giblin, and C.H. Wickens, *The Australian Tariff: An Economic Enquiry* (Melbourne: Melbourne University Press, 1929).

[3] Jacob Viner, 'The Australian Tariff,' *Economic Record*, Vol. V, No. 9 (November 1929) pp. 306–15 (reprinted as Chap. IV in Viner's *International Economics* [Glencoe, Ill.: Free Press, 1951]); W.M. Corden, 'The Calculation of the Cost of Protection,' *Economic Record*, Vol. XXXIII, No. 64 (May 1957) pp. 29–51.

[4] J.H. Young, *Canadian Commercial Policy* (Ottawa: Royal Commission on Canada's Economic Prospects, 1957) esp. Part III and Appendix A. It is ironic, to say the least, that in its Foreword the Royal Commission specifically dissociates itself from this study.

Brigden committee's concept. Young then gives reasons why this measure may overstate or understate the true economic cost.[5]

Measurement of the economic gain or loss resulting from particular economic policies is clearly an interesting aspect of the quantification of economic relationships that modern mathematical and statistical techniques make possible and that contemporary methodology insists should be the aim of scientific endeavour. In order to make such measurements, it is first necessary to clarify the nature of the gains or losses and specify them in a measurable way. Thus the main purpose of the present paper is to reformulate the theory of tariffs in order to specify a method of measurement of the cost of protection. The calculation of the cost of protection is the subject matter of the first section, which begins by following to a large extent a recent article by Corden on the same subject,[6] but then proceeds to an analysis that has been strongly influenced by the work of my colleague Arnold Harberger.[7] Consideration of the cost of protection, however, suggests a balancing of these costs against other results of the tariff, which might be held by supporters of the tariff to be beneficial. This leads to the concept of a scientific tariff, meaning a tariff that achieves these other results at minimum cost to the economy.[8] The scientific tariff is the subject of the second part of the paper, for the

---

[5] See also the study made for the Congressional Joint Committee on the Economic Report by Howard S. Piquet (later published under the title *Aid, Trade and the Tariff* [New York: Thomas Y. Crowell Co., 1953]) of the effects of liberalization of trade barriers on American imports, which provides the raw material for a calculation of the cost of protection to the United States economy; also Beatrice Vaccara's *Employment and Output in Protected Manufacturing Industries* (Washington, D.C.: Brookings Institution, 1960), which appeared after this chapter was accepted for publication.

A referee has pointed out the existence of a literature on the cost of the German grain duties (see A. Gerschenkron, *Bread and Democracy in Germany* [Berkeley: University of Califomia Press, 1943] p. 64, where reference is made to Brentano's *Die deutsche Getreidezolle*).

[6] *Op. cit.*

[7] See, for example, his 'The Fundamentals of Economic Progress in Underdeveloped Countries: Using the Resources at Hand More Effectively,' *American Economic Review*, Vol. XLIX, No. 2 (May 1959) pp. 134–46.

original idea of which I am indebted to Young.[9]

I. THE COST OF PROTECTION

In general terms the cost of protection to a country can be conceived of as comprising two elements: first, the gain in real income that could be obtained by abandoning protection in favour of unilateral free trade and, second, whatever additional gain in real income might be achieved by using the readiness to abandon protection to obtain tariff concessions from the rest of the world.[10] This second gain might be quite substantial, even for a small country, if that country's trade is narrowly concentrated on a large neighbouring country, as in the case of Canada and the United States. Nevertheless, it will be left out of account in the remainder of the argument on the ground that it depends on the concessions that can be obtained in tariff bargaining, which cannot be predicted by economic methods.[11]

The effect of abandoning protection and adopting free trade would be to induce a re-allocation of factors among industries and of consumption among goods, with corresponding changes in goods and factor prices and in international trade. In short, a new world general equilibrium would tend to be established. The cost of protection to the country can be measured in terms of the goods that could be extracted from the economy in the free-trade situation without making the country worse off than it was under protection — some variant of the Hicksian compensating variation. Such a measure presupposes that the country's

[8] Various commentators have suggested that the term 'scientific tariff' misuses the adjective 'scientific.' The use of the term in this chapter is justified (a) by the established use of the concept in the tariff literature and (b) by the *Concise Oxford Dictionary*, according to which one meaning of the adjective is 'assisted by expert knowledge.'

[9] *Op. cit.*, Chap. IV

[10] This second element of gain is stressed by Young (*op. cit.*, *passim*). The exchange of unilateral free trade for tariff concessions must be distinguished from the formation of a customs union or preference area, which does not entail unilateral free trade.

[11] If the concessions could be predicted reliably, the total gain on both scores could be measured by extending the method developed below.

welcome — welfare can be considered as a unit, which in turn implies either that internal income distribution can be ignored or that the country implements a definite policy regarding it. When applied to a country as a whole, it also raises certain problems of consistency whose solution complicates the measure.

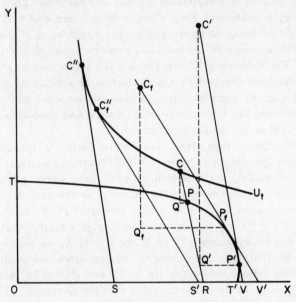

Fig. 1

The effects of the adoption of free trade and the problem of measuring the resulting gain are illustrated for the standard two-good general equilibrium model of international trade in Figure 1. In the figure, TT' is the country's transformation curve between goods Y and X, and U_t is the community indifference curve reached with the tariff. Initially, C is the country's consumption point, and P its production point; CQ its imports of Y, and PQ its exports of X; the slope of CP corresponds to the international terms of trade, and the slopes of the tangents at C and P correspond to the internal (tariff-inclusive) price ratio between the goods.

The country's national income and output, valued in international prices and calculated in terms of its exportable good,

191

is OR. If consumers were allowed to buy goods at the international exchange ratio, they could obtain the same level of satisfaction at C'' with a national income of OS instead of OR. The difference SR represents the *consumption cost* of the tariff, the loss imposed by the distortion of consumption from the optimal pattern corresponding to the international price ratio. Similarly, if producers were allowed to produce and sell at the international terms of trade, production would be at P', and the international value of the national product would be OV instead of OR. The difference RV represents the *production cost* of the tariff, the loss imposed by the distortion of production from the optimal pattern corresponding to the international price ratio. SV represents the total of the consumption and production costs of the tariff at the initial terms of trade.

Unless the foreign offer curve were perfectly elastic (that is, unless the country's terms of trade were independent of the volume of trade), the adoption of free trade would change the terms of trade adversely to the country; at the initial terms of trade the country would now desire to export $P'Q'$ of X in exchange for $C'Q'$ of Y, whereas the foreign country would only be willing to exchange CQ of Y for PQ of X, as before. With free trade, therefore, the country's consumption- and production-equilibrium points would not lie at C' and P' but in locations corresponding to less favourable equilibrium terms of trade, such as C_f and P_f. The gain from trade would not be SV but a smaller, and possibly negative, quantity, $S'V'$. The difference between SV and $S'V'$ represents the benefit derived by the country from the favourable effect of the tariff on its terms of trade.

The cost of protection is measured by $S'V'$ if the terms of trade are not constant. But this does not represent a quantity of goods that could be extracted from the economy, leaving it as well off under free trade as it was with the tariff. If $S'V'$ of exportables were extracted, the economy would reduce its demand for exportables by less than $S'V'$, reducing its demand for importables by an amount determined by its marginal propensity to import at the free-trade price ratio. Thus the terms of trade would turn in the country's favour. The gain from free trade is not $S'V'$ but $S'V'$ *divided between exportables and importables*

in accordance with the country's marginal propensity to import.
To put the point another way, if the gain is to be extracted
entirely in exportables, it will not be $S'V'$ but some larger
quantity, the extraction of which would involve better equilibrium terms of trade, and if the gain is to be extracted entirely
in importables, it will not be the quantity of importables for
which $S'V'$ exchanges in equilibrium but some smaller quantity,
the extraction of which would entail worse terms of trade. In
general, the gain must be conceived of as a set of combinations
of quantities of exportables and importables which could be
extracted from the economy while leaving it in free-trade equili-
librium at the level of satisfaction achieved under the tariff.[12]

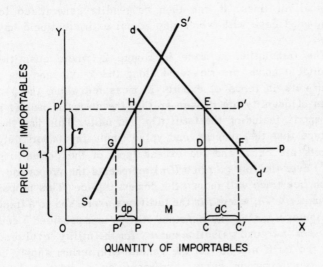

Fig. 2

[12] For an extended treatment of the gains from trade, see Jagdish
Bhagwati and Harry G. Johnson, 'Notes on Some Controversies in
International Trade Theory,' *Economic Journal*, Vol. LXX, No. 277
(March 1960) pp. 74—93.

To summarize, the cost of protection is the sum of the consumption cost and the production cost less the terms of trade gain, and may be negative. The terms-of-trade gain arises when the foreign-offer curve is not perfectly elastic, and in this case the cost (possibly net benefit) of protection must be measured in terms of a quantity of each good, not merely of one of them. Because of this complication, and also because in many cases the terms-of-trade gain from protection may be negligible, it seems most convenient to begin by estimating the consumption and production costs of protection at constant terms of trade and to introduce later the effects of a worsening of the terms of trade under free trade as a deduction from the estimate. This procedure has the advantage of allowing the foregoing argument to be translated into partial-equilibrium analysis on neo-Marshallian lines. It can then be readily generalized to the many-good case with which any actual estimate would have to cope.

The translation is made in Figure 2, where quantities of importable goods are measured along the X-axis and the price of imports in terms of exports is measured along the Y-axis. Units of quantity are chosen so that the domestic market price of imports including the tariff (Op') is unity. This has the advantage that the quantity and value (including import duty) of imports are equal and the excess (pp') of the domestic price (Op') over the foreign price (Op) represents the proportion τ by which free trade will reduce the domestic price. This proportion τ equals $t/1 + t$, where t is the tariff rate expressed as a fraction. In Figure 2, dd' is the constant-utility ('compensated') demand curve, or 'marginal valuation curve,' for the utility level reached with the tariff and SS' is the general-equilibrium supply curve (the transformation curve, expressed as a relation between relative price of importables and the quantity of them produced domestically). These curves are drawn as straight lines for geometrical convenience; they may be regarded as approximations to curvi-linear curves.

With the tariff, consumption is OC, domestic production OP, imports PC. If the tariff were removed and consumers were simultaneously deprived of export goods to the extent required to keep their utility level constant, consumption would expand to OC', and domestic production would fall to OP'. Consumers' surplus would be increased by $pp'EF$. Of this, $pp'HG$ would be offset by a reduction in producers' surplus, and $HJDE$ by the loss of import duties formerly collected. The remainder, consisting of GHJ and DEF, represents the increase in the value of production and the reduction in the cost of consumption made possible by free trade, which must be extracted if utility is to remain constant; that is, GHJ is the production cost, and DEF the consumption cost, of protection.

The consumption and production costs of protection, GHJ and DEF, can be expressed symbolically as $\frac{1}{2}\tau dC$ and $\frac{1}{2}\tau dP$, respectively, where dC is the increase in consumption and dP the decrease in domestic production resulting from (compensated) tariff elimination. Making use of the fact that by choice of units $p' = 1$, the total cost of protection can be expressed as

$$\frac{1}{2}\tau(dP + dC) = \frac{1}{2}\tau\left(\frac{dP}{dp'}\tau - \frac{dC}{dp'}\tau\right)$$
$$= \frac{1}{2}\tau^2\frac{d}{dp'}(P - C)$$
$$= \frac{1}{2}\tau^2\eta V,$$

where τ is the proportion of tariff protection in the final domestic price p', C and P are the quantities initially consumed and produced domestically, $V[= p'(C - P)]$ is the initial domestic market value of imports and

$$\eta\left[= -\frac{p'}{C - P}\cdot\frac{d}{dp'}(C - P)\right]$$

is the compensated arc-elasticity of demand for imports. For purposes of subsequent analysis it is desirable to express the cost, not as an absolute sum, but as a proportion of national income (expenditure) at market prices; the proportional cost is given by the same formula, with V redefined as the ratio of imports at market prices to domestic expenditure.[13]

---

[13] Alternatively, the cost as a proportion of national income at factor cost is given by $\frac{1}{2}t\tau V\eta$, where V is now defined as the ratio of the value of imports at factor cost (which is equal to the value of exports) to national income at factor prices.

The foregoing measure of the cost of protection assumes only one export good, one import good, and a single tariff rate, but it can readily be extended to the case of a country producing a multiplicity of goods, provided certain qualifications or assumptions can be made. The general case involves the elimination of tariffs levied at different rates on a variety of goods, with a consequent reshuffling of consumption and production patterns. In the process (1) production of certain importable goods may disappear completely, while others will for the first time come to be imported; and (2) substitutions will occur between imports and domestic (non-traded) goods and among domestic goods. Both require some elaboration of the simple measure, which continues to hold for goods, [14] some quantity of which is imported despite the tariff and some quantity of which continues to be produced domestically after the tariff is removed.

So far as the first type of change is concerned, the gain from complete replacement of home production by imports may exceed the formula value of $\frac{1}{2}\tau dP$, rising to a maximum of τP where none of the excess of domestic over foreign price is producers' surplus; similarly, the gain from consumption of new imports formerly excluded will be less than $\frac{1}{2}\tau dC$, where τ is calculated from the exclusive tariff rate. In the former case the formula can be amended to $k\tau P$, where k is the proportion of the excess of domestic over foreign price which is not rent. When imports do not completely replace domestic production, $k = \frac{1}{2}\tau\epsilon$, where ϵ is the arc-elasticity of domestic supply at the production point with the tariff. In the latter case, τ can be defined as calculated for the tariff rate at which the goods concerned would be on the margin of exclusion (the 'effective' tariff rate). [15]

The second type of change, substitutions between imports and domestic goods and substitutions among domestic goods,

---

[14] In the form $\frac{1}{2}\tau(dP + dC)$, though not in the form $\frac{1}{2}\tau^2\eta V$, since the change in the quantity imported is determined by changes in the domestic prices of other goods as well as the commodity's own price.

[15] Where the tariff previously gave sufficient protection for domestic products to satisfy demand without the need for imports, and the domestic industry is competitive, the 'effective' tariff rate is calculable from the difference between domestic and foreign prices.

requires elaboration of the measure to the extent that domestic goods bear taxes or, due to imperfections of competition, carry a margin of price over cost. A decrease in consumption of such goods reduces welfare, since the value of the consumption foregone is greater than the resources released for the purchase of imports; the converse is true if the consumption of such goods increases. The measure of gain or loss in this case is the excess of price over cost multiplied by the change in quantity.

If it is assumed that, on the average, the excess of domestic price over cost is no greater for domestic goods than for the imports which replace them, this source of complexity can be disregarded, and will therefore be ignored in what follows, although, as with terms of trade effects, it may need to be re-introduced as a correction to a specific calculation.

On these assumptions the measure of the cost of protection becomes the sum of the measures for the individual goods,

$$\sum_i k_i \tau_i P_i + \sum_i \tfrac{1}{2} \tau_i dC_i,$$

where P_i is domestic production of the protected good, dC_i is the total change in consumption of it resulting from a compensated elimination of tariffs, k_i is the non-rent portion of the excess of the domestic price over the foreign, and τ_i is the proportion of the 'effective' tariff rate in the domestic price.

The aggregate production cost of protection can be rewritten as

$$\sum_i \tau_i P_i - \sum_i r_i \tau_i P_i,$$

where $r_i = 1 - k_i$ is the proportion of rent in the excess of the domestic over the foreign price of the ith good. The first part of the expression is identical with the Brigden committee's 'excess cost of protected production' and Young's 'cash cost of protection'; the second measures the extent to which these measures overstate the real production cost by ignoring economic rent.

Since the changes in quantities of the different goods consumed are restricted by the condition of maintenance of a constant utility level, the aggregate consumption cost can be rewritten as

197

$$\frac{1}{2} \sum_i \sum_j S_{ij} \tau_i \tau_j,$$

where S_{ij} is the pure substitution slope (with reversed sign) $-\partial q_i / \partial p_j$, restricted by the conditions

and

$$\sum_j S_{ij} = 0, \quad S_{ij} = S_{ji}, \quad S_{ii} > 0,$$

$$\sum_i^m \sum_j^m S_{ij} \lambda_i \lambda_j > 0$$

for any m less than the number of commodities,[16] and the summation runs over all the goods consumed with $\tau_i = 0$ for goods not initially protected. This expression can in turn be rewritten as

$$\frac{1}{2} E \sum_i e_i (\eta_i - m_i) \left(\tau_i^2 - \sum_{j \neq i} s_{ji} \tau_j \tau_i \right),$$

where E is aggregate expenditure at market prices, e_i is the proportion in it of expenditures on the ith good, η_i is the usual (uncompensated) own-price elasticity of demand for the ith good, and m_i the marginal propensity to spend on it (so that $\eta_i - m_i$ is the compensated elasticity of demand for the ith good), and s_{ji} is the proportion of the substitution of the ith good for other goods when the price of the ith good falls that is made at the expense of the jth good. (If the jth good is a complement of the ith good, s_{ji} is negative.)[17]

With the foregoing substitutions, the aggregate production and consumption cost of protection is given by the formula

[16] These are simply the four Hicksian restrictions on the substitution terms, modified in accordance with the reversal of sign of the substitution terms adopted here for convenience, and the simplification permitted by measurement of commodity quantities in units with a tariff-inclusive price of unity (see J.R. Hicks, *Value and Capital* [Oxford: Clarendon Press, 1939] p. 311).

Marc Nerlove has commented on the similarity between the cost formula using this version of the consumption cost and the loss formula developed by Marcel Boiteux ('Le "Revenue distribuable" et les pertes économiques,' *Econometrica*, Vol. XIX, No. 2 [April 1951] pp. 112–33). Boiteux expresses the production cost of a non-optimal situation, as well as the consumption cost, in terms of a substitution matrix; this assumes that the economy produces all goods for both situations, an assumption which is not generally acceptable for an open economy.

$$C = \sum_i \tau_i P_i - \sum_i r_i \tau_i P_i + \tfrac{1}{2} E \sum_i e_i (\eta_i - m_i) \left(\tau_i^2 - \sum_{j \neq i} s_{ji} \tau_j \tau_i \right).$$

Expressed as a proportion of national expenditure at market prices, this total cost is given by the formula

$$c = \frac{C}{E} = \sum_i \tau_i \pi_i - \sum_i r_i \tau_i \pi_i + \frac{1}{2} \sum_i e_i \ (\eta_i - m_i) \left(\tau_i^2 - \sum_{j \neq i} s_{ji} \tau_j \tau_i \right),$$

where π_i is the proportion of purchases of domestically produced commodity i in total expenditure. Both formulas show that the Brigden–Young calculation overstates the cost of protection

[17] Since $S_{ij} = S_{ji}$,

$$\sum_j S_{ji} = \sum_j S_{ij} = 0,$$

and

$$\sum_{j \neq i} S_{ji} = -S_{ii};$$

definition of s_{ji} by $S_{ji} = -s_{ji} S_{ii}$ permits the substitution

$$\sum_i \sum_j S_{ij} \tau_i \tau_j = \sum_i \left(S_{ii} \tau_i^2 + \sum_{j \neq i} S_{ji} \tau_j \tau_i \right) = \sum_i S_{ii} (\tau_i^2 - s_{ji} \tau_j \tau_i).$$

Since

$$\eta_i = -\frac{p_i}{q_i} \cdot \frac{dq_i}{dp_i} = -\frac{p_i}{q_i} \cdot \frac{\partial q_i}{\partial Y} \cdot \frac{\partial Y}{\partial p_i} - \frac{p_i}{q_i} \cdot \frac{\partial q_i}{\partial p_i}$$

$$= -\frac{m_i}{q_i} \cdot \frac{\partial Y}{\partial p_i} + \frac{1}{q_i} S_{ii},$$

where Y is real income and m_i is the marginal propensity to spend on the ith good, and since $\partial Y / \partial p_i$ may be approximated by $(-q_i)$, S_{ii} may be replaced in the foregoing expression by $e_i E (\eta_i - m_i)$, where

$$e_i = \frac{q_i}{\sum_j q_j}$$

is the proportion of expenditure on the ith good in total expenditure.

The consumption cost could also be rewritten in the more symmetrical form

$$\tfrac{1}{2} E \sum_i \sum_j e_i \left(\eta_{ij} - m_i \frac{e_j}{e_i} \right) \tau_i \tau_j,$$

by the amount of economic rent earned in the domestic production of import substitutes and understates it by the amount of the consumption cost.[18]

Even if the simplifying assumptions outlined earlier can be justified, the application of the measure of the production and consumption cost of protection to an actual economy would obviously require a major statistical effort, involving econometric analysis of both demand and cost functions for at least the major goods produced and consumed. Without making such detailed measurements, it is nevertheless possible to show that the production and consumption cost of protection, taken as a proportion of national expenditure, is likely to be rather low. Also, if the cost is not low, this is likely to be attributable to production cost rather than to consumption cost. These conclusions follow from the nature of the cost formulas, together with the general empirical observation that tariff rates in force are almost invariably fractions, usually running below 50 per cent, and the fact that statistical estimates of elasticities of both consumption and import demand have generally

Footnote continued

where

$$\eta_{ij} = -\frac{p_j}{q_i} \cdot \frac{dq_i}{dp_j}$$

$$= -\frac{p_j}{q_i} \cdot \frac{\partial q_i}{\partial Y} \cdot \frac{\partial Y}{\partial p_j} - \frac{p_i}{q_i} \cdot \frac{\partial q_i}{\partial p_j}$$

$$= -\frac{m_i}{q_i} \cdot \frac{\partial Y}{\partial p_j} + \frac{1}{q_i} S_{ij},$$

$\partial Y/\partial p_j$ is approximated by $-q_j$, *and*

$$e_j = \frac{q_j}{\sum_j q_j}$$

is the proportion of expenditure on the jth good in total expenditure. This form would correspond more closely to econometric concepts; but the form used in the text is better adapted to the subsequent argument.

[18] This is apart from the tariff-bargaining, terms-of-trade, and domestic-repercussion effects discussed and set aside earlier in the argument.

produced low figures.[19]

Consider first the two-goods model, which can be taken to approximate an aggregative treatment of imports and tariff rates. The most extreme possible assumption is that the country consumes none of its export good, producing only importables for domestic consumption,[20] and that the excess of the internal over the external price of importables is accounted for entirely by higher real costs of domestic production. In this case, the whole of the cost of protection is production cost, and its amount, measured as a proportion of national income at market prices, is $\tau(1 - V)$, where V is the ratio of the value of imports to national expenditure at domestic prices and τ is the proportion of the tariff in the domestic price of imports as before. This expression is the product of two fractions, and, while the second is likely to lie near the upper end of the range between $\frac{1}{2}$ and 1, the first is likely to be well under $\frac{1}{2}$ ($\tau = \frac{1}{2}$ corresponds to a 100 per cent duty), so that even in this extreme case the cost of protection is likely to be appreciably less than half the national income.

On the more realistic assumption that the country would produce some importables and consume some exportables even under free trade, the formula for the proportional cost of the tariff in the two-goods model is $\frac{1}{2}\tau^2 \eta V$, τ being the proportion of the tariff in the domestic price, V the share of imports in domestic expenditure, and η the compensated elasticity of demand for imports. Unless the compensated elasticity of demand for imports is very high, the cost calculation is bound to turn out small because it involves multiplying the elasticity by half

---

[19] Harberger takes an elasticity of consumption demand of unity 'to be a reasonable central value for the range of price elasticities that have been reliably estimated in demand studies. The price elasticity of demand for food appears to be about −0·4 and this is almost surely at the low end of the scale; at the other extreme, price elasticities for housing and for refrigerators appear to be in the range between −1 and −2. Higher elasticities have been measured only in cases where the good in question has been so narrowly defined as to exclude an obvious close substitute' (*op. cit.*, p. 138). He also regards an elasticity of import demand of 5 as a maximum likely value (*op. cit.*, pp. 135−36).

[20] This is equivalent to assuming that exportables and importables are perfect substitutes in consumption.

the product of three fractions, each of which is likely to be substantially below ½. For example, supposing a tariff rate of 33⅓ per cent ($\tau = \frac{1}{4}$) and an import share of 25 per cent, the compensated elasticity of demand for imports would have to be slightly above 5 for the cost to amount to 4 per cent of national income. With a tariff rate and import share of 20 per cent, the elasticity would have to be 14·4 for the same result.

Now consider the measure for the general case. It is convenient to take up the consumption cost and production cost separately.

The consumption cost may be written as

$$\frac{1}{2} \sum_i e_i (\eta_i - m_i) \tau_i^2 - \frac{1}{2} \sum_i e_i \ (\eta_i - m_i) \sum_{j \neq i} s_{ji} \tau_j \tau_i.$$

Since s_{ji} is positive for substitutes and negative for complements, the second part of the expression will constitute a deduction from the total consumption cost unless there is substantial complementarity among the commodities bearing the highest tariff rates. The first part of the expression is comparable to the elasticity formula for the two-goods case and is likely to be small for the same reason — it involves multiplying the compensated elasticity of demand by half the product of three fractions, each of which is likely to be small. [21] The resulting figure will be a very small fraction unless high expenditure proportions, high elasticities, and high tariff rates go together. Thus, unless high elasticities of demand are correlated with high tariffs and large expenditure proportions, and/or highly taxed imports are strongly complementary with one another, the consumption cost is likely to come to a very small proportion of national expenditure.

The consumption-cost formula is unfortunately too complicated for the foregoing considerations to be illustrated easily by calculations using specific values of the variables. For that

[21] Though the proportion of expenditure spent on consumption of a good will exceed the proportion spent on imports of it, this will be offset or more than offset by the difference between the elasticities of consumption demand and import demand. If domestic supplies of importable goods were completely inelastic, the first part of the expression would be the sum of the two-goods-case formulas for individual imports; otherwise, it would be less.

purpose it is necessary to simplify the problem. One approach is to assume: (1) that complementarity among taxed imports is not strong enough for the second part of the formula to be negative, so that the first part of it is a maximum estimate of the consumption cost; and (2) that the distributions of e_i, $(\eta_i - m_i)$, and τ_i are independent of one another. This second assumption, which does not appear to be biased toward understatement of the value of the formula, permits the first part of the formula to be simplified to

$$\tfrac{1}{2} e \, (\overline{\eta - m})(\overline{\tau}^2 + \sigma_{\overline{\tau}}^2),$$

where

$$e \;=\; \sum_i e_i (\tau_i \neq 0)$$

is the proportion in total expenditure of expenditure on commodities subject to protection, barred symbols denote arithmetic averages, and $\sigma_{\overline{\tau}}$ is the standard deviation of the τ_i about their mean.[22] Given the bunching of actual tariff rates, $\sigma_{\overline{\tau}}$ may be expected to be a fraction of $\overline{\tau}$. As an example, suppose $\overline{\tau} = \tfrac{1}{4}$, $\sigma_{\overline{\tau}} = \tfrac{1}{3}\overline{\tau}$, $(\eta - m) = 1 \cdot 5$, and $e = \tfrac{1}{3}$; then the maximum consumption cost would be just under $1\tfrac{3}{4}$ per cent of national expenditure.[23]

An alternative simplification, frequently used by international trade theorists,[24] is to assume that expenditure is divided in

[22] This result is obtained by writing each term in the formula as its average plus an error term, multiplying out, and equating all sums containing products of first-power error terms to zero.

[23] The term $\sigma_{\overline{\tau}} = \tfrac{1}{3}\overline{\tau}$ corresponds to the maximum value consistent with an approximately normal distribution of τ_i. Unless e is a small fraction, the cross-effects in the second part of the formula cannot be neglected.

On the assumed value of $(\overline{\eta - m})$, see n. 19.

The order of magnitude suggested by the example is also suggested by two computations. The Australian study mentioned in n. 2 contains a table of tariff rates on forty-nine items of protected production (Brigden committee, *op. cit.*, pp. 191–92), for which $\overline{\tau} = 0 \cdot 1982$ and $\sigma_{\overline{\tau}} = 0 \cdot 0497$. The Vaccara study mentioned in n. 5 contains a table of average duties on imports for fifty-eight import-competing industries (*op. cit.*, pp. 26–27); if these are used as substitutes for actual tariff rates, they give $\overline{\tau} = 0 \cdot 1160$ and $\sigma_{\overline{\tau}} = 0 \cdot 1013$. The corresponding consumption cost maxima are $0 \cdot 0209 \; e \, (\overline{\eta - m})$ for Australia and $0 \cdot 0119 \; e \, (\overline{\eta - m})$ for the United States. For reasons already discussed, $e \, (\overline{\eta - m})$ is likely to be less than unity, so that the numerical coefficients overstate the maximums.

constant proportions between goods. This assumption, which implies unit price and income elasticities of demand for all goods and exact offsetting of the income and substitution effects of a change in the price of one good on the quantity demanded of each of the others, permits the consumption cost formula to be simplified [25] to

$$\frac{1}{2}\left[\sum_i e_i \tau_i^2 - \left(\sum_i e_i \tau_i\right)^2\right].$$

This in turn reduces to

$$\frac{1}{2}\tau^2 e\left(1 + \frac{\sigma_\tau^2}{\tau^2} - e\right),$$

where e as before is the proportion in total expenditure of expenditure on goods subject to tariff,

$$\tau = \sum_i \frac{e_i}{e}\tau_i$$

is the weighted-average tariff proportion, the weights being total expenditures on the relevant commodities, and

$$\sigma_\tau^2 = \sum_i \frac{e_i}{e}(\tau_i - \tau)^2$$

[24] See, for example, F.D. Graham, *The Theory of International Values* (Princeton, N.J.: Princeton University Press, 1948) *passim*, esp. pp. 83 ff.

[25] Since $\eta_i = 1$ and $m_i = e_i$, $S_{ii} = e_i(1 - e_i)E$; since S_{ji} must equal $-m_j e_i E$, $s_{ji} = -S_{ji}/S_{ii} = e_j/(1 - e_i)$ (see n. 17 for definitions). Hence the consumption cost formula becomes

$$\frac{1}{2}\sum_i e_i(1 - e_i)\left(\tau_i^2 - \sum_{j \neq i}\frac{e_j}{1 - e_i}\tau_j\tau_i\right)$$

$$= \frac{1}{2}\left(\sum_i e_i \tau_i^2 - \sum_i \sum_j e_i e_j \tau_i \tau_j\right)$$

$$= \frac{1}{2}\left[\sum_i e_i \tau_i^2 - \left(\sum_i e_i \tau_i\right)^2\right].$$

The result follows much more directly from the alternative form given in n. 17, since the assumption implies $\eta_{ii} = 1$, $\eta_{ij} = 0$, $m_i = e_i$.

is the variance of the distribution of τ_i about τ.[26] The expression

$$\frac{1}{2}\tau^2 e\left(1 + \frac{\sigma_\tau^2}{\tau^2} - e\right)$$

has the maximum value of

$$\frac{1}{8}\tau^2\left(1 + \frac{\sigma_\tau^2}{\tau^2}\right)^2$$

when

$$e = \frac{1}{2}\left(1 + \frac{\sigma_\tau^2}{\tau^2}\right).$$

Thus, for example, with $\tau = \frac{1}{3}$ and $\sigma_\tau = \frac{1}{3}\tau$, the maximum possible consumption cost would be less than $1\frac{3}{4}$ per cent of national expenditure, while with $\tau = \frac{1}{4}$ and $\sigma_\tau = \frac{1}{3}\tau$ it would be less than 1 per cent of national expenditure.[27]

The consumption cost of protection is likely to be a small proportion of national expenditure because its calculation involves multiplying together for each commodity four fractions, of which one is $\frac{1}{2}$ and the others are likely to be substantially under $\frac{1}{2}$. The production cost

$$\sum_i (1 - r_i)\tau_i \pi_i,$$

on the other hand, involves multiplying together three fractions, one of which ($[1 - r_i]$, the proportion of real cost in the excess of domestic over foreign value of domestically produced importables) may be unity. This means that the production cost, and hence the total consumption and production cost, may be an appreciable proportion of national expenditure. Such will be the case if large sectors of domestic output are heavily protected and if little of the excess of the internal over the external

[26] The stated result is obtained by expanding the definition of σ_τ^2 and using the definition of τ.

[27] The average tariff rates are 50 per cent and $33\frac{1}{3}$ per cent in the two cases; assuming an approximately normal distribution of τ_i, 99 per cent of the tariff rates will be between 0 per cent and 200 per cent in the first case, and between 0 per cent and 100 per cent in the second. If all tariff rates were identical, the consumption cost would be under 1·4 per cent of total expenditure in the first case and under 0·8 per cent in the second. If $\sigma_\tau = \frac{1}{3}\tau$ is acceptable as corresponding to the maximum dispersion of τ_i, the formula for the maximum consumption cost reduces to $0·1543\,\tau^2$.

price of the product is accounted for by rent. It seems likely, however, that the tariff rate as a proportion of the final price will tend to be small unless the protected production constitutes a small proportion of national expenditure and that some part of the excess of domestic over foreign price will be accounted for by economic rent,[28] so that the production cost will not work out at a very large proportion of national expenditure. This expectation is confirmed by the two major studies previously cited. The Brigden committee estimated the excess cost of protected production at £36 million on a national income of £600 million, making 6 per cent of national income,[29] and Young's estimate of the cash cost of protection came to '3·5 per cent to 4·5 per cent of gross private expenditure net of indirect taxes.'[30] Neither of these estimates makes any deduction for economic rent.[31]

The probability that the consumption and production costs of protection will be small — and that the total will be still smaller when allowance is made for the terms-of-trade benefit it may procure the country [32] — has an important general implication. For, if the cost of protection is a small proportion of

[28] For example, protection may assist the establishment in protected industries of wage levels higher than would otherwise prevail; pressure on wage standards from foreign competition has often been an effective argument for protection. Again, protection may permit profits above the competitive level for the economy.

[29] op. cit., pp. 45, 66.

[30] Op. cit., p. 73.

[31] Cf. Harberger, op. cit., p. 135, where the cost of protection in Chile is estimated at 'no more than 2½ per cent of the national income.' Two calculations relating to the economic effects of European integration also tend to confirm the proposition under discussion, that the costs of protection tend to be small. Tibor Scitovsky estimates the gain from increased specialization at 'less than one-twentieth of one per cent of the gross social product of the countries involved' (Economic Theory and Western European Integration [Stanford, Calif.: University Press, 1958] p. 67). I have estimated the gain to Britain from the formation of a Free Trade Area as at most 1 per cent of national income ('The Gain from Freer Trade with Europe: An Estimate,' Manchester School of Economic and Social Studies, Vol. XXVI, No. 3 [September 1958] pp. 247—55). Both calculations use estimates of changes in trade patterns prepared by other writers and open to serious objections.

[32] For the two-goods case, the net cost of protection allowing for the terms-of-trade effect can readily be expressed in terms of the (compensated) elasticity of demand for imports and the foreign elasticity of supply of imports (or elasticity of demand for exports). Let $D = Ae^{-\eta p'}$ be the compensated demand for imports of the country with the tariff, p' being the internal price and η the compensated elasticity of demand for imports, and $S = Be^{\epsilon p}$ be the foreign supply of imports, p being the foreign price and ϵ the elasticity of supply (which can be replaced by the foreign elasticity of demand for exports through the relation $\epsilon = \eta - 1$). Let p_0 and $p'_0 = (1 + t)p_0$ be the initial equilibrium prices, where t is the tariff rate; equality of demand and supply initially requires that the constants in the two equations have the relationship $A/B = e^{(\epsilon + \eta + \eta t)p_0}$.

With free trade the equilibrium price p_f must be such that

$$e^{(\epsilon + \eta)p_f} = A/B = e^{(\epsilon + \eta + \eta t)p_0},$$

whence

$$p_f = \left(1 + \frac{\eta}{\epsilon + \eta} t\right)p_0.$$

The gain in consumers' surplus from the adoption of free trade is the area under the demand curve between the two domestic prices,

$$\int_{p_f}^{p'_0} Ae^{-\eta p'}\, dp' = -\frac{1}{\eta} Ae^{-\eta (1+t)p_0} + \frac{1}{\eta} Ae^{-\eta (1 + \eta t/(\epsilon + \eta))p_0}$$

$$= \frac{1}{\eta} Ae^{-\eta (1+t)p_0}(e^{(\eta \epsilon t/(\epsilon + \eta))p_0} - 1).$$

From this must be deducted the loss of tariff revenue formerly received,

$$tp_0 Ae^{-\eta (1+t)p_0}.$$

so that the net gain, simplified by putting $p'_0 = (1 + t)p_0 = 1$ and using T, is

$$\frac{1}{\eta} Ae^{-\eta}(e^{(\eta \epsilon/(\eta + \epsilon))T} - T\eta - 1).$$

The larger expression in parentheses can easily be negative, indicating a net gain from protection. For example, if foreign and domestic elasticities of import demand are equal ($\epsilon = \eta - 1$), a gain from free trade requires that they be above 6 if $T = \frac{1}{2}$ and above 11 if $T = \frac{1}{4}$. If the elasticity of domestic demand for imports is 1, the foreign elasticity of demand must be above 5 for $T = \frac{1}{2}$ and above 9 for $T = \frac{1}{4}$ for a gain to result from free trade.

the level of national income at any point of time and if protectionists happen to be correct in their claim that protection increases an economy's rate of growth, the increase does not have to be very great for its effect in raising national income to counterbalance the reduction due to the cost of protection within relatively few years. For example, if protection reduced national income by 5 per cent below the free-trade level but raised the rate of growth from 2½ per cent to 3 per cent per annum, in about 10¾ years national income would be at the level it would have reached under free trade, and growing more rapidly than it would have under free trade; if the rate of growth rose only from 2½ per cent to 2¾ per cent, the free-trade level of national income would be reached in about 21⅓ years.[33] The gain of an increasingly higher income after a relatively short space of years might well be worth the cost of a lower income in the immediate future.[34] Hence the effect of alternative commercial policies on the rate of growth may well be the quantitatively significant issue in the free trade versus protection debate.

---

[33] Let r and r' be the annual growth rates under free trade and protection, c be the cost of protection as a proportion of free-trade national income, and n be the number of years after which national income under the two alternative commercial policies would be equal. n is determined by the equation

$$(1 + r)^n = (1 + r')^n(1 - c),$$

or

$$1 + \frac{r - r'}{1 + r'} = (1 - C)^{1/n};$$

expanding the right-hand side by Taylor's series gives

$$\frac{r' - r}{1 + r'} = \frac{c}{n} + \frac{1}{2}\left(\frac{c}{n}\right)^2 (n - 1) + \frac{1}{6}\left(\frac{c}{n}\right)^3 (n - 1)(n - 2) + \dots .$$

The values of n given above are calculated from the first two terms on the right-hand side.

(Edward F. Denison has subsequently, and rightly, criticized this argument on the grounds that the small percentage point increases in the growth rate cited are in fact 20 per cent and 10 per cent increases in the growth rate, 'huge increases by any reasonable standard.' See his *The Sources of Economic Growth in the United States* [Washington Committee for Economic Development, 1962] p. 6, n. 2.)

II. THE SCIENTIFIC TARIFF

The idea of a scientific tariff is an old one, popular with propagandists and legislators as a means for lending prestige to their peculative propensities but largely discredited among economists because the way in which the idea is usually expressed — equalization of the costs of production between domestic and foreign sources of supply — is meaningless unless some standard of efficiency is laid down for domestic industry.[35] At one extreme, ability to compete in world markets implies that free trade is the only scientific tariff; at the other extreme, ability to produce at some cost level implies that prohibition is the only scientific tariff. But the ridicule of economists has so far failed to eradicate the notion of a

---

[34] The net welfare effect of an immediately lower and ultimately higher national income can only be assessed by reference to some sort of intertemporal social choice function. The simplest form of such an intertemporal choice function is a social rate of time preference, by which future income is discounted. Assuming for the sake of argument a higher growth rate with protection than with free trade, it is evident that protection must be socially preferable if the growth rate it produces exceeds the social rate of time preference; if the social rate of time preference exceeds the growth rate with protection, protection will still be superior to free trade if the proportion by which protection reduces potential national income is less than the ratio of the excess of the protection over the free-trade growth rate to the excess of the social rate of time preference over the free-trade growth rate. The free-trade income stream is $Y_t = Y_0(1 + r)^t$, and the protection income stream is $Y'_t = (1 - c)Y_0(1 + r')^t$. If s, the social rate of time preference, is less than r', the present value of the protection income stream is infinite, and the contribution of the income of progressively remoter years to the present value of the income stream is progressively greater for the protection than for the free-trade stream. If s is greater than r', the present values of the free-trade and protection income streams are

$$Y_0 \frac{1 + s}{s - r}$$

and

$$Y_0 \frac{(1 - c)(1 + s)}{s - r'},$$

the latter exceeding the former if c is less than $(r' - r)/(s - r)$.

[35] The argument of this section is confined to static analysis. The 'dynamic' arguments for protection obviously lead to the notion of a dynamic 'scientific tariff' whose structure could be analysed on lines paralleling those developed below.

scientific tariff, and it seems perfectly possible, and indeed desirable in the interests of efficient economic policy, to give content to it by applying the maximization and minimization principles of economic rationality.

Existing theory of economic welfare already suggests one approach to a scientific tariff. This would be the tariff which would correct divergences between marginal social and marginal private costs brought about by disequilibrium pricing of factors and external economies and diseconomies, including divergences between marginal revenue or marginal cost and price in the country's international trade owing to imperfectly elastic foreign demands for its exports and supplies of its imports (the 'optimum tariff' argument), wherever such divergences of social and private costs could appropriately be remedied by the tariff. By extension, a scientific tariff of this kind could comprise using the tariff where the most appropriate remedy is somehow ruled out and where the tariff would produce some improvement. In other words, the tariff might be used to implement 'second-best' welfare economics as well as 'optimum' welfare economics.[36]

Such a concept of the scientific tariff follows directly from the modern theory of welfare economics. But it is not the concept of a scientific tariff which tariff advocates who use the term seem to have in mind. Instead, these people want to use the tariff as a means of promoting non-economic objectives of various kinds, identified in one way or another with the effects of the tariff on domestic production and consumption of certain products. The notion of a scientific tariff seems to comprise an inchoate notion of a balancing of results achieved against costs incurred. So conceived, the construction of a scientific tariff presupposes definition in quantitative terms of the beneficial results to be achieved by protection and attachment of values to the achievement of different amounts of these beneficial results, values that can be weighed against the cost of protection discussed in the previous section. It entails the

---

[36] See R.G. Lipsey and R.K. Lancaster, 'The General Theory of Second Best,' *Review of Economic Studies*, Vol. XXIV (1), No. 63 (October 1956) pp. 11–32.

dual process (exactly parallel to profit maximization in the individual firm or utility maximization in the household) of minimizing the cost of achieving each amount of benefit by adjusting the structure of tariff rates in order to equalize the ratio of marginal benefit to marginal cost in each industry protected and of maximizing the benefits of protection by selecting the general level of protection at which marginal value of benefit from protection equals marginal cost of protection.[37] About the second part of this process there is little of theoretical interest to be said, but the first raises the interesting problem of the quantitative definition of the benefits of protection, and the resulting characteristics of the scientific tariff structure, that can be associated with various common arguments for protection.

To analyse this problem, it is convenient to measure the cost of protection from the free-trade rather than the tariff position; in terms of Figure 2, this involves drawing dd' for the free-trade utility level and measuring quantities in units such that the free-trade price (Op) is initially unity and the difference between it and the tariff-inclusive price (Op') is the proportional tariff rate t. To simplify the problem of the scientific tariff structure, two further assumptions are made in addition to those set out for the many-good case in Section I. The first is that demand and supply conditions are such that some of each commodity is produced domestically under free trade and imported under the tariff; this allows the cost of protection to be written as

$$\frac{1}{2} \sum_i t_i (dP_i + dC_i).$$

The second, and much more limiting, assumption is that cross-effects of a change in the price of one commodity on the

[37] As mentioned in the Introduction, this conception of the scientific tariff derives from Young's study of the Canadian tariff (*op. cit.*, Chap. IX). Young does not, however, discuss the selection of the general level of protection, assuming merely that a maximum economic cost is set for the tariff authority, and he does not discuss the tariff structures corresponding to alternative tariff objectives but confines his argument to the first objective considered below and qualifications to it.

211

quantities of the others produced and consumed can be neglected.[38] This allows the cost of protection to be written as

$$\frac{1}{2} \sum_i t_i^2 (P_i \epsilon_i + C_i \eta_i),$$

where P_i and C_i are the quantities produced and consumed under free trade and ϵ_i and η_i are (compensated) own-price elasticities of supply and demand for the ith commodity. In other words, the cost of protecting a particular commodity varies only with its own tariff rate; similarly, the decrease in quantity of consumption $(t_i C_i \eta_i)$, increase in quantity $(t_i P_i \epsilon_i)$ and value $(t_i P_i [1 + \epsilon_i + \epsilon_i t_i])$ of domestic production, decrease in quantity and value of imports $(t_i [P_i \epsilon_i + C_i \eta_i])$, increase in ratio of domestic production to consumption $([P_i/C_i][\epsilon_i + \eta_i]t_i)$, and increase in employment in the domestic industry $(l_i t_i P_i \epsilon_i$, where l_i is labour per unit of output) resulting from protection all vary only with the tariff rate for the particular commodity concerned. From these formulas it follows that a tariff imposed on the ith industry achieves a marginal decrease in consumption of $(C_i \eta_i)$, increase in quantity of domestic production $(P_i \epsilon_i)$, increase in value of domestic production $(P_i + P_i \epsilon_i + 2 \epsilon_i P_i t_i)$, decrease in quantity and value of imports $(P_i \epsilon_i + C_i \eta_i)$, increase in ratio of domestic production to consumption $([P_i/C_i]\epsilon_i + [P_i/C_i]\eta_i)$, and increase in employment $(l_i P_i \epsilon_i)$, at a marginal cost of $(t_i P_i \epsilon_i + t_i C_i \eta_i)$. These are the marginal quantities used in the following analysis.

The number of recognized common arguments for protection is large; moreover, serious consideration of the criteria of benefit that might be associated with any one of them quickly leads to recognition of a need for the drawing of complex and subtle distinctions among industries and products of various sorts. The following treatment attempts only a listing of the common arguments and a brief analysis of the criteria of benefit and corresponding scientific tariff structures that might be associated

---

[38] Compare J. deV. Graaff, *Theoretical Welfare Economics* (Cambridge: Cambridge University Press, 1957) Chap. IX 'Foreign Trade', esp. p. 131 (bottom). Scientific tariff formulas for the general case could be developed, with mathematical effort, along lines similar to Graaff's formulas for optimum taxes, or formulas developed by Boiteux, *loc. cit.*

with them, ignoring differences in the 'quality' of different industries for protective purposes.[39]

(a) *A tariff to promote national self-sufficiency and independence.* The simplest possible measure of the benefit achieved by such a tariff is the value of imports excluded by it. On this criterion, the ratio of marginal cost to marginal benefit in the ith industry is simply t_i, and the scientific tariff structure, which requires equation of this ratio in all industries, is a uniform tariff rate on all imports. This is the tariff structure usually recommended by international trade theorists to countries wedded to protectionism,[40] but it is the scientific tariff for import exclusion only on the simplifying assumptions of the present argument, which exclude cross-effects in production and consumption. Also, as will be seen, it is not the scientific tariff for other tariff objectives.

This point can be readily illustrated by considering a more sophisticated concept of national independence than import exclusion, that is, one which measures the benefit of protection by the resulting increase in the proportion of consumption supplied from domestic production. On this alternative criterion, the ratio of marginal cost to marginal benefit is

$$t_i C_i \left(1 + \frac{C_i - P_i}{P_i} \cdot \frac{\eta_i}{\epsilon_i + \eta_i} \right);$$

and the implied scientific tariff structure entails tariff rates which are higher the higher the elasticity of supply, the lower the elasticity of demand, the lower the free-trade quantity consumed, and the higher the free-trade quantity domestically produced (or ratio of domestic production to consumption) of the commodity concerned.

[39] In addition, the argument is confined to import duties; a fully worked-out scientific tariff would presumably entail interferences with exports as well.

[40] See, for example, W.M. Corden, 'Import Restrictions and Tariffs: A New Look at Australian Policy,' *Economic Record*, Vol. XXIV, No. 69 (December 1958) pp. 331–46; and Gottfried Haberler, *International Trade and Economic Development* (Cairo: National Bank of Egypt, 1959) esp. pp. 35–36.

(b) *A tariff to promote diversification, industrialization, or agriculturalization.*

A number of different arguments for protection have as their objective to change the productive structure of the economy by encouraging certain favoured lines of production. The benefit of such a policy (in the simplest case, where the various industries protected are assigned the same value) may be measured either by the increase in the quantity of desired production or by the increase in the income earned in the various industries. Where the amount of protected production is the criterion, the ratio of marginal cost to marginal benefit is

$$t_i \left(1 + \frac{C_i}{P_i} \cdot \frac{\eta_i}{\epsilon_i} \right),$$

and the scientific tariff rate will be higher the higher the elasticity of supply, the lower the elasticity of demand, and the higher the ratio of free-trade production to free-trade consumption, for the commodity subject to that rate. Where the amount of protected income is the criterion, the marginal cost to marginal benefit ratio is

$$t_i \left(\frac{\epsilon_i + \frac{C_i}{P_i} \eta_i}{1 + \epsilon_i + 2 \epsilon_i t_i} \right),$$

and the scientific tariff rate on a commodity will be higher the higher the free-trade ratio of domestic production to consumption, the lower the elasticity of demand, and the higher the elasticity of supply unless the elasticity of demand is very low — to be precise, unless

$$\eta_i < \frac{P_i}{C_i} (1 + 2t_i).$$

(c) *A tariff to promote a 'way of life'.*

This argument for protection, whose most familiar form is probably the assertion that farming is such a desirable way of life that farmers should be subsidized heavily to put up with it, indicates the amount of protected employment (as contrasted

214

with protected production or income) as the simplest measure of benefit. The ratio of marginal cost to marginal benefit in this case is

$$\frac{t_i}{l_i} \left(1 + \frac{C_i \eta_i}{P_i \epsilon_i} \right).$$

The scientific tariff rate on a commodity whose production constitutes a desirable way of life will be higher the higher its labour requirement per unit of output, the higher its free-trade ratio of domestic output to consumption, the higher its elasticity of supply, and the lower its elasticity of demand.[41]

(d) A tariff to increase military preparedness.

The argument here is that the country's military preparedness is increased by using tariff protection to maintain a higher level of domestic production of certain strategic commodities than would be produced under free trade. The simplest definition of benefit would be one or other of the two discussed under (a) above, restricted to commodities defined as strategic, and the structure of the corresponding scientific tariff would have the same characteristics. Either measure might be further elaborated by valuing industries according to their degree of strategic importance, which valuations might be related to the time required to adjust to the likely loss of imported supplies in the event of war.

The degree of military preparedness might depend on the presence or absence of minimum productive capacities in certain strategic defense industries rather than on the levels actually achieved. In that case, determination of the scientific tariff would require determining the cost of giving each such industry the protection necessary to insure the minimum required capacity and choosing that combination of industries for protection which afforded the maximum defense potential for the optimal level of defense protection.

[41] The 'way of life' argument is similar to, but essentially different from, the argument for imposing a tariff in order to increase the population-sustaining power of the economy. While the model employed here suggests the characteristics of a scientific tariff designed for that purpose, it can only provide a crude approach to the problem, which assumes that the supply of labour depends upon the real wage and that the cost of protection falls on other factors.

(e) *A bargaining tariff.*

The tariff arguments so far discussed are concerned with the attainment of objectives that can be defined in terms of domestic economic variables and the achievement of which depends on domestic elasticities and magnitudes. The bargaining tariff, in contrast, is aimed at inflicting economic damage upon another country or countries in order to obtain advantageous tariff concessions. The infliction of such damage depends on the elasticities of foreign supply of imports and demand for exports being less than perfectly elastic, so that investigation of the scientific bargaining tariff requires modification of the assumption on which most of the argument of this chapter is based — that world prices of exports and imports are constant. For simplicity, it will be assumed that export prices remain fixed, so that the foreigner can only be damaged through the dependence of import prices on quantities demanded, and that cross-relations between prices and quantities abroad can be ignored, so that the price of a particular import depends only on the quantity of it demanded and the elasticity of foreign supply of exports of it to the importing country.

The imposition of a tariff on imports of a particular commodity reduces the quantity of it demanded and so reduces its foreign price, so that the domestic price rises by less than the amount of the tariff. The cost of protecting the commodity is the production and consumption cost of the rise in the internal price *minus* the gain from the reduction in the price of the quantity of imports which survives after the tariff; this cost may be negative. The benefit from protection (loss inflicted on the foreigner) is the loss of the foreigner's exporter's surplus due to the fall in the price of his exports. The ratio of the marginal cost of protection to the marginal benefit from it is

$$\frac{\sigma_i(\sigma_i + z_i)t_i}{z_i + \sigma_i + z_i t_i - \sigma_i z_i t_i} - 1,$$

where σ_i is the elasticity of foreign supply of imports and z_i is the (compensated) elasticity of domestic demand for imports.[42] From this it follows that the scientific bargaining tariff on a particular commodity will be higher the lower the elasticity of

[42] Let M_i be the initial quantity of imports, T_i the amount of tariff collected per unit of imports, and Δp_i the reduction in the foreign price of imports from unity due to the effect of the tariff on demand. Since the reduction in imports demanded must be equal to the reduction in imports supplied, we must have

$$(T_i - \Delta p_i) M_i z_i = (\Delta p_i) M_i \sigma_i$$

whence

$$\Delta p_i = \frac{z_i}{z_i + \sigma_i} T_i,$$

where

$$z_i = \frac{P_i \epsilon_i + C_i \eta_i}{C_i - P_i}$$

is the country's (compensated) elasticity of demand for imports and σ_i is the foreign elasticity of supply of imports. The cost of protection to the country is

$$\tfrac{1}{2}(T_i - \Delta p_i)^2 M_i z_i - (\Delta p_i)(M_i - \Delta p_i M_i \sigma_i)$$
$$= \frac{1}{2} \frac{z_i T_i M_i}{(\sigma_i + z_i)^2} (\sigma_i^2 T_i - 2\sigma_i - 2z_i + 2z_i \sigma_i T_i).$$

The benefit (loss inflicted on the foreigner) is

$$(\Delta p_i)(M_i - \Delta p_i M_i \sigma_i) + \tfrac{1}{2}(\Delta p_i)^2 M_i \sigma_i$$
$$= \frac{1}{2} \frac{z_i T_i M_i}{(\sigma_i + z_i)^2} (2z_i + 2\sigma_i - \sigma_i z_i t_i).$$

The marginal cost of protection is

$$\frac{z_i M_i}{(\sigma_i + z_i)^2} (\sigma_i^2 T_i - \sigma_i - z_i + 2z_i \sigma_i M_i)$$

while the marginal benefit is

$$\frac{z_i M_i}{(\sigma_i + z_i)^2} (z_i + \sigma_i - \sigma_i z_i M_i).$$

Hence the ratio of marginal cost to marginal benefit is

$$\frac{\sigma_i(\sigma_i + 2z_i) T_i - (\sigma_i + z_i)}{z_i + \sigma_i - \sigma_i z_i T_i}.$$

But T_i has been defined as the amount of tariff collected, not the tariff

domestic demand for them (that is, the lower the elasticities of domestic demand and supply of imports and the higher the proportion of consumption supplied from domestic output).

It would be as well to reiterate that the foregoing analysis is intended to be no more than a sketch of what might be involved in the notion of a scientific tariff. The variety of scientific tariff structures implicit in different arguments for protection points to what is probably the fundamental problem in giving concrete content to the notion — the difficulty of reconciling conflicting objectives of protection in a single scientific tariff structure.

Footnote continued

rate, which as a proportion of the new price of imports is

$$t_i = \frac{T_i}{1 - \Delta p_i} = \frac{T_i(\sigma_i + z_i)}{\sigma_i + z_i - z_i T_i}.$$

Substitution for T_i from this expression gives the result in the text; in establishing the influence of σ_i by differentiation, it is necessary to make use of the fact that the denominator of the fraction is positive.

It should be remarked that the formula for the scientific bargaining tariff is different from, and more complicated than, the formula for the optimum tariff. On the present assumptions, the formula for the latter is simply $t_i = 1/\sigma_i$ (cf. Graaff, *op. cit.*, p. 132).

9. The Costs of Protection and Self-Sufficiency*

I. INTRODUCTION

One of the interesting problems in the theory of commercial policy concerns the magnitude of the gains from trade, and the extent to which protective policies may reduce real income below its potential maximum and may account for differences in real income among nations. As is well known, for a country small enough that its terms of trade are unaffected by its commercial policy, the loss of real income due to protection can be divided into two elements – the consumption cost resulting from the distortion of prices facing consumers away from the prices ruling in the world market, which represent the social alternative opportunity costs of commodities to the country, and the production cost resulting from the distortion of prices facing producers away from world market prices, which represent the social benefits from producing alternative commodities. Previous analyses of the cost of protection have applied the apparatus of the Hicksian compensation tests to these elements in the cost of protection, and have derived expressions for the total cost of protection in terms of elasticities of (compensated) demand and supply;[1] these analyses in effect explore the implications for economic welfare of small departures from free trade. This chapter presents an alternative approach to the problem, one that works with an explicit social utility function and transformation curve and is therefore not restricted to small departures from free trade. The results are, on the other hand, limited by the specific character of the utility and transformation

* The Quarterly Journal of Economics, Vol. LXXII, No. 3 (August 1965) pp. 356–72.

[1] See, for example, Harry G. Johnson, 'The Cost of Protection and the Scientific Tariff,' Journal of Political Economy, Vol. LXVII (Aug. 1960) pp. 327–45, reprinted as Chapter 8 above.

functions employed, though these functions are flexible enough to comprise a wide range of practical possibilities.

II. CONCEPTION OF THE PROBLEM

For purposes of analysis, the imposition of a tariff can be treated as equivalent to two other fiscal operations: the imposition of a tax on the consumption of the protected commodity, the proceeds of which are returned to the community as a general income subsidy, and the granting of a subsidy to domestic production of the protected commodity, the cost of which is financed by a general income tax. (To the extent that net imports occur, the income subsidy exceeds the income tax, the difference representing the excess of the domestic over the world market cost of imports.) The consumption tax, by making domestic prices to consumers different from foreign prices, induces a socially nonoptimal consumption pattern, reducing the level of utility achieved with a given real income (valued at world market prices) below the maximum attainable if consumers were free to allocate their incomes to consumption at world market prices. This reduction in utility below the attainable maximum measures the consumption cost of protection. The production subsidy, by making domestic prices to producers different from foreign prices, induces a socially nonoptimal production pattern, reducing the real output of the community (valued at world market prices) below the maximum attainable if producers were free to allocate resources to production at world market prices. This reduction in real output measures the production cost of protection. Protection, which has the joint effect of a consumption tax and a production subsidy, reduces the utility enjoyed by the community both by reducing real output below the maximum attainable and by reducing the utility attainable by the expenditure of the reduced real output below the potential maximum. The total reduction in utility from these two causes is the total cost of protection.

The analysis that follows is concerned with the quantitative magnitudes of the consumption, production, and total costs of protection. For this purpose, I assume a country consuming and capable of producing two commodities, X and Y, and specify a utility function and transformation curve representing its tastes and transformation possibilities. Without loss of generality, the two goods can be measured in units such that they exchange at a price ratio of one for one in the world market. It should be observed that while the analysis is confined to the two-good case, both the utility function and the transformation curve can be readily extended to any number of commodities. The analysis begins by treating the consumption cost and the production cost of protection separately — these sections can be interpreted as analyses of the 'burdens' of consumption taxes and production subsidies — and then proceeds to the total cost of protection. The analysis of consumption and production costs deals with the costs of protection at various tariff rates; the analysis of the total cost of protection concentrates for simplicity on the cost of the protection required to achieve self-sufficiency. The chapter concludes with some remarks on the general impli-cations of the findings.

III. THE CONSUMPTION COST OF PROTECTION

The social utility function is assumed to be of the C.E.S. or homohypallagic type[2]

$$U = (AX^{-\beta} + aY^{-\beta})^{-(1/\beta)}$$

where A and a are constants governing the division of expendi-ture between commodity X, assumed in what follows to be the export good, and commodity Y, assumed in what follows to be the import good, and β is a constant incorporating the elasticity of substitution σ through the relationship $1/(\beta + 1) = \sigma$. This function implies unit income elasticities of demands for the two goods; but the elasticity of substitution is a parameter that can be varied according to choice. The function also

[2] For a detailed description of the properties of this function, see B. Minhas, 'The Homohypallagic Production Function, Factor-Intensity Reversals, and the Heckscher-Ohlin Theorem,' *Journal of Political Economy*, Vol. LXX (April 1962) pp. 138—56; unfortunately, this refer-ence contains some mathematical errors.

implies that the marginal utility of income is constant.[3]

The marginal utilities of the two goods are

$$U_x = A\left(\frac{U}{X}\right)^{\beta+1}$$

$$U_y = a\left(\frac{U}{Y}\right)^{\beta+1}.$$

(2)

Given a tax t on the consumption of Y, utility will be maximized when

$$\frac{U_y}{U_x} = \frac{a}{A}\left(\frac{X}{Y}\right)^{\beta+1} = 1 + t;$$

(3)

or

$$\frac{X}{Y} = \left[\frac{A}{a}(1+t)\right]^{1/(\beta+1)}.$$

(4)

Given a total income fixed in terms of world prices,

$$M = X + Y,$$

(5)

implying that tax revenues collected on consumption of Y are returned to the community as income subsidies, consumption of the two goods, determined by equations (4) and (5), will be

$$X = \frac{\left[\frac{A}{a}(1+t)\right]^{1/(\beta+1)}}{1 + \left[\frac{A}{a}(1+t)\right]^{1/(\beta+1)}} M$$

(6)

---

[3] Economists have customarily assumed that the marginal utility of income falls as total income and consumption increase. The assumption of constant marginal utility of income can be defended as an adequate approximation for small changes, such as most of those considered in this article turn out to be; and it is implied by the common use of national income per capita as a measure of economic welfare. If the marginal utility of income is assumed to be falling instead of constant, the figures in the subsequent tables will overstate the percentage losses of utility resulting from protection; readers can make whatever corrections they wish on this basis. It is scarcely necessary to remark that assumptions about the marginal utility of income represent a welfare judgment, and that hypotheses about its behaviour can only be tested in situations of choice involving risky alternatives.

and

$$Y = \frac{1}{1 + \left[\frac{A}{a}(1 + t)\right]^{1/(\beta + 1)}} M \qquad (6)$$

Hence, substituting (6) into (1), total utility as a function of real income and the tariff rate will be

$$U = \left[\left(\frac{A}{a}\right)^{1/(\beta + 1)} (1 + t)^{-\beta/(\beta + 1)} + 1\right]^{-1/\beta} \frac{a^{-1/\beta} M}{1 + \left[\frac{A}{a}(1 + t)\right]^{1/(\beta + 1)}} \qquad (7)$$

The ratio of utility enjoyed with the tax to utility enjoyed in the absence of the tax (income at world prices remaining constant) will be

$$\frac{U_t}{U_0} = \frac{\left[\left(\frac{A}{a}\right)^{1/(\beta + 1)} (1 + t)^{-\beta/(\beta + 1)} + 1\right]^{-1/\beta}}{\left[\left(\frac{A}{a}\right)^{1/(\beta + 1)} + 1\right]^{-1/\beta}}$$

$$\times \frac{1 + \left(\frac{A}{a}\right)^{1/(\beta + 1)}}{1 + \left[\frac{A}{a}(1 + t)\right]^{1/(\beta + 1)}} \qquad (8)$$

From (4), it follows that $(A/a)^{1/(\beta + 1)} = R$, where R is the ratio of X to Y consumed in the absence of a tariff. In turn, $R = r/(1 - r)$, where $r = X/M$ is the proportion of income spent on consumption of X in the absence of the tariff and can be conveniently used as a parameter representing different preference possibilities. Substituting for A/a in terms of R and for β in terms of σ, the elasticity of substitution, (8) becomes

$$\frac{U_t}{U_0} = \frac{[R(1 + t)^{\sigma - 1} + 1]^{\sigma/(\sigma - 1)}}{1 + R(1 + t)^{\sigma}} (R + 1)^{1/(1 - \sigma)}. \qquad (9)$$

It can readily be shown that U_t/U_0 decreases as t increases.

The expression given in equation (9) is difficult to manage for the case of a unit elasticity of substitution; for that special case, however, direct manipulation of the Cobb-Douglas utility

223

function $U = X^r Y^{1-r}$ yields the simpler expression

$$\frac{U_t}{U_0} = \frac{(1 + t)^r}{1 + rt.} \tag{10}$$

The ratio U_t/U_0 given in equations (9) and (10) represents the consumption cost of protection: the difference between U_t/U_0 and unity is the proportion by which the tariff-induced distortion of the prices facing consumers away from social opportunity costs reduces the utility attainable from a given real income (measured at world market prices) below the maximum attainable from spending that income at world market prices.

Calculated values of the consumption cost of protection $[1 - (U_t/U_0)]$ for ranges of values of r and σ and selected values of t are shown in Tables IA to IC. A general feature of the Tables is that the cost increases steadily with the elasticity of substitution, while for any given elasticity of substitution the maximum cost for a given tariff rate at first rises and then declines with r (the proportion of income spent on the untaxed good in the absence of the tariff), the maximum-cost value of r falling as t increases and as σ increases. The significant characteristic of the numbers themselves is that the consumption cost of protection turns out to be relatively small, except for combinations of high tariff rates and high elasticities of substitution. Thus for a tariff rate of 20 per cent and an elasticity of substitution of 2·50 or less, the maximum consumption cost barely surpasses 1 per cent, and does not rise to 1¼ per cent even with an elasticity of substitution of 3·00. For a tariff rate of 60 per cent, the maximum consumption cost is less than 5·4 per cent for elasticities of substitution up to 2·00, and less than 7·8 per cent for $\sigma = 3·00$. For the highest tariff rate shown, 100 per cent, the maximum consumption cost is less than 3 per cent for an elasticity of substitution of 0·50, and less than 6 per cent for a unit elasticity of substitution, though it rises to nearly 16 per cent for an elasticity of substitution of 3·00.

TABLE IA. *Consumption cost* $(1 - U_t/U_0)$ *of a 20 per cent tariff for various values of r and σ (in percentages of U_0)*

$r\backslash\sigma$	0·25	0·50	0·75	1·00	1·25	1·50	1·75	2·00	2·50	3·00
·05	0·02	0·04	0·06	0·08	0·11	0·13	0·16	0·19	0·25	0·31
·10	0·04	0·07	0·11	0·16	0·20	0·25	0·29	0·34	0·45	0·57
·15	0·05	0·11	0·16	0·22	0·28	0·34	0·41	0·48	0·62	0·77
·20	0·07	0·13	0·20	0·27	0·35	0·43	0·51	0·59	0·76	0·94
·25	0·08	0·16	0·24	0·32	0·41	0·49	0·58	0·68	0·86	1·06
·30	0·09	0·17	0·26	0·36	0·45	0·55	0·64	0·74	0·94	1·15
·35	0·09	0·19	0·29	0·38	0·48	0·58	0·69	0·79	1·00	1·21
·40	0·10	0·20	0·30	0·40	0·51	0·61	0·71	0·82	1·02	1·23
·45	0·10	0·21	0·31	0·41	0·52	0·62	0·72	0·83	1·03	1·23
·50	0·10	0·21	0·31	0·41	0·52	0·62	0·72	0·82	1·02	1·21
·60	0·10	0·20	0·30	0·39	0·49	0·58	0·67	0·76	0·93	1·09
·70	0·09	0·17	0·26	0·34	0·42	0·50	0·57	0·64	0·78	0·91
·80	0·07	0·13	0·20	0·26	0·31	0·37	0·42	0·47	0·57	0·65
·90	0·04	0·07	0·11	0·14	0·17	0·20	0·23	0·26	0·31	0·35

TABLE IB. *Consumption cost* $(1 - U_t/U_0)$ *of a 60 per cent tariff for various values of r and σ (in percentages of U_0)*

$r\backslash\sigma$	0·25	0·50	0·75	1·00	1·25	1·50	1·75	2·00	2·50	3·00
·05	0·12	0·26	0·42	0·60	0·81	1·04	1·30	1·59	2·26	3·08
·10	0·23	0·50	0·79	1·12	1·48	1·89	2·32	2·80	3·87	5·09
·15	0·33	0·70	1·11	1·56	2·04	2·56	3·12	3·72	5·01	6·39
·20	0·42	0·88	1·38	1·91	2·49	3·09	3·73	4·39	5·77	7·19
·25	0·50	1·03	1·60	2·20	2·83	3·49	4·17	4·86	6·25	7·62
·30	0·56	1·15	1·77	2·43	3·09	3·77	4·46	5·15	6·51	7·78
·35	0·61	1·25	1·90	2·58	3·26	3·95	4·63	5·30	6·58	7·74
·40	0·65	1·31	1·99	2·67	3·36	4·03	4·68	5·32	6·50	7·54
·45	0·67	1·35	2·04	2·71	3·38	4·02	4·64	5·23	6·31	7·22
·50	0·69	1·37	2·04	2·70	3·33	3·94	4·62	5·06	6·01	6·80
·60	0·67	1·31	1·93	2·52	3·06	3·57	4·04	4·46	5·18	5·73
·70	0·59	1·15	1·67	2·14	2·57	2·96	3·31	3·61	4·11	4·46
·80	0·46	0·88	1·26	1·59	1·89	2·15	2·37	2·56	2·86	3·06
·90	0·26	0·50	0·70	0·87	1·02	1·15	1·26	1·35	1·48	1·56

TABLE 1C. *Consumption cost* $(1 - U_t/U_0)$ *of a 100 per cent tariff for for various values of* τ *and* σ *(in percentages of* U_0)

	0·25	0·50	0·75	1·00	1·25	1·50	1·75	2·00	2·50	3·00
·05	0·26	0·57	0·95	1·40	1·94	2·56	3·29	4·13	6·15	8·65
·10	0·49	1·08	1·77	2·57	3·48	4·51	5·66	6·92	9·74	12·81
·15	0·70	1·52	2·46	3·52	4·69	5·97	7·34	8·79	11·82	14·83
·20	0·89	1·90	3·03	4·28	5·61	7·03	8·50	10·00	12·96	15·67
·25	1·05	2·22	3·50	4·86	6·29	7·77	9·25	10·71	13·47	15·82
·30	1·19	2·48	3·86	5·30	6·76	8·23	9·67	11·05	13·53	15·52
·35	1·30	2·69	4·12	5·59	7·05	8·47	9·83	11·10	13·28	14·92
·40	1·39	2·83	4·29	5·75	7·17	8·51	9·77	10·91	12·80	14·13
·45	1·45	2·92	4·37	5·79	7·14	8·39	9·52	10·53	12·13	13·19
·50	1·48	2·94	4·37	5·72	6·97	8·11	9·13	10·00	11·34	12·16
·60	1·45	2·83	4·11	5·27	6·30	7·19	7·95	8·57	9·45	9·90
·70	1·30	2·48	3·53	4·44	5·21	5·85	6·37	6·77	7·29	7·49
·80	1·02	1·90	2·65	3·27	3·78	4·18	4·48	4·71	4·96	5·01
·90	0·59	1·08	1·47	1·79	2·03	2·21	2·34	2·43	2·51	2·54

IV. THE PRODUCTION COST OF PROTECTION

The transformation curve is assumed to be of the form

$$x^2 + mxy + y^2 = K^2, \tag{11}$$

where lower-case letters are used to denote quantities produced (as distinct from quantities consumed, denoted in the preceding section by upper case letters).[4] In the equation, K^2 is a constant, and m is a parameter which may range between $+2$ and 0 without violating the usual restrictions on the shape of the transformation curve. If $m = +2$, the transformation curve is a straight line; if $m = 0$, the transformation curve is a quarter circle (for x, $y \geqslant 0$).

---

[4] Though it would be both more elegant and more in keeping with modern trade theory to derive the transformation curve from the underlying production functions for the two commodities, the results of attempting to do so are unmanageably cumbersome.

The marginal rate of transformation of x into y is

$$-\frac{dx}{dy} = \frac{mx + 2y}{2x + my}. \tag{12}$$

Maximum value of output at domestic prices requires equality of the marginal rate of transformation of x into y with the price of y in terms of x,

$$\frac{mx + 2y}{2x + my} = p = 1 + t, \tag{13}$$

where t is the tariff rate or rate of subsidy on domestic production of y. Setting $x = 0$ yields the tariff or subsidy rate required to induce the economy to specialize entirely on the production of y,

$$\bar{t} = \frac{2 - m}{m}, \tag{14}$$

which varies from zero to infinity.

Since m is an unfamiliar parameter, it may be helpful to understanding to translate it into the equivalent form of the elasticity of the supply of y at the free-trade price ratio. Solving equation (13) for x as a function of y and p and substituting the result into equation (11) yields the expression for y as a function of p,

$$y^2 \left(\frac{pm^3 - p^2m^2 - m^2 - 4mp + 4p^2 + 4}{m^2 - 4mp + 4p^2} \right) = K^2. \tag{15}$$

Denoting the expression in parentheses by A for simplicity, differentiating equation (15) totally by p, and rearranging terms yields the elasticity of supply of y with respect to p,

$$\sum = \frac{1}{y} \cdot \frac{dy}{dp} = \frac{1}{2} \cdot \frac{1}{A} \cdot \frac{dA}{dp}. \tag{16}$$

Performing the differentiation and simplifying the result yields the elasticity formula

$$\sum = \frac{1}{2} \cdot \frac{(m + 2)(m^3 - 2m^2 - 4m + 8)}{(2p - m)(pm^3 - p^2m^2 - m^2 - 4mp + 4p^2 + 4)}, \tag{17}$$

whence, substituting $p = 1$, the elasticity of supply of y at the free trade point is

$$\Sigma_0 = \frac{1}{2} \frac{2+m}{2-m}. \tag{18}$$

From this it follows that as m decreases from $+2$ to 0, Σ_0 falls from infinity to one-half.

Rearrangement of equation (13) permits the expression of the relation of production of x to production of y as a function of the tariff rate,

$$x = \frac{m(1+t)-2}{m-2(1+t)} y. \tag{19}$$

(Under free trade production of the two goods would be equal, as is implicit in the symmetry of the transformation curve.) Substituting this value of x into equation (11) yields the result

$$y^2 = \left\{ \frac{[2(1+t)-m]^2}{(4-m^2)[2+2t+t^2-(1+t)m]} \right\} K^2, \tag{20}$$

or, taking the positive root only,

$$y = \left\{ \frac{2(1+t)-m}{\sqrt{(4-m^2)[2+2t+t^2-(1+t)m]}} \right\} K. \tag{21}$$

Solving for x from equation (19) and adding x to y yields the value of output at world market prices

$$M = x+y = \left\{ \frac{(2-m)(t+2)}{\sqrt{(4-m^2)[2+2t+t^2-(1+t)m]}} \right\} K \tag{22}$$

From this expression it follows that the ratio of national income (at world market prices) produced under protection to what would be produced under free trade is

$$\frac{M_t}{M_0} = \frac{(t+2)\sqrt{2-m}}{2\sqrt{2+2t+t^2-(1+t)m}}. \tag{23}$$

This expression measures the production cost of protection; the difference between M_t/M_0 and unity is the proportion by which protection reduces real national output (at world market prices) below what it would be under free trade.

Values of M_t/M_0 computed for various values of m and t are presented in Table II; for obvious reasons only values of t less than $\bar{t}$, the complete specialization tariff or subsidy rate, are presented.

TABLE II. Values of M_t/M_0 for various values of m and t (%)

m/t	·05	·10	·15	·20	·25	·30	·40	·50	·60	·70	·80	·90	1·00	1·25	1·50
1·9	98·86														
1·8	99·44	97·91													
1·7	99·64	98·63	97·13												
1·6	99·73	99·00	97·88	96·48	94·87										
1·5	99·79	99·22	98·34	97·23	95·94	94·53									
1·4	99·83	99·36	98·65	97·74	96·68	95·50	92·95								
1·3	99·86	99·47	98·87	98·07	97·21	96·22	94·03	91·68							
1·2	99·88	99·55	99·04	98·39	97·62	96·76	94·87	92·85	90·80						
1·1	99·90	99·61	99·17	98·61	97·94	97·19	95·53	93·75	91·92	90·11					
1·0	99·91	99·66	99·28	98·78	98·20	97·54	96·08	94·49	92·86	91·22	88·35				
0·9	99·92	99·70	99·36	98·93	98·41	97·83	96·53	95·11	93·64	92·17	89·63	88·08			
0·8	99·93	99·74	99·44	99·05	98·59	98·07	96·91	95·64	94·31	92·97	90·71	89·30	86·60		
0·7	99·94	99·77	99·50	99·15	98·74	98·28	97·23	96·09	94·89	93·68	91·65	90·36	87·95		
0·6	99·95	99·79	99·55	99·24	98·87	98·46	97·52	96·48	95·39	94·29	92·47	91·29	89·11	86·22	
0·5	99·95	99·81	99·60	99·32	98·99	98·61	97·76	96·82	95·84	94·83	93·19	92·10	90·14	87·46	83·67
0·4	99·96	99·83	99·64	99·39	99·09	98·75	97·98	97·13	96·23	95·31	93·82	92·83	91·05	88·57	85·08
0·3	99·96	99·85	99·67	99·45	99·18	98·87	98·17	97·40	96·58	95·74	94·39	93·48	91·86	89·57	86·35
0·2	99·96	99·86	99·70	99·50	99·25	98·98	98·34	97·64	96·90	96·13	94·90	94·06	92·58	90·47	87·50
0·1	99·97	99·88	99·73	99·55	99·33	99·07	98·50	97·86	97·18	96·48	95·36	94·59	93·24	91·28	88·54
0·0	99·97	99·89	99·76	99·59	99·39	99·16	98·64	98·06	97·44	96·80	95·77	95·07	93·83	92·03	89·54

The figures indicate that substantial inelasticity of supply of the protected good combined with a high tariff rate is necessary for the production cost to be substantial — the loss of real income is less than 10 per cent for tariff rates up to 70 per cent, and the greatest loss shown in the Table is just under 16½ per cent. The Table also confirms a theoretical presumption that the production cost is likely to be of a higher order of magnitude than the consumption cost.

V. THE TOTAL COST OF PROTECTION

Substituting the value of M from equation (22) into equation (7), the equation for the utility attainable from a given real output, yields the expression for utility as a function of the tariff rate

$$
U = \left[\left(\frac{A}{a}\right)^{1/(\beta+1)} (1+t)^{-\beta/(\beta+1)} + 1\right]^{-1/\beta}
$$
$$
\times \left\{\frac{a^{-1/\beta}}{1 + \left[\frac{A}{a}(1+t)\right]^{1/(\beta+1)}}\right\}
$$
$$
\times \left[\frac{(2-m)(t+2)}{\sqrt{(4-m^2)(2+2t+t^2)} - (1+t)m}\right] K. \tag{24}
$$

From this expression, with appropriate substitutions, it follows that the ratio of utility enjoyed with the tariff to utility enjoyed under free trade is

$$
\frac{U_t}{U_0} = \frac{[R(1+t)^{\sigma-1}+1]^{\sigma/\sigma-1}}{1+R(1+t)^{\sigma}} \left[(R+1)^{1/(1-\sigma)}\right]
$$
$$
\times \left[\frac{(t+2)\sqrt{2-m}}{2\sqrt{2+2t+t^2} - (t+1)m}\right]. \tag{25}
$$

In the special case of unit elasticity of substitution [equation (10)] the corresponding equation is

$$
\frac{U_t}{U_0} = \frac{(1+t)^r}{1+rt} \left[\frac{(t+2)\sqrt{2-m}}{2\sqrt{2+2t+t^2} - (1+t)m}\right]. \tag{26}
$$

These expressions measure the total cost of protection: the difference between U_t/U_0 in this equation and unity measures the proportion by which the consumption and production costs of protection reduce utility below the maximum attainable under free trade.

These expressions are, of course, valid only if production of y does not exceed domestic consumption of Y. Since under free trade the quantities produced of y and x are equal, and the ratio of quantities consumed of Y and X is $(1 - r)/r$, r must be less than one-half for Y to be an import good, and only values of t such that Y remains an import good (does not become an export good) can be considered.

Values of U_t/U_0 could be computed for various combinations of r, σ, and m, and values of t below the corresponding self-sufficiency level; but it is simpler and less tedious to concentrate on the values of t that make the country just self-sufficient (at various assumed values of r, σ, and m) and the corresponding ratios of the self-sufficiency level of utility to the free trade level. This section is therefore concerned with the cost of self-sufficiency, rather than with the cost of protection at different levels of the tariff rate.

From equation (6), with substitutions,

$$\frac{X}{Y} = R(1 + t)^{\sigma};$$

and from equation (19)

$$\frac{x}{y} = \frac{m(1 + t) - 2}{m - 2(1 + t)}.$$

Equating these two expressions to find the self-sufficiency tariff rate τ as a function of the production and consumption parameters yields the equation

$$R(1 + \tau)^{\sigma} = \frac{2 - m(1 + \tau)}{m - 2(1 + \tau)}. \tag{27}$$

This equation is unfortunately too complex to be solved for an explicit functional relationship of τ to r, m and σ. It can, however, be simplified in two alternative ways. One is to confine σ to the value of unity; this permits analysis of the interaction of m and r in determining τ and the total cost of protection. The other is to set m equal to zero; this permits analysis of the

TABLE III. *Self-sufficiency tariff rate (%) for various values of r and m*

Depend-ence on trade	r/m	1·75	1·50	1·25	1·00	0·75	0·50	0·25	0·00
0·05	0·45	1·26	2·53	3·83	5·14	6·47	7·81	9·17	10·55
0·10	0·40	2·54	5·15	7·84	10·61	13·46	16·38	19·39	22·47
0·15	0·35	3·84	7·87	12·10	16·52	21·15	25·98	31·03	36·28
0·20	0·30	5·18	10·73	16·67	23·01	29·78	36·99	44·65	52·75
0·25	0·25	6·55	13·75	21·64	30·28	39·72	50·00	61·16	73·21
0·30	0·20	7·97	16·97	27·13	38·60	51·51	65·99	82·13	100·00
0·35	0·15	9·44	20·45	33·33	48·43	66·12	86·76	110·66	138·05
0·40	0·10	10·98	24·26	40·51	60·56	85·41	116·23	154·14	200·00
0·45	0·05	12·59	28·51	49·12	76·50	113·78	165·54	237·67	335·89
Elasticity of supply of y at free-trade price ratio		5·50	3·50	2·17	1·50	1·10	0·83	0·64	0·50

TABLE IV. *Percentage utility loss for various values of r and m*

Depend-ence on trade	r/m	1·75	1·50	1·25	1·00	0·75	0·50	0·25	0·00
0·05	0·45	0·03	0·06	0·09	0·13	0·16	0·19	0·22	0·25
0·10	0·40	0·12	0·25	0·38	0·50	0·63	0·75	0·88	1·00
0·15	0·35	0·28	0·56	0·85	1·13	1·41	1·69	1·98	2·26
0·20	0·30	0·50	1·00	1·51	2·01	2·52	3·02	3·53	4·03
0·25	0·25	0·78	1·57	2·37	3·16	3·96	4·75	5·54	6·33
0·30	0·20	1·13	2·27	3·42	4·58	5·74	6·89	8·05	9·19
0·35	0·15	1·54	3·11	4·69	6·28	7·88	9·48	11·07	12·65
0·40	0·10	2·02	4·08	6·17	8·29	10·43	12·57	14·71	16·81
0·45	0·05	2·56	5·19	7·89	10·64	13·44	16·28	19·12	21·91
Elasticity of supply of y at free-trade price ratio		5·50	3·50	2·17	1·50	1·10	0·83	0·64	0·50

interaction of r and σ in determining τ and the total cost of protection.

If σ is set equal to unity, the equation reduces to a quadratic, the positive root of which is

$$\tau = \frac{-(4r - 2rm + m) + \sqrt{(4r - 2rm + m)\ - 8r(2 - m)(2r - 1)}}{4r}$$

(28)

Table III shows the self-sufficiency tariff rates for various combinations of r and m. Table IV shows the percentage loss of utility under self-sufficiency as compared with free trade, for the same selected values of r and m, obtained by substituting the value of τ from equation (28) into equation (27) and subtracting the result from unity.

It is noteworthy that for each value of r the percentage loss is an approximately linear function of m, while for any given m the first difference of the percentage loss is an approximately linear function of r; the percentage loss can in fact be closely approximated by the expression

$$L = (8 - m) [\tfrac{1}{2} (9 - r) (10 - r) (\cdot 07) + \cdot 08], \qquad (29)$$

where m is measured in units of $\cdot 25$ and r in units of $\cdot 05$.

For convenience of interpretation, the first column in each of the Tables shows the value of $0 \cdot 50 - r$; this is the proportion of national income that would be spent on imports (earned by exports) under free trade, and represents the degree of natural dependence of the economy on international trade. The last row in each Table shows the elasticity of supply of y (at the free trade price ratio) corresponding to the assumed value of m, calculated from equation (18); this may be taken to indicate the flexibility of the economic structure of the country.

The calculations presented in Table IV show that the percentage loss of national income under self-sufficiency is relatively small in this case (say, under 5 per cent) unless the economy is both naturally heavily dependent on international trade and inflexible in economic structure. (These conditions are reflected in the high tariff rates necessary to establish self-sufficiency shown in the lower right-hand corner of Table III). The maximum percentage loss from self-sufficiency for free-trade shares of trade in national income and expenditure up to 25 per cent is 6·33 per cent, and for supply elasticities of 3·5 or more is 5·19 per cent. For the percentage loss from self-sufficiency to exceed 10 per cent requires both dependency on

233

TABLE V. *Self-sufficiency tariff rate (%) for various values of r and σ*

$\sigma \backslash r$	·05	·10	·15	·20	·25	·30	·35	·40	·45
0·25	954·39	479·95	300·56	203·14	140·82	96·96	64·09	38·32	17·41
0·50	612·04	332·67	217·85	151·98	108·01	75·92	51·09	31·04	14·31
0·75	437·92	250·98	169·45	120·82	87·34	62·28	42·44	26·07	12·15
1·00	335·89	200·00	138·05	100·00	73·21	52·75	36·28	22·47	10·55
1·25	270·11	165·53	116·18	85·17	62·95	45·73	31·67	19·75	9·33
1·50	224·71	140·82	100·14	74·11	55·18	40·34	28·10	17·61	8·36
1·75	191·74	122·33	87·90	65·55	49·11	36·08	25·25	15·89	7·57
2·00	166·84	108·01	78·28	58·74	44·23	32·64	22·92	14·47	6·92
2·25	147·44	96·61	70·53	53·20	40·22	29·78	20·98	13·29	6·37
2·50	131·93	87·34	64·15	48·60	36·87	27·39	19·35	12·28	5·90
2·75	119·28	79·67	58·81	44·73	34·04	25·35	17·95	11·42	5·50
3·00	108·78	73·21	54·29	41·42	31·61	23·59	16·74	10·67	5·14
4·00	80·20	55·18	41·47	31·95	24·57	18·47	13·18	8·45	4·10
5·00	63·35	44·23	33·52	25·99	20·09	15·17	10·87	6·99	3·40
Dependence on trade	0·45	0·40	0·35	0·30	0·25	0·20	0·15	0·10	0·05

TABLE VI. *Percentage utility loss for various values of r and σ*

$\sigma \backslash r$	·05	·10	·15	·20	·25	·30	·35	·40	·45
0·25	24·85	20·59	16·50	12·64	9·11	6·02	3·48	1·58	0·40
0·50	23·91	19·26	15·05	11·28	7·97	5·18	2·95	1·32	0·33
0·75	22·92	17·99	13·77	10·14	7·07	4·54	2·56	1·14	0·29
1·00	21·91	16·81	12·65	9·19	6·33	4·03	2·26	1·00	0·25
1·25	20·92	15·73	11·67	8·38	5·73	3·62	2·02	0·89	0·22
1·50	19·96	14·75	10·81	7·70	5·23	3·29	1·83	0·81	0·20
1·75	19·05	13·87	10·06	7·12	4·80	3·01	1·67	0·73	0·18
2·00	18·19	13·07	9·41	6·61	4·44	2·77	1·53	0·67	0·17
2·25	17·38	12·35	8·82	6·17	4·13	2·57	1·42	0·62	0·15
2·50	16·63	11·69	8·30	5·78	3·86	2·40	1·32	0·58	0·14
2·75	15·92	11·10	7·84	5·44	3·62	2·24	1·23	0·54	0·13
3·00	15·27	10·56	7·42	5·13	3·41	2·11	1·16	0·51	0·13
4·00	13·06	8·81	6·11	4·19	2·76	1·70	0·93	0·41	0·10
5·00	11·37	7·55	5·19	3·53	2·32	1·42	0·78	0·34	0·08
Dependence on trade	0·45	0·40	0·35	0·30	0·25	0·20	1·15	0·10	0·05

trade under free trade conditions exceeding 30 per cent of national income, and a supply elasticity of around 1·50 or less.

If m is set equal to zero, the self-sufficiency tariff rate becomes

$$\tau = R^{-1/(\sigma+1)} - 1. \tag{30}$$

From this formula the self-sufficiency tariff rates can be computed for given values of r and σ; these rates are presented in Table V for ranges of values of the independent variables. Table VI presents the percentage loss of utility under self-sufficiency as compared with free trade, for the same range of values of the independent variables, obtained by substituting the values of τ from Table V into equation (25) and subtracting the result from unity.

For convenience of interpretation, the last line of each Table shows the value of $0.50 - r$, representing the degree of natural dependence of the economy on international trade. The elasticity of substitution may be interpreted (in parallel with the treatment of the previous case) as indicating the flexibility of preferences of the country.

The figures in Table V show that the tariff rate required for self-sufficiency is lower, the lower the dependence of the economy on international trade and the greater the flexibility of the economy's preferences. The former relationship is intuitively obvious. The latter is worth noting, since the fact that the consumption cost of a given tariff is higher the higher the elasticity of substitution might wrongly be taken to imply that the cost of self-sufficiency increases with the flexibility of preferences; in fact, flexibility of preferences operates to reduce the tariff rate required for self-sufficiency, and so to reduce both elements in the cost of protection.

In interpreting the numbers presented in the Tables, it is important to bear in mind that they relate to the case of $m = 0$, the maximum degree of inflexibility of economic structure allowed by the model. As is illustrated by Tables III and IV, positive values of m, representing higher degrees of flexibility of economic structure, would produce substantially smaller numbers. Interpreted as outer extreme values, the numbers presented in Table VI show the percentage loss of utility under self-sufficiency to be relatively small, unless the economy is not only extremely inflexible in economic structure, but either naturally heavily

235

dependent on international trade or inflexible in its preferences, or (especially) both together. The percentage loss is less than 5 per cent, for example, for a 20 per cent dependence in trade and substitution elasticity of 0·75 or greater, or a 25 per cent dependence on trade and substitution elasticity of 1·75 or greater; it is less than 10 per cent for trade dependence of 25 per cent and substitution elasticity of as little as 0·25, or trade dependence of 30 per cent and substitution elasticity of unity.

VI. CONCLUSION

While the model used in this chapter is far too simplified to permit the drawing of any very firm conclusions about reality, the results support a number of propositions about the gains from trade and the costs of protection that seem plausible on broader grounds of analysis and common sense. One such proposition is that both the total gains from international trade and the cost of protection are likely to be relatively small in the large advanced industrial countries, owing to their relatively flexible economic structures, probably high elasticities of substitution among the goods on which this consumption is concentrated, and relatively low natural dependence on trade; while they are likely to be appreciably larger, relative to maximum potential national income, in the smaller and less developed countries, whose economies tend to show the opposite characteristics. Another is that the costs of protectionist policies are unlikely to be large enough, relative to potential maximum national income, to account for much of the existing major differences between the real per capita national incomes of various countries. (The maximum percentage utility loss shown in Table VI is 25 per cent, which implies that utility could be increased at most by one-third by changing from self-sufficiency to free trade.) This does not imply, however, that the income sacrificed by protectionist policies is negligible. On the contrary, it may be very substantial, when measured against the appropriate standard of the cost in terms of additional resources or time of obtaining an increase in real income comparable to what could be obtained by trade liberalization. (The increase of one-third just mentioned corresponds to an investment equal to a year's national income with a marginal capital/output ratio of 3, and to nearly ten years of growth at an annually compounded rate of 3 per cent.)

10. An Economic Theory of Protectionism, Tariff Bargaining, and the Formation of Customs Unions*

I. INTRODUCTION

The traditional approach to the theory of tariffs, which is embodied in the recently elaborated analysis of the effects of customs unions pioneered by Viner, Meade, Lipsey, and others, is concerned with such matters as the possibility of increasing real income by using the tariff to exploit monopoly or monopsony power in world markets, the 'welfare costs' of the tariff in terms of foregone real income, and the effects on real income of changes in particular tariffs or in tariff structures, such as are entailed by the formation of customs unions and free-trade areas. Implicit in this approach is the assumption that 'real income' is identifiable, on social welfare function lines, with the utility derived by individuals from their personal consumption of goods and services; and, except in the optimum tariff analysis, the further assumption that tariffs are arbitrary interferences with the freedom of international exchange, which may be changed equally arbitrarily by governments.

In two previous papers, written within the traditional approach, I have called attention to the special and restrictive nature of these assumptions and the implications of abandoning them. In my 'The Cost of Protection and the Scientific Tariff'[1] I assumed that the authorities of a country were attempting to achieve certain non-economic objectives by the use of the tariff, and worked out the implications for the structure of tariff rates of a 'scientific' effort to achieve these objectives at minimum cost in terms of foregone real income. In my 'Optimal Trade Intervention

---

* The Journal of Political Economy, Vol. LXXIII, No. 3 (June 1965) pp. 256–83.

[1] Journal of Political Economy, Vol. LXVIII (August 1960) pp. 327–45, reprinted as Chapter 8 above.

in the Presence of Domestic Distortions,'[2] I remarked that the relevance of the traditional theory to the problems of economic policy depends on a particular assumption about the nature of government, namely, that government seeks to maximize real income but is ill informed about how to do this. I also pointed out that under different assumptions about the nature of government the analysis would have to be interpreted differently: if government were assumed to be all wise, the traditional measures of marginal welfare loss would have to be reinterpreted as measures of the divergence of social from private costs or benefits of protection; if, on the other hand, government is regarded as an extra-market system for modifying the distribution of income and wealth, interest would focus on the tariff structure as measuring the political power of various claimants to the national income, and the traditional welfare costs would measure the inefficiency of the political process as a redistributor of income.

The traditional approach explicitly adopts the orthodox economist's judgment of what economic welfare consists in, which runs in terms of individual consumption of goods and services. This definition of welfare leads virtually automatically to the recommendation of what Meade has called the 'modified free-trade position,'[3] a position exemplified by my paper on "Distortions", previously mentioned. This policy recommendation, in turn, puts the economist in opposition to dominant strands in the actual formulation of international economic policy, which have to be treated by definition as 'irrational' or 'non-economic,' or as arbitrarily constraining analysis to the realm of 'second-best theory.' At the same time, the economist is left without a theory capable of explaining a variety of important and observable phenomena, such as the nature of tariff bargaining, the commercial policies adopted by various countries, the conditions under which countries are willing to embark on customs unions, and the arguments and considerations that have weight in persuading countries to change their commercial policies.

[2] In R.E. Caves, H.G. Johnson, and P.B. Kenen (eds.), *Trade, Growth and the Balance of Payments: Essays in Honor of Gottfried Haberler* (Chicago: Rand McNally Co., 1965); reprinted as Chapter 4 above.

[3] J.E. Meade, *The Theory of International Economic Policy*, Vol. I: *The Balance of Payments* (London: Macmillan & Co., 1951).

This chapter attempts a sketch of such a theory.[4] The theory derives from the underlying analysis of my two previous papers, in that it accepts the relevance of 'non-economic' objectives and utilizes the suggested hypothesis that government action represents a rational attempt to offset divergences between private and social costs or benefits. But it departs from that analysis in abandoning the distinction between economic and non-economic objectives, which is ethically biased in favour of private consumption as the exclusive measure of welfare, in favour of a distinction between private and public consumption goods, and between 'real income' in the sense of utility enjoyed from both private and public consumption and 'real product' defined as total production of privately appropriable goods and services. The theory employs building blocks provided by a variety of recent contributions, notably Downs' economic theory of democracy, Becker's theory of discrimination, and Breton's economic theory of nationalism.[5] The theory presented does not claim to account for all aspects of commercial policy formation, only to

[4] The stimulus to develop this theory comes partly from my former colleague J.A. Knapp, of Manchester University, who has persistently posed the question why, if reduction of tariffs is economically beneficial, tariff negotiators always regard a tariff reduction as a concession that must be compensated by reciprocal tariff reductions by the other party to the bargain.

[5] See Anthony J. Downs, 'An Economic Theory of Political Action in a Democracy,' *Journal of Political Economy*, Vol. LXV (April 1957) pp. 135–50 and his *An Economic Theory of Democracy* (New York: Harper & Bros., 1957); Gary S. Becker, *The Economics of Discrimination* (Chicago: University of Chicago Press, 1957); and Albert Breton, 'The Economics of Nationalism,' *Journal of Political Economy*, Vol. LXXII (August 1961) pp. 376–87.

From Downs I take the notion of government policy in a democracy as a rational response to the demands of the electorate; Becker's work contributed the notion (already present in my analysis of the scientific tariff) of conceptualizing 'irrational' behavior as a preference and measuring it by the marginal premium (discount) individuals would pay (give) to gratify it; Bretons work contributed the notion of conceptualizing certain kinds of government policies as providing a collective consumption good. I have used these building blocks in an earlier and more general paper prepared for the University of Chicago Committee for the Comparative Study of New Nations Seminar on Nationalism and Economic Policy in Developing Nations ('A Theoretical Model of Economic Nationalism in New and Developing States,' *Political Science Quarterly*, Vol. LXXX, No. 2 (June 1965) pp. 169–85.

provide a tool for dealing with some practically important aspects; in particular, it concentrates on industrial protection, to the exclusion of agricultural protection, though the latter may be dealt with by obvious extensions of the theory.[6]

II. THE THEORY OF PROTECTIONISM AND TARIFF BARGAINING: INDUSTRIAL PRODUCTION AS AN AGGREGATE

The theory assumes, following Downs, that political parties in democratic countries (and, to a sufficient extent, in dictatorial systems) seek to gain and hold power by promising and implementing policies desired by the electorate; and that competition for office will result in the adoption of policies that tend to maximize the satisfaction enjoyed by the electorate. That satisfaction flows from two sources; private consumption of privately provided goods and services, and collective consumption of goods and services provided through the government at the cost of sacrifices of private consumption. (Consumption is used here as shorthand for both investment and consumption proper.) Competition among parties will tend to carry the allocation of the economy's productive resources between private and collective consumption to the point where the marginal return of satisfaction per unit of resources expended is the same in the two uses.

It is further assumed that there exists a collective preference for industrial production, in the sense that the electorate is

---

[6] The theory presented below is derived from the assumption of a 'preference for industrial production'; by extension, agricultural protectionism can be explained by an assumed 'preference for agricultural production.' Since industrial protectionism is a major common policy of less developed countries (which are predominantly agricultural in economic structure) and agricultural protectionism is a major common policy of advanced countries (which are predominantly industrial in economic structure), the two preferences could be synthesized in the concept of a 'preference for economic balance.' This concept was indeed suggested by R.A. Mundell, in discussion of an early draft of this article. Such a concept has the appeal of formal elegance and symmetry in explaining the commercial policies of countries at all stages of development. I have not pursued it, however, for two reasons: (1) policies of agricultural protection are implemented by different means than policies of industrial protectionism, and, more important, agricultural commodities are treated differently than industrial commodities under GATT; (2) advanced countries protect their industry or parts of it as well as their agriculture, and do bargain over reductions of tariffs on industrial goods in a manner explained by the theory presented here.

241

willing to spend real resources through government action in order to make the volume of industrial production and employment larger than it would be under free international competition. Industrial production, in other words, appears as a collective consumption good yielding a flow of satisfaction to the electorate independent of the satisfaction they derive directly from the consumption of industrial products. The origins of the preference for industrial production may lie in any one of a number of sources — nationalist aspirations and rivalry with other countries, the power of owners of and workers in industrial facilities to achieve a redistribution of income toward themselves by political means,[7] or the belief that industrial activity involves beneficial 'externalities' of various kinds. The precise source of the preference for industrial production will influence the form of expenditure of resources through government action, and especially the distribution of resources so spent among particular industries. In a detailed analysis of a particular nation's tariff policy, the nature of the preference for industrial production would be an important question, and could be inferred from the relative magnitudes of the premiums the public is willing to pay for different kinds of industrial production; for the present purpose, however, it is sufficient to work with a generalized preference for industrial production.

Resources for the support of industrial activity as a collective consumption good have to be provided by government action, since it is in no one's individual interest to provide them voluntarily. Such resources could be supplied in various ways: fundamentally, the choice lies between direct subsidy from tax revenue, indirect subsidy through tax concessions involving loss of tax revenue, and indirect subsidy through a tariff. The tariff involves the equivalent of an excise tax on the consumer the proceeds of which are paid to the producer to the extent that he produces the good and to the government to the extent that the producer is

---

[7] Downs (op. cit.) explains the dominance of producer over consumer interests in a democracy by the costs of acquiring information and taking action, which generally exceed the potential benefits for the consumer. whose economic interests are diffuse, but not for the producer, whose interests are concentrated; the dominance of producer interests in political decisions is therefore a consequence of economic rationality.

unable to compete with imports. Subsidy through tax concessions depends on the existence of sufficiently heavy taxes on productive activity, and hence has only become an important technique since World War II. Direct subsidy can be shown to be more efficient than the tariff as a means of promoting production, since it avoids the consumption cost of the tariff. But the tariff is invariably favoured, generally on the grounds that the revenue to finance a subsidy is difficult to collect. Other explanations are that the politicians and businessmen who exploit the preference for industrial production do not wish its alternative opportunity costs to be readily ascertainable, and that the preference for industrial production includes the specification that the country's industry must appear to be able to compete with imports without explicit governmental support. In other words, the collective utility derived from industrial production is conditional on the maintenance of the appearance of competitiveness.

On the assumption of the rationality of governmental processes, the government will tend to carry protection to the point where the value of the marginal collective utility derived from collective consumption of domestic industrial activity is just equal to the marginal excess private cost of protected industrial production. In so doing, the government will be maximizing the country's real income, properly defined. But it will not be maximizing the country's real product, since maximization of real income requires sacrificing real product in order to gratify the preference for collective consumption of industrial production.

The marginal private excess cost of protected industrial production consists of two components, the marginal production cost and the marginal private consumption cost. The marginal production cost, expressed as the proportion by which domestic cost exceeds world market cost, would be measured by the tariff rate, in the usual simple model of trade in which goods are assumed to be produced by production processes employing only original factors of production. In a more complex input—output model of production, the marginal production cost, similarly expressed as a proportional excess above world cost, would be measured by the tariff rate minus the proportion of world cost by which other tariffs on goods used as inputs raised domestic costs above world costs, all divided by the proportion of the value of the final product considered to constitute collective consumption. (If, for example, the country derives collective satisfaction from the sales value of automobiles assembled in the country, the divisor is unity; if it derives satisfaction from the value added in assembly, the divisor will be substantially less than one, for the automobile assembly industry.)

The marginal private consumption cost of protected industrial production comprises the loss of consumers' surplus due to the restriction of consumption by the increase in the tariff rate necessary to induce the marginal unit of domestic production. The magnitude of this marginal cost depends on the tariff rate and on the price sensitivity of demand relative to supply, increasing with the relative price sensitivity of demand.[8]

If account were taken of the variety of industrial products

[8] According to a well known formula, the welfare cost of a small increase in the tariff rate, for a simple model ignoring cross-effects in production and consumption and input—output complications, may be written

$$- \frac{dW}{dt} = t \frac{dP}{dp} - t \frac{dC}{dp},$$

where t is the tariff rate, p the domestic price, P domestic output of the protected good, and C domestic consumption of it (quantities being measured in unit values at free-trade prices, so that $dp = dt$); the two terms on the right-hand side are, respectively, the marginal production and marginal consumption costs of protection (dC/dp being negative). The present analysis, however, is concerned with the welfare cost, not of an increase in the tariff rate, but of an increase in protected output. Division of the foregoing expression by dP/dp yield this welfare costs as

$$- \frac{dW}{dP} = t - t \left(\frac{dC/dp}{dP/dp} \right),$$

the second expression on the right-hand side being the marginal private consumption cost of protected industrial production. The ratio $[(dC/dp)/(dP/dp)]$ is a ratio of the price slopes of the demand and supply curves, referred to in the text as 'the relative price sensitivity of demand.' The marginal excess private cost of protected industrial production may also be expressed in terms of elasticities of supply and demand as

$$- \frac{dW}{dP} = t \left(1 + \frac{P}{C} \cdot \frac{\eta}{\epsilon} \right),$$

where η and ϵ are, respectively, the elasticities of consumption demand and domestic supply.

available for protection, and the possibility that their contributions to satisfaction of the collective preference for industrial production might well vary were recognized, the foregoing principle that the government would equate marginal social utility of collective consumption of domestic industry to marginal excess private cost of protected production would have to be elaborated into the principle that the government would equate the values of the marginal utilities derived from the various lines of industrial production to their marginal excess private costs. This principle would not imply equalization of tariff rates, both because the marginal collective utility of a dollar's worth of industrial production might depend on what was produced, and because the relation of the proportional excess cost of marginal protected production to the tariff rate associated with it would vary, for two reasons. First, the relation of the tariff rate to the marginal excess production cost would vary due to the input—output complications just mentioned,[9] second, the relation of the consumption to the production cost component of the marginal excess private cost of protected production would, as already mentioned, vary with the price sensitivity of demand relative to supply. For all these reasons, the real-income-maximizing tariff structure would not entail equal tariff rates on all protected products. Thus variations in the tariff rates levied under existing national tariff structures cannot be adduced as evidence of 'irrationality' in tariff-making, contradicting the theory presented here. In what follows, these complications will be ignored, and industrial production treated as a single aggregate, produced entirely with domestic inputs.

In equilibrium, the proportional marginal excess private cost of protected production measures the marginal 'degree of preference' for industrial production. Its magnitude reflects the interaction

---

[9] An important implication of the theory is that inputs not counted as part of 'industrial production' will not be subject to protection. This implication is confirmed empirically by the escalation of tariff rates by stage of production typical of national tariff structures. On the protective effects of such escalation see my 'The Theory of Tariff Structure with Special Reference to World Trade and Development,' in Harry G. Johnson and Peter B. Kenen, *Trade and Development* (Geneva: Etudes et Travaux de l'Institut Universitaire de Hautes Etudes Internationales, 1965), reprinted as Chapter 12 below.

of the demand for collective consumption of industrial production and the cost of supplying it. This interaction is depicted in Figure 1.

In Figure 1, $1S_f$ is the supply curve of industrial products (measured in unit values at world market prices) from the world market, assumed to be perfectly elastic (probably a reasonably realistic assumption for most countries), and DD is a compensated (constant-utility) demand curve for such products (at the free-trade private utility level). S_hS_h is the domestic supply curve, and PS_{h+u} is the marginal private cost curve of protected production, including excess private consumption cost, the

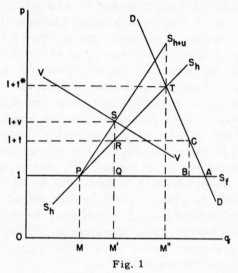

Fig. 1

vertical distance between PS_{h+u} and S_f representing the marginal excess private cost, of protected production, geometrically, PS_{h+u} must be so constructed in relation to S_hS_h that, for any tariff t, the area PSR is equal to the area ABC. The height of the curve VV above S_f represents the marginal value of industrial production in collective consumption, measured in units of world purchasing power. The maximization of real national income is achieved at the intersection S of VV with PS_{h+u}, requiring the use of the tariff rate t to induce an increase in industrial production from OM to OM', and involving the marginal degree of preference for industrial production v.

The marginal 'degree of preference' for industrial production v will be higher, the higher is VV and the more elastic it is at the free-trade output, and the farther left and less elastic is PS_{h+u}. Given the slope of DD relative to that of S_hS_h, which determines the ratio of SR to RQ and hence of v to t, the higher also will be t, the tariff rate. It follows that, if the demand conditions and the preference for industrial production tend to be the same in all countries, the lower is a country's ability to compete in industrial production (as represented by the location of P. relative to A, the free-trade production and consumption points, respectively), the higher will be its marginal degree of preference for industrial production, and (except in certain circumstances detailed in the next footnote) the higher will be its tariff level (degree of protection). In other words, the degree of protection will tend to vary inversely with ability to compete with foreign industrial producers. This is a testable implication of the theory, which seems confirmed by reality. Similarly, if a country's competitive ability should change adversely (that is, S_hS_h shift leftward), continued maximization of real income would require an increase in the degree of protection; and vice versa. This is another testable implication of the theory, which again seems confirmed by reality.[10]

As Figure 1 is drawn, the preference for industrial production is satisfied with the country producing less industrial goods than it consumes. The limit to the gratification of the preference for industrial production that can be achieved by protection is

---

[10] Using the mathematical expression of n. 8, and the equality of the marginal degree of preference for industrial production v with its marginal private excess cost,

$$\frac{v}{t} = 1 - \left(\frac{dC/dp}{dP/dp}\right) = 1 + \frac{P}{C} \cdot \frac{\eta}{\epsilon}$$

If $- [(dC/dp)/(dP/dp)]$ is constant, v/t will be constant, and t will vary with v. If, on the other hand, η/ϵ is constant, v/t will decrease with P/C (which may be taken as an index of ability to compete with foreign producers). In both cases, differences in v due to differences in P/C must necessarily be accompanied by differences in t in the same direction. A decrease in t could accompany an increase in v only if the slope (elasticity) of the demand curve increased relatively to the slope (elasticity) of the supply curve as t (and P/C) increased.

the level of industrial production OM'' achievable by the self-sufficiency tariff rate t^*. Beyond that point, the country can gratify the preference for industrial production only by resorting to export subsidies. Since the domestic price is unsubsidized, and must rise with increased output if domestic sales are to be profitable to producers, the tariff must be increased along with the export subsidy to prevent imports (and reimports) from undercutting sales in the domestic market; thus this policy will continue to involve both excess production costs and excess consumption costs. The marginal private cost of such a policy would be represented in Figure 1 by an extension of PS_{h+u} beyond S_{h+u}.

Figure 1 assumes that the country depicted would be a net importer of industrial products under free trade. Countries that are net exporters of industrial products may also have a preference for industrial production. The preference of exporting countries for industrial production may be satiated by the level of industrial production their exports permit them (that is, VV may joint $S_h S_h$ at a point below the world market price of industrial goods). If the preference is not satiated, the only policy open to the country is export subsidization coupled with a tariff

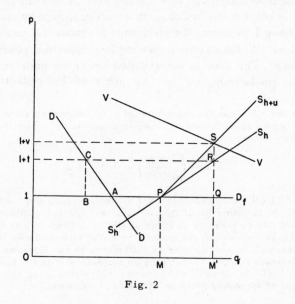

Fig. 2

at the same rate as the subsidy to prevent reimportation. This case is shown in Figure 2, which is the same as Figure 1 except that the locations of P and A are reversed, the world demand curve $1D_f$ replaces the world supply curve, and s, the subsidy and tariff rate, replaces t.

These last two implications of the theory — subsidization of industrial exports by both high-cost protectionist countries and countries competitive in the world market — are again testable and confirmed to some extent by practical experience. Examples are the practice of subsidizing exports of the products of 'new industries' in the less developed countries such as India, and the various arrangements for subsidizing exports through tax incentives, easy export credit, and so forth maintained by countries that have no balance-of-payments reason to transfer real product to foreigners by these means. Another implication, again in conformity with experience, is that industrial exporting countries faced with adverse changes in their international competitive position will introduce export subsidies or raise existing export subsidies. (For possible exceptions to this proposition, refer back to the discussion of the effects of the same change on the industrial importing countries, and especially n. 10.)

The subsidization of exports just discussed is, however, not a widespread practice and is usually disguised in some subtle fashion. The reason is that there is an international convention against explicit export subsidization, incorporated in the principles of GATT and backed up by national antidumping legislation. This convention and the associated national legislation are themselves explainable by reference to the preference for industrial production and the free enterprise philosophy that underlies the preference for tariffs over production subsidies. Export subsidization by a foreign country appears as an attempt by the foreigner to increase his collective utility from industrial production at the expense of one's own by unfair means. What is more important, direct export subsidization is visible and can be counteracted by use of one's own tariff. Enforcement of a prohibition on export subsidization implies that only industrial importing countries are free to maximize their real incomes by gratifying the preference for industrial production: industrial exporting countries are (or may be) confined to a suboptimal level of real income by the inability to subsidize exports. This constraint has important consequences for tariff policy and bargaining, which will be developed subsequently.

The analysis thus far has implicitly assumed a typical country small enough for changes in the volume of its imports or exports of industrial products to make no difference in the price it pays for its imports (if it is a net industrial importer) or receives for its exports of the other products (if it is a net industrial exporter).[11] If this is not true, and the terms of trade are affected by the country's tariff policy, the conditions of optimum tariff theory exist; and by the initial assumption of governmental rationality they will be exploited. It is clear, however, that importers of industrial products will adopt a higher tariff level (against industrial products) than the optimum tariff of conventional analysis, and conversely that countries that are net exporters of industrial products will adopt a lower tariff level (against nonindustrial products) then the conventional optimum tariff — always provided that the preference for industrial production does not become satiated.[12] In both cases real income is maximized, and thus is higher than it would be under the conventionally determined optimum tariff. But in the net industrial importing country real product must be lower than it would have been under the conventional optimum tariff, and may be lower than it would have been under free trade; whereas in the net industrial exporting country, real product, though less than it would have been under the conventional optimum tariff, must be higher than it would

---

[11] For simplicity, industrial products are here taken as *numéraire*, so that all terms of trade effects appear as changes in the prices of nonindustrial goods.

[12] The orthodox optimum tariff formula for the two-commodity case may be derived as follows. Maximization of social welfare requires $U_m/U_x = dX/dM$, where X and M, respectively, represent export and import quantities and U_x and U_m the marginal utilities of X and M in domestic consumption. Here dX/dM is the marginal cost of additional imports, derived from the balance of trade equality $X = pM$ or $M = \pi X$ (where $p = 1/\pi$ is the price of M in terms of X) and the foreign supply of imports or demand for exports,

$$\frac{dX}{dM} = p\left(1 + \frac{1}{\epsilon}\right) = \frac{1}{\pi} \cdot \frac{\eta}{\eta - 1}$$

have been under free trade — provided that the preference for industrial production is not strong enough to lead to free trade (or to export subsidization, if that is possible) rather than a tax on imports.

The introduction of monopoly—monopsony power in the world market into a model in which industrial production is treated as a single aggregate provides a motive for industrial exporting countries as well as industrial importing countries to have tariffs, and therefore introduces the possibility of negotiation for the reciprocal reduction of tariffs. To investigate this possibility, I assume a world of two countries only, an industrial exporting ('advanced') country and an industrially importing ('less developed') country, each with a tariff on imports.[13] To allow scope

---

Footnote continued

where ϵ is the elasticity of foreign supply of imports and η the corresponding elasticity of foreign demand for exports as functions, respectively of p and π. Welfare maximization requires the imposition of an import tariff such that

$$\frac{U_m}{U_x} = (1 + t) p = \frac{dX}{dM}, \text{ that is,}$$

$$t = \frac{1}{\epsilon} \quad \text{or} \quad t = \frac{1}{\eta - 1}$$

With a preference for industrial production, however, the loss of social utility from an additional unit of exports for the industrial exporter is not U_x but $U_x - vaU_x$, where v is the proportional marginal preference for industrial production and a is the proportion of the increase in exports effected by increased domestic industrial production; similarly for the industrial importer, the gain in utility from an additional unit of imports is not U_m but $U_m - vbU_m$, where v is defined as before and b is the proportion of the increase in imports effected by decreased domestic industrial production. Substitution of these expressions yields the results $t = 1/\epsilon - av(1 + 1/\epsilon)$ for the industrial exporter, and $t = 1/(\eta - 1) + bv$ for the industrial importer.

[13] The problem of many countries, which involves the possibility of preferential tariff reductions, is most conveniently dealt with in conjunction with differentiation of industrial production. It is difficult to deal with in the present model, since industrial exporting countries will have tariffs only if they possess monopoly—monopsony power, and this creates analytical complexities in a multicountry system.

for tariff bargaining, these tariffs must be assumed to have been arrived at by some process of independent tariff formation in the two countries, though this process may or may not be assumed to have involved recognition of the dependence of the welfare-maximizing tariff policy of each on the tariff policy of the other, without affecting the conclusions. [14]

Under what condition will a reciprocal reduction of tariffs by the two countries be mutually beneficial, in the sense that some combination of tariff reductions can be found that will raise the real income of both countries? In the traditional analysis, where the initial existence of tariffs is derived from the exercise of monopoly—monopsony power on the part of each country, reciprocal tariff reduction is always beneficial, and it can be shown that tariff bargaining would proceed to reduce tariffs until at least one country had eliminated its tariff entirely. [15] In the presence of a preference for industrial production, however, this proposition no longer holds, since this preference gives the less developed country a motive for imposing a tariff independent of the exploitation of monopoly—monopsony power, so that the existence of its tariff does not necessarily imply the presence of such power. In this case, mutually beneficial tariff reduction is possible only to the extent that the less-developed country's tariff involves the exploitation of monopoly—monopsony power, and

Footnote continued

The terminology of 'advanced' and 'less developed' employed in the text is, of course, misleading, since neither real product nor real income is necessarily higher for net industrial exporting than for net industrial importing nations; but the terminology does reflect a judgement that follows naturally from the preference for industrial production.

[14] The adjustment of the tariff of one country to changes in the other, based on the objective of maximizing national welfare, is to be distinguished from 'tariff retaliation' in the pure sense, which implies that a country derives utility by reducing the welfare of the other country through increasing its tariffs. The latter means that one country's welfare is a function of the other's, and introduces considerations that are excluded at this point, though they will be introduced briefly later in the argument.

[15] One country may possess sufficiently superior monopoly power to be better off when both follow optimum tariff policies than it would be under free trade; negotiation for reciprocal tariff reduction cannot bring such a country to practice free trade.

would never lead to that country's abandoning protection in favour of free trade.

The point may be illustrated, without loss of generality, by considering the attractiveness to the two countries of a proposed slight reciprocal reduction of tariffs, so designed as to expand trade without changing the terms of trade. In the traditional model the presence of tariffs means that in each country the marginal private value of an increment of imports exceeds its price (the tariff having been imposed because the marginal social cost of imports exceeds price), so that each country will gain by the reciprocal reduction of tariffs, and tariff reduction will proceed until one country reaches the free-trade point. In the present model, the marginal private value of an increment of imports also exceeds its price, owing to the tariff. But in the advanced country the marginal social value of an increment of imports is above the marginal private value, because an increment of imports carries with it an increment of exports and therefore of industrial production and the utility of collective consumption associated with industry. In the less developed country, on the other hand, the marginal social value of an increment of imports is below the marginal private value, because an expansion of trade entails a contraction of industrial production and a loss of utility from the collective consumption of industry. Given rational maximization of real income, the country will have fixed its tariff so that the marginal social value of an increment of imports is initially just equal to its marginal social cost, and unless the presence of monopoly—monopsony power makes marginal social cost exceed price, the country will derive no gain in real income (as distinct from real product) from an expansion of trade at constant terms of trade. In fact, a non-infinitesimal expansion of trade would impose a loss on it. Thus while the advanced country will have an incentive to accept the proposed reciprocal tariff reduction, the less developed country will have no incentive to do so unless it possesses monopoly—monopsony power that its tariff has exploited. If it possesses no monopoly—monopsony power, it would only accept a reciprocal tariff reduction proposal that promised an improvement in its terms of trade; but the advanced country would have no incentive to offer such a proposal since to do so would entail an unrequited sacrifice of the exploitation

253

of its own monopoly—monopsony power.[16] If it does possess monopoly—monopsony power, it would be willing to accept reciprocal tariff reduction of the type described, but only to the point at which its tariff rate equalized the marginal excess private cost of protected production with the marginal degree of preference for industrial production. Thus reciprocal tariff reduction could only lead to one country's following a free-trade policy if that country were the advanced country; and this would require that that country's monopoly—monopsony power be relatively less, in some sense difficult to define except by its results, than that of the less developed country.

The case in which the less developed country has no monopoly—monopsony power is of special interest, since for the analysis of tariff bargaining (though not of the actual results of bargains) it can be taken to represent the more realistic situation in which there are a large number of less developed countries, each too small to exercise any independent monopoly—monopsony power, even though the aggregate of less developed countries may possess such power. To be acceptable, a tariff-reducing bargain in this case must promise to improve the terms of trade of the less developed country and turn them against the advanced country; in monetary terms, it must threaten to worsen the advanced country's balance of payments at the existing exchange and money wage rates. If, as a matter of rational exploitation of monopoly—monopsony power (as in the preceding analysis), or more generally of bargaining tactics, balance of payments considerations or other reasons, the advanced country's negotiators insist that equity of bargains necessitates reciprocal tariff reductions that would produce a balanced expansion of trade at unchanged terms of trade (that is, equal increases in export and import values at current prices) the less developed country will refuse any bargain proposed, as involving a loss of real income to it. This point explains one aspect of the dissatisfaction that the less developed countries have recently been manifesting with respect to the GATT mechanism of bargaining for tariff

[16] Recall that the exercise of this monopoly—monopsony power is assumed to have already been tempered by the preference for industrial production.

reduction. Given the preference for industrial production, bargaining on GATT rules appears to offer no attractions to countries that do not export industrial products and lack monopoly—monopsony power in world markets; instead, it appears to such countries as a mechanism designed to enable the advanced countries to win benefits at their expense.[17]

The aggregated two-good model of this section does not lend itself readily to extension to tariff-bargaining among a number of countries, which introduces the possibility of preferential arrangements. The analysis does, however, indicate the reasons why preferential arrangements between advanced and less developed countries may be attractive to both sides. The convention against export subsidies may prevent the advanced country from achieving a level of industrial production high enough to maximize its real income, and this may make it willing to pay a price, in terms of a preference-created increase in the cost of its imports of non-industrial goods, for a preference-created increase in its exports. To the less developed country, on the other hand, a preference toward a particular advanced country has the advantage that its price is an increase in the social cost of existing imports, rather than a decrease in the country's industrial production, which loss may be more than offset by the increased prices the country may obtain for its exports of non-industrial products.

III. THE THEORY OF PROTECTIONISM AND TARIFF BARGAINING: VARIETY OF INDUSTRIAL PRODUCTION

In this section, I abandon the assumption that industrial production is a single aggregate, with countries having varying comparative advantage in industry as opposed to non-industrial production. Instead, I assume that industrial production comprises a variety of products, in which countries have varying degrees of comparative advantage. Such differences in comparative advantage among industries may be assumed to result from

[17] Both the theoretical conclusion and its application to the contemporary situation are strengthened if the less developed country of the analysis is assumed to derive positive disutility from its 'collective consumption' of the industrial production of the advanced country.

differences in the local availability of natural resources, in the general level of labour or management skill, in the availability of capital, in technological level, or in the size of the domestic market combined with the existence of economies of scale in certain industries, I continue to assume that countries differ in their over-all comparative advantage in industry as compared with non-industrial production.

The variety of industrial production allows countries to be both importers and exporters of industrial products, and in combination with the preference for industrial production will motivate each country to practice some degree of protection. It is therefore not necessary to appeal to monopoly—monopsony power in world markets to provide an environment of universal protection within which reciprocal tariff reduction is possible; and for analytical simplicity it will be assumed that no country has such power. It will also be assumed that the convention against export subsidization is fully effective; this is an important assumption, in that it creates an opportunity for mutually profitable tariff reduction, and in certain circumstances a motive for protection itself.

In the circumstances posited, a country can gratify its preference for industrial production only by protecting the domestic producers of commodities it imports. Acting rationally, it will carry protection to the point where the marginal social value of collective consumption of industrial production is equal to the marginal excess cost of industrial production. The latter, however, will be constituted somewhat differently in this model than in the previous one. Protection of import-competing industries will tend to some extent to reduce industrial exports, as well as non-industrial production; hence, in order to increase total industrial production by one unit, it will be necessary to increase protected industrial production by more than one unit to compensate for the induced loss of industrial exports, so that the marginal excess private production cost and consumption cost must be reckoned accordingly.[18]

[18] Another way of making this point is to say that the marginal cost of protected industrial production in this case includes an additional element not encountered in the previous case, namely, the loss of utility from collective consumption of industrial production due to the decrease in industrial exports induced by protection.

256

Protection of import-competing industries reduces industrial exports by raising their cost of production, either by raising the prices of factors of production common to the two sectors of industry, or by raising the cost of outputs of the protected sector used as inputs in the export sector. The stronger are these effects of protection, other things equal, the higher will be the marginal excess cost of industrial production. These effects are likely to be larger, the larger the size of the total industrial sector relative to the non-industrial sector and the larger the size of the protected industrial sector relative to the exporting industrial sector.

These relationships would imply that the same marginal degree of preference for industrial production would entail (a) lower tariff rates in a country with a relatively small non-industrial sector than in one with a relatively large non-industrial sector, and (b) higher tariff rates in countries a relatively small proportion of whose industrial production is protected than in countries a relatively large proportion of whose industrial production is protected. These would appear to be testable implications of the theory: and the former seems in conformity with reality, while the latter does not. The tests, however, are not valid ones, because the marginal degree of preference for industrial production is not independent of the characteristics of the economy to which the implication refer. A country with a small non-industrial sector is virtually certain to be a net industrial exporter, and vice versa, so that with identical preferences for industrial production among nations a country with a small non-industrial sector would necessarily have a more fully gratified preference and hence a lower marginal degree of preference for industrial production: hence its tariff rates would tend to be lower anyway. Similarly, a country that protects relatively much of its industrial production presumably does so because it has a comparative disadvantage in industrial production, so that its marginal degree of preference for industrial production and hence its tariff rates would tend to be higher than those of a country which protects relatively little of its industrial production. Higher tariff rates in the former than in the latter are therefore not inconsistent with the theory.

As in the previous model, the theory implies that the degree of protection practiced by the various countries will vary inversely with their net industrial export position; and that an improvement in a country's comparative advantage in industrial production as against non-industrial production will lead it to reduce its degree of protection, and vice versa. As already mentioned, these implications are consistent with experience — countries whose competitiveness in world markets is improving tend to move in the free trade direction, while countries whose competitiveness is deteriorating tend to move toward increased protectionism.[19]

The analysis just presented assumes that domestic and international trade is organized competitively, so that protection tends to divert resources away from production for export. If production is assumed to be carried on by monopolistic enterprises, so that discrimination by the producer between markets is possible, and these enterprises are assumed to be multiproduct firms operating under joint cost conditions, so that discrimination between the domestic and the foreign markets can be effected by loading different products with different proportions of overhead cost rather than by charging different prices for the same product in the two markets (thus circumventing the convention against dumping), the foregoing conclusions will be altered. A tariff will permit the protected producer to charge his overheads against the home-market consumer and, indirectly, to subsidize exports. By so doing, monopolistic market organisation may permit the country, through its tariff policy, to achieve a given level of industrial production at a lower marginal excess cost than would rule under competition. Under these conditions, the tariff might increase rather than decrease industrial exports, thus yielding a double gain from protection. The implications of monopolistic market organization for the theory of tariff bargaining are obviously both complex and interesting; the former characteristic prevents them from being pursued further in this chapter.

The analysis thus far has provided a rationale for the existence

---

[19] Outstanding examples are the adoption of free trade by Britain in the nineteenth century and her retreat into protectionism in the period after World War I, the espousal of freer trade by the United States and Canada in the period after World War II, and the growth of protectionism in both countries when they encountered difficulties in international industrial competition after 1957.

of universal tariff protection of industrial production and examined some of the implications of differences or changes in countries' circumstances for their protectionist policies. I now introduce the possibility of bargaining for reciprocal tariff reduction. To begin with, I assume a world of only two countries, though this does some violence to the assumption that no country has monopoly—monopsony power in the world market. One of these countries must be a net exporter, and the other a net importer, of industrial products; but it is no longer true (as in the previous model) that the expansion of industrial production in one must entail a contraction of industrial production in the other, since industrial production in both can expand at the expense of production of non-industrial products.

At the outset, it should be emphasized that for each country the prospective gain from reciprocal tariff reduction must lie in the expansion of exports of industrial products. By assumption, each country has been willing to reduce its real product by protection of domestic industrial producers against foreign competition in order to maximize its real income (including utility from collective consumption of industrial production), and any reduction in industrial production due to an expansion of imports adds less to real product than it subtracts from collective utility. Thus reduction of one's own tariffs is a source of loss, which can only be compensated for by a reduction of the other country's tariff. On the other hand, a reduction of the other country's tariff is a source of gain, since it expands one's own industrial production and yields an increased flow of utility from collective consumption of industrial production. The theory therefore accounts for the form and logic of bargaining for reciprocal tariff reduction, phenomena which are incomprehensible to the classical approach to tariff theory, according to which the source of gain is the replacement of domestic production by lower-cost imports, whereas increased exports yield no gain (improved terms of trade apart) to the exporting country, but a gain to the foreigner through the same replacement of domestic production by lower-cost imports. Since these gains are attainable by unilateral action, the classical approach provides no explanation of the necessity and nature of the bargaining process.

The gains from reciprocal tariff reduction are nevertheless of the same basic nature in this model as in the classical analysis, though their outward character is different; they result from the substitution of lower-cost for higher-cost sources of want satisfaction. The difference is that in the classical analysis it is lower-cost satisfaction of private consumer wants that is involved, and this could be achieved without the co-operation of the other country through unilateral tariff reduction; whereas in the preference for industrial production model it is lower-cost satisfaction of the demand for collective consumption of industrial production that is involved, and this can only be achieved through the co-operation (via bargaining) of the other country. Because of the convention preventing export subsidization, a country enters the bargaining situation in a 'second-best' equilibrium position, in which the marginal excess cost of industrial production achieved by additional exports is zero, whereas the marginal excess cost of additional industrial production achieved by protection is positive. Each country therefore stands to gain, in terms of real income, by exchanging a reduction of its industrial production through its own tariff reduction for an equal expansion of its industrial production through the other country's tariff reduction. Actually, however, reciprocal tariff reductions can be arranged that will increase each country's industrial production while lowering its marginal excess cost, since reciprocal tariff reduction will increase each country's aggregate consumption of industrial goods at the expense of its consumption of non-industrial goods.[20] And an individual country could gain from negotiated reciprocal tariff reductions that reduced its aggregate industrial production, providing that the resulting increase in real product outweighed the loss of utility from collective consumption of industrial production; at the initiation of bargaining

---

[20] The reduction in a country's industrial production will be less than the increase in its industrial imports to the extent that its consumption switches from non-industrial products to industrial imports, and that contraction of protected industrial production increases industrial production in the non-protected sector. Each country will therefore have an incentive to offer the other concessions on items that are close substitutes for non-industrial products in consumption and for non-protected industrial products in production, rather than on items that are close substitutes in consumption for its other industrial products and in production for its non-industrial products.

it could gain from any reciprocal tariff reduction that offered it any slight increase in exports.[21] It follows that reciprocal tariff-cutting would proceed so long as each country could offer the other a tariff reduction that would increase the other's exports. Consequently, just as in the classical model in which tariffs exist due to monopoly—monopsony power in world markets, bargaining for mutually beneficial tariff reductions would eliminate tariffs in one of the countries, and possibly in both.

This result depends, of course, on the assumptions of the model, and especially on the assumption that the preference for industrial production does not discriminate between industries. If countries attached separate collective consumption utility to different industries, a position could be reached in which a country could not be compensated for further reductions in the tariff on one of its (more highly valued) industries by a reduction in the other country's tariff or one of its (less highly valued) industries. Also, if a country's production is concentrated in the hands of monopolistic enterprises capable of effective price discrimination between the domestic and foreign market, reciprocal tariff reduction might involve a loss rather than a gain for that country.

The assumption of a two-country world and a general preference for industrial production leads to the conclusion that bargaining will result in the elimination of the tariffs of at least one of the countries. This result is due to the fact that in a two-country world it is always possible to arrange reciprocal tariff reductions that will increase industrial production in both countries while reducing the excess cost of industrial production. I now abandon the two-country assumption and assume the existence of many countries. In this case, as will be shown, there are limits to the extent of the reciprocal reduction of tariffs that can be negotiated on a most-favoured-nation basis; furthermore these limits introduce the possibility that reciprocal preferential tariff reduction, that is, tariff reductions discriminating among foreign

[21] At the margin, the marginal excess cost of protected industrial production is just equal to its marginal social utility; a small contraction of protected production occasions negligible loss, while an expansion of industrial exports yields a surplus of utility from collective consumption of industrial production.

countries, will be more attractive than non-discriminatory tariff reduction, a possibility that would not exist apart from the preference for industrial production.

Assume that all reciprocal tariff reductions must be arrived at on a most-favoured-nation basis; that is, that each partner in the negotiation must extend the tariff reduction to all other nations, not merely to the negotiating partner. Reduction of a country's tariff on a particular item will then increase its total imports of that item by more than it increases imports from the partner country; it may or may not decrease the country's industrial production by more than it increases industrial production in the partner country, depending on the magnitudes of the parameters involved. [22] The same holds for a reduction of the partner country's tariff.

It follows, first, that countries negotiating for reciprocal tariff reductions will offer concessions on those items for which a reduction in their own tariff will yield the maximum increase in partner industrial production per unit reduction in domestic industrial production, and demand concessions on those items for which a reduction in the partner's tariff will yield the maximum increase in their own industrial production per unit reduction in the partner's industrial production. By so doing, they maximize their joint gains from the combination of substitution of lower-cost (exported) for higher-cost (protected import-competing) industrial production and expansion of aggregate industrial production. In other words, each country has an incentive to choose items for negotiation in a fashion that discriminates against expansion of trade with third parties in favour of expansion of trade with the partner country. In this way the most-favoured-nation principle,

---

[22] The relative magnitudes of the reduction in domestic production and the increase in imports will depend on the elasticities of demand and domestic supply of the good in question and the extent to which demand shifts from, and production shifts to, non-industrial production; the share of the increase in demand for imports that goes to the partner country depends on the magnitude of its elasticity of supply of exports relative to those of other countries, and the magnitude of the increase in the partner's industrial production relative to the increase in its exports depends on the relative magnitudes of the elasticities of domestic demand and supply of the commodity in the partner country. In all cases the elasticities have to be weighted appropriately by ratios of quantities initially produced, consumed, or traded.

which proscribes tariff discrimination among countries, leads to indirect discrimination among countries through the choice of commodities for reciprocal tariff reduction.

Second, it follows that the process of reciprocal tariff reduction is likely to come to a halt well before either country approaches anything like complete elimination of tariffs. This is so because sooner or later the only reciprocal tariff reductions possible will be the ones that will reduce the aggregate industrial production of one or both countries. And while reciprocal reductions of this kind will be mutually advantageous over a certain range, in the sense that the loss of utility from collective consumption of industrial production in a country whose industrial production fell would initially be outweighed by the gain in real product resulting from tariff elimination, this must cease to be the case before the country's tariffs have been completely eliminated, because the loss of utility is constant or rising per unit of industrial production sacrificed while the gain of real product must fall as the tariff is reduced.[23]

The foregoing propositions relate to the nature and effects of bilateral negotiation for reciprocal tariff reduction, subject to the rule of non-discrimination, in a multicountry world; and they bear a reasonably close relationship to the nature and results of tariff negotiations under the GATT system. In a rational world, however, negotiations for reciprocal tariff reduction would not be confined to bilateral negotiations between pairs of nations; and this is not entirely the case under GATT. What would be the results of multilateral negotiations for reciprocal tariff reductions?

It seems likely, on the analogy of Marcus Fleming's treatment

---

[23] Suppose the value of the marginal utility of collective consumption of industrial production is a constant v, initially equal to the marginal excess cost of protected production e; and that for every unit reduction in protected industrial production through reduction of its own tariff the country receives an increase in its industrial exports equal to $1 - a > 0$, from the reduction in the partner country's tariff. Its net gain is initially $e - av > 0$; but it gains from further reciprocal tariff reduction only so long as e does not fall to av.

A simple mathematical model designed for analysis of the limits of non-discriminatory reciprocal tariff reduction is presented in the Appendix. It is there shown that such tariff reduction can only reach free trade if it would increase industrial production in the two countries combined.

of the problem of making the best of balance-of-payments restrictions on imports,[24] that the outcome would be a situation in which countries could be arranged in an order of decreasing industrial strength (comparative advantage in industrial production) and increasing protectionism – though it is difficult to construct a rigorous formal argument leading to this conclusion, owing to the difficulty of defining 'industrial strength.' The basic logic behind the conclusion stems from the preceding analyses of two-country models, where it was shown (in the aggregate industrial production model) that a country with no industrial exports and no monopoly–monopsony power would have no incentive to negotiate tariff reductions; and (in the disaggregated industrial production model) that both countries would gain from negotiating reciprocal tariff reductions until at least one of them practiced free trade. Multilateral negotiation, it may be presumed, will permit one country to deal with the rest as if they constituted a single country.

In a multicountry world it should always be possible to find at least one country ('the strongest industrial country') so situated with respect to its initial trade position in industrial products and the elasticities of demand and supply governing them that universal adoption of free trade would increase its industrial exports more than its industrial imports. Such a country could always gain by offering to pursue a free-trade policy in exchange for tariff concessions by the others, providing that it received sufficient concessions for its aggregate industrial production to remain unchanged or increase; and the other countries – except for the non-exporters of industrial products, who would have no incentive to participate – should always be able to find some set of individual non-discriminatory tariff concessions that, in combination with the effects of free trade in the strongest industrial country, would leave unchanged or increase their individual

---

[24] J.M. Fleming, 'On Making the Best of Balance of Payments Restrictions on Imports,' *Economic Journal*, Vol. LXI (March 1951) pp. 48–71, esp. 48–54. Fleming's problem is analytically both more interesting and more clear cut than the present one, since it explicitly comprehends discrimination among countries, and can use the equivalent of a simple 'bargaining' rule, that the trade of all countries must always be exactly balanced.

aggregates of industrial production.[25] Thus one country at least would end up with a commercial policy of free trade. After this negotiation, the next strongest industrial country would have an incentive to negotiate reciprocal tariff reductions with the rest; but the free-trade country would now appear as the third party in the preceding analysis of bilateral negotiation, since it would gain automatically from the non-discriminatory reciprocal tariff reductions of the rest without being able to offer them export-increasing tariff concessions in return. Thus this negotiation might or might not bring the second-strongest industrial country to free trade. At the opposite extreme, countries with no comparative advantage in industrial production — countries all of whose industrial production has to be protected — would have nothing to gain from reciprocal tariff negotiation, but industrial production to lose, and would retain their original tariffs. Thus some arrangement of countries in order of increasing protectionism and decreasing industrial strength would emerge from multilateral negotiation of reciprocal tariff reduction. But this arrangement would be subject to some indeterminacy, since the outcome would depend in part on the order in which negotiations took place and the way in which the gains from negotiated tariff reductions were divided among the participating countries.

Now introduce, in place of the most-favoured-nation principle, the possibility of preferential (discriminatory) reciprocal tariff reduction, that is, of reciprocal reduction of tariffs on imports from the partner country, tariffs on imports of the same commodity from third countries remaining unchanged. Starting from an initial position of non-discrimination, discriminatory tariff reduction has the advantage over non-discriminatory tariff reduction that it permits a country to offer its partner an increase in exports and industrial production without suffering any loss of its own industrial production, through diverting imports form third countries to the partner. After all such possible trade diversion has occurred,

[25] Though the argument is couched in terms of increased industrial production, it will be recalled from the preceding analysis that within limits a country could gain from reciprocal tariff reduction that reduced its aggregate industrial production, if the resulting increase in its real product exceeded the value of the corresponding loss of utility from collective consumption of industrial production.

further discriminatory tariff reduction has the advantage over non-discriminatory tariff reduction of yielding the partner the whole of any increase in the tariff-cutting country's imports (which now occur partly at the expense of its domestic industrial production), whereas under non-discriminatory tariff reduction the partner's exports would expand less than the tariff-reducing country's imports, so that the partner's industrial production expands more under the former than under the latter type of tariff-cutting. Thus discriminatory reciprocal tariff reduction costs each partner country less, in terms of the reduction in domestic industrial production (if any) incurred per unit increase in partner industrial production, than does non-discriminatory reciprocal tariff reduction. On the other hand, preferential tariff reduction imposes an additional cost on the tariff-reducing country, the excess of the cost of imports from the partner country over their cost in the world market.

For the initial slight preferential tariff reduction, this cost will be smaller, the smaller the amount of the partner country's exports to the world market. (Under the assumed conditions of perfect competition, the partner's exports may be sold anywhere under non-discrimination, but any slight preference will divert them to the market of the preference-granting country. It is obvious that the preference-receiving country will only benefit from the preference if its initial export sales are less than the import quantity that would be demanded by the preference-granting country under free trade, since only in this case can the preference increase its sales; this sets limits on the conditions under which preferential arrangements can be mutually beneficial.) For subsequent preferential tariff reductions, the marginal cost per unit of increased imports will rise, both because the excess cost of the marginal unit of imports increases and because this excess price is paid on a larger volume of intramarginal trade with the partner. Once the partner country's exports have replaced imports from other countries, further preferential tariff reductions entail an additional element of cost through replacement of domestic by partner industrial production and a consequent loss of collective utility.

That part of the cost of the preference that corresponds to the higher price paid for intramarginal imports, however, is an income transfer to the partner, whose gains from the preference comprise this transfer and the collective utility derived from whatever expansion of its industrial exports results. Since the excess marginal cost of the increment of partner industrial exports resulting from an initial slight preferential tariff reduction is negligible, while there must be some increase in the partner's industrial production if the preference is to benefit it, it follows that an exchange of slight preferential tariff reductions between the partners must always be mutually beneficial. For further recip-

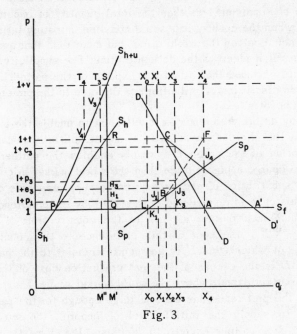

Fig. 3

rocal tariff reductions, however, the increasing marginal cost of preferential tariff reductions to the two partners is likely to mean that preferential tariff reduction will not proceed to the point of 100 per cent preferences (reciprocal free trade in the commodities under negotiation). This conclusion parallels a proposition in standard customs union theory, to the effect that a partial preferential arrangement is more likely to raise the real income (real product, in the present terminology) of the preference-granting countries than a 100 per cent preferential arrangement.

The cost of giving a preference is illustrated in Figure 3, which reproduces the relevant parts of Figure 1. For simplicity, it is assumed that the quantity of resources used in domestic production of the imported commodity has no influence on the quantity of resources used in the country's production of other industrial products, and that the marginal degree of preference for industrial production v is constant. The partner country's supply curve is represented by S_pS_p, quantity supplied being measured from the vertical SM'; the partner is assumed to be capable of supplying less than the total quantity of imports demanded when the country imposes a non-discriminatory tariff and the partner receives the world price, but more than that quantity of imports if it receives the domestic price. For simplicity, it is arbitrarily assumed that all of the exports of the partner in the initial non-discriminatory situation are directed to the preference-granting country.

So long as the preference is insufficient to enable the partner to supply the whole of the quantity of imports initially demanded, the granting of the preference simply enables the partner suppliers to charge a higher price than the world market price, and induces substitution of partner for foreign supplies (trade diversion). This case is represented in the figure by the preference p_1, which increases partner exports to the country from $M'X_0$ to $M'X_1$ (by X_0X_1); the cost of this preference to the country is $QH_1J_1K_1$, of which QH_1J_1L is an income transfer to the partner and J_1K_1L is the excess of the real production cost of the additional partner exports above the world market price.

Once the preference has become large enough for the partner country to supply the initial level of imports, the situation changes. For partner exports to increase, the domestic price must fall, to induce increased consumption and decreased domestic production (trade creation). In the figure, the effect on the quantity of imports demanded of the contraction of domestic production as the domestic price falls is represented by shifting the demand curve DD to the right below the point C by the amount of the corresponding contraction of domestic output, to give the demand curve for imports CA' continued (in the figure, $PQ = AA'$). The necessity for the domestic price to fall to induce increased imports means that part of any additional preference is absorbed in price reduction to domestic consumers, so that only a part of it accrues as an increase in the price received by partner suppliers. To represent this in the figure, the vertical distance between the horizontal line at $1 + t$ and CA' is added to $S_p S_p$ to give the line BF, which represents the locus of the preferences necessary to induce various quantities of partner exports. With the preference p_3, for example, imports from the partner would be $M'X_3$; the excess of the price received by the partner over the world market price would be e_3; the domestic price would be above the world market price by c_3 and below the price in the absence of the preference by $t - c_3$; and domestic production would be below its level under non-discriminatory protection by the amount $M''M'$. The cost of the preference p_3 would consist of two parts: $QH_3 J_3 K_3$, the excess of the cost of imports from the partner country above world market prices, of which $QH_3 J_3 L$ is an income transfer to the partner and $J_3 K_3 L$ is the excess of the real production cost of the additional partner exports above the world market price; and $ST_3 V_3$, the excess of the loss of utility from domestic industrial production over the saving of excess private cost of protected production.

Figure 3 can also be used to depict the gains from preferential tariff reduction to the partner country, if it is assumed that the increase in partner exports represents the net increase in its industrial production resulting from the preference and that the partner country's marginal preference for industrial production is also v. Under the preference p_1, the partner gains an increment of producer's surplus (income transfer) equal to $QH_1 J_1 L$, and an increment of collective utility from industrial production $LX_0' X_1' K_1$; under the preference p_3, the corresponding gains are $QH_3 J_3 L$ and $LX_0' X_3' K_3$.

Taking the two countries together, and cancelling out the income transfer, there is for preference p_1 a net benefit for the two together of $LX_0' X_1' J_1$; for preference p_3, there is a net benefit of $LX_0 X_3' J_3 - ST_3 V_3$. From the assumptions on which the figure is constructed it is obvious that the latter measure must be positive and must increase as the preference increases up to a 100 per cent preference (a change from a preference p_3 to a preference t involves an addition to net benefit of $J_3 X_3' X_4' J_4 - $

$T_3 V_3 V_4 T_4$, and since $T_4 T_3$ is less than $X_3' X_4'$, and $T_3 V_3$ and $T_4 V_4$ are less than $X_3' J_3$ and $X_4' J_4$, this must be positive). If these assumptions held in both countries, the partners would therefore negotiate 100 per cent preferences (reciprocal free trade) in the commodities concerned. The assumptions of the figure are highly restrictive, however: if the industrial production of the preference-receiving country increases by less than its exports, the gain of collective utility to the partner country will be less (say) than the area $LX_0' X_3' K_3$ and may fall short of the sum of the areas $LJ_3 K_3$ (the excess real production cost of the increased exports) and $ST_3 V_3$ (the net loss of real income to the home country from the reduction of its domestic production).

The potential benefit from discriminatory reciprocal tariff reduction, it should be noted, derives from two assumptions of the model: the preference for industrial production, and the convention against export subsidization. The first involves a willingness to sacrifice real product for the sake of greater industrial production, the second prevents countries from implementing the preference for industrial production by direct subsidization of exports. Reciprocal preferential tariff reduction is in fact an arrangement by which each partner indirectly subsidizes its own industrial exports by subsidizing its industrial imports from the other, the subsidy being given in the disguised form of preferential relief from tariffs otherwise payable.

It should also be noted that the foregoing analysis involves both of the effects considered in the standard analysis of preferential tariff reduction — trade diversion and trade creation — and that contrary to the standard analysis trade diversion as well as trade creation yields a gain to the partners; in fact, trade diversion is preferable to trade creation, for the preference-granting country, because it entails no sacrifice of domestic industrial production. This reversal of the usual conclusions is due to the presence of the preference for industrial production, and its frustration by the convention against export subsidization. In these circumstances, the gain of real product from trade creation to the importing country is insufficient to compensate for the loss of real income due to the resulting sacrifice of utility from collective consumption of domestic industrial production; and trade diversion is preferable because, though it involves a real product loss, it does not involve a sacrifice of domestic industrial production.[26] In both cases, however, the gain in a country's real income comes, not from a preponderance of the real product gains from trade creation over the real product losses from trade diversion resulting from the effects of the country's own preferential tariff reduction on its own imports, but from the increase in the country's exports of industrial products resulting from the trade-diverting and trade-creating effects of the partner country's preferential tariff reduction in its favour. Consequently, preferential reciprocal tariff reductions may be negotiated even if they lead to a loss of real product for one or both parties.[27]

The foregoing analysis also indicates the conditions under which reciprocal preferential tariff reduction will be beneficial to the countries concerned, and will therefore be resorted to. Implicit in the analysis are the assumptions that the parties concerned have a strong preference for industrial production, and a weak comparative advantage in industrial production, so that they each export relatively small quantities of industrial products, and gratify their preference for industrial production largely through protection of domestic industry against imports. A country with strong comparative advantage in industrial production would both be able to seek expansion of its industrial production through multilateral tariff bargaining, and might be unable to benefit (in the competitive conditions of the model) from preferential entry to the other country's market, because such preferential entry might merely divert its exports from other countries' markets without significantly affecting their prices. The analysis also requires that the partners have differing comparative advantages (disadvantages) in the various lines of industrial production, so that each can benefit from preferences given by the other. In the preceding analysis, this was implicit in the assumption that each could export some quantity of a

[26] Trade diversion will be relatively still more attractive if the discriminating countries attach positive disutility to the industrial production of the countries discriminated against.

[27] Whether a country's real product rises or falls depends on the net outcome of the trade-creating and trade-diverting effects of the reciprocal tariff reductions, as the standard theory has demonstrated.

product that the other imported in spite of its protection of its domestic industry; that assumption is unnecessarily strong, all that is required being that tariff rates vary so that domestic costs of production of the various commodities exceed their world prices by different proportions in the two countries, the lower costs being found sometimes in one country and sometimes in the other.

Since in the model of protectionism presented above the marginal degree of preference for industrial production is equal in all industries, differences in tariff rates among industries must be due to differences in the behaviour of the consumption cost of protection among industries, or to differences in the extent to which resources employed in one branch of industry reduce production in others, and differences in tariff rate structures among countries must be due to differences in these factors among countries. For tariff rates to be sometimes higher and sometimes lower in one protectionist country than in the other, the latter differences must outweigh any differences in the marginal degree of preference for industrial production among countries. This last requirement implies that only countries with comparable degrees of preference for industrial production are likely to be in a position to benefit extensively from preferential reciprocal tariff-cutting schemes, a point relevant to the the prediction of what countries or groups of countries are likely to engage in such schemes.[28]

Under these conditions, countries can obtain increases in their individual aggregates of industrial production through preferential reciprocal tariff reduction that they could not obtain otherwise, while at the same time increasing their real incomes, and possibly but not necessarily their real products. The benefits accrue primarily through balanced exchanges of lower-cost industrial production in one country for higher-cost industrial production

[28] In the real world, preferences have frequently been exchanged between industrially advanced countries and their less developed colonies or close political allies; these cases can be fitted into the argument by postulating that the advanced country includes the less developed territory in its concept of 'domestic.' Preferences given unilaterally to an industrially advanced country by its colonial dependencies of course fit perfectly into the theory presented here, which offers another way of looking at the phenomena of economic imperialism.

272

in the other (trade creation) and through balanced substitutions for foreign production of domestic industrial production whose collective consumption value exceeds its excess cost (trade diversion). There is, however, a further possible source of gain not comprehended in the preceding analysis: if the reason for the excess cost of domestic industrial production is inefficiency promoted by the small scale of the domestic market and the monopolistic tendencies fostered by the tariff in each country, the trade-creating and especially the trade-diverting effects of reciprocal preferential tariff reduction may permit the harvesting of economies of scale. The preference for industrial production on which the analysis is posited will require that industries subject to the economies of scale be fairly divided up among the participants in the preferential arrangements. This consideration, however, is more relevant to the theory of customs union formation, the subject of the next section.[29]

IV. THE THEORY OF CUSTOMS UNION FORMATION

Preferential tariff arrangements of the type discussed at the end of the previous section are inconsistent with the most-favoured-nation principle, and are frowned on for the quite valid reason that they are likely to be used mainly for protectionist rather than trade-liberalizing purposes. The most-favoured-nation principle can in fact be interpreted as a convention designed to protect the third parties at the expense of whose industrial production the mutual benefits of preferential reciprocal tariff reduction are in part obtained. Under the rules of GATT, however, an exception to the most-favoured-nation principle is made for customs unions and free-trade areas, on the quite questionable assumption that, since these arrangements demand 100 per cent preferences across the board, they are likely to constitute movements in the free-trade rather than the protectionist direction. The standard theory of customs unions has shown that this is not necessarily so, if by 'the free-trade direction' is meant the

[29] A number of the propositions stated in this and the preceding three paragraphs have been arrived at independently by C.A. Cooper and B.F. Massell, 'Toward a General Theory of Customs Unions for Developing Countries,' *Journal of Political Economy*, Vol. 73, No. 5 (October 1965) pp. 461—76.

direction of maximization of real product, while the emergence of the European Common Market has provided a practical demonstration of the protective potentialities of customs unions.

That customs unions will be formed with a protective intent is one of the implications of the analysis of protectionism in the preceding sections, and especially of the assumption of a preference for industrial production. The analysis of preferential tariff reduction is especially relevant, the customs union differing from preferential tariff reduction only in that preferences granted to participants in the arrangement have to be at the rate of 100 per cent, and to apply across the board, and that the tariff rates of members against imports from the rest of the world have to be unified. The purpose of the present section is to apply the theory developed in the preceding sections to various aspects of the formation of customs unions (free-trade areas can be analyzed by obvious extensions of the analysis).

The first problem to be considered is the nature of the gains that are generally alleged to follow from the formation of customs unions. The standard economic analysis of customs unions stresses the gains from trade creation, against which must be weighed the losses from trade diversion; and some weight is put on economies of scale and the promotion of efficiency through competition in a larger market area. These arguments, however, are equally arguments for unilateral tariff elimination, which would have the advantage of entailing no losses from trade diversion; and, apart from the economies of scale argument, which begs the question of why such economies are not exploitable through the world market but can be obtained by customs union, the only economic argument on classical lines for pursuing these gains through customs union rather than unilateral tariff elimination must rest on the possible terms-of-trade loss from unilateral tariff reduction and on the possible terms-of-trade gain for the union as a whole from discrimination against the outside world. The arguments usually advanced for customs unions in political discussion, however, generally ignore any possible gain from trade creation, in the sense of replacement of domestic production by cheaper imports, and instead regard this as a price to be paid for the benefits of expanded export markets, those benefits to result from both trade creation and trade diversion in favour of domestically produced products; and stress is laid on the gains to domestic industry from economies of scale and increased competition in a large market, as well as the 'growth potential' of a larger market area. In these arguments, trade diversion is valued for its effects in increasing production within the union, not for its effects in improving the terms of trade with the outside world; this is significant, because the conditions under which a customs union will divert the most trade are those under which its terms-of-trade effects will be least.

The difference between the two sets of arguments is clearly explainable by the hypothesis that standard economic analysis is concerned with maximization of real product, whereas political discussion derives from a preference for industrial production and is concerned with the maximization of real income conceived to include utility from the collective consumption of industrial production. The latter concern is bound to concentrate on the potentialities of a customs union for increasing the industrial output of the country and the efficiency of its industrial production, rather than on its potentitalities for satisfying private consumption demand at lower cost by increased imports; and to regard such imports as a necessary cost of rather than a benefit from joining a customs union.

A second problem is the characteristics of countries likely to be successful in forming a customs union. As the preceding analysis of preferential reciprocal tariff reduction has shown, an arrangement of this kind will be attractive to countries with a strong preference for industrial production that are (or feel themselves to be) at a comparative disadvantage in industrial production in relation to the world market. A customs union enables them to gratify the preference for industrial production through trade creation and trade diversion, to an extent that would not be possible through negotiation of non-discriminatory tariff reduction.

In contrast to preferential tariff reduction, however, a customs union involves 100 per cent preferential treatment of partners on an across-the-board basis. Instead of being able to pick and choose among commodities on which to give and demand preferences, a country must choose whether or not to participate in the customs union; and it will only choose to participate if there is

275

a reasonable probability of a net gain, by comparison with *either* the situation in the absence of a customs union, *or* the situation in the presence of a union to which it does not belong. In either case, broadly speaking, a country will be motivated to join the union only if it judges that its industrial competitiveness or comparative advantage in industrial production is strong enough for its industrial production to increase within the union (or for any loss in aggregate industrial production to be compensated by increased efficiency). Conversely, the other members will be willing to have it join only if its membership does not threaten to increase its industrial production unduly at the expense of their own. Consequently, customs unions are most likely to be negotiable among countries with a similar degree of preference for industrial production, and with a similar degree of comparative advantage in industrial production,[30] or, as it is sometimes put, countries at a similar stage of economic development. This implication of the theory of protectionism advanced here is confirmed by the formation of the European Common Market, and by the actual and prospective formation of customs unions among groups of less developed countries, in both of which connections much has been made of the 'similar stage of economic development' argument.

A third and final problem concerns the internal arrangements of the customs union. Standard trade theory would suggest that these arrangements would seek to maximize efficiency of production within the union, regardless of where production was located. The preference for industrial production hypothesis, however, would imply that any customs union agreement would include provisions to insure that each member obtains a 'fair share' of industrial production, and particularly that the growth of production in the union does not concentrate in one or a few countries at the expense of the rest. Such provisions are written into the Treaty of Rome, in the arrangements for a Development Fund, and incorporated more generally in the Common Market through the recognition of an obligation to contribute to the development

---

[30] These prerequisites are suggested by consideration of the determinants of the impact of customs union on trade — the initial individual country tariff levels and the industrial structures of the countries — and also by the necessity of the members agreeing on a common tariff level.

of southern Italy. They are even more explicit in the provisions of the Latin American Free Trade Area Treaty, which envisage the Treaty as applying mostly to the establishment of new industries, and are concerned with a fair allocation of the new industries among the participating countries.

V. CONCLUDING COMMENTS

This chapter has departed from the conventional assumptions of international trade theory and welfare economics, that welfare depends on private consumption of goods and services, in an attempt to construct a theory of protectionism, tariff bargaining, and customs union formation. In order to do so, it has posited a 'preference for industrial production,' involving the treatment of industrial production as a collective consumption good the quantity of which is governed by commercial policy. The intention has been to provide a logically coherent explanation of why commercial policy is conducted the way it is.

Any such attempt runs the risk of being misinterpreted as a justification of whatever countries have chosen or choose to do, and a demonstration that economics has nothing to say about what public policy should be. These are misinterpretations, because they fail to distinguish between two separate levels of analysis. At one level an economic decision unit is treated, as in this chapter, as an objective actor in the economic process, with certain preferences whose satisfaction it seeks to maximize, the assumption being that the actor rationally connects means with ends. At a different level of analysis, the analytical problem is precisely what the actor should do to maximize its satisfaction, the assumption being that the actor does not, or does not fully, understand the connections between means and ends. Thus one branch of economics is concerned with the consequences of the assumption that firms act rationally to maximize profits, while another branch is concerned with devising decision rules and operations on data that will yield the profit-maximizing decisions. In this chapter, problems at the second level of analysis have been deliberately concealed in the concept of 'a preference for industrial production,' in order to explore and rationalize the behaviour of governments. That preference, it will be recalled, was so defined as to comprise the effects of electoral ignorance and the influence of power groups on government policy. There is nothing in the analysis of this chapter to prevent an economist from asking whether industrial production yields the economic benefits believed to flow from it, from calculating the real product cost of protection and asking whether the benefits repay this cost, or from insisting that the consumer's interest in low-cost consumption, as contrasted with the producer's interest in high-priced production, deserves more representation in government policy-making than it usually receives.

Appendix:
The Limits of Non-Discriminatory Reciprocal
Tariff Reduction

This appendix develops a simple and somewhat artificial model to demonstrate the proposition stated in the text, that bilaterally negotiated reciprocal tariff reduction on a non-discriminatory basis may cease to be profitable before free trade is reached.

Assume that each country produces exports at constant cost, and import substitutes at increasing cost. Let each country's import demand function (imports being measured in dollar's worth at world market prices) be $M_i(1 - m_i t_i)$, where M_i is the free-trade level of imports, m_i is the slope of the demand curve for imports, and t_i is the tariff rate (expressed as a proportion). The slope of the import demand curve is the absolute sum of the consumption demand and domestic supply curves; let x_i be the proportion of m_i ($0 < x_i \leqslant 1$) composed of the domestic supply slope. Assume further that each country j receives a fixed share s_{ij} in country i's imports

$$0 < s_{ij} \leqslant 1, \qquad \sum_{j \neq i} s_{ij} = 1,$$

this share being determined by some economic mechanism not investigated here. (In fact, these shares can be defined less restrictively, as applying only to the imports excluded by country i's tariff.) Finally, assume that each country attaches a constant social value v_i to a unit increase in industrial production achieved through an increase in exports or in production for the domestic market (by protection). The cost of protection, is, of course, approximately equal to $\frac{1}{2} m_i t_i^2 M_i$.

The difference between the real income of the country under general protection and under general free trade is

$$R_i = - v_i \sum_{j \neq i} s_{ji} M_j m_j t_j + v_i x_i m_i t_i M_i - \frac{1}{2} m_i t_i^2 M_i. \tag{1}$$

If each country takes the tariffs of the others as given, it will maximize its real income by setting its tariff rate at the level required by

$$\frac{\partial Ri}{\partial t_i} = m_i M_i (v_i x_i - t_i) = 0, \tag{2}$$

that is, it will establish the tariff rate $t_i = v_i x_i$. This is the tariff rate from which bilaterally negotiated tariff reductions are assumed to commence.

Now consider reciprocal tariff reduction by countries i and j. Assume that the negotiation comprises a series of exchanges of small tariff reductions, symbolized by $T_i = -dt_i$ and $T_j = -dt_j$. The effects on the respective real incomes of the two countries at each step will be

$$dR_i = v_i s_{ji} m_j M_j T_j - (v_i x_i - t_i) m_i M_i T_i, \tag{3}$$

$$dR_j = v_j s_{ij} m_i M_i T_i - (v_j x_j - t_j) T_j, \tag{4}$$

where t_i and t_j represent the tariff rates established at the termination of the previous step. Note that there must be some gain from non-discriminatory tariff reduction at the first step, because in each equation the first term on the right-hand side is positive, while at the beginning of negotiations the second term on the right-hand side is zero [by the maximization condition of eq. (2)].

The limits to which non-discriminatory reciprocal tariff reduction may go can be investigated by using equations (3) and (4) to define two 'boundary' loci of possible reciprocal tariff reductions, representing successive pairs of marginal tariff reductions that would leave one of the two countries no better off in terms of real income than it was initially. These loci, obtained by setting dR_i and dR_j, respectively, equal to zero are

$$\frac{T_i}{T_j} = \frac{v_i s_{ji}}{v_i X_i - t_i} \frac{m_j M_j}{m_i M_i}, \tag{5}$$

$$\frac{T_i}{T_j} = \frac{v_j x_j - t_j}{v_j s_{ij}} \frac{m_j M_j}{m_i M_i}. \tag{6}$$

Reciprocal tariff reductions on a non-discriminatory basis that will benefit both countries will be possible only so long as the value of T_i / T_j given by equation (5) exceeds the value given by equation (6); that is, so long as

$$\frac{v_i\, s_{ji}}{v_i\, x_i\, -\, t_i} \;>\; \frac{v_j\, x_j\, -\, t_j}{v_j\, s_{ij}}. \tag{7}$$

This condition must hold for the first step of tariff reductions from the initial level, since initially the denominator of the left-hand side and the numerator of the right-hand side are zero. Thereafter, however, the left-hand fraction falls and the right-hand fraction rises, as the tariff rates are reduced.

Will it be possible to reach free trade in the two countries by non-discriminatory reciprocal tariff-cutting? Substitution of $t_i = t_j = 0$ into equation (7) yields the necessary condition

$$\frac{s_{ji}\, s_{ij}}{x_i\, x_j} \;>\; 1. \tag{8}$$

This condition can be given an economic interpretation in several ways; the simplest approach is to express it in terms of conditions on the (geometric) average values of the parameters. Alternative statement of the condition can then be made as follows. Free trade on both sides is attainable through non-discriminatory reciprocal tariff reduction if

(a)   the average share of a country in the expansion of the other's imports exceeds the average proportion of the increase in a country's imports resulting from tariff reduction by which its domestic production of import substitutes is reduced $(s_{ji}\, s_{ij} > x_i\, x_j)$, or

(b)   on the average an increase in a country's imports reduces its domestic production by less than it increases the other country's exports $[(x_j\, /s_{ji})(x_i\, /s_{ij}) < 1]$.

Version (b) amounts to the requirement that reciprocal tariff reduction must increase total industrial production in the negotiating countries, as stated in n. 23. Note that this condition is incapable of fulfilment unless an expansion of imports involves some increase in total consumption, and does not merely replace domestic production (in the latter case, the condition reduces to $s_{ji}\, s_{ij} > 1$, which is by assumption impossible). In general terms, the condition implies that the possibility of reciprocal non-discriminatory tariff reduction proceeding to free trade will be greater, the larger the shares of the negotiating countries in each other's markets, and the more responsive their domestic demand and the less responsive their domestic supply of import substitutes to reduction in the landed price of imports,

Finally, the condition of equation (8) can be used to illustrate the proposition, presented in the text, that preferential arrangements may be more attractive than tariffs. By preferential arrangements, s_{ji} and s_{ij} can be made equal to or greater than unity, so that a free-trade area between the two countries would always be mutually beneficial. This conclusion, however, is limited to this particular model: since exports are assumed to be in perfectly elastic supply, a country incurs no loss from trade diversion effected by preferential tariff reduction.

PART IV:
The Theory of Effective Protection

PART IV.
The Theory of Effective Protection

11. The Theory of Content Protection*

I. INTRODUCTION

In 1960 Dean V.W. Bladen of the University of Toronto was appointed a Royal Commissioner on the Canadian Automotive Industry, and in 1961 he produced a report recommending an 'extended content plan' to improve the competitive situation of the industry in the Canadian and American markets. In May 1963 I published an elaborate critique of the Report and the plan. Since the objectives of the plan were eventually implemented in a substantially different form, through the Canadian-American Automotive Agreement of 1965, there is no point in republishing my detailed critique of that particular plan. However, consideration of it led me to make some general observations on the nature of content protection, and to construct a model of how it works and of how the extended content plan would have worked, which may be of general interest, as content protection has been widely employed, especially in less developed countries.

II. THE CANADIAN SYSTEM OF CONTENT PROTECTION IN 1960

The present system of protecting the automotive industry dates from the tariff revision of 1936. Basically, the present system seeks to protect not merely the assembly of motor vehicles in Canada – which is achieved by the 17½ per cent MFN tariff on completed vehicles – but also the production of parts. The production of parts is protected in two ways: directly by a MFN tariff of 17½ per cent on a long list of parts if these are of a class or kind made in Canada, and of 25 per cent on other parts

---

* An abridged version of 'The Bladen Plan for Increased Protection of the Canadian Automotive Industry,' *The Canadian Journal of Economics and Political Science*, Vol. XXIX, No. 2 (May 1963) pp. 212–38, with an explanatory introduction added.

not specifically provided for; and indirectly by free entry of parts of a class or kind not made in Canada, which increases the effective protection of parts that are made in Canada. In the case of automobile and commercial vehicle manufacturers free entry of parts not made in Canada is conditional on a certain minimum proportion of the factory cost of production during the year being incurred in the British Commonwealth. In automobile manufacturing the content requirement depends on the number of vehicles produced annually, and is 40 per cent for production up to 10,000 units, 50 per cent for production over 10,000 but not exceeding 20,000 units, and 60 per cent for production exceeding 20,000 units; for commercial vehicles the content requirement is 40 per cent regardless of scale of production. Entry of British vehicles and parts under the 1936 tariff was duty-free; but since British participation in the Canadian market at that time was negligible, and since the application of the extended content plan presumes reduction of British preference to a token level, the economic analysis of the two systems of protection can be simplified without loss by disregarding the preference provisions, and assuming that content is purely Canadian.

The analysis of the economic effects of the 1936 system of protection is best approached by comparing the two 'pure' systems of which it is a hybrid, namely tariff protection of parts production at the same rate as applies to imported vehicles, and content protection, abstracting temporarily from the effects of the 'class or kind' distinction and the facts that some rates on parts differ from the rate on imported vehicles and that the content requirement varies with scale of production. In each case our interest is in the maximum degree of protection afforded to Canadian production, the efficiency of protection, and its effects on Canadian production and the cost of protection to the Canadian economy. Maximum degree of protection is measured by the proportional excess of cost of production in Canada that it would be worth the manufacturer's while to incur rather than import and pay duty; efficiency is measured by the extent to which the protective system minimizes the excess real cost per dollar's worth of protected Canadian production; the cost of protection to the economy rightly includes both the excess cost of Canadian production and the loss of consumer's surplus due to the protection-induced increase in price over the world price, but only the production cost will be considered here. It is important to notice that the object of protection is assumed to be total Canadian production of the industry and not the protection of particular Canadian production processes and parts. This assumption is fundamental to the Commissioner's analysis of the industry, and is adopted here as the most economically sensible simple assumption, though it does not necessarily accord with the object that would follow from defence considerations, a closer analysis of the 'external economies' argument or the industry's own definition of society's responsibility towards it.

A tariff on all imported parts equal to the tariff on imported vehicles would afford an equal maximum degree of protection to all stages of the production process, that maximum being equal to the uniform tariff rate. This system would also be efficient, in the sense that at the margin the excess cost of all elements of Canadian production would be equalized at the tariff rate. The system would be efficient in another sense, namely that a firm that could increase its volume of operations sufficiently to permit domestic production of parts subject to economies of scale would thereby acquire a competitive advantage over smaller firms that had to import those parts and pay the duty on them, and ultimately the excess cost of Canadian production would be minimized by the exploitation of all possible economies of scale. The maximum degree of protection being fixed by the tariff rate, moreover, both the volume of protected production and the production cost of the tariff to the economy would vary inversely with the industry's comparative disadvantage in world markets.

The system of protection just described could be converted into one of content protection by waiving all duties on imported parts on condition that manufacturers of vehicles achieved a certain minimum domestic content. The effect of such conversion would be greatly to increase the maximum degree of protection afforded to Canadian production up to the content requirement, since by fulfilling the content requirement the manufacturer would receive a subsidy equal to the duty waived on the imported parts; for example, with a 17½ per cent tariff and a 40 per cent content requirement, the maximum degree of protection would be 59 per cent, and with a 60 per cent content requirement 33 per cent, respectively over three times and nearly twice the nominal degree of protection expressed in the tariff rate.[1] This is, of course, only a particular example of the well-known principle that reduction of the tariff on an input increases the effective protection of the output. It should be noted that the increase in maximum degree of protection just mentioned is an average applying to all the Canadian content; if, as seems certain, some part of the Canadian content can be produced at little or no excess cost, the degree of protection on the remainder can be so much the higher. On the other hand, the degree of protection on Canadian production in excess of the content requirement is zero, and this has implications for the efficiency of this system of protection.

So far as the attainment of each individual manufacturer's required content is concerned, content protection is efficient inasmuch as each manufacturer has the incentive to earn his content with the least possible excess cost of Canadian production. But the fact that the degree of protection is zero after content is earned removes the incentive which the other system provides to the large-volume car manufacturer to produce parts as soon as his scale enables him to produce them at a cost

[1] Let a be the proportion of the value (measured at world prices) of a car produced domestically, c be the required domestic content as a proportion of factory cost of production, and t be the proportional tariff rate on imported cars and parts, and let x be the maximum proportion by which the domestic cost of the production included in a can exceed its world market cost. The value of x is to be derived from the equality of the cost of an imported car, $1 + t$, with the cost of a car produced in conformity with the content requirement, $1 + xa$, or $x = t/a$. The minimum value of a is derived from the content requirement

$$\frac{(1 + x)a}{(1 + x)a + (1 - a)} = c.$$

By substitution,

$$a = c(1 + t) - t$$

and

$$x = \frac{t}{c(1 + t) - t}.$$

below the foreign price plus the tariff, because both he and his smaller competitor can import them free of duty. Thus the system contains no mechanism, or at best a discontinuous mechanism, for improving the efficiency of protection through economies of scale, except to the extent that larger scale enables Canadian content to be fulfilled at lower excess cost. But in the present tariff system and the extended content plan, this last possibility is offset to an unknown extent by the imposition of a higher content requirement on larger-scale output, which reduces the maximum degree of protection afforded to the larger-scale producer and increases the cost of achieving it, to an extent which may or may not be outweighed by economies of scale.

Since the conversion of a uniform tariff system into a content protection system automatically raises the maximum degree of protection afforded on the Canadian content, it is obvious that a content requirement can always be chosen that will increase Canadian output above what could be secured by the alternative uniform tariff. In so doing, it would of course raise the cost of protection to the economy; moreover, this increase could well be accompanied by lower prices of cars to consumers made possible by the waiver of duty on imported parts — consumers would simply have to pay more in general taxation than they gained in lower prices, to make up the loss of tariff revenue to the government. Further, since a well-chosen content requirement would probably leave a considerable margin between the maximum degree of protection and the actual costs of Canadian production firms would have to incur to fulfil their content requirement, there would be a considerable margin of reserve protection to cushion Canadian producers against having to adjust production to changes in comparative advantage.

The Canadian tariff system established by the 1936 revision is, as already mentioned, a hybrid of the two 'pure' systems just discussed, with some additional complications which generally reduce its efficiency by comparison with either of them. The eligibility for conditional free entry of parts of a class or kind not made in Canada increases the effective maximum degree of protection afforded to assembly processes; and the higher tariffs on non-specified parts distort Canadian production towards items with a higher excess cost of Canadian production, while decreasing the effective maximum degree of protection afforded to the automobile manufacturers. Viewed as a system of content protection, as the Commissioner considers it, it is less effective than it could be because conditional free entry applies only to specified parts of a class or kind not made in Canada, and inefficient because in planning their Canadian content production manufacturers are influenced by the existence and differentiation of rates on parts that they cannot escape by fulfilling the content requirement.

The Commissioner is particularly disturbed by the fact that the small-scale producers are obliged to pay duty on parts which they cannot produce, but which the large producers can produce and which therefore become of a class or kind made in Canada, a situation which he regards as inequitable. This position is questionable, on grounds of both equity and efficiency: the large producers are in a sense already taxed by the imposition of higher content requirements, which among other things induces them to develop domestic production of parts that could be more cheaply imported if they could obtain conditional free entry; and for reasons explained above, the undercutting of small-scale producers by larger-scale producers is a part of the process of developing a more efficient industry. The Commissioner, however, regards such undercutting as 'inequitable' and 'inexpedient in a market already dominated by a few producers."

The extended content plan is designed to remedy the defects the Commissioner sees in the present system of content protection. More positively, it is designed to secure the automotive industry, and particularly the parts industry (the Commissioner writes as if the sole intent of the Canadian automotive tariff schedule were to provide a market for Canadian parts), the market opportunity for larger-scale production at lower cost, and this without the risk that a bilateral free trade arrangement would entail. Much is made of the notion of a step towards freer but still safe trade, and some elements of freer trade the plan certainly contains; something is also made of the notion of lower prices for consumers — though almost nothing is said about the expense in lost revenue to the government. Basically, however, the plan is a plan for a much more severely protective scheme of content protection, coupled with a device for extending content protection into export subsidization by the equivalent of tied sales and purchases.

III. AN ILLUSTRATIVE ARITHMETICAL MODEL OF THE CANADIAN AUTOMOTIVE INDUSTRY AND TARIFF SCHEDULE

The economic analysis of the effects of the Canadian automotive tariff, and of the Royal Commissioner's proposed revision of it, is an extremely complex problem for several reasons. In the first place, the 'industry' comprises both the assembly of motor vehicles and the production of parts, the assembly industry providing the market for the parts industry. In the second place, both industries, but essentially the parts industry, are characterized by economies of scale. In the third place, because of economies of scale, the assembly industry contains few producers, and is characterized by an oligopolistic market structure, with all the problems that raises; the same is true of certain sections of the parts industry. In the fourth place, a large proportion of both industries is foreign-owned; the importance of this is that abnormal profits created by protection cannot in this case be treated merely as domestic income transfers involving no net loss to the country.[2] Fifthly, there is the complexity of the tariff schedule itself, due to the combination of the Canadian content provisions, the variation of the content requirement with scale of production of vehicles, the fact that duty-free entry under the content provisions does not apply to parts of a class or kind made in Canada or to the residual category of non-specified parts, and the fact that rates on parts not eligible for duty-free entry vary, and in particular that the rate on non-specified parts is higher than the rate on specified parts. Finally, there is the additional complication of duty-free entry of British-made cars and parts.

[2] The mere earning of profits in a country by foreign enterprise is frequently objected to by the economically illiterate as constituting a loss to the country. In fact, of course, provided such profits are competitively determined they constitute a payment for services rendered by foreign capital and enterprise. In addition, under present international tax arrangements, a country derives a net profit from foreign investment in it, since the taxes it collects on the profits earned by foreign enterprises are not added to the taxes those enter-

In order to facilitate analysis of the essential issues, it is necessary to simplify the problem by constructing a model of the industry and of the tariff schedule applying to it. While an elegant and relatively simple mathematical model could be constructed, it seems more useful to work with an arithmetical model containing actual figures. To simplify the model, the following assumptions are made:

(1) *Technology.* The manufacture of a car consists of assembling four separately produced parts. The assembly process and the production of the separate parts each constitute 20 per cent of the cost of a finished car, the costs of assembly and parts production and the price of the car being reckoned at world market prices. The parts are numbered 1, 2, 3 and 4; only the production of parts 2 and 3 are subject to economies of scale. The assembly process and the separate parts are assumed to cost $200 each at world prices, and the costs of domestic production of the parts are assumed to be: for part 1, $220; for part 2, $260 at a low volume and $240 at a high volume; for part 3, $300 at a low volume and $270 at a high volume; for part 4, $300. Producers are assumed to prefer to import when importing and domestic production cost the same. The cost of assembly in Canada is not specified, for reasons that will appear later.

prises would have had to pay had they operated in their own countries (and so borne by the domestic consumer), but instead are offset against profit taxes otherwise due to the governments of those countries, and so in effect are collected from the foreign taxpayers. American corporation tax law benefits other countries in which American companies conduct business not only in this way but in a number of others, notably through the subsidization of oil exploration by depletion allowances.

The point at issue here is the quite different one that in so far as the tariff creates opportunities for abnormal profits, that is, profits above the competitive level, and these profits accrue to foreign capitalists, only the taxes on these profits represent an internal income transfer (from the consumer to the taxpayer), the remaining untaxed portion representing a transfer to foreigners and therefore a cost to the country. It should be noted that what matters here is foreign ownership, not foreign enterprise; to the extent that domestic residents own stock in the foreign enterprise (or its parent company), abnormal profits earned by that foreign enterprise still involve only a transfer of income between residents.

(2) *Market structure.* Parts production is assumed to be carried on by assemblers, or by independent contractors who sell exclusively to one assembler at a price equal to cost. (This assumption prevents the small-scale assembler from sharing the economies of large-scale production of parts obtainable by the large-scale assembler.) Domestically produced vehicles are assumed to be close but not perfect substitutes for imported vehicles. The assembly industry is assumed to be characterized by oligopoly; this permits three possible competitive strategies — fix price at the level set by world cost of production plus the tariff and appropriate any excess of that price over domestic costs as excess profit; set price in the same way but spend the potential excess profits on non-price promotion of sales of domestically produced cars; set prices equal to domestic costs of production to promote sales by price competition. The model assumes that the automobile manufacturers follow the first course; the effects of the alternatives on the average cost of protection to the consumer, and the volume of Canadian production, are explained briefly at the outset.

(3) *Company ownership and taxation.* By the above assumptions, all excess profits accrue to the manufacturers of cars. The manufacturing companies (car-makers) are assumed to be entirely foreign-owned, so that all excess profits accrue to foreigners. It is assumed that there is no Canadian tax on company profits; this is an important abstraction, for reasons explained in footnote 1 above, and at various points the consequences of assuming instead that 50 per cent of excess profits return to the Canadian economy as taxes or dividends will be indicated.

(4) *The tariff structure.* The tariff is assumed to apply to all imports regardless of origin (i.e., British preference is ignored). The tariff rate is assumed to be 20 per cent (i.e., $40) on imported vehicles and imports of parts 1 and 2, 40 per cent (i.e., $80) on part 3, and 30 per cent (i.e., $60) on part 4. The Canadian content provision is 40 per cent for low volume production and 60 per cent for high volume production and applies to parts 1, 2, and 3 if they are of a class or kind not made in Canada, part 4 not being specified for conditional free entry and carrying

293

a higher rate than the general tariff rate. To avoid a complication of the present content provision, that the excess cost of Canadian production is reckoned into the value of Canadian production and the Canadian content, it is assumed that the content provision specifies the proportion of the world cost of the car that must be produced in Canada. The 40 per cent rate on part 3 does not correspond to anything in the present tariff schedule, so far as can be determined, but is inserted to illustrate a particular theoretical point.

For simplicity, the analysis concentrates on the effect of the tariff in determining the proportion of a given total annual rate of purchase of cars that is produced in Canada and the cost of this to the Canadian economy. On the assumptions about prices and profits made above, this problem can be simplified to the effect of the tariff on the proportion of a Canadian-manufactured car actually produced in Canada, and the cost of protection per car produced, expressed as a total and as a proportion of the Canadian content achieved — the excess cost per car, and the excess cost ratio — since the assumed price-profit policy can be taken to fix the number of Canadian cars produced to meet a given total demand. Where the relation between the domestic price fixed at world price plus tariff and domestic costs yields excess profits, these excess profits might, instead of being appropriated as such, be used to expand sales of Canadian produced cars by price reduction or by non-price competition. The effects of the former strategy on the cost of protection to the Canadian economy would be a combination of a gain in consumers' surplus due to increased consumption of cars, a gain due to the transfer of the excess profits of the foreign owners of domestic car-manufacturing firms into lower prices to consumers, and a loss due to the higher costs incurred in replacing imported cars by Canadian cars. The effects of the latter strategy would be a loss from substitution uncompensated by lower prices, though the methods by which Canadian car sales were increased by non-price competition might yield some psychic gain to consumers; in this case there would be no gain from reduced foreign owners' profits, since these profits would be transformed into real costs of sales promotion.[3]

With this preliminary out of the way, we proceed to analyse the effects of the Canadian tariff on the assumption that any excess of price over the cost of producing a car in Canada is absorbed in excess profits to foreign owners of manufacturing companies. The analysis proceeds in stages, introducing the complications of the Canadian tariff schedule in succession.

First, consider the case of a tariff at a uniform rate of 20 per cent on imports of complete cars and all parts. If assembly and all parts produced in Canada cost more than $40 above world cost, all cars consumed will be imported; if assembly costs less than $40 more than, but all parts cost above $40 more than, world costs all parts will be imported and assembled in Canada. If one or more parts can be produced in Canada at less than $40 above world price, but assembly in Canada costs more than $40 extra, cars will be imported, or the parts in question produced in Canada and assembled in Canada along with imported parts, depending on whether the total costs of assembly plus parts production in Canada average more or less than 20 per cent above world costs. In the latter case, it will be noted, cars will be assembled in Canada at an advance on assembly costs of more than 20 per cent over world assembly costs, some of the protection accorded to parts being transferred to assembly; and the country could reduce the average excess cost of Canadian production by exporting the parts in question for assembly abroad and reimporting assembled cars.

[3] Competitive pricing would be more likely to benefit the consumer the greater the proportion of excess profits that would accrue to foreigners (here assumed to be 100 per cent), the greater the elasticity of total demand for cars and the smaller the Canadian share in the market, and the smaller the cross-elasticity of demand for foreign cars with respect to the price of Canadian cars; whether the Canadian economy gained or lost on balance, by comparison with the competitive strategy assumed here, the excess cost per unit of Canadian content produced would be lower, because the excess production cost per car produced would be the same, the excess foreign profits would be eliminated, and the loss of consumers' surplus in car consumption would be smaller and averaged over a larger volume of Canadian car production; the total excess cost of protected production might therefore be lower, even if more cars were domestically produced. Non-price competition would be likely to increase the total cost of protected production by increasing the production volume, though there would be some reduction in the excess cost per car owing to the spreading of the loss of consumers' surplus over more units.

The fact that the capacity to produce parts at below the advance in cost permitted by the tariff on parts adds to the maximum of protection afforded to assembly, which protection may be used in the form of either excess assembly cost or excess profits, is crucial to understanding the effects of the automotive tariff and of revisions in the rates accorded to automobiles and parts and in the content percentages required. For the purposes of the subsequent argument we take as a reference point the cost of assembly in the world market, and concentrate on the proportion by which the tariff schedule permits the price charged for assembly of Canadian cars — subsequently termed the excess-cost-cum-profit of assembly — to exceed the world price. This reference point, incidentally, accords with the implicit assumption of the Commissioner's *Report*, that the purpose of the tariff is to protect parts production and not assembly.

Given the schedule of costs stated above and the assumed preference for importing when costs of domestic production and imports are equal, a uniform tariff on cars and parts would lead both high-volume and low-volume producers to assemble cars and produce part 1 in Canada. In this case, the excess cost of a Canadian produced car would be $80, of which $20 would be the excess production cost of part 1 and $60 the excess-cost-cum-profit of assembly — an effective rate of protection of 30 per cent on assembly; the remaining $120 of the higher price of a Canadian car would be a transfer from the consumer to the taxpayer and not a real cost to the economy. The excess cost ratio for the Canadian content would be 20 per cent ($80 on a world value of Canadian content of $400).

Now assume that the tariff schedule grants free entry to parts of a class or kind not made in Canada. The effect of this is that the duty becomes excess profit to the assembly companies and therefore excess cost to the economy. The excess cost is now $200 instead of $80, a rate of excess cost of 50 per cent on Canadian content; of this cost $20 is excess cost of Canadian-made parts, and $180 excess-cost-cum-profit of assembly. For this increased excess cost, there is no increase in the proportion of the car produced in Canada, which remains at 40 per cent.

Now assume that the free entry of parts is made conditional only on the fulfilment of a Canadian content requirement. If the requirement is fixed at 40 per cent for small-volume producers and 60 per cent for large-volume producers, the small-volume producer continues to assemble cars and produce part 1, and retains his cost-cum-excess-profit of $180. The large-volume producer has the choice of not fulfilling the content requirement, and returning to an excess-cost-cum-profit of assembly of $60, or of meeting the content requirement by producing part 2, the cheapest he can make. It will be worth his while to incur up to $120 excess cost — the excess profit he would obtain by saving the tariffs on parts 2, 3, and 4 — in producing an additional part, i.e., part 2.

If he had to produce at a low volume, as the low-volume manufacturer would be obliged to do by a 60 per cent content requirement, he would have to spend $60 and for so doing obtain an excess-cost-cum-profit in assembly of $120; instead, by exploiting economies of scale, he can spend only $40 extra and obtain an excess-cost-cum-profit of $140, as contrasted with the $180 of the small-volume producer. The content requirement forces him, in effect, to spend $40 — and in the absence of economies of scale would have forced him to spend $60 — of the excess profit given him by the conditional free entry of parts on the excess cost of producing more of his car in Canada. The total excess cost to the economy of producing a car in Canada is $200 as in the absence of the content requirement, but for the small-volume producer the excess cost of Canadian-produced parts is $20 and the excess-cost-cum-profit $180, whereas for the large-volume producer the excess cost of Canadian produced parts is $60 and the excess-cost-cum-profit $140; the excess cost ratio for Canadian content production is 50 per cent for the small-volume producer and 33⅓ per cent for the large-volume producer.[4] By raising the content requirement for large-volume producers to 80 per cent, the large-volume producer could be forced to produce part 3 in Canada as well, reducing his excess-cost-cum-profit in assembly back to the $60 he would obtain by not fulfilling content and reducing the excess cost ratio for Canadian content production to 25 per cent. At

---

[4] These ratios would be 35 per cent and 26⅔ per cent if half the increases in excess-cost-cum-profit (from $60 to $180 in the one case and to $140 in the other) were recaptured in taxes and dividends.

this point, however, the manufacturer would be cost-indifferent between an 80 per cent and a 40 per cent Canadian content, and by assumption would return to the latter, making the excess cost ratio of large-volume production again 20 per cent. In that case the content requirement would merely have increased the excess cost of Canadian content produced by low-volume manufacturers, without increasing total Canadian production.

The analysis thus far brings out an important feature of content protection. The remission of duty on imported parts increases the effective protection to the assembly industry; it does so indirectly at the expense of the taxpayer rather than directly at the expense of the consumer. The content requirement, when effective, forces the manufacturer to spend the increased profits he would obtain, not on lower prices to the consumer, but on the excess costs of parts production in Canada.[5] As a means of protecting Canadian automotive and especially parts production it may be ineffective for two reasons. The first is that the content requirement may be fixed too high for the free entry of parts conditional on its fulfilment to be used. The second, which has been hidden by our assumption that assembly and production of part 1 would be profitable at the uniform tariff rate without conditional free entry, is that the excess cost of assembly may exceed the excess-cost-cum-profit provided under the uniform tariff, and the content requirement may use up too much of the additional protection provided by conditional free entry to allow the excess cost of assembly in Canada to be met. If the excess cost of assembly exceeded $140 in the above example, the large-volume producer would have to go out of business, though the small-volume producer could remain in business at an assembly cost up to $180.

In the preceding example, the remission of duty on parts was conditional only on fulfilment of the content requirement. Now suppose that it is additionally conditional on the part being

---

[5] There is an interesting parallel between content protection and the regulation of broadcasting by private enterprise: broadcasting regulation attempts to force private broadcasters to spend part of the profits of a natural monopoly on socially desired program content; content protection seeks to force the manufacturer to spend part of the profits of an artificial monopoly created by the tariff on socially desired domestic production.

of a class or kind not made in Canada. In this case, if the large-volume producer produced part 2, the small-volume producer would not be able to obtain duty-free entry of that part, would have to pay duty of $40 on it, and would therefore obtain an excess-cost-cum-profit of only $140, the same as the large-volume producer. Both producers would receive the same increased protection for their assembly operations, but the excess cost ratio for Canadian production would be 40 per cent ($160 excess cost on $400 of Canadian content) for the small-volume and 33⅓ per cent ($200 on $600 Canadian content) for the large-volume producer,[6] so that protection, though equitable as between assembly operations, would be inefficient as a means of encouraging production in Canada. If the large-volume producer could reduce the excess cost of part 2 below the $40 that his rival has to pay in duty, his excess-cost-cum-profit on assembly would rise above that of the small-volume producer; on the assumptions employed here, this would not alter the cost of protection to the economy, though if Canadians had any share in the profits of assembly through dividend receipts or taxes the the cost of protecting large-volume production would be reduced relative to small-volume production and the excess cost ratio of large-volume production in Canada would be reduced.

It should be emphasized that the class-or-kind provision is essential to the preservation of equity between manufacturers subject to different content requirements; otherwise the imposition of a higher content requirement on the larger producer amounts purely to a progressive tax, which he (or those who buy his cars) must pay in the form of excess cost on the additional Canadian content required. In the view of the small-volume producer, however, the operation of the class-or-kind provision gives an unfair advantage to the large-volume producer whenever the latter can produce parts more efficiently than the former can import them. This claim, however, overlooks the fact that the imposition of a higher content requirement places the large-volume producer at a disadvantage by comparison with the small-volume producer; or else it rests on implicit acceptance of the

[6] These ratios would be 30 per cent and 26⅔ per cent if half the advance in excess-cost-cum-profit from the initial level were recaptured.

principle that large businesses should be taxed progressively more than small businesses, a principle which is inherently inefficient economically and can derive no support from the ethics of equality between persons.

For purposes of theoretical analysis it has been assumed that part 3 carries a double rate of duty as compared with part 2 and imported cars. This assumption allows the possibility that, given the class-or-kind provision, the large-volume producer would not in fact make up his content requirement by producing part 2; instead he might produce part 3, since by producing that part he would, given the assumed costs of small-volume and large-volume production of it, oblige his rival to pay $80 duty for a part that he can produce for $70. By this means his excess-cost-cum-profit, which without conditional free entry of parts would be equal to his rival's at $20, would become $70, whereas his rival's would be only $60. In this case the excess cost ratio for Canadian production would be 33⅓ per cent for large-volume production, and only 30 per cent for small-volume production; this reversal of excess cost ratios is a consequence of the tariff on part 3 being above the tariff on part 3 when the latter is imported as part of an assembled car, a fact which enables the government to extract part of the small producer's excess-cost-cum-profit on assembly; and the superior efficiency of small-volume production in this case is a consequence of the small producer's inability to produce a part on which the government has levied a specially heavy tariff. The purpose of this example is to show that the parts tariff can only raise the excess cost ratio of large-volume production above that of small-volume production when the parts tariff rate is higher than the rate on imported cars.

The final complication of the Canadian tariff is the levying of a tariff above the general level on non-specified parts, which parts are not eligible for conditional free entry. In the complete absence of conditional free entry, the imposition of parts tariffs above the level of the tariff on imported automobiles would increase the cost of assembly of cars in Canada, and reduce the effective protection afforded to assembly by the tariff on imported cars and any excess of that tariff over the cost of parts produced in Canada, in the extreme making the excess-cost-cum-profit of assembly too low for assembly and parts production in Canada to be profitable. Short of that extreme, higher duties of this kind would give an incentive to produce the relevant parts in Canada, provided the cost fell short of the world cost plus the (higher) tariff, even though other parts enjoying less protection could be produced at a lower absolute cost, though still at a cost exceeding the world price plus the (general) tariff. In other words, a higher-than-average parts tariff would encourage an inefficient choice of parts for production. This possibility is excluded in the present case, however, by the assumption that the Canadian cost of production exceeds the world cost plus the (higher) tariff.

With free entry of the other parts conditional on content fulfilment only, the picture changes. The small-volume manufacturer simply loses the subsidy that remission of the tariff on this part would have given him — his excess-cost-cum-profit being reduced to $120 — but continues to assemble and produce part 1. The large-volume producer's choice of what part to produce to earn his content is, however, now influenced by the consideration that if he produces parts 2 or 3 he does not escape duty on part 4, but that if he produces part 4 he escapes duty on all three. In the example, if he chooses to produce part 2 at an excess cost of $40 he saves $120 duty on parts 2 and 3 and has to continue to pay duty on part 4; if he produces part 4 at an excess cost of $100 he will save $180. He thus obtains a net gain of $80 in each case, and might produce either part; but a slight decrease in the cost or increase in the tariff on part 4 would induce him to choose that part. If he chooses to produce part 2, the excess cost ratio for his Canadian production is $23\frac{1}{3}$ per cent ($140 on $600 of Canadian content), whereas if he chooses to produce part 4, the excess cost ratio for his Canadian production is $33\frac{1}{3}$ per cent ($200 on $600 of Canadian content). In the latter case, the effect of the higher tariff on part 4 and that part's ineligibility for conditional free entry is to induce a pattern of production whose excess cost ratio is higher than necessary; note that the incentive to such a pattern is primarily the ineligibility for free entry, which prevents the manufacturer from escaping the duty on this part except by producing it, though the excess of the tariff rate above the general rate increases the incentive.

Now consider the effect of making the free entry of scheduled parts conditional on their being of a class or kind not made in Canada. This introduces the additional complication that by producing part 4 instead of part 2, the large-volume producer relieves the small-volume producer of the obligation to pay duty on his imports of part 2. In the example, the choice of part 2 instead of part 4 would impose an extra cost on the small-volume producer of $40, reducing his excess-cost-cum-profit to $80, the same as the large-volume producer would receive.

This situation, in which the small-volume producer assembles and produces part 1, and the large-volume producer assembles and produces parts 1 and 2, and each has an excess-cost-cum-profit of assembly of $80, is a convenient starting point for the analysis of the potential effects of the extended content plan. The situation may be described more fully as follows. The small-volume manufacturer sells cars at an advance on world price of $200, of which $20 is laid out on the excess cost of producing part 1 in Canada, $40 on the duty on part 2, and $60 on the duty on part 4; to protect his $400 of Canadian production, the country is incurring a net cost of $100 — $40 each on assembly and production of part 1, plus $40 duty remitted on part 3, less $20 duty collected on part 4 in excess of the difference between the world price of that part and its Canadian price when imported as part of a car — an excess cost ratio for small-volume Canadian production of 25 per cent. The large-volume manufacturer also sells cars at an advance in price of $200, of which $20 is laid out on the excess cost of producing part 1 and $40 on the excess cost of producing part 2 in Canada, and $60 on duty on part 4; to protect his $600 of Canadian production, the country is incurring a net cost of $140 — $40 each on assembly and production of parts 1 and 2, plus $40 remitted on part 3, less $20 excess duty levied on imports of part 4 — an excess cost ratio for large-volume Canadian production of $23\frac{1}{3}$ per cent. For both producers, the assembly process is protected at the rate of 40 per cent, the excess of 20 per cent over the 20 per cent tariff on imported cars being made up of 10 per cent corresponding to the excess of the Canadian price of part 1 over the cost of producing it in Canada, and of 10 per cent corresponding to the net effect of remission of the 20 per cent duty on part 3 and the charging of a 10 per cent excess duty on part 4 (above the 20 per cent charged on imported cars).

The extended content plan has four constituents, which for the present purpose can be grouped into three — free entry for all parts, provided only that the content requirement is met; revision of the content requirement schedule to increase its progressivity and extension of its base to include imports; and extension of eligibility for satisfying the requirement to exports. These will be taken up in turn.

In terms of the example, free entry of all parts conditional only on content fulfilment would involve two changes. First, providing the content requirement is fulfilled, the duty on part 4 would be remitted. Remission of this duty would increase the excess-cost-cum-profit of assembly for both small-volume and large-volume manufacturers by $60, to $140, thus increasing the effective rate of protection on assembly from 40 per cent to 70 per cent. This increase would be given at the expense of the taxpayer, and would increase the cost of protecting the small-volume producer to $160, and of protecting the large-volume producer to $200, per vehicle, thus raising the excess cost ratios on Canadian production to 40 per cent and $33\frac{1}{3}$ per cent respectively.[7] Second, the duty on part 2 paid by the small-volume manufacturer would be remitted; this would increase the excess-cost-cum-profit of small-volume assembly to $180, and the rate of protection on small-volume assembly to 90 per cent, as contrasted with the 70 per cent received by the large-volume assembler.[8] Put another way, in the example the elimination of the class-or-kind provision and of the distinction between scheduled and non-scheduled parts would give $2\frac{1}{4}$ times the previous effective tariff rate on assembly to the small-volume manufacturer, and $1\frac{3}{4}$ times the previous effective tariff rate on assembly to the large-volume manufacturer, the differential increase for the small-volume manufacturer being due to the elimination of the class-or-kind requirement.

[7] With 50 per cent recapture of the advance in excess-cost-cum-profit these ratios would be $32\frac{1}{2}$ per cent and $28\frac{2}{3}$ per cent.

[8] The excess cost ratio for small-volume Canadian production would be 50 per cent, or $37\frac{1}{2}$ per cent with 50 per cent recapture of increased profits.

The elimination of the class-or-kind provision discriminates against the large-volume manufacturer. This discrimination is reinforced by the second constituent of the extended content plan, the revision of the schedule relating content requirement to volume and extension of the base to which it applies to include imports of cars. The revision of the schedule apparently reduces the content required of the small-volume manufacturer, while leaving that required of the large-volume manufacturer in its present neighbourhood; but the extension of the base in fact increases the content requirement imposed on large-volume manufacturers by including imported cars, which are an important part of the sales of the large companies. In terms of the example, suppose that the effective content requirement is reduced to 30 per cent for the small-volume manufacturer and increased to 70 per cent for the large-volume manufacturer.

Assuming that the small manufacturer meets his content requirement by producing half his supply of part 1 in Canada and importing the other half, the reduction in content requirement would give the small-volume manufacturer an excess-cost-cum-profit of $190 as contrasted with the $180 mentioned above, increasing the rate of protection of small-volume assembly to 95 per cent and the excess cost ratio of small-scale Canadian production to $66\frac{2}{3}$ per cent ($200 on Canadian content of $300).[9] By contrast, if the large manufacturer could split production of part 3 half and half between domestic production and imports without losing the economies of large-scale production, his excess-cost-cum-profit of assembly would be reduced from $140 to $105, decreasing the rate of protection of large-volume assembly to 52·5 per cent and the excess cost ratio of large-scale Canadian manufacturing to 28·57 per cent ($200 on $700 of Canadian content).[10] If, on the contrary, the large-volume manufacturer had to choose between just fulfilling his content by producing half his supply of part 3 in Canada at low-volume cost or over-fulfilling his content requirement by producing all his supply of part 3 in Canada at high-volume cost — both of which alternatives would involve a higher cost than the case

[9] With 50 per cent recapture of increased profits, $48\frac{1}{3}$ per cent.

[10] With 50 per cent recapture of increased profits, 26·79 per cent.

just described — he would (on the cost figures assumed) choose the former alternative. This would reduce his excess-cost-cum-profit of assembly to $90 (as compared with $70 on the second alternative), decreasing the rate of protection of large-volume assembly to 45 per cent, the excess cost ratio of large-scale Canadian manufacturing being 28·57 per cent as before.[11]

These two constituents of the extended content plan therefore discriminate severely against the large-scale manufacturers. The small-volume manufacturer would benefit from elimination of duty on non-scheduled parts, elimination of the class-or-kind provision, and a reduction in his content requirement. The large-volume manufacturer would benefit only by the elimination of duty on non-scheduled parts, and would lose by the increase in his content requirement. He necessarily loses relative to the small-scale manufacturer, and he may well lose absolutely (the arithmetical example is dominated by the assumption of a very large remission of duty on non-scheduled parts to both manufacturers).

This discrimination against the large-volume producer involves substantial economic inefficiency, owing to the sharp differentiation of the excess cost of protected Canadian production between small-volume and large-volume manufacturing. The effects of the discrimination might be so sharply adverse to the large manufacturers as to produce results the reverse of what the plan is intended to achieve. Suppose, for example, that the small manufacturer had a volume of 10,000 cars, and the large manufacturer a volume of 100,000 cars, and that the discrimination led to the replacement of the large manufacturer by ten small manufacturers. On the assumptions previously made, the Canadian content of production of the 110,000 vehicles in question would fall from the equivalent of 64,000 to the equivalent of 33,000 instead of rising to 73,000 as expected — a reduction equivalent to 31,000 vehicles instead of an increase equivalent to 9,000. At the same time, the excess cost of production of the 110,000 vehicles would rise (in terms of the example) from $14,100,000 to $22,000,000, i.e. by $7,900,000 — the country would have paid $7·9 million for a 31,000 vehicle-

[11] With 50 per cent recapture of increased profits, 27·86 per cent.

equivalent decrease in Canadian production, all of it of course incurred in parts production. It should be mentioned, however, that of the $14·1 million only $8·8 million, while of the $22·0 million $20·9 million is excess-cost-cum-profit of assembly; if half the increase were recaptured in taxes or dividends, the increase in the cost of protection would be reduced to $1·85 million.

The third element of the extended content plan is the inclusion of imported cars in the base for content requirement and of exported parts in the category of production fulfilling content requirement; this provision allows an escape from the excess costs imposed by the content requirement. In the arithmetical example, the large-volume manufacturer could, by exporting 2½ units of part 1 for every one incorporated in a Canadian car, achieve his 70 per cent content requirement and at the same time increase his excess-cost-cum-profit of assembly from $105 to $130, less whatever foreign tariffs he had to pay on exported parts (he could afford, therefore, to pay foreign duties up to 10 per cent of the world price of part 1). If the excess cost of Canadian assembly were higher than the excess cost of the cheapest part, it would pay him to shut down his Canadian assembly operations and import finished cars. If, for example, the excess cost of Canadian assembly were $80 (the excess cost plus profit of both producers before the extended content plan was applied), he would increase his excess profit from $25 to $110 by going entirely into the parts business. Note that the small-volume manufacturer would also increase his excess profit by $60 (from $100 to $170) by converting to parts production.

12. The Theory of Tariff Structure, with Special Reference to World Trade and Development[*][1]

The formal theory of tariffs, like most of the theory of international trade, has been constructed on the assumption of a world in which commodities are all final goods — goods destined for final consumption — and are produced entirely with the use of original factors of production. Yet in the real world, many commodities are raw materials, fuels, intermediate goods, or capital goods destined for use in production processes making other goods; and the production processes for making commodities use other commodities as inputs, in addition to using original factors of production. Similarly, in the real world international trade comprises not only goods destined for final use, but raw materials, fuels, semi-finished goods and capital goods destined for use in the production processes of other goods. Moreover, the tariff schedules or structures of countries take account of these differences between goods, levying duties at rates that differ not only between commodities but according to the nature of the goods and the stage of the production process at which they enter the country.

The fact that internationally traded goods enter the production process at different stages and with different functions, and are subject to duties varying according to stage of production, has important implications for tariff theory, tariff policy, and tariff negotiations. These implications have only begun to be explored by economists.[2] Their significance has only begun to become

[*] From Harry G. Johnson and Peter B. Kenen, *Trade and Development* (Geneva; Librairie Droz, 1965) pp. 9–29.

[1] A lecture delivered at the Institut Universitaire de Hautes Etudes Internationales, Geneva, June 3, 1964. The research underlying this chapter was supported by a grant from the Rockefeller Foundation.

[2] The most important references are:
   Clarence L. Barber, 'Canadian Tariff Policy', *Canadian Journal of*

apparent to governments and the educated general public in connection with the problems encountered in the preparations for the forthcoming 'Kennedy Round' of tariff negotiations under GATT, as a result of the fact that the Common Market method of across-the-board reciprocal tariff reductions, adopted by the United States in the Trade Expansion Act, has thrown emphasis on the characteristics of tariff structures in connection with the so-called problem of 'tariff disparities' and the increased protectionism inherent in the Common Market's common agricultural policy.[3] The most important of these implications are the necessity of recognizing that a tariff on a good used in a productive process is equivalent to a tax on the output of that process, and the consequent necessity of distinguishing sharply between the structure of tariff rates on commodities entering international trade, and the structure of rates of protection accorded by the tariff structure to the specific processes or stages of production that make up the productive system. The latter are commonly

Footnote continued

Economics and Political Science, Vol. XXI, No. 4 (November 1955) pp. 513–30;

W.M. Corden, 'The Tariff', in Alex Hunter (ed.), *The Economics of Australian Industry* (Melbourne: Melbourne University Press, 1963);

Harry G. Johnson, 'The Bladen Plan for Increased Protection of the Canadian Automotive Industry', *Canadian Journal of Economics and Political Science*, Vol. XXIX, No. 2 (May 1963) pp. 218–38, reprinted as Chap. 11 of *ibid*, *The Canadian Quandary* (Toronto: McGraw-Hill of Canada, 1963); and condensed in Chapter 11 above;

William P. Travis, *The Theory of Trade and Protection* (Cambridge: Harvard University Press, 1964).

[3] The problem of 'tariff disparities' refers to disparities between rates levied by different countries on the same commodity, which disparities are alleged to make equal percentage reductions in tariff rates unfair to the low-tariff country. Strictly speaking, this is not a problem of tariff structure in the sense dealt with in this paper, and therefore is not discussed below. In the early stages of the discussion of tariff disparities, however, the French argued for 'harmonization' of tariff rates as a solution to the problem, 'harmonization' meaning the establishment of standard tariff rates of say, 0 per cent for raw materials, 5 per cent for semi-manufactured products, and 10 per cent for manufactures. (See *Common Market*, Vol. 4, No. 2 (February 1964) p. 23.) As will be shown in the analysis below, 'harmonization' of this type would have little to recommend it, since the implicit rates of protection would necessarily escalate and might differ widely among commodities.

referred to as rates of protection of value added, or 'implicit' or 'effective' rates of protection.

The purpose of this chapter is to explore some of the implications of tariff structures in the light of this distinction, with special reference to the effects of typical tariff structures on patterns of world trade and development. For this purpose I shall use rather different analytical tools than are usually employed in conventional tariff theory, namely the techniques of the Leontief input-output system. This analytical apparatus is generally considered to be too restrictive for most analytical purposes, since it assumes constant costs and ignores all possibilities of substitution between outputs in consumption and between inputs of commodities and or original factors in production, but it is useful for bringing out the main points raised by the present problem. In using the apparatus, I shall not only ignore its limitations but also confine attention to the implications of tariff structures for the protection of processes of production; I shall not, except incidentally, attempt to delve into the difficult problem of the effects of tariff structures in protecting the use of factors of production and hence influencing factor prices.[4]

An input-output system can be written in the form

$$(I - a_{ij})(x_j) = (x'_j)$$

where I is the unit matrix, a_{ij} is the technical coefficient expressing the input of the ith commodity into the jth process per unit of output of that process, and x_j and x'_j are respectively the gross and the net outputs of the jth commodity in the system. For simplicity, it is customary to measure quantities of goods in unit values, so that a_{ij} is the value of the input of the ith good per unit value of the output of the jth good. In the application of the input-output relationships to tariff problems, it is the price rather than the production aspects of the system that

---

[4] The problem is difficult because, by affecting factor prices, the tariff structure will influence the determination of the processes actually carried on and the prices of the goods for which protection is effective in establishing domestic production; see Travis, *op. cit.*, Chap. 4 for fuller discussion.

are relevant; these may be written

$$(v_j) = \left(1 - \sum_i a_{ij}\right)$$

where v_j is the value added or income earned by the factors used in the jth production process, per unit of output. Also, due to the presence of tariffs (which make domestic prices diverge from world market prices), it is necessary to choose whether to value commodities at domestic or world market prices; the latter method of valuation is easier to handle symbolically, but the former is necessary for practical applications since input-output tables are generally constructed from data expressed in domestic prices. The following analysis is for completeness conducted initially in terms of both methods of valuation, primed symbols being used for domestic values and unprimed symbols for world market values. It is important to note that throughout the analysis the basic technological input-output relationships are assumed to be the same in domestic and in foreign production; this assumption is acceptable, of course, only as a first approximation.

The analytical problem may now be stated as follows: given the input-output system and a tariff structure t_j consisting of tariff rates on imports of the commodities j, to find τ_j, the set of rates of protection of value added in producing the commodities j afforded by the tariff structure t_j, the τ_j's being defined as the maximum proportions by which the tariff structure allows the domestic value of the factors used in the jth production process to exceed their value at world market prices. It should be noted that for consistency with the assumption that international trade takes place, it is necessary to assume that one or more of the commodities is exported, which means that the relevant tariff rate is either zero or non-effective.

To take first the input-output system expressed in world market values, we have in world production

$$v_j = 1 - \sum_i a_{ij}$$

and in domestic production

$$v'_j = 1 + t_j - \sum_i a_{ij}(1 + t_i).$$

Using the definition of the rate of protection of value added or effective rate of protection

$$v_j' = (1 + \tau_j)v_j$$

we obtain the result

$$\tau_j = \frac{t_j - \sum_i a_{ij}t_i}{v_j} = \frac{t_j - \bar{t}_j \sum_i a_{ij}}{v_j} = t_j + \frac{(t_j - \bar{t}_j)\sum_i a_{ij}}{v_j} \quad (1A)$$

where $\bar{t}_j = \sum_i a_{ij}t_i / \sum_i a_{ij}$ is the weighted average tariff rate on inputs of commodities into the jth production process.

Similarly, taking the input-output system expressed in domestic values, we have in domestic production

$$v_j' = 1 - \sum_i a_{ij}'$$

and in world production

$$v_j = \frac{1}{1 + t_j} - \sum_i a_{ij}' \frac{1}{1 + t_i}.$$

Again using the definition of the implicit rate of protection

$$v_j' = (1 + \tau_j)v_j$$

we obtain with some manipulation the result

$$\tau_j = \frac{v_j't_j + \sum_i a_{ij}' \dfrac{t_j - t_i}{1 + t_i}}{v_j' - \sum_i a_{ij}' \dfrac{t_j - t_i}{1 + t_i}} = t_j + (1 + t_j)\frac{\sum_i a_{ij}' \dfrac{t_j - t_i}{1 + t_i}}{v_j - \sum_i a_{ij}' \dfrac{t_j - t_i}{1 + t_i}} \quad (1B)$$

Appearances to the contrary, the right-hand side of (1B) is identical with that of (1A);[5] since (1A) is so much simpler symbolically, it is used for purposes of further discussion.

[5] By using the relationship $a_{ij} = (1/1 + t_i)a_{ji}^t$, the numerator of the right hand side of (1B) can be reduced to $(1 + t_j)\sum_i a_{ij}(t_j - t_i)$, and by using this relationship and the definition of v_j' the denominator can be reduced to $1 - \sum_i a_{ij}(1 + t_j) = (1 + t_j)v_j$; hence the whole right hand side reduces to

$$t_j + \frac{\sum_i a_{ij}(t_j - t_i)}{v_j},$$

which is identical with the right hand side of (1A). Note that in this case $v_j + \sum_i a_{ij} = 1/(1 + t_j)$, not unity.

The first and most obvious implication of equation (1A) is that the rate of protection of value added in a production process can differ widely from the tariff rate applicable to the commodity produced in that process. The two rates of protection will in fact be equal only if $\bar{t}_j = t_j$, that is, if the weighted average tariff rate on inputs into the process is equal to the tariff rate on the product produced by that process.

The implicit rate of protection will be higher than the explicit tariff rate if the weighted-average tariff rate on imported inputs is lower than the tariff rate on the output; it can in fact attain a maximum of t_j/v_j if all inputs enter the country free of duty.[6] The implicit rate of protection will be lower than the explicit tariff rate if the weighted-average tariff rate on imported inputs is higher than the tariff rate on the output. The implicit rate of protection can indeed be negative (implying a tax on domestic production) even though the explicit tariff rate is positive and substantial; the condition for this, derived from equation (1A), is obviously $t_j < \bar{t}_j \sum_i a_{ij} = \bar{t}_j(1 - v_j)$; that is, the tariff rate on the output must be less than the weighted average tariff rate on the inputs multiplied by the ratio of value of inputs to selling price. This condition will necessarily be fulfilled for exports, the tariff rate on which is zero or ineffective; exports will be subject to negative protection to the extent that they employ inputs that are subject to tariff protection.

The divergence of implicit from explicit rates of protection results from the fact that in an input-output system tariffs simultaneously provide subsidies to domestic production of the goods on which they are levied and impose taxes on the domestic production of other goods using the protected goods as inputs. The complexities resulting from this dual role of tariffs have long been recognized in tariff legislation, and exploited in tariff bargaining, though not always with a clear understanding of the issues.

---

[6] The implicit protection rate can of course exceed this maximum if some inputs are subsidized, either directly, or indirectly through the taxation or prohibition of exports of them if they are exportable.

In the first place, the fact that a tariff on an input is a tax on the output has been generally recognized in national tariff legislation in the form of provision for 'drawbacks' or remission of tariffs paid on imports incorporated in goods subsequently exported. 'Drawbacks', however, can only be effectively administered if the imported inputs are clearly distinguishable, and their use is obviously confined to cases where the purpose of the tariff is to raise revenue and not to protect domestic production of the inputs in question. Where the purpose of the tariff on inputs is protective, its imposition raises a problem for the policy-makers, since by taxing the process employing the input the tariff may destroy the market for the product it seeks to protect. To avoid this, it is usually necessary to grant a tariff also to the product in whose production the protected input is used; such a tariff is primarily 'compensatory' rather than 'protective', in the sense that it seeks to offset the competitive disadvantage imposed by the tariff on the input rather than to grant a competitive advantage. In terms of equation (1A), a tariff at the rate of $t_j = \bar{t}_j \sum_i a_{ij}$ is necessary to compensate the jth production process for the tariffs levied on its inputs; a tariff at this rate would put the jth process in the same competitive position with respect to the home (but *not* the foreign) market as it would enjoy under free trade. Recognition of the compensatory argument for tariffs is exemplified by the *Report of the Royal Commission on the Canadian Automotive Industries*, where the view is taken that the primary purpose of the Canadian tariff on automobiles is to provide a market for the output of the protected Canadian automotive parts industries, and the handicap imposed on the automobile manufacturers by the protection of parts production is advanced as an argument against continued free entry of British automobiles under Imperial Preference.[7] A similar example is provided by President Kennedy's action in imposing a duty on imports of cotton textiles when U.S. sales of raw cotton in the world market at prices below the supported domestic price encouraged foreign manufacturers to manufacture textiles from U.S. cotton for export to the U.S. market. The problems imposed by the use of the tariff to protect goods that

7 See Harry G. Johnson, *op. cit.*

function primarily as inputs are, however, often inadequately appreciated — as witness the prolonged difficulties encountered by the United States in its attempt to protect both its ship-building industry and its ocean shipping industry.

In the second place, the fact that a reduction in tariffs on the inputs is equivalent to an increase in the tariff on the outputs has influenced tariff legislation and negotiation in various ways. By granting free entry to some or all inputs, a country can increase the protection afforded by the tariff on the finished product. This possibility is incorporated in the provisions of certain countries' tariff legislation by which duties are applicable only to goods of a type produced domestically. It is exploited in the system of 'content protection' practised in various countries, according to which free entry of components is allowed providing a certain proportion (by value, and sometimes by weight) of the final product is produced domestically; the consequence is to increase the protection afforded to that part of the product that is domestically produced by transferring to it the protection that would otherwise have to be shared with the imported part. It has also been exploited in tariff negotiations; by negotiating tariff reductions on imported raw materials and semi-finished goods a country can increase the degree of protection afforded by its tariff structure to its production of finished goods while seeming to lower its protective barriers. Moreover, since the height of these barriers is generally measured in a rather naive fashion, by weighting tariff rates by import volumes or simply dividing total duties collected by total value of imports, such a policy will tend to reduce the measured degree of protection by encouraging the low or zero duty imports of materials and semi-finished goods and discouraging the higher-duty (and still higher effective protection rate) imports of finished goods.

The fact already mentioned, that a tariff on inputs constitutes a tax on output, and specifically that a tariff on inputs used in export industries necessarily constitutes a tax on exports, has some interesting implications for economic development policy as currently practised in the underdeveloped countries. Developing countries typically rely heavily on industrialization fostered by policies of protection and import substitution; the argument for such a policy generally involves the assertion that either domestic agriculture or the traditional primary export industry, as the case may be, is backward and incapable of embarking on the development process by modernizing itself. Protection of industrialization on the basis of this assertion, it should be noticed, involves the imposition of taxation on exports or domestic agriculture, to the extent that these activities employ manufactured inputs, and thereby tends itself to provide evidence justifying the assertion that these sectors are incapable of providing the basis for economic growth. Further, insofar as import substitution policies, by raising the costs of manufactured inputs, discourage their use, they tend to create the appearance of technical backwardness and remove the incentive to modernization through greater use of produced inputs. In these ways development policies of industrialization and import substitution, far from providing the solution to underdevelopment, may be a major cause of its continuance.

The analysis thus far has demonstrated that the implicit rates of protection offered by a tariff structure can differ widely from the explicit tariff rates, and may be much higher or much lower than the explicit tariff rates, and even negative. This is a general analytical finding; to illustrate its relevance and importance, it is appropriate to quote some calculations of the rates of protection of value added implicit in the United States tariff structure, performed by Giorgio Basevi, formerly a student at the University of Chicago. Basevi's method conformed to equation (1B), and made use of an input-output table at domestic values in conjunction with a set of matching tariff rates for 1958; since the origin of some material inputs was unspecified, Basevi made two alternative calculations, one [estimate (a)] assuming these materials to be subject to the average tariff rate collected on imports (7·0 per cent), the other assuming them to enter free of duty [estimate (b)]. A few of the more striking results are set out in Table I.

The first three results illustrate the conversion of positive tariffs on commodities into negative protection of processes through the influence of protection of inputs; the results for rice milling and textile bags are especially interesting, since

315

TABLE I. *Some implicit rates of protection in the United States tariff structure*

Industry	Tariff Rate (%)	Implicit Rate of Protection (%)	
		(a)	(b)
Poultry dressing plants	5·9	−10·3	−6·1
Rice milling	14·3	−27·9	−27·2
Textile bags	10·1	−16·1	−12·3
Cigars	53·0	+98·2	+99·4
Venetian blinds and shades	40·0	+106·6	+126·3
Watches and clocks	51·9	+143·1	+175·3

Source: Giorgio Basevi.

the nominal tariff rates are high enough to afford what many people would regard as a quite substantial degree of protection. The second three results exemplify effective protection far in excess of the nominal tariff rate as a consequence of low tariff rates on inputs. In two cases [both estimate (a) and estimate (b)] the effective rate of protection exceeds one hundred per cent. This is particularly interesting because the U.S. Congress has in the past made it a point not to legislate tariff rates of 100 per cent or over — the American Selling Price method of valuation, which applies to rubber footwear and coal tar products, was invented specifically to permit a lower tariff rate to give protection beyond the 100 per cent level — but as the figures show protection at an effective rate well over 100 per cent can also be attained with nominal tariff rates of 50 per cent or less.

The foregoing analysis has been concerned with the relation between the explicit tariff rates embodied in a tariff structure and the implicit rates of protection of productive processes or of value added in these processes afforded by the tariff structure. I now turn to the application of this analysis to the implications of the tariff structures typical of the modern world. The typical tariff structure of an advanced industrial country, as these tariff structures have emerged from tariff legislation and its amendment and from bargaining under the Reciprocal Trade Agreements Acts and in the postwar period under GATT, entails escalation or 'cascading' of tariff rates such that rates are zero or low on raw materials and fuels, higher on semi-manufactures, and highest on final products. (This feature is illustrated by Tables II and III.[8] The tariff structures of under-developed countries also tend to follow this pattern, especially after allowance is made for protection by exchange controls, import restrictions and tax concessions in addition to protection by tariffs.

A tariff structure escalated in this way is frequently defended as 'modern' or 'rational', and at one point in 1963 it was even urged by the EEC that the objective of the Kennedy Round negotiations should be to 'harmonize' the tariff rates of the

TABLE II. *Arithmetic average tariff rates, France and Germany*, 1953–55

Item	Germany (%)	France (%)
All tariffs	15·5	18·1
Food, drink and tobacco	24·8	23·0
Raw materials, other than mineral fuels	6·4	8·1
Mineral fuels and related material	49·7*	6·8
Chemicals	13·3	19·9
Manufactured products	13·5	18·5

*These duties consist mainly of high consumption taxes on petroleum; the degree of refinery protection was estimated to be 6 per cent in Germany and 8 per cent in France in 1957.

Source: William P. Travis, *op. cit.*, p. 211.

industrial countries at standard and rising levels for successive stages of fabrication. The only explicit argument in favour of an escalated tariff structure that I have found is presented by Clarence L. Barber, who argues that if the effective rate of protection on goods at the first stage of production is greater than the nominal tariff rate, tariff rates at subsequent stages must be still higher to give these stages the same degree of effective protection as is afforded at the first stage.[9] One might notice in passing that though the concept of equal effective rates

[8] These two Tables are drawn from much fuller Tables and supporting analysis in Travis, *op. cit.*, to which the reader is referred for more extensive treatment of many of the points sketched out in this section of the chapter.

[9] Clarence L. Barber, *op. cit.*, p. 524.

TABLE III. *Arithmetical average tariff rates by sector, Japan, 1960*

Intermediate Primary Production		Intermediate Manufactures		Final Manufactures	
Subsector	Tariff Rate (%)	Subsector	Tariff Rate (%)	Subsector	Tariff Rate (%)
Metal mining	0.0	Iron and steel	15.0	Machinery	19.5
				Transport equipment (excluding ships)	22.5
				Ship-building	15.0
Agriculture and Forestry	4.4	Paper and products	13.6	Lumber and wood products	7.6
				Printing and publishing	33.3
				Processed foods	23.5
		Textiles	13.3	Textiles (final consumption)	22.7
		Leather and products (excluding apparel)	20.0	Apparel (including rubber and leather)	25.9
		Rubber products (excluding apparel)	17.5		

Source: Travis, *op. cit.*, p. 199.

of protection appears superficially to be fair and equitable, there is in fact no reason to think that it represents the most efficient way of achieving the objectives of protection,[10] and that in any case it is impossible to apply to exported goods.[11] Ignoring that objection, however, let us investigate the validity of Barber's argument.

It turns out that the proposition is correct only in one special case: if production processes can be arranged in a chain such that each process uses as inputs only original factors of

[10] There are two reasons for this. First, some lines of production may have greater social value in the eyes of protectionists than others, and so warrant more protection. Second, though equalization of effective rates of protection will tend to equalize the marginal social cost of protected production in all lines, this is not a valid standard for minimization of the social cost of protection, since protection imposes a consumption cost through the distortion of consumers' choices, and there is no reason to think that the marginal consumption cost will be equalized by equal effective rates of protection.

[11] This is, of course, the insuperable obstacle to all efforts to rationalize protection by tariffs; exports can be 'protected' by subsidies, but a general effort to protect all industries by import tariffs or export subsidies would have virtually the same effect as a devaluation, yielding no protection.

production and the output of the preceding process in the chain, then if the effective rate of protection exceeds the nominal tariff rate at the first stage, the nominal tariff rates must be successively higher at each subsequent stage to afford the same effective rate of protection to all stages.

For proof, consider the ith stage, and set the desired common effective rate of protection at τ; to obtain this effective rate of protection, it is necessary to choose t_i such that

$$\frac{t_i - a_{i-1, i} t_{i-1}}{v_i} = \frac{t_i - (1 - v_i) t_{i-1}}{v_i} = \tau.$$

On rearrangement, this requires

$$\begin{aligned} t_i &= v_i \tau + t_{i-1} - v_i t_{i-1} \\ &= t_{i-1} + v_i (\tau - t_{i-1}) \\ &= \tau - (1 - v_i)(\tau - t_{i-1}). \end{aligned}$$

From this it follows that if t_{i-1} is less than τ, t_i must be greater than t_{i-1} and less than τ; hence if t_1 is less than τ, to achieve the same effective rate of protection on all stages requires $t_1 < t_2 < - - < t_n < \tau$, where n is the number of stages. It should be noted, however, that $t_1 = v_1 \tau$; hence, for the tariff rate at the first stage to be less than the effective protection rate, the first stage must employ some inputs that are either exported, or imported free of duty (to make $v_1 < 1$).

The assumption that the productive system can be arranged in a chain such that each process uses only original factors and the output of the preceding process, or in a set of parallel chains of this kind, is however clearly unrealistic. And even if the production processes can be ordered so that each uses only original factors and outputs from processes lower in the order, the proposition ceases to be true. To see this, consider a three-process production system of this type, in which commodity 1 enters as an input into the process of production of commodity 2, and both enter as inputs into the process of production of commodity 3. The tariff rates required to afford equal rates of effective protection to the three processes are determined by the three equations

$$\frac{t_1}{v_1} = \frac{t_2 - a_{12}t_1}{v_2} = \frac{t_3 - a_{13}t_1 - a_{23}t_2}{v_3} = \tau.$$

The solutions are

$$t_1 = v_1\tau$$
$$t_2 = [v_1 + v_2(1 - v_1)]\tau$$
$$t_3 = [v_1 + (1 - v_1)(v_2 + a_{12}v_3 - a_{13}v_2)]\tau.$$

If v_1 is less than unity, t_2 must be greater than t_1; but t_3 must be greater than t_2 only if $(v_3/v_2) > (a_{13}/a_{12})$, which depends on the empirical magnitudes of the input coefficients.

In the general case, where commodities enter as inputs in preceding as well as succeding processes of production, an equal rate of protection of each process requires selecting the t_js so that $t_j - \sum_i a_{ij}t_i = v_j\tau$, or in matrix notation $[I - A'](t) = \tau(v)$, where A' is the transpose of the matrix of input-output co-efficients $[a_{ij}]$. The solution is $(t) = \tau[I - A']^{-1}(v)$, and it is obvious that no general solution for the relative magnitudes of the tariff rates to be applied to different stages of production can be obtained; the required rates will depend on the specific values of the input coefficients.

The validity of the proposition that escalation of tariff rates with stage of production is required to give equal degrees of effective protection is therefore limited to the special case in which production processes can be arranged in a 'chain' or a set of parallel 'chains'. In the latter case, it should be noted, each chain of tariff rates should escalate, but there is no reason to expect tariff rates to be similar at corresponding stages of the different chains since the required rates will depend on the value added coefficients for the first and succeeding stages of production in the chain; consequently even in this case the proposition would provide no support for the notion that tariff rates at comparable stages of production should be 'harmonized'.

In the general case, failing concrete evidence to the contrary, it is reasonable to assume that the escalation of tariff rates with stage of production typical of modern tariff structures

320

implies a corresponding but steeper escalation of effective rates of protection with stage of production. Such a pattern of effective tariff rates has important implications for the patterns of world trade and economic development.

So far as the pattern of world trade is concerned, the tendency of protective tariff structures escalated by stage of production is obviously to bias trade towards raw materials, fuels, and semi-fabricates; towards producers' goods (capital goods) rather than consumers' goods; among manufactured consumers' goods, towards goods of a luxury nature capable of bearing high tariffs; and towards both producers' and consumers' goods distinguished by technical superiority sufficient to overcome the competitive disadvantage imposed by tariffs. These biases are especially evident in the trade policies and patterns of the underdeveloped countries; in the advanced countries they are frequently inter-mingled with the effects of policies of protection of domestic agriculture and primary production adopted to prevent or mitigate the reduction of income in these sectors consequent on technical progress in the face of inelastic demands.

With respect to economic development, it is necessary to consider separately the implications of tariff escalation in both the advanced and the underdeveloped countries.

The escalated tariff structures of the advanced countries obviously create serious barriers to the development of the underdeveloped countries on the basis of their resources of relatively cheap labour, and instead bias the opportunities for development of the underdeveloped countries through international trade towards dependence on the exploitation of natural re-sources. It is somewhat paradoxical that in their dealings with the advanced countries the underdeveloped countries have been almost exclusively concerned with the level and variability of the prices of their primary products and with schemes for raising and stabilizing these prices; and that they have paid so little attention to the escalation features of the advanced countries' tariff structures, which tend to confine the comparative advan-tage of the underdeveloped countries to natural resource products and to prevent them from exploiting their advantages in the form of cheap labour on the basis of a large world market. In particular, the escalated tariff structures of the advanced countries tend to prevent the underdeveloped countries from taking what would seem to be the most natural first steps towards industrialization, the establishment of first processing of their own natural resources.

This point may be illustrated both by a hypothetical example and by some concrete cases. To take the hypothetical example first, suppose that advanced countries permit free entry of a certain raw material, but impose a 10 per cent duty on it after it is first processed; and that one quarter of the value after first-processing represents the cost of (value added in) first-processing. To be able to compete in the advanced country market for the first-processed product over the 10 per cent tariff, the underdeveloped country would have to be able to produce that product for 10/11 (= 91 per cent approximately) of the advanced country price. But since 75 per cent of the advanced country price is the cost of raw materials, the same in both countries, the cost of first-processing in the underdeveloped country must be only 16 per cent of the advanced country price, as compared with 25 per cent in the advanced country, for the underdeveloped country to be able to supply the first processed product competitively. In other words, the cost of value added can be up to 9/16 (over 50 per cent) greater in the advanced country, or down to 9/25 (over 33⅓ per cent) less in the underdeveloped country, without the latter being able to overcome the competitive disadvantage imposed by the 10 per cent advanced country tariff on first processing. Nor is this all: the cost of value added includes both labour costs and capital charges, and presumably is internationally mobile, so that the competitive position of the underdeveloped country depends on its relative labour costs. If half the value added in the advanced country (12½ per cent of the price) is capital costs, and these would be the same in both countries, the underdeveloped country must have labour cost of 3½ per cent of the advanced country price as compared with labour cost of 12½ per cent of the price in the advanced country: to be able to compete over a tariff of 10 per cent on first processing, the underdeveloped country must have labour costs less than 30 per cent of those in the advanced country.

The heavily protective effect of apparently low duties on first processing is illustrated by the following concrete examples furnished by my colleague D. Gale Johnson. These examples actually relate to the hypothetical effects of free entry of raw products combined with a 10 per cent duty on first processing on U.S. exports of agricultural products to the Common Market, developed as part of an analysis of the effects of the Common Market's agricultural policy on U.S. agricultural exports, but they illustrate the general point being made here.

1. *Cottonseed*. In recent years the processing cost of cottonseed into oil, meal, linters and hulls has been about $25·00 per short ton. The price of cottonseed in the U.S. at mills in 1962 was $47·90 per ton. The price in Western European ports is estimated at $60·00 a ton. Assuming the same transport costs on raw and processed cottonseed, a 10 per cent duty on oil, meal and other products would come to $8·50 per ton, equivalent to a duty rate of 34 per cent on the processing cost of $25·00.

2. *Soybeans*. In recent years, processing cost of soybeans into oil and meal has averaged approximately 20 cents per bushel of soybeans. In 1962, the average price of No. 2 Yellow in Chicago was $2·51 per bushel. The price in Western European ports was estimated at $3·00 per bushel. Thus, assuming equal transport costs on processed and unprocessed soybeans, a 10 per cent duty on soybean oil and meal would amount to an effective tariff of 160 per cent (32 cents on a 20 cent processing cost).[12]

[12] Data source: U.S. Department of Agriculture, *Agricultural Statistics* 1963, pp. 118 and 121 for cottonseed processing costs and prices, pp. 138 and 140 for soybean processing costs and prices. Note that in these examples the effective protection rate is increased by the fact that the tariff applies to landed cost including transport cost, a factor not considered in the main argument of this chapter; also that European processing costs in the soybean case could be as high as 30 cents, and the U.S. be unable to compete even if processing cost nothing.

Some estimates of the effective protection afforded by the Canadian tariff structure to processing industries are presented by Barber, *op. cit.*, p. 525; these show effective tariff rates running about double the nominal rates. The British Monopolies and Restrictive Practices Commission *Report on the Supply and Export of Certain Semi-Manufactures of Copper and Copper Based Alloys* (1955) contains the information that the *ad valorem* duty rate of 15 to 20 per cent amounts to some 80 per cent or more of the conversion cost at contemporary copper prices (pp. 94, 101,. I am indebted to Gerard Curzon for this reference.)

The escalated tariff structures of the advanced countries are therefore a potentially powerful inhibitor of economic growth in the underdeveloped countries. This may be especially so with respect to industrial products that demand a mass market to permit efficient exploitation of economics of scale, a market not available within the underdeveloped countries themselves.

Turning to the underdeveloped countries, their pursuit of protection by escalated tariff structures or the equivalent use of foreign exchange and import controls, tax incentives, and public investment may also be a potentially powerful deterrent to their economic growth. The reason for this is the waste of resources involved in protection – through high-cost domestic production of goods that could be imported more cheaply from other countries – combined with the fact that the waste of resources involved in protection may be much greater than appears at first sight from tariff rates or from the difference between the domestic and the foreign prices of protected commodities. A variety of arguments have of course been advanced in recent years to the effect that the excess cost of protected production in underdeveloped countries is not 'really' waste – the external economies argument, the infant industry argument, the terms of trade argument, the argument that wages in industry exceed the opportunity cost of labour to the economy, and so on – but it is extremely likely that in many cases the excess money costs of protected production are greater than can be justified by any of these alleged sources of divergence of money cost from social opportunity cost, especially as the excess cost may be considerably greater than it appears to be.

To discuss this point it is necessary to alter the analytical approach somewhat, in order to focus on the excess cost of protected production rather than the degree of protection afforded by the tariff structure; this change of viewpoint also permits attention to some aspects of the cost of protection not considered in conventional tariff theory.

The cost of protection to a country is frequently judged by the extent to which it raises prices to consumers above world market levels. This is not, however, an accurate measure of the excess cost of protected production to the economy, for a variety of reasons. In the first place, the higher price due to protection discourages some consumption of the protected commodity,

324

thereby causing a loss of consumers' surplus – the 'consumption cost' of protection – additional to the increased cost of the goods actually consumed. Second, insofar as some part of total consumption is supplied by imports, the duty collected on these imports returns to the community and must be offset against the higher domestic price. Third, insofar as the protected commodity is produced with the aid of imported materials or components, any duties collected on these inputs should be deducted from the higher domestic price. On the other hand, the use of imported inputs implies that the domestic productive activity fostered by protection is less than the value of the final product, since part of the domestic price paid for that product is indirectly a purchase of imports, so that the excess cost per unit of protected productive activity is greater than the excess price of the final product. It is this factor in particular that tends to make the excess cost of protection greater than it appears. Fourth, if protection is provided by tax concessions or subsidies rather than by tariffs or other restrictions on imports, its cost appears as a loss of government revenue rather than as an increase in prices to consumers. Finally, the excess money cost of protection may overstate the true social cost of the factors employed in producing protected output, for a variety of reasons some of which have been mentioned earlier, and others of which have to do with fiscal considerations.

To elaborate on these complexities in the assessment of the cost of protection, it is convenient to work with the domestic costs of protected production rather than directly with the tariff. Assume a commodity available in the world market at a unit price made up of v_j of value added and $\sum_i a_{ij}$ of produced inputs, and produced domestically under protective policies at a domestic price of $1 + \rho_j$. Assuming for simplicity that the whole of the domestic market is supplied from protected domestic production, and ignoring cross-effects on the demands for other goods, the total consumption cost of protection is approximately[13]

[13] For the method of deriving this formula, which measures the area of the lost triangle of consumers' surplus, see Harry G. Johnson, 'The Cost of Protection and the Scientific Tariff,' *Journal of Political Economy*, Vol. LXVII, No. 4 (August 1960) pp. 327–45, Chapter 6 above.

$$\frac{1}{2}\left(\frac{\rho_j}{1 + \rho_j}\right)^2 \eta_j(1 + \rho_j)C_j$$

and the consumption cost per unit of final product is $1/2 \times (\rho_j^2/1 + \rho_j)\eta_j$, where η_j is the elasticity of consumption demand for the product, and C_j is the quantity consumed under protection. On the production side, assume that domestic productive activity comprises only the value-added component (for this purpose, domestically-produced inputs can be lumped in with value added in both domestic and foreign production) and that the inputs are imported. Further, assume that importing the inputs in original form costs a fraction d_i more than would importing the inputs embodied in the finished good — this is a realistic assumption, given packing costs and pricing policies for components — and that some imported inputs are subject to tariffs t_i. Finally, let the excess of the domestic over the foreign cost of value added be represented by the fraction e_j. On these assumptions, the domestic cost of production per unit is

$$1 + \rho_j = (1 + e_j)v_j + \sum_i (1 + t_1)(1 + d_i)a_{ij};$$

the excess of the domestic price over the foreign price is

$$\rho_j = e_j v_j + \sum_i (d_i + t_i + d_i t_i)a_{ij}.$$

The excess production cost per unit of final product, however, is

$$e_j v_j + \sum_i d_i a_{ij},$$

and the total excess cost (production and consumption) per unit of final product is

$$e_j v_j + \sum_i d_i a_{ij} + \frac{1}{2} \cdot \frac{\rho_j^2}{1 + \rho_j}\eta_j = \rho_j - \sum_i (1 + d_i) t_i a_{ij} + \frac{1}{2} \cdot \frac{\rho_j^2}{1 + \rho_j}\eta_j.$$

Footnote continued
Note that if some consumption demand is supplied from imports, the consumption cost per unit of final product will be

$$\frac{1}{2} \cdot \frac{\rho_j^2}{1 + \rho_j}\eta_j \frac{C_j}{P_j},$$

where C_j and P_j are respectively the numbers of units consumed and produced.

The excess cost per unit of final product, in other words, is less than the difference between the domestic and the foreign price by the tariff revenue collected on inputs, and greater than the price difference by the consumption cost imposed by the price difference. What matters in assessing the cost of protection, however, is not the excess cost per unit of the final product, but the excess cost per unit of protected activity (value added), which is

$$
e_j + \frac{\sum_i d_i a_{ij} + \frac{1}{2} \cdot \frac{\rho_j^2}{1 + \rho_j} \eta_j}{v_j}
$$

$$
= \rho_j + \frac{(1 - v_j)\rho_j - \sum_i (1 + d_i) t_i a_{ij} + \frac{1}{2} \cdot \frac{\rho_j^2}{1 + \rho_j} \eta_j}{v_j}
$$

$$
= \rho_j + \frac{\sum_i a_{ij}[\rho_j - (1 + d_i) t_i] + \frac{1}{2} \cdot \frac{\rho_j^2}{1 + \rho_j} \eta_j}{v_j} .
$$

This excess cost consists of three parts: the excess cost of domestic value added, the excess cost of imported inputs, and the consumption cost of protection; and it can be substantially greater than the excess price of the final product, especially if v_j is small and inputs are imported at little or no excess cost and low or zero duty rates.

As an example, suppose $t_i = d_i = 0$ (inputs enter duty free at their foreign cost) $v_j = 1/2$ (value added is half the foreign price) and $\rho_j = 1$ (the domestic price is double the foreign price), and ignore the consumption cost element. Then the excess cost per unit of protected activity would be 2 — the country would be paying 3 units of domestic resources to replace foreign productive activity worth one unit. This would only be economical if the alternative opportunity cost of domestic resources were one-third or less of their money value — if, for example, domestic resources in the protected industry were priced at three times their value in other sectors of the economy, or the marginal revenue from exports were only one third or less of the average

327

revenue, implying an elasticity of foreign demand for exports of $1\frac{1}{2}$ or lower. Moreover, if the d_i were positive the country would be replacing less than one unit of foreign activity by domestic activity, and the overpricing of resources or inelasticity of foreign demand would have to be even stronger for protection to be economical. Note also that the consumption cost element, ignored in the foregoing argument, may be substantial; if the elasticity of demand were unity, the excess cost per unit of protected productive activity would be $2\frac{1}{2}$ instead of 2.

The analysis just presented refers to protection the cost of which is borne by the consumer in the form of higher prices. In the development policies of the underdeveloped countries, however, it has become increasingly common to provide protection or stimulate import substitution by tax incentives of various kinds. The same effect can be obtained through the establishment of public enterprises exempt from taxation, since the exemption is a form of subsidy. Subsidies provided by tax exemption should be reckoned in the cost of protection if the enterprise is domestic, since presumably the factors employed would otherwise have been employed elsewhere in the economy and would have paid taxes. For example, suppose that through tax exemptions the government in effect provides a subsidy at the rate of σ_j on the domestic cost of value added; this will increase the excess cost per unit of protected activity by $(1 + e_j)\sigma_j$.

The proposition that tax concessions should be included in the cost of protection is, however, confined to protection of enterprises employing domestic factors of production. If protection serves the purpose of attracting foreign enterprise, as it may be specifically designed to do and frequently does even if not intended to, the situation and the appropriate calculation of the cost of protection are different. The reason is that, because of double-taxation arrangements, the location of a foreign enterprise in a country enables it to tax foreign capital (and possibly labour and management). In this case, instead of adding the value of any tax concessions, it is necessary to deduct the net gain of tax revenue in calculating the cost of protection: from the formula presented above for the cost of protection per unit of protected activity must be subtracted an amount $(1 + e_j)T_j$, where T_j is the proportion of domestic value added that consists of taxes on foreign factors of production that without protection would not be present to be taxed. The production cost of protection per unit of protected activity (i.e., excluding the consumption cost) would then be

$$e_j + \frac{\sum_i d_i a_{ij}}{v_j} - T_j(1 + e_j)$$.

This might well be negative, showing a net gain from protection on the production cost side: if, for example, half of domestic value added consisted of the earnings of foreign capital, and this capital were taxed at the rate of 50 per cent, making T_j 25 per cent, the country would enjoy a net gain on the production cost of protection so long as the domestic cost of value added were less than one-third greater than the foreign cost (assuming $d_i = 0$) or so long as the excess of the prices of imported inputs above their embodied cost averaged less than a quarter of foreign value added (assuming $e_j = 0$). Such a net gain from protection, of course, would be obtained at the expense of making world production as a whole less efficient than it otherwise would be, and also at the direct expense of the foreign government that would otherwise collect the taxes on the capital.

It is unlikely, however, given normal levels of tax rates and shares of profits in value added, that the opportunity to tax foreign capital provided by protection will justify very high degrees of protection. Nor is it likely that foreign elasticities of demand for exports will be low enough, or domestic factors used in import-substituting activities over-priced enough or the source of sufficiently great external economies, to justify protection on the scale frequently found in underdeveloped countries. (This is, of course, a personal judgment based on observation of some underdeveloped countries and on consideration of the likely magnitudes of the variables in the formulas presented above — unfortunately, almost no empirical work has been done on the cost-benefit analysis of protection in underdeveloped countries.) Rather, it seems likely that protection at current levels is prone to waste resources through the real excess costs of import substitution, and by so doing reduce both actual real income and the potential for economic growth.[14] Further, since many underdeveloped countries have been following policies of progressive import substitution — policies which fit naturally into a syndrome of inflationary development programmes, balance-of-payments difficulties, and import-substitution policies to cope with balance-of-payments deficits — it is probable that the waste of resources increases over time, thereby cancelling out part or all of the gains in productivity that should normally accrue from the accumulation of experience, the improvement of skill, and the reinvestment of profits. This may indeed be a partial explanation of why so many underdeveloped countries, in spite of having invested so much of their own and the advanced countries' çapital in economic development programmes, have had so much difficulty achieving the take-off into a self-sustaining growth of income per head.

[14] In his 'An Economic Justification of Protectionism', *Quarterly Journal of Economics*, Vol. LXXII, No. 4 (November 1958) pp. 496—514, Everett Hagen presents data on the ratio of the unskilled urban wage to the (male) agricultural wage in various advanced countries (Table 2, p. 502), the modal ratio being 1.4; he also refers to Arthur Lewis's observation that in the underdeveloped countries wages in the 'capitalist sector' are usually equal to income in the 'subsistence sector' plus 30 per cent or more. If these differentials are assumed to correspond entirely to an artificial premium on industrial labour — which is questionable on a variety of grounds — and the consumption costs of protection are ignored, they would justify import duties ranging downwards from 40 per cent to 30 per cent respectively, depending on the share of labour cost in total cost according to the formula $t = dw$ or $t = w'd/(1 + d - w'd)$ where t is the tariff required to offset the wage differential and w and w' are the shares of labour cost in total cost valued respectively at the agricultural and the industrial wage rate.

The *Economic Survey of Asia and the Far East*, 1963, Table II. 13, pp. 41—43, presents data on the import duties applicable to the import-substitution industries of various Asian countries. For comparison with the foregoing argument, the unweighted average tariff rates are as follows: China (Taiwan) 37 per cent (37 items); India 36 per cent (35 items); Republic of Korea 44 per cent (9 items); Pakistan 64 per cent (12 items); the Philippines 40 per cent (13 items); Thailand 35 per cent (4 items). Some of these items bore (and presumably needed) no duties. Imports of some were subject in addition to controls; on the other hand, part of the tariff protection was undoubtedly offset by currency overvaluation.

13. The Theory of Effective Protection and Preferences*[1]

In the past five years, international trade specialists concerned with the theoretical analysis and practical measurement of the impact of commercial policy on world trade and specialization patterns have been developing and applying a new approach to this range of problems, the concept of effective protection, or as it is variously termed, implicit protection or protection of value added.[2] Interest in these policy problems, which had subsided to a low level in the immediate postwar phase of concern with chronic dollar shortage on one hand and with import-substituting policies of promoting economic development on the other, has been revived as a result of three developments. First, the preparations for the Kennedy Round of negotiations under the General Agreement on Trade and Tariffs (GATT), and specifically the replacement of commodity-by-commodity negotiations by the new principle of bargaining for so-called 'linear' tariff reductions across-the-board, raised in an acute form the question of the relative levels of national tariff barriers, which would determine the 'fairness' or otherwise of equi-proportionate reciprocal tariff reductions, and therefore the hoary problem of how to measure national tariff levels. Second, the 1964 United Nations Conference on Trade and Development (UNCTAD), the convocation and the ideological basis of which derived in large part from the belief that the existing GATT system of regulating

* *Economica*, Vol. XXXVI, No. 142 (May 1969) pp. 119–38.

[1] This chapter was originally presented as a paper to the Annual Conference of the Association of University Teachers of Economics, Reading, 1967. It has benefitted particularly from comments by Bela Balassa and W.M. Corden, and has been revised to take account of some subsequent developments in the theory.

[2] See references listed at the end, and also the brief history of contributions to the literature in Corden [3(b)]. (References in square brackets are to the list at the end of this chapter.

international trade barriers discriminates unfairly against the export interests of the less-developed countries, and especially against their exports of manufactured goods to the developed countries, stimulated interest in the empirical investigation of the evidence for this contention.[3] Third, scholars working on the development policies of the less-developed countries have been increasingly concerned with the apparent irrationality of the protectionist policies of these countries, and with the measurement of the economic waste that such policies may entail.[4] In all three contexts the concept of effective protection has proved illuminating, and its application in empirical research has produced a mounting volume of evidence on the influence of commercial policy on international trade, specialization and development.

In this chapter I shall not attempt any sort of comprehensive survey of the contributions to empirical knowledge that have been accumulating in consequence of the application of the new concept, though I shall refer to some of them in the course of the argument. Instead, I shall attempt, first, to outline the essentials of the new approach, second, to apply it to the problems of the measurement of tariff barriers and the cost of protection, and third, to develop some of its implications for customs-union theory, in the particular case of the proposal advanced at UNCTAD for the granting of preferences for the manufactured exports of the less-developed countries in the markets of the developed countries. In the first part of the chapter I must necessarily be brief; such brevity can be excused on the grounds that the main points are rather simple, and that several good expositions are available in print.[5] In the second and third parts, I shall deliberately use very crude models of the economic system, essentially partial-equilibrium models or general-equilibrium models from which most of the substitution possibilities of such models have been removed. The reason for proceeding in a fashion so 'contrary to the general-equilibrium

[3] See the three papers by Balassa [1(a), (b), (c)], and my study [7(d)] of the issues raised at UNCTAD.

[4] See Soligo and Stern [10], and Krueger [8].

[5] See, for example, Johnson [7(a)], Balassa [1(a)] and Corden [3(b)].

spirit of modern international trade theory is two-fold; to avoid the use of complex mathematical formulae, and to make the results potentially applicable to empirical study.

I. THE THEORY OF EFFECTIVE PROTECTION

The foundation of the effective-protection approach to the analysis of tariffs and their impact is the recognition that an industrial society is a complex of economic activities or processes each of which uses as inputs the products of other processes and produces outputs that in part serve as inputs into other processes. In such a system, the tariffs embodied in a national tariff structure influence the location of activities as between that nation and others exporting to it in two contrasting ways: as tariffs on outputs they provide a subsidy to location of the activity within the nation; as tariffs on inputs they impose a tax on the location of the activity within the nation. To determine the influence of national commercial policy on the international location of productive activities, therefore, requires determination of the net subsidies to or taxes on the various activities — specifically, on value added in these activities — implicit in the whole national tariff structure. More accurately, one should perhaps refer to the intended influence of national commercial policy, since the actual outcome will depend on other countries' policies, domestic cost conditions, and so forth.

There are two possible alternative empirical approaches to the problem. One consists in detailed study of the influence of the tariff structure on a particular narrowly-defined industry or output process; this approach has the virtues of desirable disaggregation, but raises the problem of aggregating the results, which are arduous to obtain, into general conclusions about the effects of tariff structures. The other makes use of the information contained in input-output tables; in order to do so, however, it is necessary to accept a high degree of aggregation, and also to assume that domestic prices are equal to world market prices plus tariffs and ignore any substitutions between inputs induced by protection. Both approaches assume that world prices can be taken as given — an assumption legitimate for most countries of the world.

333

To expound the central concept, I shall use the input-output system approach; and for algebraic simplicity, I shall assume that the input-output table provides inputs per unit of output, valued at world market prices, though in practice input-output tables are generally expressed in domestic values. I shall also for the time being ignore the influence of other taxes than tariffs, and of transport costs, and treat value added as being added by a homogeneous original factor. Then for every commodity j, reckoning at world market prices,

$$1 = v_j + \sum_i a_{ji}, \tag{1}$$

where v_j is value added and the individual a_{ji} represent the inputs of commodity i into the output of a unit of commodity j. In the domestic market of the tariff-imposing country, however, assuming that all goods are traded and that their domestic prices are kept by international competition equal to the world price plus tariff,

$$1 + t_j = v_j' + \sum_i a_{ji}(1 + t_i), \tag{2}$$

where v_j' is the value added in domestic production, per unit of output. (For consistency with the assumption that trade occurs, it must be assumed that some product is exported and hence unprotected; the analysis can however easily be extended to take account of export taxes or subsidies.)

We now define the effective protection rate accorded to the jth process by the tariff structure — the proportion by which the tariff structure permits value added domestically at the margin to exceed what it would have to be for the domestic industry to exist under free trade,

$$v_j' = (1 + \tau_j)v_j. \tag{3}$$

On substitution, this yields the formula for the effective protection rate for value added in the jth process,

$$\tau_j = \frac{t_j - \sum_i a_{ji} t_i}{v_j}. \tag{4}$$

This formula[6] can usefully be expressed in the alternative forms

$$\tau_j = t_j + (t_j - \bar{t}_j) \frac{\sum_i a_{ji}}{v_j}, \tag{5}$$

where $\bar{t}_j = \sum_i a_{ji} t_i / \sum_i a_{ji}$ is the weighted average tariff rate on inputs into the jth process; and

$$\tau_j = \frac{t_j}{v_j} - \frac{\sum_i a_{ji} t_i}{v_j} = S_j - T_j, \tag{6}$$

where S_j may be described as the gross subsidization rate per unit of value added in the jth process accorded by the tariff imposed on imports of the jth commodity, and T_j may be described as the implicit tax rate per unit of value added in the jth process imposed by the tariffs on inputs into that process.

Equation (6) brings out the dual subsidy-tax influence of the tariff structure on the jth activity, and is particularly relevant for the analysis of the effects of tariff changes; in particular, it suggests that tariff reductions may have predominantly protection-increasing effects if they are concentrated on commodities that serve mostly as inputs. Equations (4) and (5), on the other hand, bring out the important point that the effective rate of protection accorded to a *process* may differ widely, and in either direction, from the nominal rate of protection of the *commodity* produced by the process. At one extreme, with no inputs subject to tariff, the effective protection rate may be a multiple of the nominal rate, its ratio to the latter being equal to the reciprocal of the

---

[6] If domestic input-output tables are used, we have, with primes representing the domestic input coefficients per unit domestic value of output,

(i) $$1 = v'_j + \sum_i a'_{ji}.$$

Deflating to obtain international values,

(ii) $$1/(1 + t_j) = v'_j/(1 + \tau_j) + \sum_i a'_{ji}/(1 + t_i);$$

whence

(iii) $$\tau_j = \frac{v'_j}{1/(1 + t_j) - \sum_i a'_{ji}/(1 + t_i)} - 1.$$

value-added coefficient, becoming in fact equal to the gross subsidization rate; at the other extreme, with no tariff protection of the product — the case of unsubsidized export goods — the effective protection rate may be negative, and will be equal to the implicit tax rate. Even with a positive nominal protection rate, the effective protection rate may be negative. Instances both of effective protection rates well in excess of nominal tariff rates, and of negative effective protection rates allied with significant positive nominal rates, have been found by several empirical investigators.[7]

The interest of the effective protection approach, however, derives not so much from the fact that effective protection rates on processes may depart widely from the nominal tariff rates on the output commodities, as from the fact that national tariff structures tend to have a common form, and moreover a form which differentiates among commodities according to their place in the input-output system in a way that imparts systematic biases to the influence of protection on trade and industrial location.

In general terms, the tariffs of the developed countries tend to be escalated by stage of production, being zero or low on raw materials, higher on intermediate products made primarily from those materials, higher still on intermediate products of greater complexity, and higher still on finished goods. This pattern, however, is modified by the imposition of relatively lower duty rates on capital goods, and also by the imposition of relatively low duties on technologically-sophisticated consumer goods.[8] The result is that the barriers imposed by the developed countries against imports of the relatively technologically-unsophisticated and relatively unskilled-labour intensive manufactures that the less-developed countries might hope to export to them are significantly higher than the barriers these countries impose against the imports they are likely to be capable of exporting to one another. A particular feature of the tariff structures of the developed countries that discriminates

[7] Balassa [1(a)], Basevi [2].

[8] Balassa [1(a)].

against the industrialization of the less-developed countries through exporting is the common practice of imposing zero duties on foodstuffs and materials in their raw state, and apparently modest but in effective-protection terms very high duty rates on the processed product, the effective-protection rate being high because the value-added ratio in processing is frequently very low.[9]

For their part, the less-developed countries typically apply the same type of tariff structure as the developed countries, or obtain the same effect by their use of tariffs, quotas and tax subsidies — though frequently their tariff structures have evolved in a topsy-turvy manner, and display no rationality whatsoever. The effect of the policy of imitating the tariff structures of the developed countries is, as several experts (including Dr Prebisch) have noted, to produce a self-limiting type of growth, based on import-substitution in consumer goods for the home market, discriminating against the production of capital goods and of exportable manufactures, and entailing increasingly severe dependence on imported capital equipment and materials and parts and consequently increasing vulnerability of the growth programme to balance-of-payments crises. These consequences are largely responsible for the demands of the less-developed countries, voiced at UNCTAD in 1964, for preferences for their manufactured exports in the markets of the developed countries — and also for the belief of many experts that such preferences would have little positive effect unless the less-developed countries at the same time made drastic reforms in their protective policies.

These observations, while explaining the importance of the effective-protection approach, take us away from the theory into its application. To return to the theory, it is interesting first to consider relaxation of the assumptions of the analysis and to consider the influence of other taxes than tariffs, and of transport costs, on effective protection.

With respect to taxes other than tariffs, it is a convenient first approximation to assume that personal and corporate income taxes are general taxes, and that their incidence falls on the

9 Johnson [7(d), ch. 3], Balassa [1(b)].

337

original factors that make up the value-added component of costs. The interesting question, then, concerns the influence of excise taxes, which are generally designed to fall on consumption rather than on production, this being achieved by border-tax adjustments which impose excise taxes on the after-tariff value of imports and exempt exports from such taxes. Let e_j be the excise tax levied on the jth commodity; then

$$(1 + e_j)(1 + t_j) = (1 + e_j)[v_j' + \sum a_{ji}(1 + e_i)(1 + t_i)] \qquad (7)$$

and

$$\tau_j' = \frac{t_j - \sum_i a_{ji}(e_i + t_i + e_i t_i)}{v_j} = \tau_j - \frac{\sum_i a_{ji} e_i (1 + t_i)}{v_j}. \qquad (8)$$

The effective-protection rate in the presence of excise taxation with border-tax adjustments must be lower than it would be with the same tariff structure in the absence of excise taxation. This is because, while an excise tax on the output of a domestic industry applied equally to imports of the product and remitted on exports does not affect the industry's international competitive position, excise taxes on its inputs reduce its effective protection against foreign competition (or, in the case of exports, increase its negative effective-protection rate). This point is relevant to the evaluation of the relative heights of national barriers to imports, because it means that for the same tariff rates effective-protection rates will be lower in countries that rely primarily on excise taxation than in countries that rely primarily on income taxation — or for that matter on value-added taxation without border-tax adjustments, the system towards which the Common Market countries are moving. [10]

As is well known, transport costs have an effect on the location of production similar to tariffs, the difference between them being that, in so far as transport charges correspond to the actual cost of transport (which may be questionable), the 'natural protection' afforded to domestic industries is consistent with economic efficiency and does not entail economic waste. [11]

---

[10] For an empirical study of the interaction of tariffs and excises in the Common Market countries, see Grubel and Johnson [5].

[11] This paragraph and the next draw on Balassa [1(b)].

'Natural protection' can be analysed in the same way as tariff protection; that is, the rate of natural protection afforded a process j is

$$\mu_j = \frac{d_j - \sum\limits_i a_{ji} d_i}{v_j}. \tag{9}$$

where d_j is the proportional charge for transport ('distance charge') on the jth commodity. Natural protection will be equally distributed among industrial processes if distance charges are proportional to value of item carried. If, instead, the proportional charge were an increasing function of stage of fabrication, either for inherent cost-of-transport reasons or as a result of mono-polistic pricing practice in charging 'what the market will bear', natural protection would be biased towards encouraging location of the higher processes of production in the final market for the goods, and so would tend to discriminate against the exports of manufactured goods by less-developed to developed countries. In so far as variations of percentage distance charges of this kind reflected monopolistic pricing rather than real cost differ-ence, they would have the same effect as escalated tariffs on the efficiency of world resource allocation. However, in fact distance charges by themselves seem to be biased in the opposite direction; moreover, the effects of distance charges have to be considered in conjunction with tariffs, and in some cases also with the pricing policies of monopolistic producers of raw materials.

Let us now consider the interaction of tariffs and transport charges. There are two systems of valuing goods for customs purposes: the Canada-United States-Australia system of levying duty on f.o.b. value and the European system of levying duty on c.i.f. value. Under the former system,

$$1 + d_j + t_j = (1 + \tau_j')v_j + \sum_i a_{ji}(d_i + 1 + t_i), \tag{10}$$

and total tariff and natural protection is

$$\tau_j' = \tau_j + \mu_j. \tag{11}$$

339

Under the latter system,

$$(1 + t_j)(1 + d_j) = (1 + \tau_j'')v_j + \sum_i a_{ji}(1 + d_i)(1 + t_i), \quad (12)$$

and total tariff and natural protection is

$$\tau_j'' = \tau_j + \mu_j + \frac{t_j d_j - \sum_i a_{ji} d_i t_i}{v_j}. \quad (13)$$

If proportional distance charges were equal for all goods, net effective-protection rates would be greater in absolute terms for the same tariff structure under the latter than under the former system, the levying of duty on the transport costs serving to increase effective-protection rates in absolute value. On the other hand, the c.i.f. valuation basis does preserve one (limited) condition of international efficiency, relevant if protection of domestic producers against foreigners is accepted as legitimate, namely equalizing marginal cost among competing sources of imports, whereas the f.o.b. valuation basis subsidizes goods produced at a greater distance, as compared with goods produced close by, when both have the same total landed cost.[12]

Thus far, this chapter has been concerned with the concept of effective protection, as expressed in effective-protection rates, and the extension of the concept to include interactions between the tariff structure and the domestic tax structure, and the effects of the treatment of distance charges in customs valuation procedures. Other extensions of the theory along this line are obviously possible, for example, inclusion of the discriminatory effects of corporation taxes (superimposed on personal income taxes) between the primarily incorporated and the primarily unincorporated activities in the economy, and the effects of private tax systems operated by monopolies and trade unions. The latter may indeed absorb the price-raising effects of the tariff in higher factor incomes in the more protected than in the less protected sectors, thereby cancelling out the effects of the tariff structure in erecting barriers to international trade.

---

[12] For an analysis of the relative efficiency of the two tariff valuation bases, with special reference to the effects of preferences, see Johnson [7(b)].

The more interesting line of analysis, however, concerns the influence of effective-protection rates on the allocation of domestic resources; for this problem the effective-protection concept is only a first step, as has been demonstrated in an important recent article by W.M. Corden.[13] In the first place, the tariff, nominal or effective, so to speak influences only the demand side of the allocation process. There is a supply side, the factor supplies available to the economy. If, as assumed earlier, these can be treated as a homogeneous entity, it is necessary for consistency with the theoretical assumption of a long-run tendency to full employment to assume that the protective effect of the tariff structure requires an accommodating alteration of either the exchange rate or the money price of the original factor of production. Contrary to expectation, as I have shown elsewhere, it is possible for a tariff structure to require a depreciation of the exchange rate or fall in money wages, rather than an appreciation of the currency or of wages.[14] This will be the case if negative effective-protection rates have a more powerful influence in discouraging exports or encouraging imports than positive effective-protection rates have in discouraging imports; and the possibility may well be relevant to the difficulties that various less-developed countries have experienced in balancing their balances of payments while pursuing inflationary import-substitution policies. Whether the normal wage or currency appreciation, or an abnormal depreciation, is required, this consequence of protection has to be taken into account in assessing the net protection rates accorded by the tariff structure to particular activities. In the case under discussion this can be done simply by deducting the percentage appreciation from (or adding the percentage depreciation to) the effective-protection rate of the activity concerned. (The same kind of adjustment would have to be made if the country's terms of trade were assumed to be a function of its trade volume.) In a more general model, involving say two factors of production, the imposition of the tariff structure would require adjustment

---

[13] Corden [3(b)].

[14] Johnson [7(b)].

of both factor prices in a fixed exchange rate system or of one factor price and the exchange rate in a floating rate system, with differential effects on the various protected activities.

Calculation of the exchange rate or factor price adjustments in question would, however, necessitate solving a general equilibrium system involving supply elasticities and cross-elasticities in the fixed terms of trade case assumed so far, and demand elasticities and cross-elasticities as well in the variable terms of trade case, the supply elasticities in question involving value added only, on the assumption of invariant input-output coefficients for produced inputs. This brings us to the second point, that the effects of the net effective-protection rates provided by the tariff structure on the actual outputs of the protected activities will not be simply related to the magnitudes of the effective-protection rates themselves, but will be determined by the supply elasticities and cross-elasticities which these effective-protection rates call into play.[15]

A third point is that in a general analysis account would have to be taken of such problems as the determination of the prices of non-internationally-traded goods, and their influence on effective-protection rates and the effects of protection,[16] and also of substitution between value-added and other inputs. This last is an important problem in the estimation of effective-protection rates from domestic input-output tables. Corden has shown that, with one produced input other than original factors, calculation from a domestic input-output table will always overstate the effective-protection rates.[17] More generally, it can be shown, by a simple application of index number theory, that computations from post-tariff input-output tables will always tend to overstate, and computations from free-trade input-output tables always tend to understate, the true rates of

---

[15] On the four different possible concepts of protection, see Corden [3(b), pp. 225—6].

[16] Corden's solution [3(b), pp. 226—8] of including such goods in value added is not really satisfactory.

[17] Corden [3(b), pp. 234—5].

effective protection implicit in a tariff structure.[18]

A final point on this aspect of the subject is that, naturally, tariffs being essentially taxes imposed on trade, and imposable by all countries, the actual production structure of a country will reflect not only its own tariff structure and effective-protection rates but the corresponding structure of tariffs and effective protection in the countries with which it trades.[19] One consequence — derived from the similarity of national tariff structures — is that the effect of reciprocal tariff reduction — whether along GATT lines or in a customs union or free trade area — might well be to induce little change in the broad contours of national economic structure, while effecting significant

[18] Let v_j, a_{ji} be quantities of original and produced factors employed under free trade, and v_j' and a_{ji}' be factor quantities employed under protection, these quantities being defined so that prices are unity under free trade. Let τ, τ_0, τ_1 be respectively the true effective-protection rate, the rate calculated from free-trade input coefficients, and the rate calculated from post-protection input coefficients. By definition,

(i) $$v_j + \sum_i a_{ji} = 1,$$

(ii) $$(1 + \tau)v_j' + \sum_i a_{ji}'(1 + t_i) = 1 + t_j.$$

By the principle of cost minimization

(iii) $$v_j' + \sum_i d_{ji}' \geq 1,$$

(iv) $$(1 + \tau)v_j + \sum_i a_{ji}(1 + t_i) \geq 1 + t_j.$$

Subtracting (i) from (iv),

(v) $$\tau v_j + \sum_i a_{ji} t_i \geq t_j.$$

Manipulating (ii) and subtracting (iii),

(vi) $$\tau v_j' + \sum_i a_{ji}' t_i \leq t_j.$$

Hence

(vii) $$\tau_1 = \frac{t_j - \sum_i a_{ji}' t_i}{v_j'} \geq \tau \geq \frac{t - \sum_i a_{ji} t_i}{v_i} = \tau_0.$$

I am indebted for this proof to a paper by Joseph M. Finger of Duke University [4].

[19] This is one of many points made by Travis [11(b)] in criticism of the applications of the effective-protection concept made by Balassa [1(a)] and Basevi [2].

gains of specialization and division of labour. There is considerable recent evidence supporting this empirical prediction.

II. THE MEASUREMENT OF TARIFF BARRIERS AND THE COST OF PROTECTION [20]

Traditional methods of measuring the height of tariff barriers aim at calculating an average of tariff rates, either by taking an unweighted average of tariff rates or by using weights derived from import volumes – which is equivalent to dividing tariff revenue by total value of imports. The statistical defects of these methods of averaging are well known; they stem from the arbitrariness of the tariff classifications that give rise to the individual tariff rates in the first case, and from the inter-correlation of tariff rates and trade volumes in the second case. In addition, recognition of the input-output nature of production, and of the fact that tariffs may both subsidize and tax domestic productive activities, raises the question of the meaningfulness of an 'average' tariff rate as an index of the protectiveness of a national tariff structure. The most fundamental criticism of tariff averages, however, is that the objective is to measure the extent to which the tariff structure restricts trade, and this depends on the relevant elasticities as well as on the tariff rates. In this part of the chapter I develop an approach to the measurement of the restrictiveness of national tariff structures that takes account of the input-output nature of the production system. [21]

For theoretical simplicity, I assume as before that world prices of imports and exports are fixed (and normalized to unity) and that all goods are traded; also, to avoid problems of exchange rate or factor price change, I assume that the country possesses at least one export good that uses no dutiable import good as an input, and into or out of which domestic productive resources (treated as a homogeneous entity) can be transferred

---

[20] This section is based on notes written early in 1965 in connection with Basevi's research on effective protection, and furnished to Balassa for incorporation (with developments by him) in his empirical study [1(a)].

[21] See Corden [3(a)] for a parallel discussion.

at constant costs of production. I also simplify the economic structure of the tariff-imposing country by assuming that input coefficients in each productive activity are fixed, but that the cost of value added, in terms of original factors required, rises with output, ϵ_j denoting the elasticity of supply of value added with respect to the price paid for it; ϵ_j is related to the elasticity of supply of the final product as normally defined (e_j) by the value-added ratio, so that $\epsilon_j = v_j e_j$. I also assume that the demand for each final product has the own-price elasticity η_j (defined to have a positive sign) and that cross-elasticities in demand can be neglected.

Let the free-trade production of import substitutes be P_j, value added in production be $V_j = v_j P_j$, and final consumption of importable goods be C_j. Impose the tariff structure t_j, entailing the effective protection rates τ_j; the domestic price of the protected goods to consumers is raised in the proportion t_j, and the domestic price of value added in the protected processes is raised in the proportion τ_j. The effect of the tariff structure in reducing the quantity of each import demanded involves three elements, two positive and one negative (note that exports that use protected inputs will have negative protection, and may be turned into imports — this possibility is neglected in the ensuing analysis):

(a) a reduction in final consumption of the commodity:

$$\eta_j C_j t_j; \tag{14}$$

(b) an increase in domestic production of the commodity:

$$\frac{1}{v_j} \tau_j \epsilon_j V_j = \tau_j \epsilon_j P_j; \tag{15}$$

(c) an increase in demand for imports of the commodity to be used as inputs in the expanded production of other protected goods:

$$- \sum_i a_{ij} \epsilon_i P_i \tau_i. \tag{16}$$

[This increase in demand for the good falls entirely on imports, because the increase in domestic production is already accounted for under (b)].

345

Summing over all imports, the total effect of the tariff structure on the quantity of imports demanded will be

$$
\begin{aligned}
-dM &= +\sum_j \eta_j C_j t_j + \sum_j \epsilon_j P_j \tau_j - \sum_j \sum_i a_{ij} \epsilon_i P_i \tau_i \\
&= \sum_j \left[\eta_j C_j t_j + \epsilon_j P_j \tau_j \left(1 - \sum_i a_{ji} \right) \right] = \sum_j (\eta_j C_j t_j + \epsilon_j v_j P_j \tau_j) \\
&= \sum_j (\eta_j C_j t_j + \epsilon_j V_j \tau_j).
\end{aligned} \tag{17}
$$

The restriction of imports by the tariff structure might more relevantly be expressed as a proportion of free-trade imports,

$$
R = -dM/M = \sum_j (\eta_j c_j t_j + \epsilon_j v_j p_j \tau_j) m_j, \tag{18}
$$

where c_j is the ratio of consumption to imports of the jth commodity, p_j the ratio of production to imports of the jth commodity, and m_j the ratio of free-trade imports of the jth commodity to total imports. Under certain statistical conditions unlikely to be approximated in reality, but which might have to be assumed for lack of data, this formula could be approximated by

$$
\mu \approx \bar{\eta} \bar{c} \bar{t} + \bar{\epsilon} \bar{v} \bar{p} \bar{t}, \tag{19}
$$

where the bars denote average values of the elasticities, 'structural' ratios, and nominal and effective tariff rates. In this form, the formula calls attention to the frequently-overlooked fact that economic structure, as reflected in the ratios of domestic consumption and production to imports, is as important as tariff rates and elasticities of demand and supply in determining the restrictiveness of a country's tariff structure. Specifically, the more self-sufficient a country would be under free trade, the more restrictive of trade would a given tariff structure be, elasticities being assumed similar in different countries.

As the various versions of the formula show, the measurement of the restrictiveness of a tariff structure involves applying the nominal tariff rates to consumption demand, and the effective tariff rates to value added in the various processes. Since, as already mentioned, effective tariff rates for certain commodities may be negative, with respect to these commodities the tariff structure will tend to create rather than restrict trade. This

346

possibility, which arises from the dual tax-subsidy nature of a tariff on a commodity in an input-output system, can be illustrated by substituting for the effective tariff rate in terms of the nominal tariff rates in (17), which yields the result

$$-dM = \sum_j (\eta_j C_j + \epsilon_j P_j - \sum_i \epsilon_i P_i \, a_{ij}) t_j. \qquad (20)$$

The traditional approach, which assumes that production employs only original factors, yields only the first two terms of this expression, and hence tends to overstate the restrictiveness of a tariff structure.

The foregoing analysis refers to the imposition of a tariff in initially free-trade conditions. The practical problem, however, usually is to predict the effects on imports of tariff reduction or free trade, starting from an initial position of protection. Consider a linear tariff cut, of the type contemplated in the Kennedy Round, in which all tariffs are cut to a proportion a of their former level; this will reduce the domestic price of protected goods in the proportion $at/(1 + t)$, and the domestic price of value added in the proportion $a\tau/(1 + \tau)$. The total increase in the quantity of imports, derived along the lines of the previous argument, will be

$$dM = a \sum_j \left(\eta_j C_j \frac{t_j}{1 + t_j} + \epsilon_j V_j \frac{\tau_j}{1 + \tau_j} \right). \qquad (21)$$

It is important to note that in this formula C_j and V_j are valued at world market and not domestic prices.

Turning to the cost of protection, this can be approximated, according to the usual loss-of-consumers'-surplus triangle and excess-production-cost triangle analysis[22] by the formula

$$\frac{1}{2} \sum_j (\eta_j C_j t_j^2 + \epsilon_j V_j \tau_j^2). \qquad (22)$$

The production-cost term of the summation here must be read to include any export goods on which the tariff structure imposes negative protection.

Since, as already mentioned, effective tariff rates are generally found to be substantially higher than nominal tariff

[22] For the relevant theory, see Harberger [6].

rates, it might appear that the production cost of protection is greater than is suggested by the traditional formula, $\frac{1}{2}\sum_j e_j P_j t_j^2$. The reverse is likely to be the case, however, since

$$\frac{1}{2}\sum_j \epsilon_j V_j \tau_j^2 = \frac{1}{2}\sum_j e_j P_j \left(t_j - \sum_i a_{ji} t_i\right)^2, \tag{23}$$

and this will necessarily be less than $\frac{1}{2}\sum_j e_j P_j t_j^2$, unless the tariff structure contains negative protection rates absolutely greater than the gross subsidization rates on the corresponding production processes.

Analysis in terms of effective protection therefore uncovers no unexpected additional source of economic waste from protection with which to confront the protectionist. It does, however, point to two aspects of the waste of protection that tend to be overlooked. One is the waste entailed in implicit taxation of export industries, via the taxation of their inputs through protection. The other is that when the costs of protection are related to its object of increasing domestic output of the protected good, and the latter is defined as it should be in terms of value added in the industry rather than in terms of gross output, the cost-benefit ratio may be extremely (and unexpectedly) high. The ratio in question, for any commodity j, is

$$\frac{1}{2}\tau_j + \frac{1}{2}(\eta_j C_j t_j^2)/(\epsilon_j V_j \tau_j). \tag{24}$$

The second term is likely to be large because it involves the ratio of the total value of domestic consumption to the value added in the process producing the protected good.

III. THE THEORY OF PREFERENCES[23]

The introduction of tariff preferences in the markets of the developed countries for exports of industrial products from the developing countries has been advocated as a means of making good the deficiency of the present volume of development aid as a source of foreign exchange for the finance of economic development programmes. Trade and aid, however, are not perfect or even close substitutes; aid properly defined and measured

[23] This section provides a more mathematical, and less comprehensive, formulation of analysis presented in my book [7(d), ch. 6].

entails a net transfer of real resources from developed to developing countries, whereas trade yields additional resources to the developing country only to the extent that it gives rise to rents above the resource cost of producing the exports concerned. Hence, in analysing the effects of preferences, it is necessary to analyse their effects both on the value of exports and on the rents earned in export production. For this purpose I employ two alternative extreme assumptions: (a) that the resources required to produce industrial exports are drawn from an export industry of the type assumed in the previous section, i.e. one subject to constant returns to scale and utilizing no produced inputs (such as a peasant export sector); and (b) that these resources are drawn from a subsistence sector at zero alternative opportunity cost. A more realistic intermediate assumption might be that the resources are drawn from import-substituting activities involving excess costs of production over world market prices, so that the alternative opportunity cost of these resources is less than their value in the export industries; this case could easily be handled by attaching a 'shadow premium' to foreign-exchange earnings, corresponding to the marginal excess-cost ratio in import substitution. To simplify a very complex problem, I consider a preference of 100 per cent of an initial non-discriminatory tariff, granted on a single commodity; and I assume that the producers of all three 'countries' involved — the preference-giving country, the preference-receiving country and the non-preferred country — are initially selling in the market of the preference-giving country and continue to do so after the preference is given. This assumption, which permits the usual elasticity concepts to be employed, implicitly assumes that the preference-receiving country is a relatively small supplier to the market, a not unreasonable assumption for the specific problem in hand. For simplicity, also, I confine attention to two extreme cases: one in which the product is homogeneous, so that shifts in trade induced by the preference depend only on supply parameters; and one in which national production costs are constant and the product is differentiated, so that the shifts in trade resulting from preferences depend only on demand parameters.

349

The two central propositions that will emerge from the analysis are, first, that in the presence of intermediate goods, contrary to the traditional analysis of the preference problem, the trade-creating and trade-diverting effects of a tariff preference cannot be related directly to the preference margin given on the final product; and second, that the effects of the preference on world welfare cannot be discussed correctly in terms of the net balance of trade-creating and trade-diverting effects. This last proposition has two separate origins, one in the theory of effective protection, and the other in the abandonment of the assumption that social costs correspond to private costs.

The initial tariff of the preference-giving country gives effective protection to producers in the jth activity of $\tau_j = S_j - T_j$, the difference between the gross subsidization rate and the implicit tax rate; the granting of a 100 per cent preferential tariff on the jth commodity alone, with no change in other tariff rates would leave producers in the preference-giving country subject to the negative protection rate $-T_j$. The gross subsidization rate S_j, which may be interpreted as the effective rate of preference given with respect to domestic producers, will govern the response of domestic producers to the preference if the domestic price falls to the world market price — the limit of the trade-creating effect in production. For purposes of welfare analysis, this trade-creating effect in production can be separated conceptually into two parts, divided by the notional proportional preference rate

$$r_j = 1 - T_j/S_j \qquad (25)$$

at which the domestic producer in the preference-giving country would receive exactly enough protection from producers in the preference-receiving country to compensate him for the tariffs levied on his inputs, and so be in the same competitive position relative to his rival as he would be under free trade. For the part of the 100 per cent preference corresponding to this rate, trade creation would involve substitution of lower-cost production in the preference-receiving country for higher-cost domestic production, and a resulting gain in economic efficiency. For the remainder of the 100 per cent preference the domestic producer would be taxed by comparison with his rival, and the corresponding trade creation would involve substitution of higher-cost production in the preference-receiving country for lower-cost domestic production, and a resulting loss of economic efficiency — a loss associated with implicit subsidization of imports. On the usual assumption of approximate linearity of supply response, the trade creation resulting from the preference would involve a net gain or net loss, according as S_j is greater or less than twice T_j (or, what is the same thing, τ_j is greater or less than one-half of S_j).

The foregoing argument applies to trade creation on the production side in the preference-giving country, when the domestic price falls to the world price. Suppose instead that the preference-receiving country is small enough so that its export price rises to the domestic price in the preference-giving country — which might entail either trade creation or trade diversion. For the preference-receiving country in this case, the preference would raise the price offered for value added by

$$\rho_j = t_j/v_j', \tag{26}$$

where v_j', value added per unit, is not necessarily the same as v_j, the value-added coefficient valued at world market price in the preference-giving country; thus it is necessary to define a separate 'effective-preference rate' for producers in the two countries, according to whether it is assumed that supply in the preference-receiver or demand in the preference-giver determines the outcome. Moreover, in analysing the welfare effects of trade diversion, it is necessary to take account of the possibility that the money price of exports from both the preferred and the non-preferred countries may overstate real costs, both because of tariffs on inputs and because factor prices overstate alternative opportunity costs. For simplicity, I consider this possibility only in the case of the preference-receiving country. Its result is to make it possible for trade diversion to produce a social gain, by shifting trade towards nominally higher-cost but actually lower-real-cost sources of supply.

After this somewhat lengthy preamble on the central analytical points, I am ready to consider the two extreme cases.

The first is the case in which the product of the preference-receiving country is a perfect substitute for the product either of the preference-giving country or of the non-preferred country, and in which the elasticity of supply of the product from the rival source is infinite. The quantum of exports of the preferred product by the preference-receiving country would increase in the proportion $dX_j/X_j = \epsilon_j \rho_j$, where ϵ_j is the elasticity of supply of value added in the production of commodity j in that country. Value added in the industry would increase by

$$\rho_j V_j' (1 + \epsilon_j + \epsilon_j \rho_j), \tag{27}$$

the three terms corresponding to the increase in initial value added due to the price increase permitted by the preference; the increase in value added, valued at world market prices, prompted by the preference; and the increase in the value of this increase in quantity due to the price increase. Under assumption (b) (no alternative opportunity cost of value added), all of this would be additional export earnings. Under assumption (a) (full alternative opportunity cost of value added),

$$\rho_j V_j' (\epsilon_j + \tfrac{1}{2} \epsilon_j \rho_j) \tag{28}$$

of this would be foregone export earnings and the remaining

$$\rho_j V_j' (1 + \tfrac{1}{2} \epsilon_j \rho_j) \tag{29}$$

would be additional export earnings accruing as rent. In addition to this increment of rent, the preference-receiving country would gain additional tariff receipts (and foreign exchange) equal to

$$\rho_j V_j' \epsilon_j \sum_i a_{ji}' t_i / v_j' \tag{30}$$

on the additional imports required to produce the increment of exports.

The preference-giving country would suffer the loss of the tariff proceeds initially collected on the original volume of imports, $\rho_j V_j = X_j t_j$, which amount would accrue to the preference-receiving country as rent on value added on the pre-existing export volume through the rise in prices. This part of the effect of the preference would therefore be a pure income transfer from the preference-giving to the preference-receiving country.

If the product of the preference-receiving country were a perfect substitute for the product of the preference-giving country – the case of trade creation – and assuming that supply of the latter is perfectly elastic, the preference-giving country would lose any tariff revenue it would have received on imports of inputs for producing the commodity in which trade has been created. Trade creation frees resources from domestic production worth

$$(1 + \tau_j)dV_j = (1 + \tau_j)\frac{v_j}{v_j'}dV_j' = (1 + \tau_j)\frac{v_j}{v_j'}\epsilon_j\rho_jV_i', \quad (31)$$

where the unprimed symbol denotes value added in the preference-giving country, valued at world market prices as before. In case (a), the resource cost of replacing the output formerly produced by these resources is

$$\rho_jV_j'(\epsilon_j + \tfrac{1}{2}\epsilon_j\rho_j), \quad (32)$$

the net saving of resource cost being

$$(v_j/v_j' - 1)\epsilon_j\rho_jV_j' + \epsilon_j\rho_jV_j'(\tau_j \cdot v_j/v_j' - \tfrac{1}{2}\rho_j), \quad (33)$$

or, on the simplifying assumption that $v_j \approx v_j'$,

$$\epsilon_j\rho_jV_j'(\tau_j - \tfrac{1}{2}\rho_j). \quad (34)$$

To this must be added the tariff receipts of the preference-receiving country, to obtain the net change in world welfare

$$\epsilon_j\rho_jV_j'(\tau_j - \tfrac{1}{2}\rho_j)\frac{\sum_i a_{ji}'t_i}{v_j'} \quad (35)$$

Note that there may be a loss from trade creation, if the effective-protection rate in the preference-giving country is less than half the effective-protection rate accorded the preference-receiving country. This result has already been derived, in a slightly different form.

On the alternative assumption (b) (no alternative opportunity cost of resources in the preference-receiving country), there must obviously be a world welfare gain equal to

$$\epsilon_j\rho_jV_j'\left[(1 + \tau_j)\frac{v_j}{v_j'} + \frac{\sum_i a_{ji}'t_i}{v_j'}\right]. \quad (36)$$

On the alternative assumption that the product of the preference-receiving country is a perfect substitute for that of the non-preferred country — the case of trade diversion — and assuming that supply in that country is perfectly elastic and money cost there corresponds to real cost, the preference-giving country would lose tariff revenue on the diverted imports in the amount $V_j' \epsilon_j \rho_j$, of which half would be matched by the marginal rents received by the preference-receiving country and half would pay the excess money costs of marginal production in the preference-receiving country over those of the non-preferred country. On assumption (a) (full alternative opportunity cost), the net change in world welfare would be

$$\rho_j V_j' \epsilon_j \left(\sum_i \frac{a_{ji}' t_i}{v_j} - \tfrac{1}{2} \rho_j \right) \tag{37}$$

which might conceivably be negative. On the alternative assumption (b) (no alternative opportunity cost of resources to the preference-receiving country), the net change in world welfare would be

$$\rho_j V_j' \epsilon_j \left(1 + \frac{\sum_i a_{ji}' t_i}{v_j} \right), \tag{38}$$

which must be positive.

For the second extreme case, it is assumed that the products of the various countries are imperfect substitutes for one another in consumption, and that they are competitively produced at constant costs in their countries of origin. For simplicity, it is further assumed that the commodities substitute only against one another, and that their value-added coefficients (at world market prices) are the same. Let C_{jh}, C_{jp} and C_{jf} stand for the quantities of goods initially consumed in the preference-giving country from the home, preference-receiving, and non-preferred countries respectively, the quantities being chosen to standardize values at world market prices at unity, and let η_{jh} and η_{jf} stand for the cross-elasticities of demand for the sub-scripted goods with respect to the tariff-inclusive price of the preferred country's good, defined to have a positive sign. With the preference,

354

$$dC_{jp} = dC_{jh} - dC_{jf} = C_{jh} \frac{t_j}{1 + t_j} \eta_{jh} + C_{jf} \frac{t_j}{1 + t_j} \eta_{jf}. \quad (39)$$

On assumption (a), the preference-receiving country obtains no direct gain of foreign exchange, but an indirect gain of

$$\frac{t_j}{1 + t_j} (C_{jh} \eta_{jh} + C_{jf} \eta_{jf}) \sum_i a'_{ji} t_i; \quad (40)$$

on assumption (b) it obtains a gain of foreign exchange equal to

$$\frac{t_j}{1 + t_j} (C_{jh} \eta_{jh} + C_{jf} \eta_{jf}) \left(1 + \sum_i a'_{ji} t_i\right). \quad (41)$$

On the usual welfare analysis, the preference-giving country gains approximately $\frac{1}{2} t_j dC_{jp}$ from the expansion of imports from the preferred country, and loses approximately $-t_j dC_{jp}$ from the contraction of imports from the non-preferred country; on the contraction of consumption of the domestic good, it loses approximately $-(\sum_i a_{ji} t_i) dC_{jh}$. Its net gain or loss, in terms of the gross subsidization rate, gross tax rate, and value added is therefore

$$\frac{1}{2} \frac{t_j}{1 + t_j} [V_{jh} \eta_{jh} (S_j - 2T_j)] - \frac{1}{2} \frac{t_j}{1 + t_j} V_{jf} \eta_{jf} S_j. \quad (42)$$

The first term here represents the welfare effect of trade creation, which as previously remarked may be a loss rather than the traditional gain; the second term represents the welfare loss from trade diversion. For the world as a whole, on assumption (a), the welfare effect of the preference is

$$\frac{1}{2} \frac{t_j}{1 + t_j} \left[V_{jh} \eta_{jh} \left(S_j - 2T_j + 2 \frac{\sum_i a'_{ji} t_i}{v'_j}\right) - V_{jf} \eta_{jf} \left(S_j - 2 \frac{\sum_i a'_{ji} t_i}{v'_j}\right)\right]. \quad (43)$$

On assumption (b), the welfare effect on the world as a whole is

$$\frac{1}{2} \frac{t_j}{1 + t_j} \left[V_{jh} \eta_{jh} \left(S_j - 2T_j + \frac{2}{v'_j} + 2 \frac{\sum_i a'_{ji} t_i}{v'_j}\right) \right. \quad (44)$$
$$\left. - V_{jf} \eta_{jf} \left(S_j - \frac{2}{v'_j} - 2 \frac{\sum_i a'_{ji} t_i}{v'_j}\right)\right].$$

Unless the gross subsidization rate and implicit tax rate are both extremely high (substantially greater than 100 per cent), assumption (b) will yield a positive welfare effect for the world as a whole – as one would, of course, expect from the extremely strong assumption that original factors are a free good in the preference-receiving country. The results on assumption (a), on the other hand, tend to suggest that, when the dual tax-subsidy nature of tariff structures is allowed for, the likelihood that preferences will lead to welfare losses is increased, as compared with what might be inferred from the traditional analysis.

The models employed in this section to extend the theory of effective protection to the effects of trade preferences are, of course, extremely crude and over-simplified; but their very crudity underlines the complexity of the effects of commercial policy in an input-output system of production.

REFERENCES

[1] (a) Balassa, B., 'Tariff Protection in Industrial Countries: An Evaluation', *Journal of Political Economy*, Vol. LXXIII (1965) pp. 573–94; (b) 'The Impact of the Industrial Countries' Tariff Structure on their Imports of Manufactures from Less Developed Countries', *Economica*, Vol. XXXIV (1967) pp. 372–83; (c) 'Tariff Protection in Industrial Nations and its Effects on the Exports of Processed Goods from Developing Countries', *Canadian Journal of Economics*, Vol. I (1968) pp. 583–94.

[2] Basevi, G., 'The United States Tariff Structure: Estimates of Effective Rates of Protection of U.S. Industries and Industrial Labour', *Review of Economics and Statistics*, Vol. XLVIII (1966) pp. 147–60.

[3] (a) Corden, W.M., 'The Effective Protective Rate, the Uniform Tariff Equivalent and the Average Tariff', *Economic Record*, Vol. 42 (1966) pp. 200–16; (b) 'The Structure of a Tariff System and the Effective Protective Rate', *Journal of Political Economy*, Vol. LXXIV (1966) pp. 221–37.

[4] Finger J.M., 'Substitution and the Effective Rate of Protection', *Journal of Political Economy*, Vol. 77 (1969) pp. 972–75.

[5] Grubel, H.G. and H.G. Johnson, 'Nominal Tariffs, Indirect Taxes and Effective Rates of Protection: The Common Market Countries, 1959,' *Economic Journal*, Vol. LXXVII (1967) pp. 761–76.

[6] Harberger, A.C., 'Principles of Efficiency: The Measurement of Waste', *American Economic Review*, Vol. LIV (1964), American Economic Association, Papers and Proceedings, pp. 58–76.

[7] (a) Johnson, H.G., 'The Theory of Tariff Structure with Special Reference to World Trade and Development', *Trade and Development* (Geneva: Institut Universitaire de Hautes Etudes Internationales, 1965); in Chapter 12 above; (b) 'A Model of Protection and the Exchange Rate', *Review of Economic Studies*, Vol. XXXIII (1966) pp. 159–63; in Chapter 17 below; (c) 'A Note on Tariff Bases, Economic Efficiency and the Effects of Preferences', *Journal of Political Economy*, Vol. LXXIV (1966) pp. 401–2; (d) *Economic Policies Toward Less Developed Countries* (Washington, D.C., 1967).

[8] Krueger, A., 'Some Economic Costs of Exchange Control: The Turkish Case', *Journal of Political Economy*, Vol. LXXIV (1966) pp. 466–80.

[9] McKinnon, R.I., 'Intermediate Products and Differential Tariffs: A Generalization of Lerner's Symmetry Theorem', *Quarterly Journal of Economics*, Vol. LXXX (1966) pp. 584–615.

[10] Soligo, R. and J. Stern, 'Tariff Protection, Import Substitution and Investment Efficiency', *Pakistan Development Review*, Vol. 5 (1965) pp. 249–70.

[11] (a) Travis, W.P., *The Theory of Trade and Protection* (Cambridge, Mass. 1964); (b) 'The Effective Rate of Protection and the Question of Labour Protection in the United States', *Journal of Political Economy*, Vol. LXXVI (1968) pp. 443–61.

14. A Model of Protection and the Exchange Rate*

One of the assumptions commonly made in the context of liberalization of trade by underdeveloped countries is that such liberalization would necessarily involve a balance of payments deficit and the consequent necessity of devaluation, which such countries are unwilling to undertake. This note presents an analysis of the problem, using a simplified production model which nevertheless allows for input—output relations among industries and hence for implicit as distinct from nominal protection. The analysis reveals the possibility that tariff structures may bring about a situation in which appreciation rather than depreciation would be necessary to preserve equilibrium under trade liberalization; this possibility is due to the fact that a tariff structure may impose a tax, rather than provide a subsidy, on particular lines of production.

It is assumed that both demands and supplies of goods in the world market are perfectly elastic, and that there are no non-traded goods. It is also assumed that production conditions and tariffs are such that all goods will be produced in both the presence and the absence of tariffs; and either that protection is in no case high enough to exclude imports, or that if it is exports are subsidized at the tariff rate, so that all tariff rates are fully effective. These assumptions permit the analysis to ignore domestic demand conditions and concentrate exclusively on supply. For simplicity, all goods are measured in units such that their world market prices are unity. Thus the domestic prices of all goods will be $p_i = (1 + t_i)r$, where r is the price of foreign exchange in terms of domestic currency and t_i is the tariff rate imposed (or equivalent degree of import restriction). For exports $t_i = 0$ by assumption, though the analysis is perfectly general and can allow for export taxes ($t_i < 0$) or export subsidies ($t_i > 0$).

* *The Reveiw of Economic Studies*, Vol. XXXIII, No. 2 (April 1966) pp. 159—63.

On the production side, it is assumed that each good is produced by combining inputs of other goods (assumed to be required in fixed proportions to final output) with original factors of production, the use of the original factor encountering decreasing returns. For simplicity it is assumed that there is only one original factor (labour), which is homogeneous and perfectly mobile between industries, and of which a fixed total supply is available at a unit price fixed in domestic currency, equilibrium in the labour market being preserved by changes in the exchange rate.

Specifically, the total cost of producing each commodity j is assumed to be

$$\sum_i a_{ji} p_i x_j + k_j x_j + b_j x_j^2 ,$$

where a_{ji} is the physical input of commodity i into the production of a unit of commodity j, and k_j and b_j are coefficients representing labour requirements. The marginal cost of production is accordingly

$$c_j = \sum_i a_{ji} p_i + k_j + 2b_j x_j.$$

In equilibrium in a particular industry, price must equal marginal cost:

$$(1 + t_j)r = \sum_i a_{ji}(1 + t_i)r + k_j + 2b_j x_j$$

or

$$\left(1 + t_j - \sum_i a_{ji}(1 + t_i)\right)r = k_j + 2b_j x_j.$$

Define $v_j = 1 - \Sigma a_{ji}$, the value added per unit by the industry in the world market; and $\tau_j = (t_j - \Sigma a_{ji} t_i)/v_j$, the implicit rate of protection of value added provided by the tariff structure. Then the equilibrium condition becomes $v_j(1 + \tau_j)r = k_j + 2b_j x_j$, which determines the equilibrium output

$$x_j = \frac{v_j(1 + \tau_j)r - k_j}{2b_j} .$$

Output in each industry is therefore a function of the cost conditions of the industry, the implicit rate of protection accorded it, and the exchange rate.

The exchange rate is determined by the condition that original factors be fully employed: $\sum_{j} (k_j x_j + b_j x_j^2) = K$, where K is the total amount of labour available (the symbols k_j and K are used for typographical clarity). Substituting the values of the x_j previously obtained, this yields an equation for the exchange rate

$$\sum_{j} \frac{[v_j(1 + \tau_j)r - k_j][v_j(1 + \tau_j)r + k_j]}{4b_j} = K$$

whence

$$r^2 = \frac{4K + \sum_{j} \frac{k_j^2}{b_j}}{\sum_{j} \frac{v_j^2(1 + \tau_j)^2}{b_j}} .$$

It can readily be verified that $\partial r/\partial K > 0$, $\partial r/\partial k_j > 0$, $\partial r/\partial v_j < 0$, $\partial r/\partial \tau_j > 0$ by differentiating r^2 with respect to the relevant variables; that $\partial r/\partial b_j > 0$ is obvious from inspection of the first equation.

Now consider the effect of substituting free trade for protectionism. Let $R = (1 + d)r$ be the exchange rate with free trade, where d represents the proportionate depreciation necessary, and may be negative, indicating appreciation.

For the individual commodity, the protection and free trade outputs are respectively

$$\frac{v_j(1 + \tau_j)r - k_j}{2b_j} \text{ and } \frac{v_j R - k_j}{2b_j} .$$

The free trade output will be higher if $v_j(1 + \tau_j)r < v_j R = v_j(1 + d)r$, that is, if $\tau_j < d$. Production will therefore expand in any industry for which the depreciation of the currency exceeds the implicit protection rate. Assuming provisionally that d will be positive, reflecting a depreciation, it follows that any industry previously subject to negative protection must expand its output.

For the determination of d, the rate of depreciation, we have

$$\left[\sum_j \frac{v_j^2(1 + \tau_j)^2}{b_j} \right] r^2 = \left(\sum_j \frac{v_j^2}{b_j} \right) r^2(1 + d)^2$$

$$(1 + d)^2 = \frac{\sum_j \frac{v^2(1 + \tau)^2}{b_j}}{\sum_j \frac{v_j^2}{b_j}}$$

This formula can be simplified by defining weights

$$w_j = \frac{v_j^2}{b_j} \bigg/ \sum_j \frac{v_j^2}{b_j}$$

and rewriting the formula as

$$(1 + d)^2 = \sum_j w_j(1 + \tau_j)^2 = 1 + 2 \sum_j w_j \tau_j + \sum_j w_j \tau_j^2$$

d will be positive, indicating depreciation, or negative, indicating appreciation, according as

$$2 \sum_j w_j \tau_j + \sum_j w_j \tau_j^2 \gtrless 0$$

d must be positive, indicating depreciation, only if there is no negative protection of any commodity. This requires (a) no explicit export taxes; (b) no implicit taxation of export industries through protection of commodities used by them as inputs; (c) no taxation of nominally protected industries by the imposition of a sufficiently higher degree of protection on commodities used by them as inputs. Conversely, free trade will require appreciation rather than depreciation if there is sufficient negative protection implicit in the country's tariff structure.

To illustrate the possibility of free trade being accompanied by appreciation rather than depreciation, consider the following three-sector model:

361

$$t_1 = 30\% \qquad a_{12} = \tfrac{3}{4} \qquad \tau_1 = 60\% \qquad v_1 = v_2 = v_3 = \tfrac{1}{4}$$

$$t_2 = 20\% \qquad a_{21} = \tfrac{3}{4} \qquad \tau_2 = -10\% \qquad b_1 = b_2 = b_3$$

$$t_3 = 0\% \qquad a_{31} = \tfrac{3}{4} \qquad \tau_3 = -90\%$$

$$(1 + d)^2 = \tfrac{1}{3}(1{\cdot}69 + 0{\cdot}81 + 0{\cdot}01) = 0{\cdot}836$$

$$d \approx -8{\cdot}5\%.$$

The general formula shows the connection between the extent of the exchange rate change required on the one hand, and the weights of the protected industries and the rates of implicit protection accorded them on the other; it should be noticed, however, that the weights and the implicit protection rates are compound expressions involving in part the same variable v_j. If it is assumed that the weights of all industries are equal, the formula becomes

$$(1 + d)^2 = 1 + 2\pi \sum_j \tau_j + \pi \sum_j \tau_j^2$$

where π is the common weight of the industries. If further the τ_js are assumed equal and positive for those industries that are protected, the formula shows that the required devaluation must be less than the implicit protection rate, and more so the smaller is the proportion of the economy protected. It is also a property of formulas of this kind that the required devaluation must be greater, for a given arithmetical average of the τ_j and given proportion of the economy protected, the greater the dispersion of the τ_j around their mean.

Thus far, the analysis has been concerned with the effects of free trade on the exchange rate. Free trade must of course maximize the country's real income, under the given assumptions, in the sense of maximizing its value added measured at world market prices. The condition for maximizing $\sum_j v_j x_j$ subject to

$$\sum_j k_j x_j + b_j x_j^2 = K \text{ is } \frac{v_i}{k_i + 2b_i x_i} = \frac{v_j}{k_j + 2b_j x_j} = \lambda \text{ for all } i,j,$$

where λ is the Lagrangean multiplier. With protection,

$$\frac{v_j}{k_j + 2b_j x_j} = \frac{1}{(1 + \tau_j)r} \quad \text{etc.}$$

For any given exchange rate, the country could achieve income maximization by giving equal effective protection to all industries at the rate appropriate to that exchange rate; this would involve subsidizing exports as well as imposing tariffs on imports, and would have exactly the same effects as adopting free trade and letting the exchange rate adjust to equilibrium.

The national income of the country at world market prices under protection is

$$\sum_j v_j x_j = \sum_j v_j \frac{v_j(1 + \tau_j)r - k_j}{2b_j}$$

and under free trade is

$$\sum_j v_j \frac{v_j(1 + d)r - k_j}{2b_j} \quad .$$

Thus the change in income resulting from the substitution of free trade for protection is

$$\frac{r}{2} \sum_j \left[\frac{v_j^2}{b_j}(1 + d) - \frac{v_j^2}{b_j}(1 + \tau_j) \right] = \frac{r}{2} \sum_j \frac{v_j^2}{b_j}(d - \tau_j) \quad .$$

The proof that this expression must be positive (or zero, if the τ_j are equal for all industries) is unfortunately rather complicated.

A proof can be developed on the following lines: rewrite the expression as

$$\left(\sum_j \frac{v^2}{b_j} \right) \frac{r}{2} [(1 + d) - \sum_j w_j(1 + \tau_j)] \quad .$$

Multiply and divide by $(1 + d)$ and substitute for $(1 + d)^2$, to obtain

$$\left(\sum_j \frac{v_j^2}{b_j} \right) \frac{r}{2} \cdot \frac{1}{1 + d} \left[\sum_j w_j(1 + \tau_j)^2 - \sum_j w_j(1 + \tau_j)(1 + d) \right] \quad .$$

363

Multiply and divide by $[\sum_j w_j (1 + T_j)^2 + \sum_j w_j (1 + T_j)(1 + d)]$ and factor out

$$(1 + d)^2 = \sum_j w_j (1 + T)^2$$

to obtain

$$\left(\sum_j \frac{v_j}{b_j}\right) \frac{r}{2} \cdot \frac{1 + d}{\sum_j w_j(1 + T_j)^2 + \sum_j w_j(1 + T_j)(1 + d)}$$

$$\left[\sum_j w_j (1 + T_j)^2 - \sum_i \sum_j w_i w_j (1 + T_i)(1 + T_j) \right].$$

The sign of the whole expression is determined by the sign of

$$\sum_j w_j (1 + T_j)^2 - \sum_i \sum_j w_i w_j (1 + T_i)(1 + T_j).$$

$$= \sum_j w_j (1 - w_j)(1 + T_j)^2 - \sum_i \sum_{j \neq 1} w_i w_j (1 + T_i)(1 + T_j).$$

Using the fact that $\sum_j w_j = 1$, the expression can be rewritten in the form

$$\sum_j \sum_{i \neq j} w_i w_j [(1 + T_j)^2 - (1 + T_i)(1 + T_j)]$$

$$= \frac{1}{2} \sum_j w_i w_j [(1 + T_j) - (1 + T_i)]^2$$

$$= \frac{1}{2} \sum_j w_i w_j (T_j - T_i)^2.$$

Since this is a sum of a series of squares, it must be positive unless $T_i = T_j$ for all j, in which case it is equal to zero.

A simpler proof, but one that depends on greater mathematical knowledge, has been suggested by the editors, as follows: the gain from the adoption of·free trade has the sign of $(1 + d) - \sum_j w_j(1 + T_j) = d - \sum_j w_j T_j$; if $d < \sum_j w_j T_j$, $(1 + d)^2 < (1 + \sum_j w_j T_j)^2$;

substituting the expression previously derived, $(1 + d)^2 = \sum_j w_j (1 + \tau_j)^2$, this requires $\sum_j w_j \tau_j^2 < (\sum w_j \tau_j)^2$, which is impossible as $\sum_j w_j = 1$; Q.E.D.

The model developed here is built on some very restrictive assumptions designed to exclude the complications that may result from demand interrelationships. With a certain amount of drudgery, however, these assumptions can be relaxed and the model made more realistic. Of particular interest are the effects of introducing non-traded goods, and the question whether free trade would raise or lower the prices and outputs of such goods. For simplicity, assume that there is one such non-traded good, that is not used as an input into the production of other goods, and that it is unimportant enough in consumption for the income effects of free trade on the demand for it to be ignored. The demand for such a good may be written as $D_j = \overline{D_j} + \sum_i X_{ji} p_i$,

where the X_{ji} are the price-slopes of demand for j with respect to the price of i and possess the usual Hicksian properties; the supply (derived from the necessary equality of the marginal cost and price) is

$$S_j = \frac{p_j - \sum_i a_{ji} p_i - k_j}{2b_j} .$$

The equilibrium price and quantity are respectively

$$p_j = \frac{\sum_{i \neq j} (2b_j X_{ji} + a_{ji}) p_i + k_j + \overline{D_j}}{1 - 2b_j X_{jj}} ,$$

$$x_j = \frac{2b_j \sum_{i \neq j} (X_{ji} + X_{jj} a_{ji}) p_i + 2b_j X_{jj} k_j + \overline{D_j}}{2b_j (1 - 2b_j X_{jj})} .$$

Under protection the prices of traded goods are $(1 + t_i) r$, and under free trade they are $(1 + d) r$, the determination of d and p_j now being interdependent.

The change in the price of the non-traded good with free trade is

365

$$\Delta p_j = \frac{\sum\limits_{i \neq j} (2b_j X_{ji} + a_{ji})(d - t_i)r}{1 - 2b_j X_{jj}} \; ;$$

and the change in the quantity of it produced and consumed is

$$\Delta x_j = \frac{\sum\limits_{i \neq j} (X_{ji} + X_{jj} a_{ji})(d - t_i)r}{1 - 2b_j X_{jj}} .$$

It is evident from these formulas that even if all goods are assumed to be substitutes ($X_{ji} > 0$ for all $i \neq j$), no generalization can be made about the effects of free trade on the price and output of the non-traded good, because the indiviudal $(d - t_i)$ may be positive or negative, as may the $(X_{ij} + X_{jj} a_{ji})$ in the equation for the quantity change.

15. Effective Protection and General Equilibrium Theory*

The theory of effective protection is based on, and owes its importance and interest to, one simple but fundamental idea: that protection is to be evaluated and analysed, not in terms of the nominal tariff rates on products, but in terms of the effective rates of protection afforded by the whole of a tariff structure (and possibly other aspects of government policy as well) to economic activities or processes. The effective rate of protection concept recognizes that a tariff provides a subsidy to the activity producing the product to which it applies, and imposes a tax on the products of other activities that use that product as an input. This change of approach is particularly relevant to commercial policy issues, especially the true heights and profiles of barriers to international trade (the concern of my own earlier work[1]) and the true economic costs of protective and import-substitutive policies. It is just beginning to be understood and applied by the officials and politicians actually concerned with commercial policy-making, their education in this respect being forwarded by the great number of empirical calculations of effective protective rates for various countries that have been

---

* This chapter embodies the results of sustained discussions with W.M. Corden and R.W. Jones, and has benefited from a reading of the manuscript of Corden's book, *The Theory of Protection* (Oxford: Oxford University Press, 1971). The chapter does not, however, pretend to deal adequately with all the issues raised by these and other authors in the now large literature on the subject.

[1] See particularly Harry G. Johnson, 'The Theory of Tariff Structure, with Special Reference to World Trade and Development', in Harry G. Johnson and Peter B. Kenen, *Trade and Development* (Geneva: Librairie Droz, 1965) pp. 9—29, reprinted as Chapter 12 above.

made recently by competent trained academic researchers.[2]

While the empirical applications and policy implications of the effective protection concept are more important than its theoretical niceties, it must be admitted that the original formulations of effective protection theory were open to theoretical criticism. These formulations rested the theory on the Leontief input–output table. This gave the theory its great strength as a tool of empirical research, but left much to be desired aesthetically and begged some serious questions in terms of more orthodox production theory and the standard Heckscher–Ohlin–Samuelson model of international trade. Specifically, standard production theory assumes substitutability among inputs into the production function, both produced inputs and original factors, whereas the Leontief system assumes fixity of input coefficients. Such fixity can be justified for a closed economy on the basis of the non-substitution theorem; but the point is precisely that our interest is in the effects on an open economy of changing the prices paid for the outputs and inputs of domestic economic activity, changes

[2] It is unfortunate, however, that two rival factions of researchers have already emerged, the 'domestic resource cost' and the 'effective protection' schools, with the usual effect of over-differentiation of what is essentially the same product; the two schools represent two different lines of initial attack on the same problem — through the aggregate information provided by input–output tables, and through the detailed information obtainable by case studies — and the differences between their treatments of particular issues should be resolvable by careful analysis. Also, one of the important early contributors to the general equilibrium analysis of protection (Travis) has attacked the new concept sweepingly, scornfully, and not altogether understandingly. Consequently, the policy-makers are being provided with support for their usual excuse for ignoring scientific economics, that 'economists never agree anyway.' See B. Balassa and D. Schydlowsky, 'Effective Tariffs, Domestic Cost of Foreign Exchange, and the Equilibrium Exchange Rate', *Journal of Political Economy*, Vol. 76, No. 3 (May/June 1968) pp. 348–60; Anne O. Krueger, 'Some Economic Costs of Exchange Control: The Turkish Case', *Journal of Political Economy*, Vol. 74, No. 5 (October 1966) pp. 466–80; subsequent discussion by Anne O. Krueger (Evaluating Restrictionist Trade Regimes: Theory and Measurement') and Michael Bruno ('Domestic Resource Costs and Effective Protection: Clarification and Synthesis') respectively, forthcoming in the *Journal of Political Economy*; also W.P. Travis, 'The Effective Rate of Protection and the Question of Labour Protection in the United States', *Journal of Political Economy*, Vol. 76, No. 3 (May/June 1968) pp. 443–61.

which may be expected to have substitution effects on the choice of optimal production techniques. Similarly, the Heckscher–Ohlin–Samuelson model assumes both constant returns to scale and substitutability, obtaining a smoothly upward-sloping supply curve of a product as a result of changes in relative factor prices induced by the necessity for factor substitution when relative outputs are changed within a constraint of fixed overall factor endowments.

To be able to obtain finite production changes in response to changes in tariff and effective protective rates without going deeply into the question of the market for factors of production and the requirements of equilibrium there, effective protection theory has to assume either that there are diminishing returns to the application of 'resources in general' to the production of value added,[3] or that there is an upward-sloping supply curve of 'resources in general' to each industry,[4] or else argue that 'resources in general' are subject to conflicting pulls from the effective rates of protection offered to the various activities.[5] On any of these devices, the unspecified concept of 'resources in general' is an attempt to marry a partial equilibrium analysis on the resources side with a general equilibrium analysis on the prices side, and to escape the need for general equilibrium analysis of the factor markets. The first device, diminishing returns to resources in adding value, also conflicts with the linearity assumptions of both the Leontief input–output table, and standard production theory, including the Heckscher–Ohlin–Samuelson model.

Finally, traditional trade theory has always been concerned at some stage (though less immediately than used to be the case,

[3] Harry. G. Johnson, 'A Model of Protection and the Exchange Rate', *The Review of Economic Studies*, Vol. XXXIII, No. 2 (April 1966) pp. 159–63, reprinted as Chapter 14 above.

[4] Harry. G. Johnson, 'The Theory of Effective Protection and Preferences', *Economica*, Vol. XXXVI, No. 142 (May 1969) pp. 119–38, reprinted as Chapter 13 above.

[5] W.M. Corden, 'The Structure of a Tariff System and the Effective Protective Rate', *The Journal of Political Economy*, Vol. LXXIV, No. 3 (June 1966) pp. 221–37, and also W.M. Corden, *The Theory of Protection*, Chapter 4.

since the rise to prominence of the Heckscher—Ohlin—Samuelson model and the elegant theoretical problems to which it gives rise) with the obvious fact that some products are so heavily protected by their nature or by transport costs as to constitute non-traded or 'non-tradeable' goods. Yet the simple theory of effective protection, based on input-output relations and the assumption that all goods have a domestic price equal to the foreign price increased by the relevant import tariff (or reduced by the relevant export tax or increased by the relevant export subsidy), ignores such goods. How do they affect the analysis?

The purpose of this chapter is to pursue some of these problems with the simplest possible tools of trade theory, i.e. without the construction of complete mathematical models of general equilibrium, in order to illuminate the issues and explain some of the apparently paradoxical results that recent theorists have been able to obtain. It should be observed in passing, however, that the production of paradoxes and counter-examples may be counter-productive of understanding, since the practical economist needs to know, not that anything is possible, but what principles are 95 per cent reliable in practice.

To begin with the final point, it is evident that the assumption that all goods are traded is tremendously useful in eliminating demand considerations from the analytical picture and enabling the analyst to concentrate on the response of the production pattern to prices that can be treated as parametric. A similar utility attaches to the assumption that world prices are given, which eliminate foreign demand conditions for exports and domestic demand for imports in relation to foreign supply conditions as factors affecting the final general equilibrium result. Once non-traded goods that are used as inputs in traded-good production processes are introduced,[6] the resources used in adding value in their production processes share in the protection or anti-protection afforded by the tariff structure to the resources so used in adding value in traded goods production; and to determine the distribution of effective protection between the supplier and the user industries will require an analysis

---

[6] Chapter 14 above deals with the demand complications, but does not deal with inputs of non-traded goods into other production processes.

incorporating the supply elasticity of the non-tradeable industry (on the partial equilibrium analysis referred to above) or a more general analysis including the implications of the presence of this industry for the effects of the tariff structure on factor prices.[7]

One point is certain, however. The costs of non-tradeable inputs should not simply be deducted from the gross value of output like other traded input costs (as has frequently been done in the empirical calculations) in determining whether an activity is effectively protected or not, if the purpose of the calculation is to determine whether investment in the industry should be encouraged or discouraged. To see this point, assume that the industry appears exactly unprotected on such a calculation. If all its inputs are traded (subject to tariffs) and the industry is (necessarily) itself tariff-protected, the losses to consumers from buying the product at a price above world market price when the industry expands will be exactly recouped by the government in the form of tariff revenue of the industry's imported inputs. But if the inputs in question are non-tradeables, whose extra domestic costs are covered by the higher domestic price of the final product, there is an excess cost associated with expansion of the user industry that is not compensated by additional government tariff revenue, this excess cost consisting of the excess of the domestic cost of non-tradeable inputs over the cost for which they could have been imported in a form embedded in the final imported good.[8]

---

[7] For a partial equilibrium analysis, allowing for the supply elasticities of non-traded inputs, see J.C. Leith, 'Substitution and Supply Elasticities in Calculating the Effective Protective Rate', *Quarterly Journal of Economics*, Vol. 82, No. 4 (November 1968) pp. 588–601; and also Corden, *The Theory of Protection*, Chapter 7.

[8] This point emerged in correspondence with Anne O. Krueger in connection with her criticism of the Balassa–Schydlowsky article cited in note 2, which criticism is forthcoming in *The Journal of Political Economy*. The point was originally made by Corden ('The Structure of a Tariff System...', *op. cit.*), who recommended that non-traded inputs be grouped with value added in calculating effective protective rates. Tradeable inputs into non-tradeable goods complicate the practical problem in an obvious way. It should be noted that the argument disregards the consumption losses from distortion of consumers' choices due to the tariff; these losses are being borne whether the domestic industry expands or not.

The other two questions — substitutions in production among produced and original factors induced by effective protection, and the constraint imposed by given factor endowments and the requirements for equilibrium in the factor markets — require to be handled together for full generality. But some issues can be disposed of before introducing the factor markets, on the temporary assumption that value added is produced by some sort of original 'resources in general'.

The term 'value added' is analytically unambiguous in a Leontief fixed-coefficient production system, since an increase in the amount of money spent on 'value added' per unit of final output must be in the same proportion as the rise in the average price per unit of the original resources that produce 'value added'. With substitution possible between these resources and other bought-in produced inputs, induced by effective protection, a semantic ambiguity arises. The concept of 'price of value added', with which effective protection theory is concerned, may be interpreted as either the *total amount spent* on original resources per unit of final output, or as the *average price per unit* of the original factors used in producing value added. And the two measures may move in opposite directions, and will do so if the rise in price per unit induces so much substitution of produced for original factors that the total amount spent on the latter per unit of final output falls.

The concept of effective protection must obviously be concerned with the price per unit of the original factors, and not with the amount spent on them per unit of final output. No-one would seriously argue that a tax on an industry is really a subsidy because, given an inelastic demand for the product, total spending on the product has risen. Yet that is a precise inverse analogue of what may happen when the 'amount spent' definition of the price of value added is used. Still, a number of authors have regarded the two alternatives as equally valid interpretations of the concept when substitution occurs, and have devoted much effort to examining the differences between them with the use of the constant-elasticity-of-substitution production function, while some have used the 'amount spent' definition in attempts to show that the concept is nonsensical.[9]

Substitution of produced inputs for original factors as effective protection of value added rises (in correctly defined 'price per unit of original factors' terms), does however necessitate drawing a distinction between the total quantity of value added (i.e. original factors used) in an activity and the gross output of that activity, since these may move in opposite directions as a result of substitution of produced for original factors used in producing gross output as the latter increases in response to protection. This may be a more important point than economists have so far appreciated. The economist's prime concern, in analysing protection, is with the allocation of original resources of production and the efficiency of their utilization. Politicians, at least until they have become educated in effective protection theory, are typically concerned with gross outputs, e.g. with what number of automobiles or tons of steel their country produces annually, regardless of what little proportion of the final output is attributable to domestic resources and how inefficiently these resources are used. The very substitution of imported for domestic factors resulting from heavy effective protection of value added that the economist regards as a waste may in fact cater to the politician's satisfaction with high gross outputs.[10]

At this level of analysis, which still does not bring in factor endowment limitations as a constraint on the production pattern and induced changes in factor prices as governing the response of production to effective protection, the most important general proposition that has emerged is Finger's proof,[11] in generalization of Corden's original special proof,[12] that the

[9] For examples, see J. Anderson and S. Naya, 'Substitution and Two Concepts of Effective Rate of Protection', *American Economic Review*, Vol. 59, No. 4 (September 1969) pp. 607–12; H.G. Grubel and P.J. Lloyd, 'Factor Substitution and Effective Tariff Rates', *Review of Economic Studies*, Vol. XXXVIII (I) No. 113 (January 1971), pp. 95–103; D. B. Humphrey and T. Tsukahara Jr., 'On Substitution and the Effective Rate of Protection', *International Economic Review*, Vol. 11, No. 3 (October 1970), pp. 488–96. Also Travis, *op. cit.*, p. 441, uses the 'amount spent' definition to criticize the theory.

[10] This point has emerged in correspondence with W. Ethier about his forthcoming paper, 'Input Substitution and the Concept of the Effective Rate of Protection', (to be published in *The Journal of Political Economy*), which takes gross output rather than quantity of value added as its standard for assessing the resource-allocation effects of protection.

true effective protective rate for an activity must lie between an upper bound calculated from post-tariff domestic input coefficients and a lower bound calculated from free-trade input coefficients. It is reproduced here[13] because of its importance in challenging the rankings of effective protective rates resulting from empirical calculations, which generally rest on domestic post-tariff input-output tables but sometimes are based on assumed free-trade input-output coefficients.

Let quantities be normalized on unit prices at pre-tariff (free-trade) coefficients. Then under free trade

$$1 = v_j + \sum_i a_{ji}$$

where v_j is quantity of value added per unit in the jth industry, and the a_{ji} are inputs of quantities of i goods into the jth process per unit of final output. Under protection the true effective protective rate $(\bar{\tau}_j)$ for the jth activity is defined by

$$1 + t_j = (1 + \bar{\tau}_j) v_j + \sum_i a'_{ji} (1 + t_i)$$

where the ts are nominal tariff rates and primes denote efficient quantity input coefficients at post-tariff prices. Hence

$$\bar{\tau}_j = \frac{1}{v'_j} \left(t_j - \sum_i a'_{ji} t_i + v_j + \sum_i a_{ji} - v'_j - \sum_i a'_{ji} \right).$$

Since, by the theory of index numbers, the cost of producing at free-trade input prices with the post-tariff input coefficients must be greater, or at least no less, than the cost of producing at those prices with the free-trade input coefficients, i.e.

[11] Joseph M. Finger, 'Substitution and the Effective Rate of Protective', *The Journal of Political Economy*, Vol. 77, No. 6 (December 1969) pp. 972–75.

[12] W.M. Corden, 'The Structure of a Tariff System...', *op. cit.*, pp. 233–35.

[13] An alternative version is given in note 18 to Chapter 13 above. For a geometric exposition of the argument, see Corden, *The Theory of Protection*, Chapter 6.

$$v_j + \sum_i a_{ji} \leqslant v_j' + \sum_i a_{ji}',$$

we must have

$$\bar{\tau}_j \leqslant \tau_j' = \frac{t_j - \sum_i a_{ji}' t_i}{v_j'},$$

where τ_j' is the effective protective rate calculated from post-tariff coefficients. Similarly,

$$1 + t_j \leqslant (1 + \bar{\tau}_j) v_j + \sum_i a_{ji}(1 + t_i),$$

that is,

$$\bar{\tau}_j \geqslant \frac{t_j - \sum_i a_{ji} t_i}{v_j} = \tau_j,$$

where τ_j is the effective protective rate calculated from the free-trade coefficients of production. Hence

$$\tau_j' \geqslant \bar{\tau}_j \geqslant \tau_j,$$

i.e. the true effective protective rate is bracketed by the post-tariff-calculated rate on the upper-side and the pre-tariff-calculated rate on the lower side. The fact that the degree of error between the calculated rate and the true one depends on the substitution possibilities in the activity concerned means that a ranking of effective protective rates on either empirical basis of calculation cannot be trusted to be a reliable ranking of the true effective protective rates.

It is now appropriate to turn to the question of factor endowment limitations and the theory of production and factor pricing. Following the Heckscher-Ohlin-Samuelson tradition, it is natural to think of the economy's production opportunities as consisting of a set of constant-returns-to-scale production functions defined in terms of the inputs of original factors of production and produced inputs. Within this general framework of a constant-returns-to-scale production function, either substitution among the individual items in the two classes of inputs may be assumed to be perfectly general, or the problem of substitution may be simplified in various ways. Specifically, original factors may be assumed to be substitutable for one another in a sub-production-function that produces 'value added'. This value added may then be assumed to be combined with produced inputs in the production of final product according to three, increasingly complex, specifications. First, each individual produced input is required in a fixed ratio to the final product. Second, produced inputs are substitutable for each other (but not for value added) in a sub-production-function that produces a single aggregate produced input that is required in a fixed ratio to final product, so that substitution occurs among original factors only and among produced factors only but not between the aggregate value added and the aggregate produced input. Third, the aggregate value added, and the aggregate produced input, both of which allow substitution among but not between items in the two categories of factors, may be assumed substitutable for one another in an aggregate production function for final product.[14]

This conception, however, raises a difficulty familiar in the theory of international trade from the vast amount of work that has been done on the factor-price-equalization theorem. There will be a unique relationship between any arbitrarily given set of prices for final products, factor prices, and the pattern of production, given the endowment of factors, only if the number of independent (i.e. non-identical) production functions is just equal to or less than (but not more than) the number of factors of production. The theory of effective protection assumes a substantial number of products, while common sense suggests that the number of separate factors is limited, at least at the level of longer-run abstract theory appropriate for a concept concerned with the analysis of 'structural' features of the economy. 'Raw' labour may be assumed to be homogeneous, while capital may be assumed for abstract long-run analysis to distribute itself among alternative opportunities for investment in material and in human forms (equipment of various kinds, and various labour skills) so as to equalize rates of return on

[14] For examples of the use of 'two-level' production functions in this connection, see W.M. Corden, 'Effective Protective Rates in the General Equilibrium Model: A Geometric Note', *Oxford Economic Papers*, Vol. 21, No. 2 (July 1969) pp. 135–41; and R.J. Ruffin, 'Tariffs, Intermediate Goods, and Domestic Production', *American Economic Review*, Vol. 59, No. 3 (June 1969) pp. 261–69.

alternative investments. And while it may ease model-building to assume that each productive activity employs, besides labour and capital, a natural resource factor peculiar to itself — which amounts in effect to assuming diminishing returns to capital and labour alone in each industry — it seems more reasonable to assume either that 'land' too is non-specific or that natural resource factors are confined to a limited number of types each with some alternative uses. The result of the assumption that production functions (commodities) outnumber factors is either that the economy produces only as many commodities as there are factors and its production pattern is determinate, given world prices, or that it produces more commodities than it has factors and its production pattern cannot be determined without the introduction of world demand conditions. This point is developed in detail, in the context of effective protection theory, in what follows.

The chief problem raised by the introduction of the factor-market-equilibrium side of the general equilibrium model is whether, as implied in particular by Corden's treatment of effective protection,[15] the direction of shift of productive activity can be predicted from the effective protective rates or not.[16]

The simplest model to use for the purpose of analysing this problem is a modification of the two-factor two-good Heckscher-Ohlin-Samuelson model, the modification consisting of introducing imported (not home-produced) goods which serve as produced inputs and therefore introduce the distinction between nominal

[15] Corden, 'The Structure of a Tariff System...', *op. cit.*

[16] For more formal and rigorous analyses of this question, see, for the case of fixed coefficients, W.M. Corden, 'Effective Protective Rates in the General Equilibrium Model: A Geometric Note', *Oxford Economic Papers*, Vol. 21, No. 2 (July 1969) pp. 135—41; and *The Theory of Protection*, Chapter 4; and for the substitution case, V.K. Ramaswami and T.N. Srinivasan, 'Tariff Structure and Resource Allocation in the Presence of Factor Substitution', forthcoming in Bhagwati et al (eds.), *Trade, Payments and Welfare, Papers in Honour of Charles P. Kindleberger* (Amsterdam: North-Holland, 1971), J. Bhagwati and T.N. Srinivasan, 'The Theory of Effective Protection', forthcoming, R.W. Jones, 'Effective Protection and Substitution, *The Journal of International Economies*, Vol. 1, No. 1 (February 1971), and W.M. Corden, *The Theory of Protection*, Chapter 6.

and effective tariff rates. If there is no substitutability between produced inputs and original factors in either production function, net production functions for value-added in the two activities can be defined and a transformation curve between the two value-added 'products' derived in the same way as in the Heckscher-Ohlin-Samuelson model; and the economy will be shifted along this transformation curve by changes in the relative domestic prices of value-added from the world market value-added price ratio, induced by effective protection, in the same way as it is shifted along the production-transformation curve by changes in the domestic product price ratio from the world price ratio by nominal protection in the more traditional analysis. If the produced inputs are assumed to be substitutable among themselves in the production of a composite intermediate products required in a fixed ratio to the final product, this conclusion will not be altered, though the computation of the precise effective protective rate relevant to this shift will obviously be complicated by the index number problem previously discussed.

Complications and possible paradoxes may arise, however, if the produced inputs (which may for simplicity be treated as a single input) are assured substitutable for original factors in the production functions for the final products. This assumption, as already mentioned, requires also the introduction of a distinction between the effects of protection on gross outputs of products and its effects on the allocation of resources to the production of value added, since with substitutability the two characteristics of an industry (gross output, and value added) will generally not change in the same proportion, and may change in opposite directions as the ratio of value added to final output changes in response to protection.

Analytically, the problem is analogous to that of the effects of technical progress on the pattern of production in a free-trade economy facing fixed terms of trade, and so are the possibilities that arise. It can be readily handled with the aid of a version of the Lerner-Pearce diagram, presented in Figure 1. The two isoquants represent now the capital (C) and labour (L) required to produce a unit of value-added input into the production functions of the final products X and Y, units being chosen so that value-addeds exchange at a one-to-one price under free

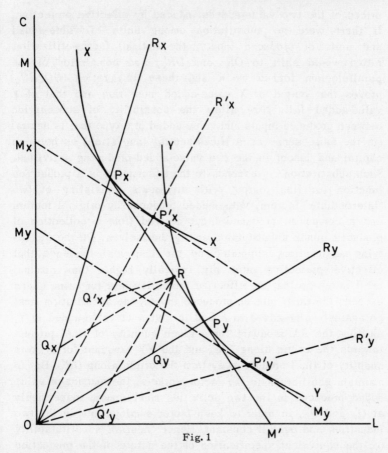

Fig. 1

trade conditions, and the isoquants being selected to represent a value of value added equal to the whole national income. Point R on the common budget line represents the economy's total endowment of capital and labour. Distances corresponding to the free-trade outputs of the two value-addeds are found by completing the parallelogram formed by R and the free-trade optimum capital-labour ratios OR_x and OR_y.

Now suppose that effective protection is given to X at the rate $M_x M_y/OM_y$, where OM_x and OM_y represent the costs of production of the original isoquantities of X and Y when factor prices have adjusted to the change in the domestic relative

379

prices of the two value-addeds induced by effective protection. If there were no substitution among units of value-added and units of produced inputs, the optimal factor-utilization ratios would shift to OR'_x and OR'_y, and completion of the parallelogram formed by R and these new ratios $(OQ'_xRQ'_y)$ proves that output of X value-added must rise and that of Y value-added fall. Now allow the possibility of substitution between produced inputs and value-added of a type that is neutral (in the same sense as a Hicks-neutral innovation) as between capital and labour in the two value-added-producing activities. Such substitution corresponds to the assumption of a production function for final output with arguments consisting of two 'intermediate' factors, value-added produced by original factors and a composite produced input derived from a collection of produced inputs substitutable among themselves. On the simplifying assumption, supported by the empirical evidence that effective protective rates are typically higher than nominal tariff rates, so that the effective protective rate for value added exceeds the tariff rate on produced inputs, the substitution must go against value-added in X and in favour of value-added in Y, shifting the XX isoquant for a given quantity of final product towards the origin along OR'_x and the YY isoquant for a given quantity of final product away from the origin along OR'_y. But to maintain equilibrium in the factor markets, the amount of value added produced in the two activities must remain respectively at Q'_x and Q'_y, in order to keep factor employments in the two industries and overall constant. Hence 'neutral' substitutability (or the equivalent specification of the nature of the production functions) does not affect the allocation of resources to the production of value added in the two industries; but because of substitution, output of the final product X increases by more and that of Y by less than it would have done in the absence of substitution between original and produced factor inputs — so that the shift in relative quantities of final products produced is greater than that in relative value-addeds produced.

The conclusion just reached implicitly assumes that the effective protective rate for the import-substituting activity is the same in the two situations being compared. If the same nominal tariff rates were imposed in the two cases, the effective protective rate on value added in import substitution will be higher with substitutability than without, for reasons of index number theory given earlier, and hence the shift of resources towards producing value added in the protected industry would be greater in the second case than in the first. Since the assumption of equal effective protective rates in the two situations thus works against the presumption that effective protective rates permit prediction of resource shifts between the two sectors, it will be retained in the subsequent argument.

If, instead of being neutral in the sense defined, the substitution between produced inputs and value added is biased towards substitution for capital rather than labour in the import-competing X sector, where substitution goes against value added and in favour of produced inputs, and towards substitution for labour rather than capital in the exporting Y sector, where substitution favours value added over produced inputs, the optimal capital-labour ratios in both sectors will fall, accentuating the shift of resources into the X sector by comparison with the case of neutral substitution (as can be seen by completing the relevant new parallelogram around R). If by contrast substitution goes relatively strongly against labour as compared with capital in the X sector, and in favour of capital as compared with labour in the Y sector, the optimal capital-labour ratios rise in both sectors by comparison with neutral substitution, and the effect may be strong enough to offset the direct substitution of labour for capital in both sectors induced by effective protection of the X sector. This last case offers the possibility of effective protection of a sector reducing its total output of value added.

This analysis of the problem has attempted to apply the standard tools of the Heckscher-Ohlin-Samuelson analysis, rather than to develop a rigorous and specific mathematical model to illuminate the possibility of exceptional cases to the general presumption that protection will shift resources into the protected sector. The analysis may well have missed something significant in the general equilibrium problem, because it compresses the production side of the economy into a transformation curve between value-addeds, the position on which is determined by the effective protective rate, and treats substitution between original and produced inputs in terms of a technical change, on the empirical assumption that substitution goes against or in favour of value added according as effective protection is positive or negative. But as it stands the necessary condition it yields for the possibility of an exceptional case — that a rise in the relative price of the original factor used relatively intensively in the production of the value added in the protected activity be accompanied by an increase in the intensity of use of that factor relative to the other factor in one or both sectors — does not convey a plausible sense of empirical relevance.[17]

The two-commodity (or activity) model of the Heckscher-Ohlin-Samuelson tradition just discussed has to be forced fairly hard to yield analytical results of interest in the construction of a more theoretically appealing analysis that nevertheless has relevance to the policy problems with which the new concept was and primarily still is concerned. More interesting and realistic models, relevant to some important practical policy problems, can be constructed by expanding the analysis to a three-commodity three-factor system (land, labour and capital) and simplifying the range of possibilities by imposing realistic restrictions on the factor-using characteristics of the productive sectors.[18] Discussion is simplified by continuing to assume (as will be done in the rest of the chapter) that the sectors can be specified as producing value added, and that the effective protective structure can be condensed into price premia given or price penalties imposed on particular value-added-producing activities, as compared with world market price

[17] In the more general anaylsis of Jones, *op. cit.*, substitution will go in favour of or against the original factors according to whether the effective rate of protection of value added falls short of or exceeds the effective rate of protection of produced inputs. But Jones's results still suggest a general presumption that resource shifts will occur in the direction indicated by relative effective protective rates. I am grateful to Jones for the suggestion to simplify the analysis by using the empirical evidence that effective protective rates typically exceed nominal tariff rates to exclude half of the possible outcomes.

[18] See for example A.H. Tan, *Differential protection, Economic Indices and Optimal Trade Policies*, unpublished doctoral dissertation, Stanford University, 1968; and ·Corden, *The Theory of Protection*, Chapter 4.

ratios. As one of the simplest possible cases, consider a country with two export-producing sectors, both employing only labour and land, and an import-competing manufacturing sector using only capital and labour. A price premium for manufactures given by protection will lead to a rise in the price of labour, pulling labour out of agriculture; agricultural production must fall, lowering the rent of land; and agricultural production will tend to shift into the land-intensive branch, with the possibility that the production and exports of that branch will actually increase. [19] A similar model, with two importable goods and one exportable good, can be used to show that a tariff on one of the import goods may either increase or decrease domestic production of the other, and so tend to decrease or increase imports of it.

We turn finally to consider the theoretically most interesting case, that in which there are more commodities than factors. For this purpose, it is convenient to revert to the two-factor Heckscher-Ohlin-Samuelson model, as depicted in the Lerner-Pearce diagram, but to abandon the usual assumption that production technologies are identical in the country under analysis and in the rest of the world, though retaining the assumption of constant returns to scale. On the latter assumption, isoquants can be drawn in the Lerner-Pearce diagram representing unit values of the commodities at world market prices; but since technology is not assumed identical in the country with that of the rest of the world, these isoquants will not have a common tangent, i.e. there will not be a relative factor-price ratio at which all commodities can be produced at equal (world) cost. The economy will seek to maximize its real income by producing that commodity or those commodities that it can produce at least cost (the costs being equal where more than one commodity is produced), cost being determined by its factor endowment in relation to its production opportunities (the isoquants). There are three possible cases, depicted in Figure 2, where X_1, X_2, X_3, and X_4 represent successively more capital-intensive commodities (factor-intensity-reversal

[19] F. Gruen and W.M. Corden, 'A Tariff That Worsens the Terms of Trade', in I.A. McDougall and R.H. Snape (eds.), *Studies in International Economics* (Amsterdam: North-Holland, 1970).

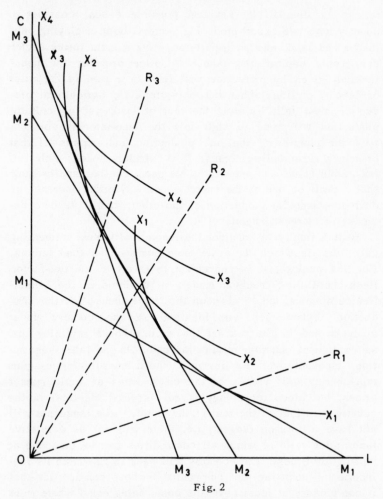

Fig. 2

possibilities are ruled out by assumption). With the endowment ratio OR_1, the equilibrium factor price ratio is M_1M_1 and the country specializes on producing X_1. With the endowment ratio OR_2, the equilibrium factor price ratio is M_2M_2 and the country produces both X_1 and X_2. With the endowment ratio OR_3, the equilibrium factor price ratio is M_3M_3 and the country drops X_1 production but can produce some of all three of X_2, X_3, and X_4. (Note that the diagram is drawn for simplicity to produce this progression as the country's overall capital-labour ratio rises; there is no reason *a priori* why the number of goods producible should vary systematically with the overall factor endowment ratio.)

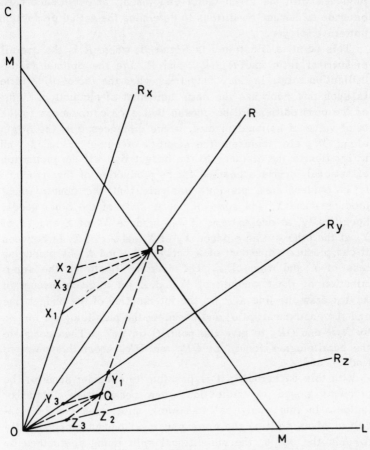

Fig. 3

In the first and second cases, the production pattern is determined by the technology available and the structure of world market prices (combined in the isoquants by choice of units) and by the country's factor endowment – in the first

385

case trivially, in the second by the requirement of full employment of factors, as previously analysed in connection with the Lerner-Pearce diagram (Figure 1). In the third case the production pattern is indeterminate over a certain range, in the sense that alternative sets of commodity quantities can be produced with the given factor endowment, and reference must be made to demand conditions to determine the actual production pattern employed.

This point is illustrated in Figure 3, where R is the overall endowment ratio and R_x, R_y, and R_z are the optimal factor-utilization ratios in three industries when the factor-price ratio is such that each has the same unit cost of production. Units of the commodities are so chosen that each corresponds to the total value of national income; hence distances from the origin along OR_x etc. represent the quantity of output produced, and in relation to the distance to the budget line MM the proportion of national income accounted for by production of that product. It is evident from previous analysis that the country must produce some X, and some of one or both of the other goods. Specifically, at one extreme it can produce X_1 of X and Y_1 of Y, at the other it can produce X_2 of X and Z_2 of Z. In between it can produce an amount of X between X_1 and X_2 by producing less of Y and more of Z. The diagram illustrates the determination of these outputs of Y and Z for a given amount of X, X_3: draw the line X_3P (to the intersection of the budget line and the endowment ratio) and complete the parallelogram formed by X_3P and OR_x to give the point Q on Y_1Z_2. Then complete the parallelogram formed by OR_y and OR_z about this point to find Y_3 and Z_3.

With this background, it is possible to consider some of the problems posed by protection when commodities outnumber factors. In this analytical framework, protection can be conceived of as shifting the corresponding isoquant proportionally towards the origin, the proportional shift being determined by the effect of the tariff rate in raising the domestic above the world market price and so reducing the quantity that needs to be produced to be worth a unit of world market value.

As a preliminary exercise, consider the standard two-good Heckscher-Ohlin-Samuelson model, considered as a special

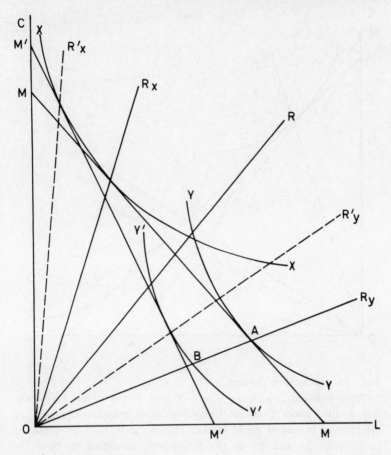

Fig. 4

case, and analysed in Figure 4. Commodity Y is taken to be the importable good, some being produced under free trade. The tariff shifts the isoquant from YY to $Y'Y'$, the tariff rate being measured by AB/OA. The equilibrium factor price ratio shifts from MM to $M'M'$, and the optimal factor-utilization ratios from OR_x and OR_y to OR'_x and OR'_y respectively. By completion of the relevant parallelograms it can easily be confirmed that production of Y increases and of X decreases. In this case, of course, there is a monotonic relation between the tariff rate

387

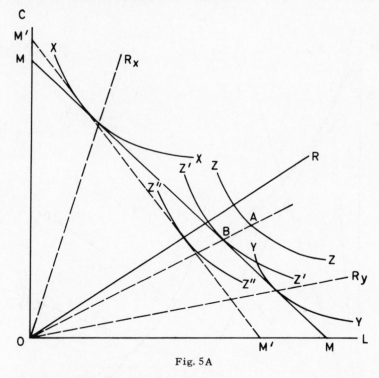

Fig. 5A

and the production pattern.

Now consider the case where X and Y are being produced, but a third good Z is not being produced because the cost of production is above world market prices. This case is depicted in Figures 5A and 5B on the alternative assumptions that Z's capital-labour ratio is intermediate between those of X and of Y, and outside their range. In each case, a tariff below the rate of AB/OA will have no effect on production. A tariff rate of exactly AB/OA will make domestic production of Z just economic. In this case the result is the indeterminacy of the production pattern discussed above. The difference between the two cases shown in Figures 5A and 5B is that in the former, any resulting production of Z takes place at the expense of both X and Y, whereas in the latter it takes place at the expense of X only and must be accompanied by expansion of

388

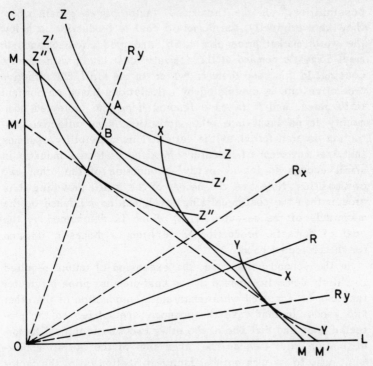

Fig. 5B

production of Y. (This can be shown by the parallelogram-completion technique developed earlier.) Since X may be either the exportable or the importable good, and vice versa for Y, the tariff on Z may increase rather than decrease the country's trade volume. This will occur if the protected good is more intensive than the existing import-substituting industry in the factor used relatively intensively in that industry. (This proposition ignores a possible qualification associated with substitution of exportables for the protected good in consumption.) The central point, however, is the indeterminacy of production of the protected good.

What happens if the tariff rate is higher than that necessary to cover the excess domestic cost of production of the protected good (diagrammatically, the new isoquant is not $Z'Z'$ tangent to MM, but $Z''Z''$, intersecting MM)? There are two polar

389

possibilities.[20] In the first case, factor prices remain where they were originally, the domestic cost of production is below the world market price plus tariff, and production expands to meet domestic demand at the domestic cost level, with imports ceasing. In this case there is 'water' in the tariff; the effective protective rate is overstated by calculations based on nominal tariff rates, and if (a case ignored here) the protected commodity is an input into other activities, some effective protection is transferred to the latter. This possibility assumes that the movement of resources into the protected industry is small enough to leave positive production of the other two commodities. Note that the height of the tariff, providing it is greater than the cost-equalizing level, has no influence on the magnitude of the resource shift, which is determined by the cost of domestic production in relation to domestic demand for the protected good.

In the second polar case, the expansion of output required to satisfy domestic demand at the cost-premium price is greater than can be achieved while maintaining production of the other two goods. In that case the economy specializes on the protected good and that one of the other two whose optimal factor-utilization ratio lies on the other side of the overall endowment ratio to its own optimal factor-utilization ratio, the factor price ratio changing so as to equalize costs of production between the goods. In the case shown in Figure 5A, production of Y would be eliminated, in the case shown in Figure 5B, production of X. Note, to avoid puzzlement, that the assumption of no transport costs permits goods not subject to tariffs to switch from being exportables to being importables, and vice versa. (Note also that, because of substitution possibilities, in the case of Figure 5A it might appear that the country might specialize completely on Z, using the overall factor-endowment ratio, but that this possibility is ruled out by the fact that sales at the protected price are limited to the quantity domestically demanded.)

[20] A third possibility, excluded by the assumption of perfect competition though important in practice, is that the difference between domestic cost and foreign price plus tariff is absorbed by monopolistic or oligopolistic market organization.

In between the two polar cases just discussed there is of course the possibility of specialization on two of the goods, with some 'water' in the tariff and factor prices not fully adjusted to equate the relative costs of domestic production of the two goods with their world price ratio as modified by the tariff. This possibility arises if output of the protected good would fall short of demand for it at the price (cost) set by the pre-tariff factor price ratio, and would exceed the domestic demand for it at a domestic price equal to the foreign price augmented to the full extent of the tariff.

The theoretical and empirical difficulty in all these cases is that there is no smooth monotonic relationship between the tariff rate and the quantity of protected production, and hence no simple traditional way to estimate either the production shifts or the welfare losses resulting from protection. The question that arises, in conclusion, is whether the theoretical elegance and authority of the constant returns to scale assumption are weighty enough to justify insistence on them at the expense of reformulating the analysis to cope with the discontinuities involved. The empirical implications of the theoretical analysis of the various possible cases just presented are not particularly appealing, since they imply for the many-good case respectively an abundance of non-protective (nuisance) tariffs, random distribution of output between domestic and imported sources, an abundance of 'water' in the tariff structure and more important of prohibitive tariffs, and specialization of domestic output on a narrow range of goods. Empirical efforts to cope with the problems by using the obvious tool of linear programming have to be buttressed by arbitrary fixation of the amounts or permissible rates of change in the amounts of a considerable number of specialized factors of production (structures, equipment, and types of labour) if they are not to produce obviously nonsensical results. It may be that the prevailing mixture of general and partial equilibrium analysis is the most reasonable approach for practical economists interested in commercial policy questions, in spite of its rather shaky foundations in pure international trade theory.

PART V:
Tariff Reduction and Policy Harmonization

16. The Implications of Free or Freer Trade for The Harmonization of Other Policies*

I. INTRODUCTION: GENERAL CONSIDERATIONS

The subject of this chapter is the extent to which a movement towards freer, and especially to free, trade among a group of countries either requires or makes desirable a harmonization of their economic policies, including those social policies that have an economic impact. This is a question that naturally concerns the governments and public opinion of countries that, on the one hand, want to improve national economic efficiency and standards of living through specialization and economies of large-scale production but, on the other hand, are fearful of the possible loss of sovereignty in economic policy and of 'national independence' that might be entailed in a commitment to freer trade.

The problem arises at two different levels of policy, which may be described, respectively, as 'structural' economic policy and balance of payments policy. Structural economic policy relates to the structure and levels of taxes and expenditures, the social security system, the regulation of public utility rates, the control of competition, and so forth; balance of payments policy relates to the choice of policy instruments for securing balance of payments equilibrium. Specifically, there are two basic questions: how far does freer trade require or make desirable the harmonization of fiscal and related policies among the participating countries; and how far does freer trade require or make desirable the coordination of balance of payments policies of the participants? These questions are most conveniently dealt with in detail separately and are so handled in subsequent sections.

* Harry G. Johnson, Paul Wonnacott, Hirofumi Shibata, *Harmonization of National Economic Policies under Free Trade* (Toronto: University of Toronto Press, 1968) pp. 1–41.

395

For purposes of clarity and relevance, this chapter concentrates on the problems of harmonization of economic policies among the member countries that might be raised by the formation of a free trade area.[1] It should be noted that this delimitation of the problem excludes from the scope of the discussion certain problems of coordination that are necessarily raised by more comprehensive and rigid schemes of economic integration. A customs union, for example, since it involves the unification of national tariff schedules, therefore necessarily involves the harmonization of whatever external economic policies and internal economic structural and development policies are embodied in such tariff schedules. A common market of the European Economic Community type goes much farther in exacting uniformity and the sacrifice of national freedom of action with respect to the control of intra-market movements of capital and labour and in requiring commitment to the standardization of competitive conditions of various kinds.[2] By contrast, a free trade area entails a commitment to the elimination of trade barriers, but no positive commitment to the harmonization either of tariffs on trade with third parties[3] or of other policies than commercial policy in the

[1] It thus excludes a set of problems that might be relevant in some circumstances: the harmonization of members' policies with those of the countries of the outside world.

[2] In addition, the form that the common agricultural policy of the European Economic Community is taking will make it extremely difficult, if not impossible, to change the exchange rates between members' currencies in future.

[3] A free trade area might generate two sorts of pressures for changes in national tariffs applicable to third parties. First, the problem of 'trade deflection' — entry of third-party goods to the market of a high-tariff member via a low-tariff member, either via trans-shipment or via substitution in the consumption or production of the low-tariff member between such goods and goods exportable to the high-tariff country — may indicate the desirability of the alignment of member tariff rates. It is usually assumed that this problem is manageable by means of certificate-of-origin procedures: and it has not in fact proved a significant problem

interests of economic integration.

In the context of a free trade area, therefore, the harmonization issue with respect to structure appears partly as an obligation on participants not to use other policies to nullify the economic consequences of the elimination of trade barriers and partly, and more importantly, as a question of what changes or alignments to make in other policies in order to facilitate the desired efficiency-increasing results of free trade or to augment those results beyond what they would otherwise be. Correspondingly, the issue with respect to balance of payments policy is: what degree of harmonization is necessary for balance of payments policies not to conflict in the short run with the longer-run economic objectives of free trade?

These issues will be the subject of detailed analysis in subsequent sections. The purpose of the present section is to place the issue of policy harmonization in a free trade area in a broad perspective and, specifically, to argue the following: first, that the need for harmonization *additional to what is already required* of countries extensively engaged in world trade is relatively slight; second, that such harmonization is more a matter of choosing to augment the benefits of free trade than of being required to harmonize as a result of free trade; third, that in many cases there is little important loss in terms of other policy objectives involved in harmonization; and fourth, that the problems of harmonization are such as can be handled by negotiation and consultation according to well-established procedures among

in the European Free Trade Association. (On this point see Gardner Patterson, *Discrimination in International Trade: The Policy Issues, 1945–65* [Princeton, NJ: Princeton University Press, 1966] p. 161, n. 89.) Second, the establishment of the free trade area may make the application of the pre-existing tariff rates to non-members no longer seem rational — for example, if their primary purpose was to protect domestic producers against competition from countries that have now become partners in the free trade area: the resulting adjustments of tariff schedules, however, would not necessarily involve closer alignment with partner's tariff schedules. Both of these pressures are consequential on the decision to free trade with the rest of the group and involve commercial policy itself rather than the implications of free trade for other policies; they therefore fall outside the scope of this chapter.

the governments concerned, rather than such as to require elaborate international agreements.[4]

To begin with, the notion that free trade (as distinct from the
present situation of substantial national tariffs but nevertheless
substantial national involvements in international trade and payments) will necessarily require major steps towards policy harmonization and a substantial loss of independence in national
economic policy is one of those black-and-white oversimplifica-
tions that frequently befog rational discussion of public policy
issues. Logically, any significant involvement in international
economic relations confronts a nation with a variety of choices

[4] That a free trade arrangement requires an elaborate harmonization of
other policies has been disputed by two well-qualified experts, on
whose thinking the argument of this section is partly based.

W.B. Reddaway, the member of the Tinbergen Committee who contributed the basic theoretical analysis of the Tinbergen Report, has
maintained very strongly that the formation of a European free trade
area would not require any agreement for 'harmonization of tax systems
and social charges.' His reasoning was that the two principles required
to avoid distortion of trade by the tax system — consistent application
of each general tax according to either the origin or the destination
principle, and remission to exporters of particular taxes that bear especially heavily on their products — are both independent of the existence or not of a free trade area, and are conformed with reasonably well
by national policies, except where governments have deliberately chosen
to distort the working of competition for other objectives. (W.B.
Reddaway, 'The Implications of a Free Trade Area for British Taxation',
British Tax Review [March 1958] pp. 71–9, esp. p. 78.)

Professor Bertil Ohlin, the eminent Swedish economist and politician,
has recently argued, with specific reference to a proposal for preferential trading arrangements between the European Free Trade Association and North America, that the main problem of harmonization in a
free trade area is for countries to maintain full employment consistently
with the relative wage-price trends necessary to preserve balance of
payments equilibrium under fixed exchange rates, and that this is a
problem they face anyway. He also argues that, so far as the static
allocation of resources is concerned, any distortions due to differences
in tax treatment of particular industries that might require harmonization
will have to be revealed and resolved by detailed study and that, in
the context of economic growth, the problems most likely to require
attention are the effect of differences in corporate tax rates and depreciation allowances on the national location of economic activity, and
the need for special policies (the reverse of harmonization) to promote
growth in backward regions. (Bertil Ohlin, 'Some Aspects of Policies
for Freer Trade', in Baldwin et al., *Trade, Growth, and the Balance of
Payments*: *Essays in Honour of Gottfried Haberler* [Chicago: Rand-
McNally; Amsterdam: North Holland, 1965].)

which range from aligning its policies with those of its trading partners in order to maximize its gain from trade to pursuing independent policies for the sake of national objectives at the cost of a certain loss in economic efficiency. Free trade is merely one end of a spectrum (of which the other end is self-sufficient isolation) and most of the advanced nations are probably much closer to the free trade end of the spectrum than to the autarky end.

This implies that these countries have probably already resolved, in the formulation of their own national 'structural' policies, the problem of balancing the contribution of such policies to national objectives against their effects on the nation's gains from trade. Similarly, in the field of balance of payments policy, whether a nation has high or low tariffs, it is necessarily obliged — at least so long as it adheres, as all advanced countries currently do, to a fixed exchange rate — to subordinate domestic objectives to the need to maintain balance in its balance of payments. The stringency of this commitment is a function, not of the level of its tariffs, but of its freedom to change its tariffs and other trade restrictions in response to changes in its balance of payments;.and the advanced industrial countries have in fact already committed themselves to severely restricting their freedom to resort to varying their trade barriers as a means of adjusting their balances of payments.

Empirically, also, the contention that a free trade area necessarily requires extensive harmonization lacks the support of experience. The long British experience with free trade is perhaps too remote historically to be very relevant but it provides at least negative evidence on the question. And in modern times, the major industrial nations have negotiated successfully among themselves for the liberalization of trade, both within the OEEC and in GATT, without having had to raise the issue of harmonization of other policies. (Experience in GATT does tend to show, however, that, as tariff barriers to trade are reduced, distortions of international competition attributable to non-tariff barriers, including various aspects of other government policies besides commercial policy, become more visible and more evocative of international concern.)

Further, the various schemes of economic integration among

399

groups of countries adopted in recent years have been consistent with the survival of much variation in both structural and balance of payments policies among the members. For example, in Benelux the Netherlands and Luxembourg continue to rely primarily on income and capital taxes for revenue, whereas Belgium relies to a much greater extent on indirect taxes. Within the Common Market the French reliance on indicative planning continues to contrast sharply with the German reliance on free enterprise, and the various countries handle their balance of payments problems in significantly different ways. The European Free Trade Association does not entail significant formal efforts at harmonization; the only serious issue that has arisen concerned Britain's application of tariff surcharges to its partner countries as well as to outsiders in 1964, and that issue merged into the broader issue of whether this technique was consistent with GATT rules. Finally, the experience of federal countries such as Canada, the United States, and Australia suggests that appreciable differences in tax and expenditure structures and levels among the component provinces or states are, in the eyes of the governments and citizens concerned, quite compatible with the enjoyment of the benefits of free trade within the national economy.

The view that a free trade area necessarily requires a great deal of harmonization of other policies derives from a variety of sources, which require some discussion if the real nature and extent of the problem are to be properly assessed.

The most important of these sources is the ignorance on the part of many 'practical' people of the principle of comparative cost and the theory of international monetary adjustment, and the associated propensity to reason in terms of absolute prices and costs and current levels of wages and/or the exchange rate. If one overlooks the basic theoretical point that in the long run[5] a country's exchange rate or wage-price level relative to those of the rest of the world must be such as to secure a rough or

---

[5] 'The Long Run' is a concept of economic theory that may be misleading in the present context; it means, not that the situation to which it refers is far off in the future, but that it constitutes a state of affairs towards which the economy gravitates under the influence of economic forces, though at any particular time there may be deviations from it in one direction or another.

400

average balancing of its balance of payments, it is easy to draw the erroneous conclusion that a higher average level of corporate taxation, of social security provision, or of wages or interest rates constitutes a competitive disadvantage for a country in domestic and foreign markets. The same oversight leads to the erroneous conclusion that differences in the general levels of taxes and other business costs lead to competitive distortions in a free trade area and thus require harmonization before a free trade area can promote economic efficiency. What in fact distorts competition and the working of the principle of comparative advantage is differentials in the incidence of such charges on goods moving in international trade and on factors of production (capital and labour) to the extent that these are internationally mobile. The result of this misconception of the problem is that harmonization is viewed as a matter of coordinating over-all policies and conditions with respect to every major factor affecting the competitive position of business enterprises. From the point of view of economic analysis, the problem of harmonization is instead likely to be concerned with particular cases in which the incidence of domestic fiscal and other policies deviates from the norm for the generality of economic activity in such a way as to impose exceptional burdens on, or provide exceptional advantages to, a particular group of domestic or foreign producers.[6]

A second source of exaggeration of the need for harmonization is the natural tendency of many people to confuse the limited objectives of a free trade area with the more far-reaching objectives of more comprehensive forms of economic integration, and especially of the ultimate form, complete economic union. They erroneously identify the requirements (or, still more misleadingly, the economic consequences) of such more comprehensive forms of integration with the harmonization requirements of a free trade arrangement. Thus it is natural enough for Canadians contemplating free trade with the United States to visualize the question in terms of Canada's becoming a state or group of states in the

---

[6] A potentially important exception concerns the influence of major differences in the levels and composition of taxation and expenditure on the international migration of factors of production, insofar as these factors are free to migrate. This subject is dealt with in greater detail below.

American union, and then to take the changes in Canadian policies and Canadian economic affairs that political union would likely entail as a measure of the harmonization of policies required by free trade arrangement. But this is a logically invalid procedure: the point of a free trade area is that it is an arrangement for obtaining the benefits of free trade over a larger economic area *without* the commitment to more far-reaching unification of policies entailed in tighter forms of economic integration or political union.

Contemporary interest in free trade on a regional basis derives primarily from the formation first of the European Coal and Steel Community and then, on the basis of its success, of the European Economic Community. The tendency previously referred to has probably been significantly reinforced by using these as examples of what is involved in a free trade area. But these examples are misleading, and specifically promote exaggeration of the harmonization required in a free trade area, for two reasons. First, the objective of the political unification of Europe in some form has always figured strongly in the background and has been reflected in both general ideas about, and concrete provisions for, harmonization of national policies that derive more from the objective of creating the outward forms of a European 'community' than from considerations of economic efficiency. Second, the economic concepts, assumptions, and analysis embodied in the economic philosophy of the two successive Communities frequently appear naive, fallacious, or questionable in the light of contemporary economic science.[7] Thus, the belief that economic integration requires harmonization of taxes and other social charges (which is deeply ingrained in Common Market economic philosophy) reflects the prevalence, even among economic experts, of the tendency to think in terms of absolute prices and costs rather

---

[7] It should be mentioned in fairness, first, that most of the work on the economics of customs unions and other forms of integration has been done contemporaneously with, or subsequent to, the establishment of the two Communities and was not available to their proponents and designers; and second, that much of that work requires a degree of economic sophistication extremely difficult to translate into the arena of popular debate.

than of comparative costs.[8] This belief also reflects the propensity of French political economists, and policy-makers in particular, to believe (or at least maintain) that industrial wages and prices bear little or no relationship to real costs of production, contrary to the assumptions of the classical theory of comparative costs and the general presumption of economic policy in the capitalist economies, and that therefore the freeing of trade, by itself, cannot be trusted to operate in the social interest unless carefully hedged by governmental control of the conditions of competition.

A third source of exaggeration or potential exaggeration of the need for harmonization of other policies entailed by a free trade area has been the evolution and content of scientific analysis of the economic effects of regional integration itself. In the first place, one of the earliest and more influential works on the subject, James Meade's *Problems of Economic Union*, was concerned with the possibility of raising standards of living by the formation of a single, integrated market for the products of the members of the economic union; and ... the implications of such action for the domestic economic policies of the countries involved.'[9] Meade's concern with *maximizing* the economic gains from integration — the formulation of the problem most appealing to the economic theorist — naturally leads to consideration of the fullest possible form of economic union, which inevitably includes freedom of migration of labour and capital, and consequently both raises and emphasizes the most far-reaching needs for harmonization. Second — a related point — the purely

---

[8] Hans Liesner records, with reference to the harmonization dispute within the ECSC that led to the appointment of the Tinbergen Committee, the existence of a 'mental barrier between the experts to whom the contestants turned,' arising from the fact that German fiscal experts traditionally think of taxes as an inseparable part of the prices of commodities, which blocked understanding of the economic issues involved in alternative systems of border adjustment of national taxes. J.E. Meade, H.H. Liesner, and S.J. Wells, *Case Studies in European Economic Union: The Mechanics of Integration* (London: Oxford University Press, 1962) p. 321.

[9] James E. Meade, *Problems of Economic Union* (Chicago: University of Chicago Press, 1953) p. vii.

theoretical approach to the problem is inherently incapable of establishing the quantitative importance to economic efficiency and income maximization of the various degrees of economic integration that might be contemplated, or the relative magnitudes of the losses that might ensue on failure to harmonize national economic policies in the various ways indicated as desirable by economic analysis. It thus tends to create the impression that all theoretically desirable measures of harmonization are both absolutely and relatively equally important to the achievement of increased income through integration. Third, while economic theorists have been by no means unaware that international differences in both the levels of taxation and public expenditure and the distribution of the burden of taxation among commodities or industries are generally the result either of fiscal expediency or of social philosophy, there is a marked tendency in the literature to treat such differences (and particularly divergences among the rates of taxation imposed on different items of consumption or production within a particular country) simply as arbitrary distortions from the conditions for efficiency of the private economy. This implication is that such distortions ought to be eliminated in the interests of economic efficiency, an implication which automatically asserts priority for harmonization of policy over national sovereignty. In a broader perspective, the economic welfare of a nation must be conceived of as depending on both private consumption provided through the market and 'public consumption' provided through the budget both by public provision of governmental services and by income transfer.[10] In this perspective, what appear to the theorist of economic integration as distortions of competition represent the outcome of the balancing in government decision-making of economic efficiency against socially desired objectives, which may comprise merely the need for collecting adequate government revenue in the most expedient way or may extend to implementing positive policies with respect to income distribution or the discouragement or encouragement of

---

[10] The government's functions in contributing to social welfare are here described as 'public consumption' for the sake of brevity only; the term has a much narrower technical meaning in the literature of public finance.

particular kinds of consumption or production. In these circumstances, there is no prima facie case for harmonization to eliminate 'distortions,' for 'distortions' may be the deliberate choice of governmental policy.

The historical origins of contemporary economic theory on economic integration and the need for harmonization bias that theory towards exaggerating the need for deliberate harmonization in two other respects. First, with respect to 'structural' policies, much of the theory was worked out against the background of the British and European situations in the postwar decade or so. During that time prices and other competitive conditions were far more distorted by direct government interventions (through price-fixing, rationing and allocation of various kinds, price and output policies of nationalized industries, balance of payments controls over imports and exports) than has since become the case. As a result the problem of coordinating government interventions consistently with free trade appeared much more serious then than it does now, and correspondingly figured disproportionately in the theoretical literature. Second, with respect to balance of payments policies, the widespread use of import restrictions, sanctioned by the needs of postwar reconstruction and the prevalence of 'dollar shortage,' and the immobility of capital associated with exchange controls and currency inconvertibility, allowed countries considerable freedom of choice among alternative methods of coping with balance of payments deficits. It also raised the question of how much of this freedom would have to be sacrificed to harmonization policies in the event of participation in a regional economic integration scheme.

Subsequent developments in international economic rules and arrangements have eliminated much of the apparent freedom and with it much of the problem of sacrificing sovereignty in balance

---

[11] This point is particularly relevant to the question of the need or otherwise for harmonization of tax rates, especially personal and corporate tax rates, when people and capital are free to move internationally. A country that chooses, say, to impose high and progressive taxes on incomes presumably does so in the assurance that the bulk of the tax-paying population approves the resulting combination of public services and income redistribution it provides, and in the knowledge that the result will be some tendency for both capital and individuals capable of earning higher net incomes elsewhere to emigrate.

of payments policy to harmonization. In particular, the end of the dollar shortage and the progressive implementation of the GATT and IMF rules regarding the use of quantitative restrictions in balance of payments policy have reduced countries' freedom of action in this respect. The progressive liberalization of capital movements and increase in the international mobility of capital since the European return to currency convertibility have drastically narrowed the freedom of choice between fiscal and monetary methods of maintaining balance of payments equilibrium which was assumed in earlier theoretical analyses of this aspect of the harmonization problem. In a regime of fixed exchange rates characterized by high capital mobility, the participating countries are obliged by the logic of the situation to rely primarily on monetary policy to keep their balances of payments in balance and primarily on fiscal policy to stabilize their domestic economies. More specifically, high international mobility of capital requires countries to keep their interest rates more or less in line, thereby resolving one of the potential problems of harmonization of balance of payments policies in a free trade area.

From the positive points made in the foregoing discussion, it may be generalized that a free trade area does not in and of itself require extensive harmonization of other policies. The most that can be said is that it may increase the urgency of problems already inherent in the participation of its members in the international economy, and the consequent need to balance domestic policy objectives against the maximization of the gains from international trade. The harmonization issue will, however, be likely to require some sort of solution, in two contexts.

First, where particular tax, expenditure, or other policies of governments appear to place a disproportionately heavy or light burden either on domestic producers in competition with other member producers in the domestic or foreign market, or on other member countries' producers competing in the domestic market. there will be pressure for remedial action to be worked out according to some agreed set of principles which will themselves constitute a species of 'harmonization.' The central problem will be to determine to what extent such cases (or their remediation) involve evasion of the free trade commitment by the substitution of fiscal for commercial policy discrimination, or the implementation of social policy by fiscal discrimination against or in favour of particular groups of domestic producers or consumers, or merely some unintended inefficiencies of the fiscal system redounding to no one's particular benefit. Clearly, such issues can be resolved only by negotiation among representatives of the parties affected, with the help of detailed information and analysis, patience, and good will. A related problem is government policy with respect to the control of monopoly and restrictive practices and competitive conditions — international differences in such policies may well be viewed by businessmen as discriminating unfairly between resident and non-resident enterprises in the domestic or member countries' markets.

Second, the decision to seek the benefits of specialization and economies of scale through establishment of a free trade area naturally raises the question of how much more of these economic benefits could be attained by appropriate modification of other government policies that result in economic inefficiency, and at what cost in terms of sacrifice or modification of other national objectives. There are three major possibilities of extending the free trade concept into other areas of public policy which might possibly have significant effects on economic efficiency. The first concerns public expenditure and contracting. In a modern economy, public expenditure constitutes a substantial proportion of total expenditure, and the rules or practices governing such expenditure generally afford substantial protection to domestic as against foreign producers, frequently extending to complete prohibition of dealings with foreign suppliers. [12] The second concerns public regulation (or public ownership and control) of the supply and pricing of public utility or natural resource products or services that are inputs in private competitive production and so affect comparative cost conditions. The outstanding examples are transport and public utility rates, which may

---

[12] Recognizing the potentially large inefficiencies consequent on such practices in certain areas, notably the purchase of defence equipment, governments have come in some cases to agreements for international specialization and division of labour in the provision of equipment. But these agreements typically attempt to arrive at an even balance of purchases and sales, which generally produces different and far less economically efficient results than would adherence to the principle of purchase in the cheapest market.

407

discriminate in various ways against foreign producers in general or in particular industries, and regulation or prohibition of the export of natural resource products and energy sources or energy (including water). Government discrimination in favour of domestic users of these inputs introduces a double distortion from the point of view of economic efficiency: it both affects the efficiency of allocation of resources between the activities supplying these services or products and other activities and constitutes protection for domestic producers of products using these inputs against their foreign competitors. The third possible area for extension of the free trade principle, which overlaps in part with the second, concerns the increased efficiency that might result from the coordinated planning of public investment on the basis of market or service area regardless of national boundaries.

All of these possibilities, it should be noted, except perhaps the third, refer to the gains that can be achieved through freedom of trade and stop short of the gains in economic efficiency that might be obtained by complete freedom of movement of capital and labour. To an important but unascertainable extent, as the theory of international trade has shown, freedom of trade is a substitute for freedom of factor movements; adoption of the former would tend to reduce the potential gains from the latter. Nevertheless, it is possible that free trade would leave substantial opportunities for additional economic gains from the freeing of factor movements. This, however, would raise the question of the relative attractiveness of these gains compared with the sacrifice of freedom of national economic policy with respect to immigration policy and the imposition of tax and other barriers to freedom of capital movement.

The foregoing argument has treated the question of harmonization in terms of a comparison of costs (in terms of sacrifice of national freedom of action in various aspects of domestic policy) and benefits (in terms of gains from increased economic efficiency). The nature and magnitude of the costs and benefits must now be explored.

The following observations are relevant to the costs of changing national economic policies to conform with the requirements of participation in a free trade area or to enlarge the benefits derivable from such participation. First, an important distinction should be drawn between those features of national policy, on the one hand, that are a consequence of past policy decisions with respect to the expediency or administrative convenience of particular taxes on, subsidies to, or special treatment of individual economic activities, and, on the other hand, those that reflect a policy choice based on some concept of the social welfare. The former reflect operational assessments of least-cost solutions which raise only peripheral questions of economic sovereignty and national independence and ought to be negotiable on a basis of reasonableness. But the latter involve national sovereignty directly and necessarily raise the issue of the choice between economic efficiency and national sovereignty. Thus it makes an important difference whether a government has chosen to impose especially heavy taxation on alcohol, tobacco, or gasoline because these taxes are comparatively easy to collect or because it wishes to stamp out (or at least charge users the social costs of repairing) the adverse social consequences of drunkenness or lung cancer or to recoup the cost of constructing highways. Unfortunately, governments often feel that national sovereignty is being challenged when what has been decided to be fiscally expedient or administratively convenient is questioned; and issues of administrative convenience or expediency are accorded an importance far beyond their economic significance.[13]

The distinction between the expedient and the policy-motivated differences in national economic policies is relevant to both the tax and the expenditure side of public financial policy. By and large, one might venture the guess that, on the tax side, very few international differences in the rates of tax on particular commodities really represent important differences in social policy but that differences in the over-all progressivity of the tax structure do correspond to significant differences in social philosophy. Similarly, on the expenditure side, one might venture the guess that differences in the general structure and progressivity of expenditure represent significant differences in social philosophy but that divergences in detail with respect to particular

---

[13] This should not be taken to imply that such issues may not be extraordinarily difficult to resolve, for purely technical reasons.

industries or areas represent considerations of expediency. These speculations assume that both the basic principles of public finance and views on what circumstances give rise to externalities deserving of special tax or expenditure treatment are fairly well understood among the countries of the Western world, so that systematic variations among countries reflect basic differences in social philosophy, and eccentric deviations reflect political expediency. It is important to note that differences in the over-all progressivity of taxation and expenditure have a distorting effect on resource allocation only to the extent that labour and capital are free to move internationally. This implies that the really serious problems of harmonization (i.e., those involving hard choices between independence and efficiency) will be raised by differences in tax-expenditure progressivity rather than by differences with respect to particular taxes or subsidies.

Second, it should be borne in mind that the budget of a modern nation, on both the tax and the expenditure side, is extremely complex and variegated and consequently offers many alternative ways of pursuing the same general social objectives. The harmonization required either to make free trade effective or to extend its benefits may therefore in many cases be made feasible and consistent with the pursuit of social objectives by switching from one fiscal method to another. For example, the objective of making automobile drivers pay the cost of road construction can be variously implemented (at least to a rough approximation) by taxing gasoline, by charging for road use by tolls, or by taxing the purchase or operation of automobiles.

Third, no country's economic policies at any point of time represent a rational implementation of social policies in the light of contemporary knowledge of economics. On the contrary, current policies generally represent a compromise between out-dated and contemporary ideas on how to implement the desired objectives. Accordingly, the pressure for harmonization of policies in a free trade area may really be pressure for a country to adopt policies that are in its own best interest, and hence not so much a challenge to its national sovereignty as a challenge to employ its sovereignty more intelligently. An important example in this connection is the pressure that has appeared in recent years in many countries for the adoption of a value-added tax in place of turnover taxes on the one hand and corporate income taxes on the other. The *real* strength of the case for change comes from the distortions of domestic resource allocation which the alternatives induce; but its *apparent* strength comes from the requirements of international competitiveness at fixed exchange rates.

Consider now the benefits of harmonization as a means of increasing the gains in economic efficiency derivable from the application of the free trade principle. The answers here depend on the increases in efficiency that such improvements in resource allocation might bring, and these depend on the degree of distortion involved in the failure to harmonize. Again, one might hazard a guess that the interest of citizens and policy-makers in various countries in freedom of trade, combined with their much less urgent (or non-existent) concern about the harmonization of policies in the other areas mentioned above, indicates that the major gains to be obtained are offered by freedom of trade *per se*, and that the gains obtainable by harmonization of policies in other areas of economic activity are of a much lower order of magnitude. This may, of course, be an erroneous judgment, and the gain from harmonization of policies other than tariff policies be far more important than the gains from freedom of trade. This could only be determined by an empirical study, case by case, of the economic consequences of tariffs and other disparities of national economic policies. But the weight of what evidence there is — both empirical and judgmental — is that free trade is the most important step to be taken first towards maximizing the benefits from international trade. [14]

[14] Unfortunately, the evidence on these points is both scarce and fragmentary. If one judges by the magnitudes of the distortions from competitive conditions, as represented by (a) the competitive disadvantage imposed on the foreigner measured by an equivalent percentage of costs, and (b) the proportion of economic activity to which the distortion applies, imposed by tariffs and other forms of discrimination, it would appear likely that tariffs are quantitatively the most important source of distortion. Discrimination in government purchasing adds a substantial distortion on top of the tariff, but such discrimination (particularly where it is extreme) applies to a relatively small part of total economic activity. Discrimination in transport costs may be severe, but its over-all effect not substantial, because transport costs are typically a small proportion of the total costs of the delivered product. (Liesner, in *Case Studies in European Economic Union*, p. 343, estimates that discriminatory railway rates applying when the ECSC was formed had a

II. FREER TRADE AND THE HARMONIZATION OF STRUCTURAL POLICIES

The case for freer trade inherently assumes that some sort of international adjustment mechanism exists and that commercial policy-making can be guided by longer-run considerations. It follows that the harmonization of structural economic policies necessary or desirable to supplement freer trade arrangements is a far more important question than that of harmonization of balance of payments policies. In considering the structural harmonization problem, it is important at the outset to distinguish between the philosophy of free trade and the philosophy of a common market. The latter, as pointed out in the preceding section, generally places an emphasis on uniformity of competitive conditions that is not logically necessary for the attainment of most of the benefits of free trade. In so doing, it suggests needs for harmonization of policy and the surrender of national sovereignty in policy-making that are not at all inherent in the more limited objective of a free trade area. [15]

The central tenet in the philosophy of free trade is that free international competition among private enterprises, unrestricted by tariff and other barriers to trade, will maximize the standards of living (and, presumably, the opportunities for economic growth

maximum distorting effect of 10 per cent of ex-works prices of the products concerned; and these were bulk products for which transport costs are an abnormally large component of final price.) Similarly, discrimination with respect to energy and natural resource inputs may be substantial in terms of its effects on these elements of cost but not very important in its aggregate effects on the efficiency of the economy. Finally, the gain in efficiency from internationalizing public investment, while it may be significant as a proportion of the costs of the individual projects, can obviously only apply to a small fraction of total economic activity.

[15] It should be noted, however, that ignorance of the theories of comparative costs and of international adjustment mentioned in the previous section may lead particular industrial interests to press for international standardization of taxes and other governmental regulations affecting competition, even though no economic case for such standardization exists. Thus, governments entering into arrangements for freer trade should be aware of the likelihood that they will have to educate their constituents (and possibly their officials) in the relevant economic principles, and also that they may have to rely more heavily on arbitration of disputes by economic experts or international committees of experts.

of the participating countries, by promoting the fullest possible exploitation of economies of specialization and division of labour and of economies of scale.[16] This proposition assumes that there is an international adjustment mechanism, operating through relative wage and price levels or through exchange rate adjustments, that operates efficiently enough to ensure broad compatibility of freedom of trade with the maintenance of full employment of the economy's resources. It also assumes, more importantly, that the economic system is in fact competitive (or will be reasonably so in a free trade system) and that the money costs and prices that guide private choices in a system of free competition represent 'social' or 'real resource' costs. If the first of these two assumptions were not true, at least as a rough approximation, freedom of trade would not lead to a competitive allocation of production according to the principle of minimum money cost; and if the second were not true (again at least as a rough approximation), the effects of competition in locating production at the least-cost source of supply and attracting demand to the least-cost source of satisfaction would provide no guarantee that free trade would maximize efficiency and living standards.

In the world of reality, these last two assumptions are not closely fulfilled, for a variety of reasons. First, the organization of industry is not always even roughly similar to the competitive model and might well continue not to be so under free trade. Second, taxes on, subsidies to, and government expenditures incurred for the benefit of particular lines of production or consumption affect the relation between private pecuniary and real social costs; moreover, some of these government activities are justified or justifiable by a divergence between costs or benefits as they appear to the private economic decision-taker and the true costs or benefits of the latter's activities to society, whereas others are the result of fiscal expediency. Third, a significant part of the consumption of the economy (using

[16] It is well known that freedom of trade among a group of countries will not necessarily have this result, since it may divert trade from lower-cost third-party sources of supply to higher-cost member sources of supply and so reduce the efficiency of utilization of the group's resources; but it may be presumed for present purposes that the membership of the free trade area is so selected that it promises a substantial improvement in efficiency.

consumption in the broad sense of absorption of resources) is conducted collectively through government expenditure, with purchases not necessarily being allocated to the cheapest source. Fourth, some part of economic activity is either performed directly by government or controlled by it. Finally, government intervenes in the operation of the competitive system so as to modify the resulting distribution of income, both through the general progressivity of its tax and expenditure policies and through special policies aimed at assisting particular sectors – most notably agriculture – or particular depressed regions.

These considerations raise the issue of harmonization of governmental policies other than commercial policy in a free trade arrangement. In the eyes of some European thinkers, as mentioned in the preceding section, the contemporary free enterprise system operates so remotely from the theoretical specifications for the beneficiality of free trade that nothing short of complete harmonization of all important policies will suffice to guarantee that free trade may be safely introduced. The position adopted here (and assumed to be acceptable as a basis for discussion of the issue) is, on the contrary, that, by and large, private money costs (apart from taxes and subsidies) do correspond to social costs, and private satisfactions (measured by what people will pay for items of consumption) to social benefits, except where policy rests explicitly on a consensus that this is not the case. It follows (as is further assumed) that the apparently substantial gains of efficiency and income obtainable by removing tariff and other barriers to trade represent real gains. The problem then is to identify those cases in which other government policies either would prevent free trade from achieving its full desired effect of increasing efficiency or would need to be altered if it were desired to obtain the full benefits intended from free trade over a larger area of the economy.

This enquiry presents some thorny problems, since in principle it is necessary to investigate the over-all impact of all relevant government policies on the competitive situation of particular industries and sectors of the economy, in order to assess the incidence of distortions of competition associated with other policies than trade policy. It is also necessary to draw a fine line between true distortions and apparent distortions deliberately created for reasons of social policy.[17] The following analysis adopts the less ambitious course of discussing the major areas of policy in which problems are likely to arise. It should be emphasized that most of these problems involve questions of degree rather than of kind, because they necessarily arise as soon as a country engages substantially in international trade.

(1) Taxes and Expenditure

According to the principle of comparative cost, a country will maximize its economic efficiency and its gains from trade by exporting those goods in which its relative domestic real costs of production are low as compared with the relative real costs of production in foreign countries, and by importing those goods in which its relative domestic real costs of production are high as compared with the relative costs of production in foreign countries. Given an adjustment mechanism to ensure that the country's price level or exchange rate establishes itself at a level consistent with full employment and a balanced balance of payments, this principle will be fulfilled under free trade if money costs of production correspond exactly to real costs. But it will also be fulfilled under free trade if money costs are distorted from real costs, in the sense of overstating or understating real costs, provided all costs are distorted in the same direction and to exactly the same degree. Thus a single-stage universal tax on production at a uniform rate would raise the prices charged by producers of each commodity above the costs of the factors of production used in producing them, but since it would do so to the same degree for each producer, the ratios of prices would accurately reflect the ratios of factor costs. Similarly, a universal tax on consumption at a uniform rate would raise prices paid by consumers above factor costs incurred by producers but leave the ratios of prices facing consumers accurately reflecting the ratios of factor costs. Finally, a universal tax on factor

---

[17] These difficulties imply, incidentally, that harmonization in practice will have to take the form of general agreement on the objectives of the free trade arrangement and the area of economic activity it should cover, with provisions for the investigation and negotiation of particular cases as they arise, based on the understanding that the parties will act in good faith and in accordance with the spirit of the agreement.

incomes at a uniform rate would make money costs incurred by producers exceed money incomes received by factor owners but would afford the latter no incentive to charge lower prices for their services in one occupation than another, so that relative money costs of production would accurately reflect relative factor costs; this proposition would continue to hold for taxes on factor incomes progressive with the total income received by factor owners.

The cases of the production tax and income tax correspond to the application of the origin principle in border tax adjustments, i.e., the principle of charging taxes on goods produced in a country, whether they are sold domestically or exported, and imposing no tax on imports. In both cases domestic prices of goods would be equal to world market prices, in the case of the production tax, domestic factor prices would have to be such that domestic production costs fall short of market prices to the extent of the tax, whereas in the case of the income tax domestic production costs would equal world costs and the tax would be reflected by incomes of factor owners being lower than those costs. The case of the consumption tax corresponds to the application of the destination principle in border tax adjustment, i.e., the principle of remitting domestic taxes on exports and imposing them on imports. In this case domestic prices would exceed world market prices to the extent of the tax, and domestic factor prices would have to be such that domestic production costs equalled world market prices.

The central point is that, provided the rate of tax is uniform across the domestic economy, either system of border tax adjustment will preclude deviation from the operation of the principle of comparative cost; and this proposition is independent of the level of the tax because any change in level will be absorbed by the adjustment mechanism.[18] Furthermore, the proposition is additive, in the sense that if two or more such general taxes are imposed, either principle of border tax adjustment can be applied to each of them without impairing the operation of the principle of

---

[18] In the case of the income tax, these propositions can be formulated in terms of uniformity of treatment of income regardless of the economic activity in which the factor yielding it is employed.

comparative cost. (In fact, this is the actual practice of nations, the origin principle being applied to income taxes and the destination principle generally to production and excise taxes.)

It follows from this that, in broad principle, there is no need to harmonize either border tax adjustment systems or rates of tax among the members of a free trade area. Such a need may, however, be felt and given political expression for various reasons. One is administrative, arising from the fact that the origin principle allows free movement of goods throughout the area without a customs and excise check at member country borders, whereas the destination principle requires such a check; since in a free trade area such checks are necessitated anyway by the existence of differences in members' tariffs on imports from third countries and the associated problem of trade deflection, this is a more important consideration for a customs union or common market than for a free trade area. This is just as well because the application of the origin principle almost inevitably creates strong pressures for the harmonization of tax rates. The imposition of unequal rates of tax on producers competing in the same market will naturally appear unfair to the more heavily taxed producers even though the adjustment mechanism may in fact be maintaining over-all competitive parity among the members of the free trade area.[19] In a free trade area, similar considerations of fairness in the eyes of producers are likely to create pressures for harmonization in the sense of adoption of the destination principle with respect to production taxes. These pressures may well even call for the harmonization of corporate income tax

---

[19] In the original version of this study, it was asserted that the favoured principle of harmonization in this case — application of the origin principle to intra-group trade and the destination principle to trade with non-members — would distort resource allocation unless members' tax rates were unified. Further reflection on the basic principles enunciated above shows that this assertion is incorrect, so long as the rates of rebate and compensating tax applied to trade with non-members are common for all members. On this point see Harry G. Johnson and Mel Krauss, 'Border Taxes, Border Tax Adjustments, Comparative Advantage, and the Balance of Payments', *The Canadian Journal of Economics*, Vol. III, No. 4 (November 1970), pp. 595–602.

rates, since these are currently applied on the origin principle and appear to businessmen as a significant source of competitive advantage or disadvantage.

The conclusion stated above is, however, an extremely abstract one, since it takes as its standard of reference a completely general tax. Any deviation from that standard will involve a distortion in the working of free competition and the possibility of a need for tax harmonization. In considering this problem, it is important to bear in mind that the argument has been couched in terms of taxes and will continue to be. But governments also affect the allocation of resources among economic activities through subsidies and direct expenditures for the benefit of particular industries. Deviations from universality really need to be conceived in terms of the net burden of governmental budgetary policy on particular activities. (This is one of the major factors that make the problem of distortions and harmonization so complex,)

To begin with, it is useful to distinguish two different ways in which deviations of the fiscal burden imposed on particular economic activities (including both production and consumption) from the average for the economy as a whole may give rise to distortions and hence to a prima facie case – and political pressure – for harmonization. The first is fiscal and concerns international transfers of the burden or benefit of taxation. Thus producers of a particular commodity in one member country may in effect be taxed by a consumption tax imposed by another member, if they constitute the main source of supply for the other country and their supply is inelastic. Similarly, consumers of a particular commodity in one member country may be taxed by a production tax imposed by another member country, if their demand for the commodity is relatively inelastic and, because of the tariff against non-member producers or for other reasons, the producing country has some monopoly power in the consuming country's market. Such cases might be particularly likely to arise where one country is the predominant supplier of certain natural resource products to another, as in the case of Canadian trade with the United States; but there is no clear basis for predicting which partner would be more open to exploitation in this way. Moreover (excluding blatant cases of exploitation of monopsony or monopoly power), the incidence of the tax-expenditure system of one country on the citizens of the other is an extremely complex problem of general equilibrium analysis into which wise governments would probably find it unrewarding to probe. For the blatant cases, if they arose, intergovernmental negotiation would be the appropriate solution; and the defence plea of 'national sovereignty' would have a very hollow sound.

The second type of problem is economic and concerns the effects of deviations of fiscal burden on the efficiency of allocation of resources in the free trade area. All such deviations, regardless of their direction, represent a departure from efficiency, but different divergences are likely to give rise to different kinds of pressures for harmonization. Thus an abnormally heavy burden on a particular line of production is unlikely to perturb the producers' competitors in other member countries,[20] while an abnormally light one will; and conversely for domestic producers.

An abnormally heavy burden of taxation on a particular item of consumption may reflect any one or a mixture of three motivations: fiscal expediency – the item lends itself readily to taxation; social policy – the item is one the consumption of which it is considered should be discouraged, or consumers of which should be taxed to compensate for the costs of various adverse social consequences of its consumption; and covert protectionism – the item is largely imported and is a close substitute for some other item that is domestically produced. The same three motivations in reverse circumstances may explain abnormally light burdens on other items of consumption. Of these three motivations, the third is clearly inconsistent with the objectives of a free trade area, and the first is a technical and practical one that does not (or need not) raise the issue of sovereignty. The hard problem is to disentangle the second motivation, which does involve an exercise of sovereignty, from the other two; and this task may be exacerbated by fundamental differences in

[20] However, if the taxes are remitted on exports and imposed on imports, according to the destination principle, strong suspicions may be aroused that the remission is too generous and the imposition excessive.

419

social philosophy regarding consumption habits among nations.[21] The same three motives may underlie international differences in the relative burdens placed on particular production activities and raise the same difficulties of disentanglement: that is, for example, a particular line of production may be lightly taxed (or subsidized) because it is difficult to tax effectively or fairly, or because it is considered to be a socially desirable activity, or because it is desired to encourage exports.[22]

Any of these cases may give rise to a demand either from the affected domestic interests or from interests in other member countries operating through their governments, for harmonization of tax or expenditure policies. The solutions proposed may, however, possess widely different merits from the standpoint of economic efficiency. In particular, the elimination of deviations of fiscal burden originating in a protective interest is both efficiency-promoting and in the spirit of the free trade arrangement. Tackling deviations of fiscal burden originating in fiscal expediency involves striking a balance between administrative cost and complexity, on the one hand, and, on the other, equality of burden as among domestic industries, which will not necessarily come out on the side of the latter desideratum. At the other extreme, deviations genuinely motivated by social philosophy represent in a sense efficiency at a higher level of social interest than the purely economic, and would seem to call for an agreement to differ rather than an effort to harmonize differences of social philosophy.

The important issue, however, is the reconciliation of *deviations* from the average fiscal burden, not necessarily or most

---

[21] The classic problem of distinguishing an exercise of national sovereignty in social policy from a protectionist device is Meade's case of the British practice of taxing the consumption of wine and subsidizing the consumption of milk. See Meade, *Problems of Economic Union*, p. 24.

[22] The conflict of fiscal expediency with efficiency was one element in the difficulty encountered in the Belgium—Luxembourg economic union over the taxation of alcohol distilleries in the two countries, though the main source of concern came to be the loss of revenue to Belgium associated with less stringent enforcement of the tax in Luxembourg. On this issue see Meade, Liesner, and Wells, *Case Studies in European Economic Union*, pp. 43—6.

fundamentally the actual tax or expenditure rates. The relevant economic analysis – the theory of the second best – offers no general rules for the harmonization of tax-expenditure policies, In particular, there is no presumption in favour of the common contentions that efficiency would be increased if tax rates on particular consumption or production items were made the same in all member countries or that harmonization should always aim to reduce particular taxes to the lowest level prevailing anywhere. If fiscal burdens differ significantly and the problem of harmonization is approached in piecemeal fashion, the most that can be said is that there is some presumption that efficiency could be increased by lowering those fiscal burdens that are exceptionally high by the standards of the country in which they are imposed and by raising those that are exceptionally low by the standards of the country in which they are imposed. Even this presumption has to be qualified by recognition that particular high or low fiscal burdens may be a deliberate result of some unique feature of national social policy.

The argument thus far has been concerned with problems of distortions in competitive conditions (from those required for free trade to ensure the proper working of the principle of comparative costs) associated with government tax and expenditure policies, on the implicit assumption of given national supplies of factors of production. But labour and capital, if not real estate, are capable of moving internationally in response to economic incentives and are unusually free to do so between Canada and the United States and also between these two countries and the United Kingdom. This fact introduces a new dimension to the problem of fiscal distortions and harmonization. It is desirable from the viewpoint of economic efficiency in a free trade area that, in so far as factors of production are free to move internationally, the incentives to do so should induce movements away from locations in which the contribution of a factor to output is lower towards locations in which its contribution is higher. The movement of factors is, however, presumably motivated by the combinations of net income after tax and government services a factor owner receives in various alternative locations. This raises two potential problems.

First, suppose the tax system in every member country were

421

such that every factor owner received back exactly the value of his contribution to production in the form of a combination of net income and government services. Even then, differences in the 'mix' of private and public consumption resulting from differences in national social policies might induce movements of factors from locations of higher to locations of lower gross-income-earning opportunities. Such factor movements, however, are unlikely to be a serious source of concern or of pressure for harmonization of social policy, because presumably the mix of private and public goods provided in each country reflects some sort of social consensus arrived at in the consciousness that it may have significant implications for the size of the country's population, among other things.[23]

Second, suppose an individual country's tax-expenditure policies are characterized by progressivity with income. The implicit income redistribution makes the incomes of low-income factor owners higher than (and those of high-income factor owners lower than) the value of the contributions of their factors to the production of income, factor incomes being defined to include both private and public consumption. If countries differ markedly in the degree of progressivity embodied in their tax-expenditure system, the resulting differences in the degree of divergence of net factor income from gross productive contribution may induce factor movements from high to low gross-income locations, thus making harmonization desirable in the interests of efficiency in the allocation of factors among countries. The potential seriousness of this problem depends on the degree of difference among countries in the progressivity of their tax-expenditure systems, and also on the international mobility of factors. As a problem arising specifically from the formation of a free trade area, its seriousness also depends on the precise effect of free trade on the relative incomes earnable in the different participating

---

[23] It is, of course, possible that, for ideological reasons or as an accident of its political processes, a country may arrive at a mix of private and public consumption that really pleases only a minority; or that, having arrived at such a mixture, it may be unwilling to accept the implications for its population and standard of living, and thus create for itself a conflict among policy objectives expressed in a problem of whether or not to harmonize its tax-expenditure policies with those of other countries.

countries by factors where owners are, respectively, in the lower and the higher income groups. If, for example, free trade raised the wages of labour and lowered the earnings of capital in the country with the more progressive tax-expenditure system relative to wages and the return on capital in another member country, the likelihood of uneconomic factor movements would be increased; and vice versa. Thus the harmonization problem is likely to be more acute if the relatively labour abundant, capital-scarce countries have the relatively progressive tax-expenditure systems than if the converse holds true.[24]

An important aspect of the problem, neglected in the foregoing analysis, is that in actual fact countries impose progressive taxes separately on corporate and personal income. People appear to be relatively immobile, at least as judged by the persistence of substantial wage differentials for comparable grades of labour skills, while corporate enterprise may be assumed to be relatively insensitive to substantial elements in the government expenditure determinant of the progressivity of the tax-expenditure systems of the various countries in which they might locate, and relatively sensitive to the tax determinant.[25] It seems reasonable to expect that the most serious questions concerning the desirability of harmonization of tax-expenditure policies would be raised in the field of corporate taxation. On the other hand, it is possible that the extra degree of harmonization that might be necessitated by a move from present tariff levels to free trade might be negligible, owing to the probability that a substantial degree of harmonization in this field has already been effected as a consequence of competitive pressures and the negotiation of double taxation treaties.

---

[24] Of course, the improvement of labour income might facilitate relaxation of the progressivity of the tax-expenditure structure.

[25] That is, for example, one would not expect corporations considering location in the United Kingdom to be particularly attracted by the presence of a National Health Service, whereas they might well be deterred by higher rates of corporate taxation required to finance the welfare state.

(2) *Public Procurement and Contracting*

In a modern state, a significant proportion of economic activity consists in the supplying of goods and services to governments, including such widely diverse items as office supplies, defence equipment, construction contracting, and research and advisory services. In procuring and contracting for these goods and services, governments generally exercise discrimination in favour of resident national suppliers, over and above the discrimination already provided by the national tariff. The decision to terminate such discrimination in favour of resident nationals in supplying the demands of the private sector, explicitly involved in participation in a free trade area, inevitably raises the question whether the principle of non-discrimination should be extended to government purchasing and contracting. This question may become acute once the free trade arrangement is under way, since producers in one member country competing on equal terms in the private sector of another country's market are likely to become increasingly aware of discrimination against them in the public sector of that market, and in some cases may come to suspect — possibly with good reason — that government orders or contracts are being deliberately used to subsidize their less efficient competitors resident in that market.

The question raises difficult political issues, for two reasons. First, there is a well-established tradition in free enterprise countries that it is the right of resident national producers to enjoy discrimination in their favour in government procurement and contracting; and this tradition plays an important part in the mechanics of political party organization and finance. Moreover, the tradition applies at all levels of government, provincial and state governments habitually discriminating in favour of their own residents against the residents of other provinces or states within the nation, and local governments discriminating in favour of local residents against outsiders. Second, such discrimination is in some important areas — such as defence expenditure and contracting, or the granting of various kinds of research contracts — motivated by broad national political and social goals rather than a narrow protectionist concern for favouring particular established industries.[26] The proposal to end it is therefore likely to raise in an acute form the conflict between economic efficiency and social policy discussed in the previous subsection.

In view of these two major difficulties — the first of which might well be incapable of resolution anyway in a federal state through lack of central power to enforce non-discriminatory purchasing in lower levels of governments — it would seem unprofitable to raise the question in the context of the formation of a free trade area, and prudent to rely, at least initially, on the conventional acceptance of genteel discrimination by governments in favour of their citizens to avoid serious international disputes. There are, in any case, economic pressures on government, stemming from the need to finance from tax revenues the excess costs entailed in national discrimination, to keep the wastes involved in such discrimination within decent bounds. It might, however, further the objectives of free trade and reduce the areas for possible dispute, without involving much sacrifice of sovereignty, if the governments of member countries were to define clearly the areas in which they believed the interests of national independence to override considerations of economic efficiency, and for the remainder to specify some maximum degree of discrimination to which resident enterprises would be entitled: for example, in the form of a maximum price premium for domestic as against other-member supplies.[27] Apart from this, governments should be able to reduce the costs of achieving national objectives through their purchasing policies by means of *ad hoc* agreements to share out contracts in such spheres as defence equipment in such a manner as to ensure 'fair' participation by the residents of each country.

[26] The line between protecting industries because they happen to be resident, and because their presence in the country contributes to broad objectives such as self-sufficient defence capability or a modern, research-oriented economy and culture, is admittedly very difficult to draw.

[27] The proper specification of such a premium is more difficult than it appears at first sight, since it raises all the difficulties of 'effective,' as contrasted with 'nominal,' protection. Thus the rule would, at a minimum, have to specify the premium as a percentage of domestic content rather than delivered price.

(3) *Transport*

The rates charged and conditions of transport imposed by the various transport agencies may introduce significant discrimination and distortions of competition among producers in comparable situations located in different member countries. Such discrimination may occur as a result of deliberate policy, as when, say, a nationalized railway pursues a policy of promoting national economic integration through subsidized rates; as a by-product of the revenue-maximizing practice of charging what the traffic will bear; or as a by-product of the natural tendency to define the market area to coincide with the national boundary, and to terminate the tapering of rates by distance and impose national terminal charges when goods cross national boundaries.

Such discrimination is inconsistent with the general efficiency-promoting objective of a free trade area and may be serious enough to raise the question of the need for harmonization. Its seriousness is likely to vary with the mode of transport in question, railways being likely, for obvious reasons, to pose more problems than road and water transport, both because of the inherent complexities of railway rate-making and because national ownership of, or public regulation of rates charged by, railway has traditionally been used as an instrument of national economic policy much more than has public control over road and water transport.

It seems likely, therefore, that any problem of harmonization in the field of transport in a Canadian-American or a North American-European free trade association would be likely to concern the harmonization of railway rates in North America to eliminate discrimination between comparable transport services according to national origin or destination. It is doubful, however — though to determine the matter would require intensive expert study — that lack of harmonization in this field would involve much less, or harmonization entail much extra, gain under the free trade arrangements, in spite of the contrary implications of the concentrated attention given to the problem in the early years of the European Coal and Steel Community. This is because there are two major contrasts between the situation confronting the ECSC in the early fifties and the situation in North America now. First, the North American countries are far more closely integrated

426

economically than were the European countries at that time, and the development of this integration has among other things involved a long history of adjustment of railway rates and transport arrangements in general. Second, the development of competition with the railways from road transport has historically in North America been in advance of Europe and has advanced rapidly everywhere since the early 1950's. With intensified competition between road (and also water and air) and rail transport, the possibility of serious distortion of competition through discrimination in transport charges and conditions has probably been reduced to a small order of magnitude.

The formation of a North American–EFTA free trade area might, however, raise one serious issue of harmonization in the area of transport that should be mentioned, though it is an issue of concerted intergovernmental action rather than of harmonization of national transport policies. The Joint Economic Committee of the United States Congress has become greatly concerned in recent years about discrimination against U.S. exports to Europe and in favour of European exports to the United States implemented through the ocean freight rates agreed on by the Atlantic Shipping Conference. An agreement to launch a concerted attack on the practices of this cartel might be made a prerequisite of U.S. participation in the free trade area. This particular harmonization of policy would, however, pose the most serious problem for the United Kingdom.

(4) *Natural Resources and Energy Policy*

Just as governments have used ownership of, or regulation of, rates and conditions set by, national railway systems to provide protection for domestic as against foreign producers, so they have used their regulatory powers over, or ownership of, natural resources and energy-supplying industries to discriminate in favour of domestic as against foreign users of these inputs. The continuation of these practices in a free trade area would entail continued distortion of competitive conditions and raise the same problem of loss of potential efficiency versus sacrifice of national independence in harmonization.

In this connection, however, the principle that distortions of competition should be considered in combination rather than

427

separately becomes relevant, at least for the question of Canadian participation in a free trade area. For many Canadian policies of promoting or favouring establishment in Canada of industries using Canadian natural or energy sources by taxing or impeding the export of these inputs have been motivated explicitly or implicilty by the desire to counteract the obstacles imposed by U.S. tariff policy to the further processing or use in manufacturing of these inputs in producing goods for exports to the American market. In effect, Canadian policy has been deviously attempting to have the Canadian public absorb the American tariff on Canadian exports to the United States. Where these policies have been effective, the right sort of allocation of resources in production between the two countries has probably been promoted at the expense of an income transfer from the Canadian public to the American government. To the extent that this is the case, removal of these discriminations in Canadian policy would be a fair *quid pro quo* for, and perhaps even an essential component in, the establishment of free trade between the two countries. Harmonization of this kind would simply mean the termination of the implicit subsidy from Canadians to Americans, and the achievement by more efficient means of the Canadian objective of increasing the proportion of further processing or manufacture of raw materials and energy produced in Canada. Insistence on the preservation of discrimination in these cases, on the other hand, would mean insistence on the right to subsidize exports of the semi-manufactures and manufactures affected by these policies, and the introduction of fresh distortions in the allocation of resources in production in the two countries.[28]

While there is no reason to expect that such a fine balancing of Canadian discrimination in favour of exporting processing industries against American discrimination against such industries prevails in fact,[29] the foregoing argument indicates that the

[28] These considerations apply to some extent also to discrimination in transport policy but were considered too peripheral to mention in the previous subsection.

[29] Even if it did, it would entail inefficiencies in consumption choices in the two countries and in the choice of technology and input combinations in the industries affected.

sacrifice of national sovereignty involved in harmonizing resources and energy policies, at least to the extent of eliminating discrimination between domestic and member-country users, may well be exaggerated if the question is not placed squarely in the context of the probable effects of free trade. Apart from these particular cases, also, it is possible that national differences in natural resources and energy policies do not involve sufficient distortions of competitive conditions to pose a serious problem of harmonization.

A further consideration is that the relevant powers of policy-making generally lie, at least to an important extent, with the provinces or states concerned, and hence do not lend themselves readily to harmonization by international agreement. This points to a general problem, touched on at other points in this chapter but not adequately dealt with in the chapter as a whole: that the distributions of relevant governmental powers in the federal structures of Canada and the United States are probably such that it is extremely misleading to conceive of free trade between the two countries as an arrangement between two sovereign powers, one much larger than the other. It is more relevant to conceive of it as an arrangement comprising ten sovereign Canadian provinces and fifty sovereign American states, at least in relation to the areas of policy harmonization with which European policy-makers and theorists of free trade arrangements and economic unions have been concerned — aside, that is, from broad questions of federal tax and expenditure policy.

(5) *Joint Planning of Public Investments*

The joint planning of public investment is a question that extends beyond the range of a free trade area arrangement into the domain of the construction of a commom market and arrangements for the free international movement of factors of production. As such, it does not seem to be a major issue in a free trade area, especially given the pragmatic approach to public investment characteristic of the governments of Canada and the United States. The established tradition of *ad hoc* collaboration between the two countries (or their states and provinces), where the pay-off from joint planning and financing of such projects is attractive enough, seems quite adequate. Nor does there seem much reason to anticipate

429

important opportunities for increasing efficiency by joint investment planning between the European and American members in the event of the formation of a North Atlantic free trade area.

(6) *The Special Problems of Agriculture and Depressed-Area Policy*

To a varying degree, most advanced countries face the problem of a chronically depressed domestic agriculture, the result of a rapid increase in agricultural productivity, low income and price elasticities of demand for agricultural products, and the inability or unwillingness of farm people to move off the land rapidly enough to evade the adverse impact of these forces on farm incomes. They have typically attempted to resolve this problem by the payment of support prices to farmers, rather than by the economically more desirable and efficacious solution of accelerating the shift of people off the land. Such policies tend to result in overproduction at the prices specified. leading agricultural exporting countries into subsidizing exports. The by-product of what is essentially intended as an income subsidy is therefore government intervention in the competitive allocation of resources on an extensive scale.

Such intervention poses a serious problem for a free trade area, the intention of which is to promote the competitive allocation of resources in production. But for political reasons and to avoid excessive disruption of established economic patterns, governments are very unlikely to contemplate subjecting their agricultural sectors to the same rules of competition as a free trade area imposes on industry in general. The problem then arises whether such an arrangement requires harmonization of agricultural policies among the members and, if so, what sort.

The European Economic Community set itself the task of establishing a common market in agricultural products, of which the central feature is a common level of support prices implemented over a large segment of agricultural production by a system of variable levies. This objective has proved extremely difficult to negotiate, for two reasons. First, the results of unification of support price levels on the levels of protection and incomes afforded to farmers in the different countries diverged widely. Second, trading at prices above world market prices entailed massive international redistributions of income among member countries. Harmonization of agricultural policies on this scale would reach far beyond the objectives and possibilities of a free trade arrangement, not only for the two reasons just given but also because harmonization would require the integration of restrictions on imports from outside sources; but it is the main purpose of a free trade area to avoid making such restrictions obligatory in other sectors of international trade.

The harmonization of agricultural policies that might be considered appropriate to a free trade area would seem to involve two major obligations for national governments. The first is to avoid encouraging the expansion of high-cost production at the expense of low-cost production in other member countries. This is in the economic interest of the producing country itself, though, given the prevalence of distortions of production costs (and especially of land rents, which are not a true social cost but a transfer payment) by agricultural policy itself, it is usually extremely difficult to determine which producers are really low-cost. The second is to conform to some agreed standard of fair play by refraining from aggressive policy actions that relieve the country's own agricultural problem at the expense of accentuating that of another member country. In this connection, a line might usefully be drawn — with relevance to the issues of sovereignty involved — between policies that determine the share of a country's producers in its own national market and policies that determine the share it captures of markets in the outside world.[30]

Given the rapidly declining importance of agriculture in the economies of Canada and the United States, the improving world market prospects of the major problem commodity, wheat, and the broad cooperation between the two countries in managing the world market for that commodity that has developed in the postwar period, harmonization of agricultural policies in the two countries

---

[30] Such a distinction, however, must rest more on the ethics of dealings among sovereign nations than on any valid economic distinction, since reductions of foreign sales due to increased protectionism in an importing country increase the problems of domestic agricultural policy in exactly the same way as a loss of foreign sales due to an increased subsidization of exports by a rival exporter.

would not seem to be a major economic problem, in the sense of such harmonization (or its absence) in a free trade area involving great gains (or correspondingly great losses) by comparison with the gains to be expected from free trade in industrial products. A broader free trade area including EFTA, however, would probably raise again the question of agricultural harmonization that has already been raised in that organization, namely, the question of special arrangements for Denmark as a country heavily specialized in the production of agricultural products and unlikely to gain substantially from industrial free trade. The magnitude of this problem is such, however, that it could probably be accommodated easily enough by offering improved access for Danish products to the Canadian and American markets, without serious disturbance to present policies or the agricultural structure.

A related but less important problem concerns national policies for the promotion of economic development in depressed regions of the country. While not of very direct relevance to the operation of a free trade area, such policies may by intent or as a by-product raise the issue of discriminatory distortion of the operation of competition by indirectly subsidizing exporting or import-competing industries. This issue is unlikely to be of any great importance, and certainly not of sufficiently great importance to suggest the desirability of harmonizing depressed-area policies, if only because such policies are rarely, if ever, successful in effecting substantial economic changes in the relative national positions of depressed regions and their industries.

(7) *The Control of Competition*

The previous subsections have been concerned with various aspects of the distorting influence of government tax, expenditure and other policies on the working of private competition as an instrument for promoting economic efficiency. Both government policies for the control of competition and the operation of private competition itself may impede the attainment of the objectives of free trade and require changes in, and harmonization of, government policies in this area.

As regards the former problem, government policies towards monopolies and business market organization usually distinguish between domestic and foreign operations and allow considerably more latitude for combinations and cartel arrangements in the export than in the domestic field. This may have the effect of allowing private business arrangements to frustrate the purpose of free trade, either by monopolistic restriction of exports or by private subsidization of them. While there is little firm evidence to show how serious or distorting an influence on competition these practices might have (and virtually none on how far they might survive the introduction of free trade),[31] the problem might require revision of national monopolies legislation to apply the same standards for competition in the market of the area as apply to domestic competition. This in turn might well suggest a need to harmonize national legislation to prevent anomalies among the different national systems of control of competition from interfering with or impeding competition, and perhaps even the establishment of an international regulatory body to supervise competition among large firms operating throughout the free market's domain. Harmonization in this area, however, raises some exceedingly complex issues in both economic theory and legal practice, and consideration of the possible need for it would probably most wisely be deferred until experience of free trade has provided evidence on the question.

The possible problem of the frustration of the competitive process by private business practices has been partly dealt with in the foregoing observations; but quite apart from monopolistic and restrictive practices, habitual definitions of market areas and spheres of interest tend to run along national or subnational lines of demarcation and may impose unconscious impediments to the free working of competition over the whole domain of the free trade area. It is, however, difficult to conceive of any remedy for this possible problem other than the educational effects of free trade itself; and it seems unlikely in any event that among countries as extensively involved in international trade as Canada, the United States, and the United Kingdom, the losses

---

[31] The introduction of free trade might, in fact, remove some or a major part of the justification for present national controls on business practices, by substituting the more pervasive and effective discipline of competition in a large free market for governmental regulation in a small protected market.

of efficiency from this source would be very significant.[32]

(8) *Concluding observations on Structural Harmonization*

This section has surveyed the main areas in which the formation of a free trade area might call, or be expected to call, for some degree of harmonization of other governmental policies. A concluding summary of the arguments presented would be difficult and not very informative. In general, it appears that the formation of a free trade area, at least between Canada and the United States and probably between these countries and the European Free Trade Association as well, would not require extensive harmonization going far beyond the arrangements that exist at present. Where the additional gains in efficiency that such harmonization might offer are or might be substantial (as in the field of public finance), it appears that a great deal of difficult research and assessment of theoretical and empirical issues is required before the desirable lines of harmonization can be established. In other cases, it appears that harmonization has little substantial benefit to offer, *provided* that the object of the exercise remains a free trade area and not a more comprehensive union. A potentially important exception, however, concerns (primarily Canadian) policies with respect to natural resources and energy, which to a significant degree have been designed to counter the adverse influence of the U.S. tariff on the location of user industries and which therefore should probably be substantially modified in the event of a free trade arrangement. The analysis has pointed to, but not fully dealt with, one significant aspect of the problem not raised by the European literature on the subject, which has had to deal with arrangements among unitary states: the extent to which the allocation of powers among the provinces of Canada and the states of the United States would make it impossible to negotiate harmonization of policies if this were considered desirable.

---

[32] It is, of course, true that observers are always coming up with products produced in one country that could, at least in their judgment, readily be exported at a profit to another. But both the acquisition of knowledge of market opportunities and the organization of facilities to exploit them involve costs for the firm, the significance of which is frequently ignored by the casual observer.

III. FREE TRADE AND THE HARMONIZATION OF BALANCE OF PAYMENTS POLICIES

The governments of the advanced countries of the world are universally committed to the maintenance of full employment, price stability, and a balanced balance of payments. Does the commitment to participate in a free trade area impose obligations which conflict with the present freedom of the potential member countries to use the customary instruments of economic policy in the pursuit of these objectives as they see fit? Does the commitment require the harmonization of the use of these policies? The customary instruments in question are primarily fiscal policy and monetary policy. But in the period when the EEC and EFTA were being established, the use of quantitative import restrictions for balance of payments control was widespread and hence figured large in the discussion. In recent years, moreover, the increased international mobility of capital consequent on the restoration of currency convertibility in Europe has prompted increased reliance on various kinds of interference with international capital movements as a means of balance of payments control, so that the use of capital controls must also be brought into the discussion.

At the outset, it should be emphasized that the problem of harmonization of balance of payments policies stems fundamentally from the maintenance of fixed exchange rates among national currencies, which is the present international monetary system; this system, in the presence of substantial international mobility of capital, itself imposes severe restraints on the individual nation's freedom of choice among policy instruments. Were it not for the maintenance of fixed exchange rates — i.e., if exchange rates were free to adjust to changing market forces — countries would have no balance of payments reason, but only domestic policy reasons, for seeking price stability. They would not be faced with conflicts between the objectives of full employment and balance of payments equilibrium, so long as they were prepared to allow their exchange rates to change. And they would not be faced with recurrent pressures to use controls on international trade and payments to safeguard their reserves. Insofar as capital were freely mobile internationally, however, they would find monetary policy a far more powerful instrument for the maintenance of full employment and price stability than fiscal policy,

435

so that their freedom of choice of instruments would be limited in that sense.

Under a fixed exchange rate system, on the other hand, countries in fact have very little freedom to pursue domestic price stability, Their price level must in the long run adjust to movements of the price level in the outside world, which in the contemporary world are dominated by economic developments in the United States. They are faced with the possibility of sharp conflict between full employment and balance of payments equilibrium, which may put strong pressure on them to resort to controls on trade and capital movements as a lesser evil than unemployment. With substantial international mobility of capital, their interest rates have to be kept in alignment with those of other countries (except to the extent that they intervene in international capital markets by controls or 'interest-equalization' taxes) and their monetary policies used to preserve balance of payments equilibrium, leaving fiscal policy to bear the burden of maintaining domestic economic stability.

It is therefore the fixed exchange rate system, essentially, and not the free trade arrangement, that raises the issue of harmonization of balance of payments policy among members of a free trade area. This consideration incidentally underlines the point made in the first section of this paper, that the harmonization issue in a free trade area is a matter of degree rather than of kind. More fundamentally, it raises the question of whether a free trade arrangement increases the desirability of members maintaining fixed exchange rates, or whether free trade arrangements would be facilitated by floating exchange rates. Briefly, there are three compelling arguments for flexible exchange rates as an adjunct of a free trade arrangement. First, they provide a more palatable and smoothly working mechanism for adjusting a country's general price level to an equilibrium relationship with those of its trading partners than the fixed-rate system's reliance on relative domestic inflation or deflation, while freeing the country from the obligation to conform to inflationary or deflationary price movements in the outside world. Second, in an environment of high capital mobility, by increasing the potency of monetary policy relative to fiscal policy, they free fiscal policy for use for 'structural' purposes, thereby both clearing the way for any harmonization of fiscal policy that may be considered desirable and avoiding the need for tax or expenditure changes that might be considered by other member countries to contravene the spirit of the free trade arrangement. Third, by making the use of controls for balance of payments purposes unnecessary, they make it unnecessary to decide how such controls should be applied consistently with the free trade arrangement.

These advantages, however, depend on the maintainance of freely floating rates, or of floating rates subject only to limited stabilization arrangements. Rates that are pegged subject to change from one level to another in case of 'fundamental disequilibrium' do not offer these advantages, and the effecting of changes in such rates is likely to cause market disruptions which will probably bear especially heavily on the trade of other members of the free trade area. Thus the adoption of a free trade arrangement among countries adhering to the present international monetary system probably involves a firmer obligation to maintain a fixed exchange rate. Whether the obligation involves a serious extra burden or restriction on national economic policy, however, is doubtful, because free trade may have a powerful offsetting effect in increasing the natural competitive pressures for preserving the alignment of national price and cost levels. This would prevent the emergence of the condition that calls for exchange rate changes, namely, a serious disparity between one nation's price-cost level and those of the rest of the world.[33]

Given a commitment on the part of its members to maintain fixed exchange rates according to the present international monetary system, the formation of a free trade area imposes on its members an extra obligation to maintain domestic economic stability, in the sense of attempting to prevent inflationary or deflationary departures from target levels of effective demand and employment. The reason is that the integration of member economies through free trade, by increasing the relative magnitude and importance of their trade with one another, increases the influence of changes in the level of effective demand in each on

---

[33] On this point see Harry G. Johnson, 'Les problèmes monétaires dans un zone de libre échange,' in *Marché commun: institutions communes* (Paris: Pichon et Durand Auzino, 1960) pp. 78–82.

the level of activity and employment in the others. This is obviously a matter of degree, since inflationary or deflationary pressures originating on one country will be transferred to some extent to others in the world economy so long as the network of international trade makes their economies interdependent. But the increased interdependence entailed in free trade might make it desirable for the members to coordinate and harmonize their domestic stabilization policies (at least in the sense of recognizing the interest of the other members in the domestic stability of each) by establishing regular arrangements, formal or informal, for consultation with other members whenever a particular member is confronted with a domestic stabilization problem or contemplates a significant change in stabilization policy. The purpose would be twofold: to exercise pressure on each member to take account of the impact of its policies on the others, and to forewarn the others of impending changes and enable them to formulate appropriate policy reactions. Such arrangements would be particularly desirable in any free trade arrangement involving the United States, owing to the overwhelming size and importance in trade of that country, and its propensity to formulate its stabilization policy with primary reference to its domestic situation. It should be noted that such arrangements would not constitute a major innovation, since the international monetary problems of recent years have prompted a rapid evolution of the concept of, and machinery for, 'multilateral surveillance' of the stabilization and balance of payments policies of the major industrial countries.

Beyond the general desirability of harmonization of domestic stabilization policies in the sense just discussed is the question of whether and how far balance of payments policies of member countries would need to be harmonized — again, by comparison with the degree of harmonization necessarily imposed by adherence to fixed exchange rates in an environment of international capital mobility.

The answer to this question obviously depends greatly on the degree and type of harmonization of structural policies adopted by the member countries. If, for example, tax rates on commodities are unified among the various countries, variations in these rates are excluded as a means of balance of payments adjustment.

The extreme form of integration envisaged by some common market theorists entails the unification of all policies affecting competitive conditions within the market area. In this case there would clearly be no scope for independent balance of payments policies, and the balance of payments of the group as a whole would have to become the object of management by concerted changes in the fiscal, monetary, or international trade and payments policies of the member countries. A free trade area, however, as argued in detail in the preceding two sections, does not require harmonization of this kind. Instead, the harmonization that may be considered desirable or necessary pertains largely to the alignment of relative tax burdens on particular commodities or activities within each member country, rather than to the relative levels of taxation as among countries. A possible exception would be the need to align the levels of taxes on mobile factors of production, especially capital, in order to avoid perverse international movements of factors from higher to lower productivity locations.

This would imply that, apart from possible effects on international factor movements, the use of fiscal policy — general increases or decreases in tax and expenditure levels — for stabilization and balance of payments policy purposes would not conflict with the allocative efficiency objectives of a free trade area, so that it would not be necessary to harmonize the use of this instrument of balance of payments policy among members. The chief practical exception arising from the desirability of not encouraging perverse factor movements would likely concern variations in corporate income tax rates, and this would be unlikely to pose serious problems both because the value of such variations in securing the relevant policy objectives is doubtful and because corporate investment would be likely to be influenced by the average level of taxation to be expected over the (business or balance of payments) cycle rather than to respond to intentionally temporary higher or lower rates of taxation.

The use of monetary policy for stabilization and balance of payments purposes, on the other hand, could conflict with the free trade area objective of efficient resource allocation, by deliberately invoking perverse movements of capital as a means of financing balance of payments deficits or disposing of balance of payments surpluses. This possibility of conflict (between balance of payments adjustment policy and efficient international allocation of resources) has in fact been stressed by a number of critics of the 'fiscal-monetary mix' solution to the problem of achieving full employment and balance of payments equilibrium in a country suffering unemployment and a deficit simultaneously. This solution calls for fiscal expansion to increase employment and tight money to attract a capital inflow to finance the resulting current account deficit. Inefficiencies of allocation arising from this source may not, however, be a serious problem in fact for a free trade area. On the one hand, governments have not in the past evinced much concern about this particular by-product of the use of monetary policy. On the other hand, and more importantly, the allocative-efficiency problem relates to the investment of real resources in material production facilities, whereas the the capital movements in question are international lendings and borrowings of liquid resources which may have little or no lasting impact on the international allocation of real investment, In any case, as already mentioned, the increasing international mobility of capital since the restoration of European currency convertibility has carried with it an increasing need for the major countries to keep their interest rate levels in alignment and to rely on fiscal policy for domestic stabilization and on relatively small deviations of their interest rate levels about the international level to control their balance of payments. The increasingly close alignment of national interest rate levels implies that any misallocation of capital arising from balance of payments policy-induced differences in interest rates could lead to only negligible losses of economic efficiency.[34]

---

[34] In a paper circulated since this study was completed. Franco Modigliani has pointed out that the system of keeping interest rates aligned and using fiscal policy to maintain domestic full employment (more correctly, using fiscal and monetary policies jointly to maintain full employment and a level of interest rates consistent with balance of payments equilibrium) does involve inefficiency, in the sense that it obliges policy to restrain or force domestic investment and savings to levels consistent with the rate of interest relative to rates in other countries at which the capital account and the current account of the balance of payments offset each other. In short, national rates of capital accumulation are constrained to be different from what the public, or government policy apart from balance-of-payments considerations, would

The general conclusion that emerges from the foregoing discussion is that participation in a free trade area probably imposes no significant additional restrictions on the use of the general instruments of fiscal and monetary policy for the adjustment of balance of payments disequilibria. However, as in the case of domestic stabilization policy, free trade could, by increasing the economic interdependence of the member countries, increase the relative impact of balance of payments policy measures taken in one country on the balances of payments and domestic activity levels of other members. This would make it desirable to establish arrangements for consultation among members with respect to balance of payments problems and the measures to be adopted to deal with them.

There remains the question of the use of controls on trade and capital movements as an instrument of balance of payments policy. Specifically, the problem is whether such controls, when considered necessary or preferable to the alternatives of deflation or devaluation, should be applied by the member country resorting to them in a non-discriminatory fashion to non-members and members alike or should be applied only to non-members. In the latter case, it is clearly necessary for the other members to apply similar controls on their transactions with non-members.

prefer. Modigliani also argues that for many reasons the movement of capital from lower to higher-interest-rate countries may not mean a movement from lower to higher social productivity uses of capital; and he concludes for both reasons that taxes and other controls on capital movements will be superior to the use of the 'fiscal-monetary-mix' policy. (Franco Modigliani, 'International Capital Movements, Fiscal Parities, and Monetary and Fiscal Policies' [Oct. 1966], mimeographed.).

The inefficiency in question, however, is a consequence of the fixed-rate system, which entails allowing the real amounts of resources internationally lent and borrowed (at full employment levels of output) to be determined by the relationships of national cost-price levels and their implications for current account balances rather than by the relative profitability of investment in different countries. There is no obvious reason to expect the problem to be exacerbated in a free trade area, and it might even be relieved by the increased competitive pressures for maintaining alignment of cost-price levels generated within a free trade area, previously mentioned. If Modigliani's reasoning came to be accepted and implemented in national policy-making it would raise the question of whether or not national controls on capital movements should be coordinated. This issue is discussed below.

441

even though they are not in balance of payments difficulties, to prevent the frustration of the purpose of the controls by inward leakages of goods through trade deflection[35] and outward leakages of capital through member-borrowing and relending to non-members. The former alternative involves a possibility of conflict with the objectives of the free trade arrangement; the latter imposes the requirement of harmonization of policies among the members of the free trade area.

In the discussions in GATT preceding the formation of the European Economic Community and European Free Trade Association, both groups reserved the right to adopt the latter alternative with respect to trade controls, even though it contravenes the GATT principle of non-discrimination in the application of quantitative restrictions for balance of payments reasons. When it came to the test, however, Britain in 1964 imposed its tariff surcharges on members and non-members alike, to the grave dissatisfaction of the other members of EFTA. In connection with the U.S. interest-equalization tax, Canada argued successfully, and in connection with the voluntary programs of capital export control unsuccessfully, that the special relation between the two countries warranted exemption of Canada from the controls, the *quid pro quo* in each case being a Canadian commitment not to contribute to a worsening of the U.S. deficit; and this argument would probably be put much more strongly in the event of a free trade arrangement between the two countries.

The first alternative — non-discriminatory application of controls to members as well as non-members — appears inconsistent with the objectives of a free trade area, while the second — application of controls only to non-members — appears consistent

---

[35] Direct trade deflection via trans-shipment of non-member goods through other member countries would be prevented by the border customs checks that would have to be retained to make national tariffs effective against non-member countries. So the problem in practice would be substitution of imports from other members for imports from non-members, the former being made available by substitution of imports from non-members for domestically produced goods in the other member countries, or diversion of exports by other members from non-member markets to the country applying the controls.

with the objective but requires harmonization of controls and their application by all members, even though not all have deficits. In principle, however, the reverse appears to be true. This becomes clear when the matter is considered in relation to the general policies alternative to controls that might be adopted, namely, devaluation as an alternative to trade controls and higher interest rates an an alternative to capital export controls. Neither of these would involve discrimination in favour of other members additional to what is already implicit in the free trade arrangement and presumably the intention of the participants in that arrangement. But application of controls only to non-members introduces an extra degree of discrimination going beyond the free trade arrangement itself. Discrimination in the application of trade controls in favour of imports from members as against non-members is equivalent to raising tariffs against non-members, as is discrimination against imports from non-members by members not in balance of payments difficulties. It amounts to a distortion of international resource allocation additional to that adopted by policy in the fixing of the tariffs applicable to non-members. It also entails, especially for other members than the one in balance of payments difficulty, a sacrifice of the sovereignty in fixing the level of barriers to trade with non-members that a free trade arrangement is intended to preserve. Similarly, discrimination in the application of capital controls in favour of other members, by the country in balance of payments trouble and the other members, introduces a distortion in the allocation of investment capital in favour of lower-yielding investments within the area as compared with higher-yielding investments outside the area, which again is not part of the intention of forming a free trade area.

[36] Trade or capital controls are, of course, not strictly alternative to devaluation or higher interest rates, since trade controls do not secure the stimulating effect on exports that devaluation would have, and capital controls have neither the attractive effect on capital inflows nor the rationing effect on domestic investment that higher interest rates would have. As is well known, the control system properly alternative to devaluation is general import restriction combined with general export subsidization; correspondingly, the control system properly alternative to higher interest rates from the point of view of efficient international allocation of capital would be a general tax on investment by residents, levied regardless of location of the investment, and not charged to foreigners.

443

The principle just stated is, however, subject to an important qualification. If the economies of the member countries are so closely integrated by trade that a devaluation by one would necessitate devaluation to the same extent by all the others, jointly implemented and harmonized trade controls would (and non-discriminatory controls applied by a single member in balance of payments difficulties would not) avoid distortion of resources allocation by balance of payments policy. Similarly, if the capital markets of the members were so highly integrated that an increase in interest rates by a member in balance of payments difficulties would evoke proportionate increases in all others, discriminatory harmonized capital controls would involve less distortion than non-discriminatory national controls. This consideration suggests that harmonized joint application of controls is more justifiable in a common market than in a free trade area, on grounds of promoting efficient resource allocation and avoiding distortions.

Determination of the issue depends, however, on the empirical facts respecting the degree of integration among members' economies and capital markets. Moreover, there is no reason to assume that in a free trade area the degree of integration will be the same among all the members, or in consequence to impose the requirement that the choice between harmonization and national autonomy in the use of controls should be resolved by the adoption of one principle for all types of controls which would be applied by the group as a whole. As a specific example, if a free trade area comprising Canada, the United States, and the EFTA countries were established, maximum efficiency in the use of controls might well be achieved by an agreement for Britain to apply controls on a non-discriminatory basis, Canada and the United States to coordinate capital (and possibly trade) controls on a basis of discrimination against other members and non-members alike, and the Scandinavian countries to do the same. It would be essential to the harmonious operation of the free trade arrangement, however, for such an agreement and the logic behind it to be already understood well in advance of any need for applying it; and it would of course be desirable for members to try to manage their balance of payments policies so as to avoid the need for resort to controls at all.

In conclusion, it should be emphasized that the discussion of balance of payments policies in this section has assumed that the objective of policy is the conventional one of balancing payments and receipts so as to avoid sustained reserve gains or losses. In some countries, and particularly in Canada, the objectives of balance of payments policy are extended to include the structure of the balance of payments and, specifically, the magnitude of the current account deficit or surplus and the corresponding capital inflow or outflow. In contrast with the objective of over-all balance, policy objectives of this kind are not necessarily mutually consistent or harmonious; and the pursuit of them, especially by methods directed at altering international trade or capital flows rather than the underlying balance of saving and investment, is likely to be inconsistent with the economic efficiency-increasing objective of a free trade area. The formation of a free trade area is therefore likely to require harmonization of such policies, at least in the sense of agreement on what targets may reasonably be set and what methods may legitimately be used to implement them consistently with the objective of economic efficiency.

Index of Subjects

447

Index of Names

Anderson, J., 373n

Balassa, B., 331n, 332n, 336n,
  337n, 338n, 343n, 344n, 356,
  368n, 379n
Baldwin, R.E., 21, 22, 46n, 55,
  55n, 117n
Balogh, T., 122, 122n
Barber, C.L., 307n, 317, 317n,
  318, 323n
Barone, E., 188, 188n
Basevi, G., 315, 316, 336n, 343n,
  344n, 356
Bastable, C.F., 145n
Becker, G.S., 145n, 240, 240n
Bertrand, T., 177n
Bhagwati, J., x, xn, xii, 3n, 37n,
  67n, 79n, 89n, 117n, 120n,
  139n, 143n, 153, 170, 180,
  180n, 193n, 377n
Black, J., 155, 167
Bladen, V.W., 285, 285n, 308n
Boiteux, M., 198n
Bowley, A.L., 153
Breton, A., 240, 240n
Brigden, J.R., 188, 188n, 189, 206
Bruno, M., 368n

Caine, S., xii
Caves, R., xii, 239n
Cooper, C.A., 273n
Copland, D,B., 188n
Corden, W.M., x, xii, 149n, 188,
  188n, 189, 213n, 308n, 331n,
  332n, 341, 341n, 342, 342n,
  350n, 356, 367n, 369n, 371n,
  373, 374n, 376n, 377, 377n,
  382n, 383n

Curzon, G., 323n

Dales, J.H., 177n
David, P., 143n, 152, 153, 166
Denison, E.F., 208n
Devons, E., ix, xii
Downs, A., 240, 240n, 241, 242n
Dyason, E.C., 188n

Eastman, H., xii
Edgeworth, F.Y., 85, 153
Ellis, H.A., 3n
Ethier, W., 373

Fei, J., 4
Finger, J.M., 343n, 356, 373, 374n
Fishlow, A., 143n, 152, 153, 166,
  167
Fisher, F.M., 174n, 175n
Flatters, F., 177n
Fleming, J.M., 100, 263, 264n

Gerschenkron, A., 189n
Giblin, L.F., 188n
Graaff, J. de V., 212n, 218n
Graham, F.D., 161, 204n
Grubel, H., 161n, 338n, 363, 373n
Gruen, F., 383n

Haberler, G., 122, 122n, 127, 130,
  131n, 139n, 167, 189, 189n,
  198n, 213n, 239n, 398n
Hagen, E., 118, 118n, 137n, 143n,
  152, 166, 167, 330n
Harberger, A.C., 152, 167, 206n,
  347n, 357
Heckscher, E., 3, 167, 183, 368,
  369, 370, 375, 377, 378, 381,
  382, 383

449